Western Garden Annual

2002 EDITION

By the Editors of *Sunset Magazine* and Sunset Books

JIM MCCAUSLAND

Rose hips wrap up the seas◌ with color and elegance (page 305).

Sunset Publishing ⟋ ⟍tion ■ Menlo Park, California

THOMAS J. STORY

SUNSET BOOKS

VP, General Manager
Richard A. Smeby
VP, Editorial Director
Bob Doyle
Production Director
Lory Day
Director of Operations
Rosann Sutherland
Art Director
Vasken Guiragossian

STAFF FOR THIS BOOK

Managing Editor
Suzanne Normand Eyre
Contributing Editors
Philip Edinger
Helen Sweetland
Indexer
Pamela Evans
Production Coordinator
Danielle Javier

SUNSET PUBLISHING CORPORATION

Senior Vice President
Kevin Lynch
VP, Publisher
Christopher D. Kevorkian
VP, Administration and Manufacturing
Lorinda Reichert
VP, Editor-in-Chief, Sunset Magazine
Katie Tamony
Consumer Marketing Director
Christina Olsen
Managing Editor/ sunset.com Editor
Carol Hoffman
Art Director
James H. McCann
Senior Editor, Gardening
Kathleen Norris Brenzel
Designers
Dennis W. Leong
Laura H. Martin
Keith Whitney

An Annual Affair

Gardeners throughout the West anticipate this annual year-in-review of *Sunset Magazine* gardening articles. Between one set of covers appears all garden and outdoor living material from all regional editions of the magazine—a handy reference to everything garden related that was newsworthy throughout *Sunset*'s western territory in 2001. In common with its eight predecessors, this volume presents the material in month-by-month installments.

Leading off each month is the Garden Guide, with its shorter, you-should-know-this features: informative pieces on diverse points of interest appropriate to the month or to the gardening period approaching. Regional checklists follow—reminders of garden tasks that might (or should) be tackled that month. Then come the month's feature articles, lavishly illustrated to inform and inspire.

Throughout these articles you will find plant adaptability keyed to numbered climate zones—24 for the Western states and 5 additional for Alaska and Hawaii. These zones are mapped and fully described in the seventh edition (2001) of the *Sunset Western Garden Book.*

Front cover: Black-eyed Susans (*Rudbeckia* 'Indian Summer') . Photographer: Norm Plate.

Back cover: Ground covers create living liners for baskets (see page 144). Photographer: Thomas J. Story.

Endpapers (hardcover edition): *Echinacea purpurea.* Photographer: Saxon Holt.

First printing: February 2002
Copyright © 2002 Sunset Publishing Corporation, Menlo Park, CA 94025. First edition. All rights reserved, including the right of reproduction in whole or in part in any form.

ISSN 1073-5089
Hardcover edition: ISBN 0376-03898-5
Softcover edition: ISBN 0376-03899-3
Printed in the United States.

All material in this book originally appeared in the 2001 issues of *Sunset Magazine.*

Sunset Western Garden Annual was produced by Sunset Books. If you have comments or suggestions, please let us hear from you. Write us at:

Sunset Books
Garden Book Editorial
80 Willow Road
Menlo Park, CA 94025
or visit our website at
www.sunsetbooks.com

Contents

Broad bronzy foliage of phormium rises over lavender-flowered catmint and heart-shaped leaves of *Houttuynia cordata*. Behind, silky flower plumes of Oriental fountain grass wave over a raised bed (see page 296).

STEVEN GUNTHER

Presenting...the Future

A review of 2001, the first year of the new millennium, shows it to be a typical year in *Sunset*'s West. But what, exactly, is the West? Geographically, it's the territory from the Rocky Mountain states to the Pacific Ocean, Alaska, and Hawaii, boasting a collection of topographic and geologic masterpieces unparalleled elsewhere on the continent. Overlaid on this larger-than-life landscape is the kaleidoscopic Western culture, a potpourri of people and cultural influences literally from all corners of the earth. Borrowed elements from Latin America, the Asian Pacific Rim, the Indian subcontinent, the Middle East, Africa, and Europe coalesce and re-form into the energetic ethos that establishes the West as the vanguard of our evolution toward a global village.

In the garden, this multiculturalism is taken for granted among *Sunset* readers. The magazine's tradition of bringing new ideas into print is so long-standing that yesterday's innovations are quickly accepted as today's standards. Just check out the feature presentation of this year's Western Garden Design Awards (pages 56–70): winning gardens carried out design ideas from Mexico, Brazil, Japan, the Mediterranean, and the tropics. And in numerous smaller articles on exemplary landscapes, garden makeovers, and garden decor, the Western embrace of world culture is abundantly on display.

But the West is not just about borrowing to create a fusion culture. Homegrown style is gaining a firmer foothold throughout the West as the "natural garden" movement gains momentum. Though its first high-profile examples were European, the natural garden is inherently regional: an assemblage of plants—native and exotic—that thrive with minimal attention under local conditions and, moreover, appear to have grown there naturally, without the obvious intervention of a garden designer. Within the West's 29 climate zones, the theory of natural gardening has a vast and varied field for expression. It is no accident that such gardens are highlighted in January, the first new-millennium month.

The spirit of innovation, of investigating the new and useful, is an intrinsic part of the wide-ranging Western outlook. This year's new-and-different presentations run the gamut of gardening interests. Dedicated plant "nuts" can read about a coleus renaissance, fuchsias that tolerate frost, ornamental grasses for containers, the best shrubs for ornamental berries, and dramatic succulent giants. Aficionados of garden styles can learn how to replicate the country casual, Asian, Mediterranean, and Mission looks. Garden techniques detailed include how to set up a drip-watering system for potted plants; how to create a fountain from large urns and other containers; and how to build sturdy raised beds. Fruit and vegetable growers are treated to the best pumpkins for pies, the tastiest tomatoes, scrumptious alpine strawberries, and a brand-new sweet corn. And for sheer novelty, what tops lining wire hanging baskets with… ground covers?

Coexisting with this Western crucible of invention is a strong element of tradition. This year saw articles long and short on such topics of timeless interest as fall bulb planting for spring display, cool-season annuals for winter color, the best roses for cutting, and all you need to know about familar plants such as columbines, ivies, nasturtiums, rosemaries, pelargoniums, and wisterias.

And as *Sunset* readers have come to expect, there are the timely region-by-region gardening tips, reviews of worthwhile new garden-related books, announcements of what-to-see-where, and basic gardening advice for tasks from planting to pruning.

An embarrassment of riches, a heady brew of ideas and activities? Perhaps. But Western gardeners expect nothing less.

CYMBIDIUMS TAKE CENTER STAGE in January at Sherman Library & Gardens in Corona del Mar, California. For advice on displaying orchids with dramatic results, see page 10.

January

Our favorite All-America Selections

THOMAS J. STORY (2)

New for 2001: Pretty flowers and a sweet pepper

■ Each year, All-America Selections (AAS) names the best new plants based on performance around the United States. Our favorite award winners for 2001 include the following.

Eustoma **'Forever Blue'.** Unlike most eustoma (lisianthus) plants, whose lanky stems make them best for cutting gardens, this cultivar tops out at 12 inches and is multibranched. Its growth habit makes it a good container candidate as well as a bedding plant. Its $2\frac{1}{2}$-inch-wide flowers are a great shade of blue.

Pepper F1 'Giant Marconi'. This is a must-grow if you love grilled red peppers, which is what these long (6 to 8 inches), meaty peppers were bred for. Excellent smoky-sweet flavor.

Zinnia **'Profusion White'.** This year's AAS Gold Medal winner—a bedding plant—pumps out a profusion of $2\frac{1}{2}$-inch-wide, single, daisylike flowers from early spring well into fall. (The powdery mildew resistance inherited from its *Z. angustifolia* parent keeps this cultivar from deteriorating in late summer like many zinnias do.) The other great virtue: It requires minimal care. You don't need to pinch back or deadhead to keep the flower show going.

— *Sharon Cohoon*

Eustoma 'Forever Blue' (above) and *Zinnia* 'Profusion White' (top left) are two winning bedding plants—new this year.

Rhubarb—the easiest, earliest vegetable

When leaves emerge from top of forcing pot, remove the pot.

■ In many gardens, rhubarb is the first crop to be harvested in spring. From the Cascades east to the Rocky Mountains, harvest takes place in May, and in milder parts of the Pacific Northwest in April—as early as March if you speed up the growing process with a rhubarb forcing pot like the one shown here.

This perennial vegetable is a snap to grow in cool-summer climates. Just plant one root crown per square yard of rich, amended soil in a sunny spot (light shade in warm-summer climates).

Many nurseries are selling rhubarb crowns now, during bare-root season. A good mail-order source is Territorial Seed Company (541/942-9547 or www.territorial-seed.com). There are dozens of varieties, from deep red 'Valentine' to the market standard 'Victoria'. For a green-stalked variety, try 'Glaskins Perpetual'.

GROWING TIPS. Mulch plants and water regularly to keep the roots moist. Apply a complete fertilizer twice a year: once when the first stalks emerge and again in early June after harvest. Let plants grow strong for two years before you pick any stalks. Then you can pull up to half the stalks after leaves unfurl. Keep picking for a month or so. Note: While the edible stalks of rhubarb are delicious, the leaves of most varieties are toxic. Do not eat them. To make stalks grow earlier and longer, you can place a bottomless terra-cotta forcing pot over a dormant rhubarb crown. The terra-cotta soaks up the sun by day and radiates warmth back to the plant at night. Rhubarb forcing pots ($100 to $160 each) are sold by some nurseries and terra-cotta suppliers, including Herban Pottery in Seattle (800/618-4742). *— Jim McCausland*

Flamboyant 'Marmalade Skies'

■ One of the most exciting roses to hit the market in years is 'Marmalade Skies', the 2001 All-America Rose Selection (AARS) winner. It isn't for the faint of heart. Like Mae West, this flamboyant rose really struts its stuff. The plant produces 2½- to 3-inch-wide tangerine orange blooms all season long (even into winter in mild climates).

'Marmalade Skies' was hybridized by the House of Meilland, the French rose company that has bred many other great roses, including 'Bonica' and 'Carefree Delight'. Its round, compact habit (to 3 feet tall) makes it perfect for low hedges, containers, and mixing into perennial and shrub beds. And its shiny, olive green, disease-resistant foliage is a foil for the brightly colored blooms.

Look for 'Marmalade Skies' in nurseries this month, or order from Edmunds' Roses (888/481-7673 or www.edmundsroses.com).

— Lauren Bonar Swezey

NORMAN A. PLATE   ABOVE: JIM MCCAUSLAND

Bountiful blueberries

■ "Our neighbors said blueberries wouldn't grow here," says Kathe Gust of Redwood City, California. But Gust's husband, Phil, was determined to try them anyway. 'Bluecrop' and 'Earliblue', from Berkeley Horticultural Nursery, were the couple's starter choices.

Because blueberries need acid soil (pH of 4 to 5), they planted the bushes in 20-inch-wide plastic containers filled with peat moss, then added drip-irrigation sprayers. To help the plants get well established the first spring, Kathe pulled off the flowers to prevent fruit formation. The second year they got their first crop of berries. Thrilled by their success, the Gusts also planted other varieties.

Phil's favorites are **'Darrow'**, featuring huge light blue berries up to an inch wide, with fine, sweet-tart flavor; **'Earliblue'**, producing average-size fruits (about ½ inch), with intense blueberry flavor; and **'Sunshine Blue'**, bearing small to average-size flavorful berries from June until August (suitable for mildest climates). 'Darrow' and 'Sunshine Blue' are

THOMAS J. STORY

available from Raintree Nursery (360/496-6400 or www.raintreenursery.com). Choose two varieties for pollination. — *L.B.S.*

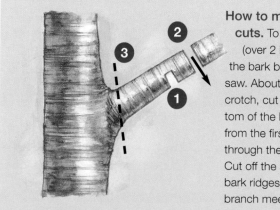

LINDA HOLT AYRISS

BACK TO BASICS

How to make proper pruning cuts. To cut off a thick branch (over 2 inches) without tearing the bark beneath it, use a pruning saw. About 12 inches from the crotch, cut halfway through the bottom of the branch (1). One inch out from the first cut, saw completely through the branch to remove it (2). Cut off the stub (3) just outside the bark ridges (which form where the branch meets the trunk). — *L.B.S.*

Cymbidiums on stage

■ Like most of us, Sherman Library & Gardens hides its cymbidium orchids in the wings for the better part of the year. (The plant's strappy leaves aren't homely, but when you have dozens potted up, the sea of unvaried green is pretty monotonous.) And, also like many of us, staffers at the California botanical garden move the orchids onto center stage during the late winter bloom peak. They cluster several potted orchids in larger containers, then raise the blooms closer to eye level, giving the orchids a theatrical presence (see photo on page 6).

Here's how to duplicate the look. Fill a 24-inch container about three-quarters full with large bark chips. You can insert a smaller, overturned pot inside first, if you like, to reduce the quantity of bark needed. Tuck in three cymbidium orchids (1-gallon size). The rims of the 1-gallon pots should be near the top of the larger container. If they're not, remove the pots and add more bark. A few 6-inch pots of variegated ivy placed close to the container's rim are a nice addition. Hide the tops of all pots with sphagnum moss, and you're done. Water about once a week when rains don't come. — *S.C.*

CLIPPINGS
•A new CD-ROM, the *UC Guide to Solving Garden and Landscape Problems* by Mary Louise Flint, et al. (University of California, Agriculture & Natural Resources Catalog, publication No. 3400, 2000; $32; 800/994-8849 or anrcatalog.ucdavis.edu) provides Western gardeners with insect and disease diagnoses and controls for crops and ornamentals.

garden guide· project

How to plant a bare-root rose

■ Inexpensive and very easy to plant, bare-root roses are sold by mail order and in nurseries between midwinter and the time roses first leaf out (around late January in mild climates, March in colder climates). In spite of the "bare-root" name, most come with roots wrapped in plastic bags or tall cartons full of damp organic matter. There's a good reason: If roots dry, plants die. The following steps will help get bare-root roses off to a good start in your garden.

1. Unwrap the rose, shake packing material from the roots, and cut off the tag that's wired to the plant. Prune off broken roots or canes, then plunge the rose into a bucket of water— its roots completely immersed—for a few hours.

While the rose soaks, dig a planting hole about 2 feet wide and 1 foot deep. If your garden soil is reasonably good (not excessively sandy or heavy with clay), you won't need to amend it. If it's bad, mix 1 cubic foot of compost into the backfill.

2. Make a 10-inch-tall cone of soil in the middle of the hole, then center the rose on top of it, with roots spread down the sides of the cone. Pull backfill into the hole, firming it with your hand (never your foot) as you go.

3. When the hole is filled, water until the soil around the plant turns to mud. Rock the rose back and forth to settle it in and to allow air pockets to bubble up through the mud. This process is called "puddling in." When you're done, the rose's topmost roots should be barely below the soil surface, and the graft (the swollen part just above the crown), if the rose has one, should be well above the soil surface.

4. After puddling, add enough backfill to level the soil. Make a 3-inch-high watering basin about 10 inches from the base of the plant. Stick a label in the ground beside the rose and you're done. — *J.M.*

Living stones and other desert flora

Visit the nursery in Tucson or shop for plants by mail or on-line

■ When Jane Evans and Gene Joseph met as horticulture majors at the University of Arizona, they discovered they had a passion for unusual succulents, cactus, and other desert plants. In 1986, when the couple's enthusiasm outgrew their Tucson backyard, they opened a retail nursery, Plants for the Southwest, and a year later launched a mail-order catalog called Living Stones Nursery. Over the years, they've cultivated a circle of collectors who appreciate distinctive specimen plants.

Evans and Joseph grow their own plants from seeds and cuttings, including many members of the genus *Lithops,* small pebble-shaped succulents commonly called living stones, and *Conophytum,* succulents with cone-shaped heads composed of pairs of leaves. They also grow and sell such exotica as boojum tree (*Fouquieria columnaris*) and Sonoran rock fig (*Ficus petiolaris*). Collections of agaves, aloes, cactus, euphorbias, and haworthias are also available. More recently they've been offering hybrid adeniums, an oleander relative with showy red or pink flowers.

With seven greenhouses and shade houses on a 1-acre site, the nursery is usually open from 9 to 5 Wednesday through Saturday, but call first to confirm. The mail-order catalog costs $2. Bare-root plants are shipped nationwide in sizes scaled mostly for 3- and 4-inch pots (a few are for 6- and 8-inch pots). When you order, request a planting instruction sheet. To contact the nursery, write to 2936 N. Stone Ave., Tucson, AZ 85705; call (520) 628-8773; or visit www.lithops.net.

— *Nora Burba Trulsson*

JACK DYKINGA

pacific northwest checklist

PLANTING

☐ **BARE-ROOT STOCK.** Zones 4–7: This month, nurseries stock bare-root berries, fruit trees, roses, vines, and shrubs. Don't let roots dry out before you get them in the ground and water them. In colder zones, plant as soon as bare-root stock is available, on a day when air and soil temperatures are above freezing.

☐ **ENGLISH PRIMROSES.** You'll find both acaulis and polyanthus primroses for sale this month. Acaulis primroses usually have one flower per stem, while polyanthus primroses have multiple flowers from a single stem. Zones 1–3: Buy acaulis primroses for indoor display (they're perfect on windowsills). Zones 4–7: Use acaulis primroses indoors or group them in outdoor containers. Plant taller polyanthus primroses in garden beds.

☐ **HARDY ANNUALS.** Sow seeds of calendulas, clarkias, English daisies, pansies, poppies (California and Iceland), snapdragons, and violas directly in the ground.

☐ **HARDY PERENNIALS.** To get a jump on spring, sow seeds of aster, delphinium, hellebore, Shasta daisy, veronica, and viola in a cold frame or greenhouse. Transplant seedlings into the garden about a month before the last spring frost.

MAINTENANCE

☐ **APPLY DORMANT OIL.** On a mild, dry day, spray dormant deciduous fruit trees and roses with horticultural oil to kill overwintering insect eggs and larvae.

☐ **CLEAN UP HOUSE PLANTS.** Feed only those that are blooming; wait until spring to fertilize other kinds. All plants should get a lukewarm shower every couple of months to wash dust off leaves and inhibit insect buildup. At the same time, prune off yellowing leaves and cut back plants that are getting leggy to force regrowth lower on the plant. Don't try this with indoor palms, as most grow from the top only.

☐ **FEED ASPARAGUS.** Top-dress beds of asparagus with a 2-inch layer of composted manure.

☐ **PRUNE FRUIT TREES.** Zones 4–7: First cut out dead, diseased, and injured branches, remove closely parallel, rubbing, or crossing branches, then prune for shape. Zones 1–3: Hold off pruning until weather turns mild.

☐ **PRUNE ROSES.** Zones 4–7: Start by removing dead, injured, or diseased canes and any suckers (growth emerging from below the graft). Then prune hybrid tea roses for shape, removing crossed or inward-growing canes. After you've removed all but the three to five strongest canes, cut the remaining ones back by about a third. Each cane should be left with one robust, outward-facing bud. Zones 1–3: Wait to prune until just before new growth begins. ◆

WHAT TO DO IN YOUR GARDEN IN JANUARY

PLANTING

☐ **FRAGRANT OLD GARDEN ROSES.** Zones 7–9, 14–17: Ten highly fragrant old garden roses to try are autumn damask, 'Baronne Prévost', 'Celsiana', 'Charles de Mills', 'Königin von Dänemark', 'Louise Odier', 'Madame Isaac Pereire', 'Marchesa Boccella', 'Rose de Rescht', and 'Sombreuil'. You can order them from Heirloom Roses (503/538-1576 or www.heirloomroses.com) or Regan Nursery (510/797-3222 or www.regannursery.com).

☐ **INSTANT COLOR.** Zones 7–9, 14–17: To dash away the winter blues, buy annuals and perennials in 4-inch containers and use them in a colorful potted arrangement for the front porch or to view from a window. Look for calendulas, candytuft, cinerarias, dianthus, English and fairy primroses, English daisies, Iceland poppies, pansies, snapdragons, stock, and violas.

☐ **ROSES.** World-famous David Austin English roses are now available by mail directly from David Austin Roses, Limited. The fall 2000 catalog contains 50 varieties of English roses, plus 100 varieties of modern and old roses. To order a free catalog, call (800) 328-8893 or visit the website at www. davidaustinroses.com.

Sunset
CLIMATE ZONES
☐ Mountain (1-2)
☐ Valley (7-9)
☐ Inland (14)
☐ Coastal (15-17)

DEBRA LAMBERT

☐ **STRAWBERRIES.** Zones 7–9, 14–17: Shop for bare-root strawberries in nurseries (or plant them from cell-packs). Three flavorful varieties to look for are 'Chandler', 'Sequoia', and 'Tristar'.

MAINTENANCE

☐ **CUT BACK HYDRANGEAS.** Zones 7–9, 14–17: Cut stems that have bloomed back to 12 inches. To produce fewer larger flowers next spring, also reduce the number of stems by cutting some of them back to the base of the plant. To yield numerous medium-size blooms, retain more stems.

☐ **FEED CITRUS.** Zones 7–9, 14–17: Feed citrus trees six to eight weeks before they bloom, according to their age. Give trees planted last season (two-year-old trees) $\frac{1}{4}$ pound of actual nitrogen, three-year-old trees $\frac{1}{2}$ pound, four-year-old trees $\frac{3}{4}$ pound, and five-year-old trees 1 pound. Trees more than five years old should get

1 to $1\frac{1}{2}$ pounds of actual nitrogen. Feed all at once, in two feedings (January and February), or in very sandy soil, divide fertilizer amount into once-a-month feedings.

☐ **MANAGE WEEDS.** When winter rain hits bare ground, it germinates weed seeds. To prevent weeds from sprouting, mulch flower and vegetable beds. Keep on top of areas seeded with wildflowers or annuals. As plants emerge, so will weeds. Hand-pull or hoe carefully.

☐ **PROTECT PLANTS FROM FROST.** Zones 7–9, 14–17: If weather forecasts warn of frost, make sure plants are well watered (dry plants are more susceptible to frost damage). Move tender container plants, such as citrus, cymbidiums, hibiscus, and mandevillas beneath overhangs or into the garage. For frost-tender plants too large to move or for those growing in the ground, protect with burlap or cloth coverings; don't let the cover touch the leaves. Remove covers first thing in the morning. ◆

southern california checklist

PLANTING

☐ **BARE-ROOT PLANTS.** Bare-root plants, those sold without soil around their roots, are a bargain, but they're also just plain fun. Watching a twiggy stick turn into a leafy plant never ceases to seem like magic. Plenty of bare-root plants are available at nurseries this month, including cane berries, grape and kiwi vines, roses, stone fruit trees, strawberries, and perennial vegetables such as artichokes, asparagus, and rhubarb. If you can, plant immediately. If the soil is too soggy, cover roots with moist soil or plant temporarily in containers.

☐ **SEEDS.** Place orders for seeds of warm-season flowers and vegetables. (Mail-order catalogs offer a much wider choice than seed displays in most nurseries.) To transplant seedlings to the garden by early spring, start seeds indoors as soon as they arrive.

☐ **SHRUBS, TREES, AND NATIVES.** Because the next few months will most likely bring rain, midwinter is a good time to plant ornamental trees, evergreen and flowering shrubs, and other landscaping plants. It's also an excellent time to plant all California natives, including ceanothus, fremontodendrons, monkey flowers (*Mimulus*), and woolly blue curls (*Trichostema lanatum*).

Bishop
NEVADA
CALIFORNIA
San Luis Obispo
Bakersfield
Tehachapi
Santa Barbara
Lancaster
Los Angeles
Palm Springs
Sunset
CLIMATE ZONES
1-3 7-9 11 13 14-24
San Diego
MEXICO
DEBRA LAMBERT

☐ **WINTER VEGETABLES.** It's not too late to start cool-season crops from seed, though seeds will be slow to germinate. The safest bets are lettuces and other greens, flat-leaf parsley, peas, radishes, and green and bulbing onions. You can also set out transplants of broccoli, cabbage, and other cole crops.

MAINTENANCE

☐ **BEGIN DORMANT-SEASON PRUNING.** Start with roses. Cut all dead wood, crossing branches, and twiggy growth, leaving at least three strong canes. Shorten remaining canes by about one-third. It's also time to prune deciduous fruit trees. Different fruit trees require different techniques: Consult a good pruning reference book before you proceed. Don't prune spring-blooming shrubs now; do it after they flower. Wait for spring to prune off any frost damage as well. The damaged portion protects tender interior growth.

☐ **FERTILIZE SELECTIVELY.** In frost-free coastal areas, feed citrus this month. Inland, wait until February. Water trees well the day before feeding. The following day, sprinkle ammonium sulfate over entire root area, then water to wash it in. Cool-season annuals, emerging bulbs, and cool-season rye or fescue lawns benefit from fertilizing now too.

☐ **MANAGE WEEDS.** To prevent weeds from sprouting, mulch flower and vegetable beds. Keep on top of areas seeded with wildflowers or annuals. As plants emerge, so will weeds. Hand-pull or hoe carefully.

PEST, DISEASE CONTROL

☐ **APPLY DORMANT OIL.** After pruning, spray roses and deciduous flowering and fruit trees with horticultural oil to smother insects such as mites, scale, and sawfly larvae. For fungal diseases, such as peach leaf curl, mix lime sulfur or fixed copper into the oil. Spray branches, crotches, trunk, and ground beneath the tree's drip line. If it rains within 48 hours, repeat. ◆

WHAT TO DO IN YOUR GARDEN IN JANUARY

PLANNING AND PLANTING

☐ ORDER VEGETABLE SEEDS. These two seed firms stock a wide selection of vegetables; call for catalogs or visit their websites. Garden City Seeds of Washington (509/964-7016 or www.gardencityseeds.com) offers two unusual beets: 'Golden' beet with yellow flesh, and 'Chioggia', an Italian variety, with alternating red and white rings and flavorful greens. Seeds Trust's High Altitude Gardens of Idaho (208/788-4363 or www.seedsave.org) offers 23 kinds of cold-tolerant Siberian tomatoes, including 'Stupice', a variety that matures in 52 days.

☐ PROVIDE WATER FOR BIRDS. Wild birds overwintering in your garden need clean water for drinking and bathing when natural water sources freeze solid. If you have a birdbath, you can prevent the water from freezing with a heater (try Avian Aquatics; 800/788-6478 or www.avianaquatics.com). Or use a shallow plastic basin in the winter. When water in the basin freezes, pour in a kettle of hot water to melt the surface ice. Rinse the basin out daily and refill with clean water.

Sunset
CLIMATE ZONES
☐ 1-3 ☐ 10-11

DEBRA LAMBERT

☐ SOW HARDY PERENNIALS. Seeds of most hardy perennials, including butterfly weed, columbine, liatris, and penstemon, require a period of chilling to germinate. Start seeds now in soil-filled pots and place them outdoors out of direct sun. Keep the pots moist, and whenever snow is available pile it on the soil in pots. After six weeks of chilling, bring pots into a greenhouse or set them on a sunny windowsill to sprout. When seedlings have two sets of true leaves, transplant them into individual containers. Continue growing them indoors until spring, then set out in the garden.

MAINTENANCE

☐ CHECK STORED BULBS. Examine bulbs, corms, and tubers for shriveling and rot. If bulbs are shriveling, sprinkle on a little water to rehydrate. Discard any that show decay (except dahlia tubers—you can cut the bad spots out of these, dust with sulfur, and store apart from the rest).

☐ MULCH FLOWER BEDS. Overlap old Christmas tree boughs and evergreen prunings on top of beds to protect newly planted and tender perennials and bulbs. Hay, straw, and pine needles also work.

☐ PRUNE TREES, SHRUBS. Winter is the ideal time to prune—you can easily see the branch structure of leafless deciduous trees and shrubs. Cut out dead, diseased, crossed, and closely parallel branches. Don't prune lilacs and other early-spring bloomers because you could be cutting off this year's flowers. Hire a tree service to prune big shade trees.

☐ WATCH FOR FROST-HEAVED PLANTS. When soil freezes and thaws in recurrent cycles, it can heave fall-planted perennials and small shrubs out of the ground. If this happens, add soil around the base of the plant to cover any exposed roots.

☐ WATER. Dry winter conditions can seriously dehydrate plants. When snow or rain has not fallen for several weeks and the ground is dry 3 to 4 inches beneath the surface (use a trowel to check), set out a sprinkler to soak all plantings thoroughly. Irrigate when the temperature is above freezing. Water at midday when the surface of the soil is not frozen solid. — *Marcia Tatroe* ◆

WHAT TO DO IN YOUR GARDEN IN JANUARY

PLANTING

☐ **BARE-ROOT FRUIT TREES.** Zones 12–13 (Tucson, Phoenix): Choose low-chill varieties of apples ('Anna' or 'Dorsett Golden'), apricots ('Gold Kist' or 'Katy'), peaches ('Babcock' or 'Flordaprince'), and plum ('Santa Rosa').

☐ **BARE-ROOT ROSES.** Zones 11 (Las Vegas) and 12–13: Set out roses (see planting tips on page 11).

☐ **COOL-SEASON COLOR.** Zones 12–13: Sow seeds of larkspurs, nasturtiums, and stock. Set out transplants of bachelor's buttons, calendulas, pansies, petunias, snapdragons, sweet alyssum, and wallflowers.

☐ **HERBS.** Zones 11–13: Sow seeds of cilantro, dill, and parsley at two-week intervals to ensure a steady harvest.

☐ **VEGETABLES.** Zone 10 (Albuquerque): Set out bare-root crowns of asparagus, horseradish, and rhubarb. Zones 11–13: Set out transplants of artichoke and asparagus root crowns.

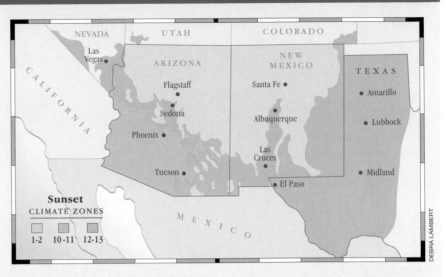

Plant Jerusalem artichoke tubers and potatoes. Start seeds of eggplant and melon indoors for transplanting outside in mid-March. Sow seeds of beets, bok choy, carrots, lettuces, radishes, spinach, and Swiss chard directly in the ground. Good regional mail-order sources are Native Seeds/Search in Tucson (520/622-5561 or www.nativeseeds. org) and Seeds of Change in Santa Fe (888/762-7333 or www. seedsofchange.com).

MAINTENANCE

☐ **CONTROL APHIDS.** Zones 11–13: Watch for aphids on tender new growth and beneath leaves. Blast them off with a jet of water from the hose or spray with insecticidal soap.

☐ **FERTILIZE BEARDED IRISES.** Zones 11–13: Late in the month, spread fertilizer around plants and scratch it into the soil. Then water thoroughly.

☐ **PRUNE HYBRID TEA ROSES.** Zones 12–13: Remove all dead canes and cut remaining canes back by a third.

☐ **TRANSPLANT PERENNIALS.** Zones 11–13: Relocate seedlings of perennials such as desert marigolds (*Baileya multiradiata*), globe mallows (*Sphaeralcea ambigua*), penstemons, and salvias.

☐ **WATER.** Zone 10: Give evergreens a deep soaking once a month if weather remains dry. Zones 11–13: If there has been no rain, deep-water trees and shrubs every three weeks and water succulents including cactus every four to five weeks. — *Mary Irish* ◆

natural gardens

Late afternoon on a warm day is a magical time in a natural garden. Rosy light bathes trees, shrubs, and colorful perennials then, and turns seed heads to spun gold. Blossoms with the ephemeral beauty of wildflowers glow as though lit from within, and a gentle breeze stirs ornamental grasses into a lyrical dance. Mornings are glorious too, when fattening buds sparkle with dew and the air is fresh and still. But then any time is special when scent and motion, plants and creatures, water, serenity, and joyous informality come together.

Much has been written in recent years about creating gardens in tune with the earth's cycles and seasons, using as models the land and its natural plant communities. But not until now, at the dawn of the 21st century, has the natural gardening movement really begun to go mainstream. Forward-thinking landscape architects and designers are installing gardens that are appropriate to their regions and climates. Gardeners too are more eager to surround their homes with natural-looking, easy-care gardens that sit lightly on the land.

As you peruse seed catalogs this month and plan ahead to spring planting, consider choosing plants and practices that will invite nature into your own backyard.

Steppingstones climb this slope through a soft cover of unthirsty Korean grass (*Zoysia tenuifolia*) in a landscape designed by Betty Edwards, Santa Monica. ABOVE: A feather-lined bird's nest fills a space between branches.

By Kathleen N. Brenzel

Ways to create an easy-care landscape

MARION BRENNER

What is a natural garden?

For some Westerners, a natural garden is decidedly green—a rich tapestry of trees, shrubs, and ornamental grasses. For others, it's a cluster of natives with endearing names that belie their toughness: fairy duster or pussy toes; woolly blue curls, shooting star, or silktassel; Mexican hat or sugar bush. For still others, it's a carnival of colorful flowers, such as cosmos and catmint, salvias and sunflowers, bloom-ing together in glorious anarchy. Or it's a backyard habitat for birds and butterflies—a nursery, grocery store, and all-night salad bar for a variety of creatures that call the garden home.

A natural garden can be all of these things or none of them. But all natural gardens have four things in common. NATURAL GARDENS ARE ALIVE. But-terflies alight here to sip nectar from a flower. Honeybees buzz, and

Softly mounding *Stipa tenuissima*, lavender, and white-flowered *Centranthus ruber* 'Alba' create a meadowlike garden that blends with the natural surroundings. Design is by Ron Lutsko Jr.

STEVEN GUNTHER   BELOW: RICHARD SHIELL

Waterfall trickles into a mirror-smooth pond in this Montecito, California, garden designed by Pat Brodie. RIGHT: A northern leopard frog surfaces among the water plants.

ladybugs scuttle among the leaves, foraging for aphids. Look closely among the foliage and you might find a hummingbird nest woven from pine needles and lined with tiny mosses and downy feathers. Birds, frogs, dragonflies, and earthworms are all part of this magnificent microcosm.

NATURAL GARDENS RESPECT NATURE'S PRICELESS RESOURCES. Where the climate is arid (as in much of the West), plants are chosen to withstand dry summers and drought, ultimately conserving water. At least some of the paving is porous enough to allow rainfall to pass through it to plant roots, rather than running off to the street.

Leaf litter is turned to compost that enriches the soil. Grass clippings left on lawns break down to form nitrogen. A healthy balance of predators and prey diminishes the need for heavy-duty chemical controls.

At the same time, a new generation of building materials—such as wood made from recycled plastic and simulated boulders that look like the real thing—helps gardeners create the look of wild habitats while leaving

Four steps to a natural garden

■ **MATCH THE PLANTS TO YOUR SITE**
Along the California coast, wind and salt spray are hard on many plants. So gardeners there should choose tough plants such as sea lavender, pride of Madeira, rockrose, or Santa Barbara daisy. For the Northwest, select ornamental grasses, rockrose, or yarrow.

In the grassy foothills, conifer forests, and dry coastal chaparral zones where wildfires are part of the scene, it makes sense to avoid highly flammable plants such as juniper, rosemary, and toyon and to maintain an irrigated greenbelt near the house. Sun and shade, bogs and dry washes, slopes and valleys—all present different challenges. But choose the right plants and they will grow lustily.

In Colorado, Utah, and other mountain states, unpredictable weather, wide temperature swings, and unexpected frosts at both ends of the growing season practically dictate the use of hardy perennials, evergreen conifers, and tough deciduous trees and shrubs.

Constant winds in the plains of Montana and Wyoming call for windbreaks and shade trees such as hackberries and cottonwoods, for well-adapted shrubs such as lilacs and smoke tree, and for wind-tolerant perennials like buckwheats, grasses, and penstemons. Where hail is a problem, gardeners favor small-leafed plants; where winters are dry and snow cover light, they compensate with mulch and extra water. Scree landscapes often leave room only for small, jewel-like alpine plants.

■ **PLANT IN LAYERS**
To replicate natural plant communities, plant in layers, tall to low: tree canopy

(Continued on next page)

to perennials to ground covers. Trees and shrubs provide a sense of enclosure. Beneath them, plant low-growers in drifts or meadows, not rows.

Treat your plants like free spirits. Let them roam, ramble, and sprawl as nature intended, rather than making them grow up pinched or sheared, squeezed or cinched. If a plant's habit is naturally stiff and upright (cactus or agave, for instance), place it to show off its sculptural qualities, to capture backlighting from the sun and uplighting from lamps, or to cast shadows that dance across paving.

■ PLANT FOR DIVERSITY

A manicured garden with a lawn and sheared shrubs is of little interest to birds, beneficial insects, and a host of other creatures that keep insect pests in check. But a diverse planting, where nectar and seed producers grow among shelter plants, is wildlife heaven.

Backyard wildlife, after all, includes gardeners' best friends—lacewing larvae, which can consume 200 to 400 aphids before adulthood, birds that dine on everything from earwigs to whiteflies, and beneficial insects that go after pesty ones. Learn to distinguish the good guys from the bad ones.

■ RECYCLE PLANTS AND MATERIALS

In nature, the cycle of life and seasons ensures recycling, as surely as trees drop leaves that turn to compost.

Likewise, a natural garden wastes nothing. Make use of what's at the site, whether rocky outcrops or hills, beach sand, sinks, or streams. Tree stumps make perfect pedestals for container plants. Fallen or pruned tree branches can be chipped for mulch or used whole to make pea stakes or brush piles for birds. Manmade materials that would otherwise go to landfills, from concrete chunks to iron gates, can find new homes among your garden's plants.

JERRY HARPUR

Artichokes, cardoon, and lavender ramble together in this garden designed by Molly Chappellet of Artforms, St. Helena, California. BELOW: Monarch butterfly pauses atop nectar-rich yarrow.

actual wild habitats intact.

NATURAL GARDENS ARE APPROPRIATE TO THE REGION. Because plants are adapted to the climate, the soil, the sun or shade, and other characteristics of the site, they thrive without heavy-handed care.

NATURAL GARDENS TEACH US. To plant with the cycle of seasons. To really see the shimmering beauty of a garden spider's web on a dewy morning. To savor the play of the moonlight over silvery leaves and snowy-hued flowers, or the reflection of light and clouds on a pond.

But perhaps the most important lesson of all is this: Working with

ROBIN CUSHMAN

Orange pincushion (*Leucospermum*), lime green euphorbia, red watsonias, and spiky blue pride of Madeira brighten this Santa Monica garden created by Susanne Jett, Jettscapes Landscape Design. RIGHT: An American goldfinch perches on a hawthorn branch.

nature teaches us to recognize that every living thing in the garden—every plant, animal, bird, insect, moth, and worm—is connected, part of an intricate web of life with a built-in system of checks and balances designed to keep our gardens, the land, and ultimately ourselves, healthy.

ADAM JONES/NATURAL SELECTION. ABOVE: NORMAN A. PLATE

The preceding natural gardens information is adapted from the seventh edition of *Sunset's Western Garden Book* (Sunset Publishing Corporation, Menlo Park, CA, February 2001; $32.95 softcover, $36.95 hardcover; 768 pages). The heavily revised new edition now includes climate zone maps for Alaska, Hawaii, and southwestern Canada, newly refined maps for the mountain states, and more than 2,000 new plant listings. The book will arrive in bookstores, nurseries, and home improvement stores beginning in mid-February. ◆

Japanese maple, ferns, gnarled wood,
and mossy rocks flank this pond,
designed by Val and Chris Moore.

Ferns, rhododendrons, and conifers grow together in this
Northwest garden.

Flowers chosen to attract butterflies—yellow yarrow and *Lysimachia punctata*, white and blue *Campanula persicifolia*, purple *Centaurea montana*, and rose pink foxgloves—fill Julie O'Donald's garden in Brier, Washington.

Purple coneflower contrasts handsomely with gray artemisia in Thomas Vetter's Portland garden.

ALLAN MANDELL

ROBIN CUSHMAN (2)

Backed by a hollowed tree trunk, a stone-edged pond is fringed on both sides by ferns in this Washington garden. Design is by Val and Chris Moore of Moorehaven Water Gardens, Everett, Washington.

White Shasta daisies and yellow potentilla surround a rustic birdhouse in this garden by Land Design by Ellison in Avon, Colorado.

Near Masonville, Colorado, yellow alyssum and daisies (*Thelesperma filifolium*), red firecracker penstemon, blue catmint, alliums, and other hardy perennials color Lauren Springer's rocky slope.

In Montana, flat slabs of stone fringed with low mounding plants step up the gentle slope in this meadowlike garden designed by Chris Wagner of Wagner Nursery and Landscape.

Near Flathead Lake in Bigfork, Montana, violet spikes of *Salvia superba* sweep around a big blowsy clump of feather reed grass (*Calamagrostis arundinacea* 'Karl Foerster') in a garden designed by Chris Moritz. White peonies, blue delphiniums, and tufted hair grass (*Deschampsia caespitosa* 'Goldgehaenge') grow behind.

In Santa Fe, a gate made of juniper poles by Tom Joyce opens to a flower- and vegetable-filled garden designed by Ben Haggard.

Aspen and fruit trees in this Santa Fe garden, designed by landscape architect Charles Pearson, are underplanted with textural perennials, such as bishop's weed and Russian sage.

LEFT: Agave, cactus, and native palms (*Washingtonia robusta*) accent this garden in Rancho Mirage, California, designed by the late Steve Chase. ABOVE: Concrete bowl displays assorted cactus.

Poolside plantings blend seamlessly with the desert beyond in this garden owned and designed by Kevin Casey and Ken Bowling of Tucson.

Gloriosa daisies and purple coneflower mingle with pink phlox.

Hollowed rock holds small, natural-looking pool in this Santa Fe yard.

Bouquet beauties

Florists pick the best 38 garden roses for cutting

By Sharon Cohoon • Photographs by Claire Curran

LEFT: Roses from Jacob Maarse's home garden are arranged in bouquets that include 'Olympiad' (red), 'Double Delight' (cream with pink edges), 'Bride's Dream' (pale pink), 'Yves Piaget' (mauve-grape), and 'Dolly Parton' (orange). RIGHT: Jan Weverka combines old roses like creamy 'Sombreuil' and modern hybrids such as 'Fragrant Plum' with garden companions like columbine, feverfew, and valerian.

■ Any rose that has a strong stem and lasts at least three days in a vase is a good rose for cutting. That's the opinion of Jacob Maarse, founder of Jacob Maarse Florists in Pasadena and Los Angeles, and Jan Weverka, owner of Roses by Jan in Monrovia, California. Both grow roses in their home gardens to sell at their respective businesses.

Notice they recommend strong—not long—stems. Weak-stemmed roses are difficult to use in arrangements, says Maarse, while short stems aren't a handicap. "Just use a shorter vase," Maarse says. If stems are very short, create the closely packed, dome-shaped, ultraromantic arrangement Europeans call a pavé. (Place a presoaked foam block in a shallow bowl and stud the block with roses, placing them as closely as tiles in a mosaic.) Or use shorter-stemmed roses near the bottom of bouquets, the way Weverka does. "Choose roses that are at least half open," she suggests. "Their weight will add ballast to the arrangement."

What else makes a rose good for cutting? Shapely blooms. Though most of us think of a cut rose as a single flower on the end of a stem, roses that flower in clusters, like floribundas and some climbing roses, look great in vases. One stem can be a bouquet in itself. A tip: Pinch off the central flower bud (terminal bud) in the cluster, so all the remaining buds will open at the same time.

About that three-day rule: If you insist that any flower worth cutting has to last at least a week, you'll miss out on some of the most fragrant roses in the world, including the big blowsy Victorians—Bourbons, Portlands, and hybrid perpetuals. (As a rule, the more fragrant the rose, the shorter its vase life.) And you can't cut the densely petaled David Austin roses in bud stage and watch them open in the vase the way you can a hybrid tea; David Austins will refuse to unfurl. Let them unfold three-quarters of the way on the shrub, then cut them and watch the rest of the show indoors.

To find the best garden roses for cutting, we talked with dozens of florists. Here are their choices.

Florists' favorite bouquet roses

'Yves Piaget' (Romantica) looks old-fashioned, but the hybrid wasn't introduced until 1989. The fragrant, mauve-grape beauty is Maarse's favorite rose.

HYBRID TEAS

'Mr. Lincoln'. Dark red, velvet texture, large flowers, very fragrant. This 1965 All-America Rose Selections winner is, by general consensus, still the best modern red.

'Olympiad'. A close second to 'Mr. Lincoln'. Bright red, long-lasting blooms. Vigorous.

'Bride's Dream'. Soft pink, large, very long buds. Productive and disease-resistant.

'Touch of Class'. Coral-pink blend with orange and cream shading.

'Double Delight'. Cream with strawberry pink edges, spicy fragrance. Possibly the most recognizable rose in the world.

'Barbra Streisand'. Mauve blend. Very fragrant.

'Sunset Celebration'. Apricot blend, large blooms. Vigorous.

'St. Patrick'. Golden yellow, tinged with green in warmer climates. Prolific bloomer. "Lasts so long you have to dust it," says Tom Carruth, Weeks Roses' hybridizer.

'Honor'. Pure white, large, perfect blooms. Unanimous favorite as best white.

'Pascali'. Close second to 'Honor'.

FLORIBUNDAS

'French Lace'. Creamy white blossoms with soft apricot centers, flower form similar to hybrid tea. Good fragrance, long-stemmed.

'Iceberg'. The most popular landscaping rose in the West is also a favorite for cutting. Ice white, heavy bloomer, very disease-resistant.

'Margaret Merril'. White with pale pink blush, ruffled petals, lemon scent.

'Sexy Rexy'. Shell pink, camellia-like flowers. Compact shrub.

'Bridal Pink'. Delicate pink blended with cream, lightly spicy fragrance.

GRANDIFLORAS

'Gold Medal'. Dark gold, red-orange tips, light tea-rose scent.

'Fame'. Deep pink with scalloped edges, long vase life. Lasts 10 days or longer, according to Lew Whitney of Roger's Gardens in Newport Beach, California.

DAVID AUSTINS

'Abraham Darby'. Pink-apricot-yellow blend, large, deeply cupped. Fruity fragrance.

'Ambridge Rose'. Pink-apricot blend, medium size, cupped form, opening to a rosette. Compact shrub, strong bloomer.

'Graham Thomas'. Rich, pure yellow, cupped, medium size. Very vigorous—almost to a fault in warm climates.

'Golden Celebration'. Dark gold fading to pure yellow. "A shorter, more freely blooming version of 'Graham Thomas'," says Gary Jones of Hor-tus nursery in Pasadena.

'Charles Rennie Mac-Kintosh'. Lilac-pink old rose, very fragrant. Vigorous plant.

'Prospero'. Like an old-fashioned Gallica in form (rosette-shaped) and color (crimson fading to purple). Reblooms, very fragrant. Small shrub.

THE NEW FRENCH ROMANTICS

'Yves Piaget' (Romantica). Large, ruffled blooms in Old World colors (mauve-grape blend).

'Martine Guillot' (Generosa). Creamy white, deeply cupped blooms blushed with peach. Petals roll back at the edges. Long vase life.

CLIMBERS

'Sally Holmes'. Huge clusters of large, single white flowers. Long vase life. A very vigorous climber in mild climates. Large shrub elsewhere.

'Sombreuil'. Flat, creamy white, quartered form, fragrant. Strong bloomer. One of the most popular old garden roses in the country, according to the American Rose Society.

'Berries 'n' Cream'. Pink-and-white stripes with gold stamens. "Flowers last 10 days or more in a vase," says Los Angeles rosarian Karen Dardick.

HYBRID PERPETUALS

'Paul Neyron'. "Hybrid perpetuals are my favorite old garden roses, and 'Paul Neyron' is my favorite hybrid perpetual," Weverka says. Rosy pink, 6 inches across, very fully petaled, fragrant. Nearly thornless canes. Tall, narrow shrub.

'Baronne Prévost'. Rose pink with quartered form, button eye, strong old-rose scent.

'Reine des Violettes'. Cerise-purple fading to lilac-mauve. Flat, quartered form. Heady fragrance. Thornless.

BOURBONS

'Madame Isaac Pereire'. Raspberry-purple, very large, heavily petaled. "Most fragrant rose in existence," says John Clements at Heirloom Roses. Tall shrub or short climber.

'Louise Odier'. Rose pink, camellia-like blooms. Richly perfumed. Vigorous.

PORTLANDS

'Comte de Chambord'. Lilac-pink, large, quartered form, richly perfumed. Good bloomer. Moderate-size shrub.

'Rose de Rescht'. Fuchsia, developing mysterious shades of gray and purple with age. Quartered form, old-rose scent. Compact.

CHINAS AND
ANTIQUE TEAS

'Irene Watts' (China). Ivory pink, fully double, fragrant. Compact shrub, good rebloom.

'Eugene de Beauharnais' (China/Bourbon). Deep magenta-purple, very fully petaled, wonderfully fragrant. Compact plant.

'Lady Hillingdon' (Tea). Apricot-yellow, classic tea form, very fragrant. Climbing version also available.

Roses by Jan, specializing in country garden wedding arrangements, is in its seventh year. "I started it in order to survive my husband, Jack's, retirement," says Jan Weverka (shown above), with a wry smile. The roses and other flowers in her arrangements are grown organically in her own garden. Weverka also publishes an organic rose gardening newsletter, *The Rose Garden* (call 626/301-0013 for a sample).

Weverka follows the classic triangle style in her arrangements. "But because I use old garden roses and simple companions, like feverfew, they look softer and more casual."

Jacob Maarse, shown below in his home garden in Sierra Madre, California, has operated a floral shop in Pasadena for over three decades. (His son Hank is now a co-owner.) Maarse's garden doubles as a flower farm. It contains more than 2,500 rose bushes that provide blooms for the shop. "Garden roses are always prettier than florist roses," he says. "They're more graceful."

"Simple but luxurious," is how he describes the Maarse style. "Most people try too hard," he says. "There's nothing wrong with a vase full of nothing but roses—as long as they're great roses and you use them generously."

Cutting tips from the pros

• Pick roses early in the morning or early in the evening, when sugar and hydration levels are both high. The flowers will last longer.

• Cut roses just above the third five-part leaf, counting down from the flower. You'll have longer stems and encourage stronger growth from the next crop.

• Recut all stems underwater before adding to bouquets. This keeps stems open so they can take up water.

• Acidify vase water. Add a commercial floral preservative, or mix one part lemon-based soda, like 7-Up, with three parts water. Or simply add a few drops of household bleach per gallon of water, as Weverka does.

• Remove all foliage that's beneath the vase water. Submerged leaves will rot quickly and shorten the life of your bouquet. ◆

Bright light lovers

Peperomia obtusifolia

Homalomena rubescens 'Emerald Gem'

Dracaena deremensis 'Janet Craig Compacta'

Sansevieria trifasciata 'Moonglow'

Calathea majestica 'Roseolineata'

Easy-care house plants

10 good choices for low or bright light

By Steven R. Lorton
Photographs by Thomas J. Story

Growing plants indoors is a bit like raising pet fish. While a collection of exotic tropical specimens can be a real challenge to care for, almost anyone can keep a bowl of goldfish alive indefinitely. Here, then, are the goldfish of the indoor plant world—10 house plants that *Sunset's* garden staff, professional growers, and interior plantscapers have found to be easy to grow and forgiving, should you miss a watering. Of course, the more attentive you are to their basic needs, the more rewarding they'll be to have around.

The plants we list should be given a generous container filled with a rich, all-purpose potting soil that provides good drainage. Water often enough to keep the soil evenly moist. Feed monthly with a complete houseplant fertilizer, following label instructions. Clip off dead foliage. Every couple of months, set the plant in the shower and spray the foliage with tepid water to wash off dust. Repot plants with fresh soil every two or three years, unless noted.

Plants that prefer bright light do well in dappled sunlight but not direct sun. Those that tolerate low light are usually happiest near an east- or north-facing window.

Six that like bright light

***Calathea majestica* 'Roseolineata'.** Prayer plant's leaves curl up at night, like hands folded in prayer. Up to 9 inches long and 5 inches wide, the leaves have pale pink stripes on glossy dark green leaves with purple undersides. The plant reaches 28 inches tall.

Dracaena deremensis. Shiny dark green leaves, 8 inches long and 2 inches wide, resemble the top of a pineapple. The species reaches 6 feet or taller; the dwarf form *D. d.* 'Janet Craig Compacta' grows to only 20 inches.

Dracaena marginata. Prized for its sculptural form, this plant's erect stems eventually reach 12 feet tall. Spiky leaves, up to 2 feet long and ½ inch wide, are glossy green with purplish red margins; rainbow dracaena (*D. m.* 'Tricolor') is gold striped.

***Homalomena rubescens* 'Emerald Gem'.** Relatively new to the market, this compact plant bears dark green heart-shaped leaves that are 4 to 5 inches wide. Give it dappled sunlight and keep the soil evenly moist. Repot infrequently; the roots don't like to be disturbed.

Peperomia obtusifolia. Trailing peperomia forms a compact bouquet of foliage. Rounded leaves, up to 3 inches wide, have creamy gold and green variegations.

Sansevieria trifasciata. Widely admired for its tough nature, it bears thick swordlike leaves up to 4 feet tall. *S.* 'Laurentii' has deep green leaves with gold margins. *S.* 'Moonglow' has extrawide (to 4 inches) silvery green leaves. Dwarf 'Hahnii' (silvery bands on dark green leaves) and 'Golden Hahnii' (golden yellow bands) form low, 6-inch-long rosettes.

Four that take low light

Aglaonema. One of the best plants for poorly lit spaces, the Chinese evergreen bears dark green leaves, 1½ feet long and 5 inches wide, in clumps 2 to 3 feet tall. For variegated leaves, choose *A.* 'Silver King' or *A.* 'Silver Queen' with silver markings; *A.* 'Emerald Star' has gold splashes.

Aspidistra elatior. As its common name implies, cast-iron plant is a toughie and very drought-tolerant. Bearing glossy dark green leaves, 1 to 2½ feet long and 3 to 4 inches wide, cast-iron plant may eventually reach 3 feet tall. Plants with white- or gold-variegated leaves are available.

Rhapis excelsa. The lady palm grows slowly to a height of 5 to 12 feet, bearing clumps of fanlike fronds up to 14 inches wide. It tolerates moderate to low light. Even 3- to 4-foot-tall specimens can be rather expensive.

Spathiphyllum. One of the few plants that blooms reliably indoors. It bears long-stemmed white flowers resembling calla lilies or anthuriums. Glossy deep green oval or elliptical leaves grow up to 18 inches long and 5 inches wide. Among named varieties, look for *S.* 'Mauna Loa' (3½ feet tall), *S.* 'Sensation' (2½ feet), and a new hybrid, *S.* 'Domino' (2½ feet), with white-streaked leaves. ◆

Low light takers

Spathiphyllum 'Domino'

Aglaonema 'Emerald Star'

Rhapis excelsa

FILL A HEART-SHAPED BASKET with English primroses to create this living Valentine. For details,
see page 44.

February

Heart and soil

Baby's tears say "I love you" in a flower bed (left); English primroses with flowers in red and pink fill the basket above.

Garden plants make these living valentines

■ Chocolates are sweet treats for Mom on Valentine's Day, as are roses for your honey. But valentines for your garden? "Why not?" ask the owners of the two hearts pictured here. Living hearts of flowers or foliage show you care on this month's loveliest day, and both endure long after February 14 has passed.

The leafy heart of baby's tears (*Soleirolia soleirolii*) pictured above grows in a corner of Desiree Nelson's garden bed just outside her bedroom window. "I was cutting back the edges of the fast-spreading ground cover to keep it away from surrounding plants when I realized how easy it was to shape," Nelson says. The chore turned into play as she cut the heart shape by plunging a trowel straight down into the soil around plant edges. Then she applied a 3- to 4-inch layer of mulch to frame the heart.

"I made it to show my love for my husband," she says. "He's so tolerant of all the time I spend gardening! But it has delighted all my visitors." To plant one like it, buy a square flat of baby's tears (Irish or Scotch moss would also work), shape it with a trowel, then plant it in prepared soil.

For the arrangement pictured above right, photographer Robin Cushman purchased a heart-shaped wicker basket (16½ inches long, 15½ inches wide, and 5½ inches deep) from a craft store and nine 4-inch pots of English primroses with flowers in shades from deep rose to hot pink. After applying a clear waterproof sealer to the basket and allowing it to dry, she lined the basket with black plastic, then poked holes through the liner for drainage. She partially filled the basket with rich potting soil, then planted the primroses from 4-inch nursery pots, setting them close together and filling in around them with potting soil. The arrangement was a hit with her family and, watered regularly, bloomed beautifully for three months before Cushman planted the primroses in garden beds.

— *Kathleen N. Brenzel*

Orchid dreams come true in Colorado

A solid pink moth orchid hybrid (above right) is one of thousands grown by Fantasy Orchids.

■ For all their exotic beauty, orchids have a reputation for being such persnickety plants that only pros can grow them. Stan Gordon, owner of Fantasy Orchids in Louisville, Colorado, hopes to change that misconception. In a 10,000-square-foot greenhouse, he stocks almost 130,000 orchids suitable for growing indoors.

The collection includes cattleyas (familiar corsage orchids); miltonias (pansy orchids), with teardrop patterns in the center of the flowers; phalaenopsis (moth orchids); and oncidiums (what florists call spray orchids).

The most popular plant that Fantasy Orchids sells is an oncidium, Sharry Baby 'Sweet Fragrance', with dark red and white flowers. Its delicious perfume is often compared to chocolate, vanilla, or cookies.

You can shop for plants directly at the greenhouse in Louisville, between Denver and Boulder, Mondays through Saturdays between 9 A.M. and 5 P.M. From U.S. 36, take the Louisville/Superior exit and drive north on McCaslin Boulevard; at the second stoplight, turn east on Cherry Street and go two blocks to the greenhouse at 830 West Cherry. Free classes on growing orchids are offered periodically on Saturday mornings.

Fantasy Orchids' website (www.fantasyorchids.com) lists most of the entire collection of about 500 varieties. Or call (303) 666-5432 to request a free catalog that lists 125 varieties. Plants cost $10 to $45 each, plus $7 for shipping and handling. — *Colleen Smith*

TERRENCE MOORE (2)

Daisies dot a desert meadow in Phoenix

■ Just below Tasha and John Vatistas's house near Camel-back Mountain in Phoenix, free-blooming African daisies paint a meadow in brilliant shades of orange, yellow, salmon, pink, and white. Blooming from January through May, the daisies are the legacy of the previous owner, Brent Turley, who started planting them in the mid-1980s.

Initially Turley broadcast by hand 5 pounds of African daisy seeds (*Dimorphotheca aurantiaca*) over a 20- by 20-foot patch. He covered the seeded area with a light mulch and kept it moist until the seeds germinated. After the daisies bloomed, he shook the spent flower heads over a cookie sheet to collect their seeds. Over the years Turley used the seeds he saved to gradually enlarge the planting (one season he used a handheld vacuum cleaner to gather seeds).

To keep the meadow from looking barren when the daisies weren't in bloom, he planted agaves and a variety of cactus, including golden barrel, prickly pear, saguaro, and night-blooming *Cereus peruvianus*.

Prickly pear and saguaros (top) punctuate the floral carpet.

Turley achieved the best results by sowing in October, raking the soil before broadcasting seeds. During fall and winter, he supplemented rainfall by watering with a hose every two to four weeks. Plants were fed with an all-purpose fertilizer in November and March. In early summer, the spent annuals were mowed and raked into the soil to supply added nutrients. — *Nora Burba Trulsson*

New plants from leaf cuttings

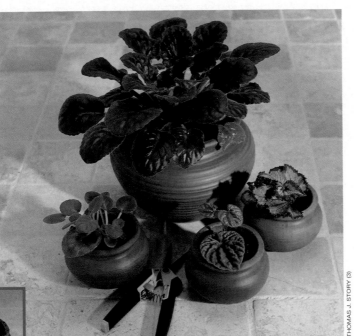

THOMAS J. STORY (3)

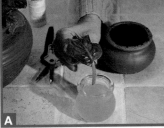

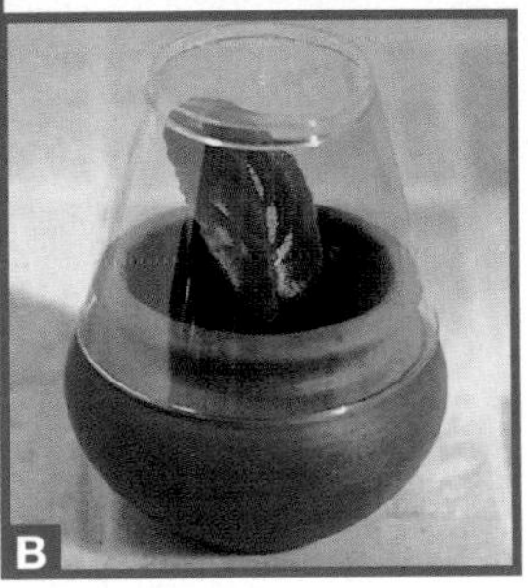

■ Some fleshy-leafed house plants can be propagated quickly and easily from leaf cuttings—one of the best methods for ensuring identical new plants. Try this technique to expand your collection of African violets, Cape primroses, gloxinias, peperomias, some begonia species, and many succulents.

Leaf cuttings take at least six weeks to form new leaves, depending on conditions and the season (growth is faster in spring and summer).

TIME: A few minutes per pot

COST: 50 to 75 cents per pot

TOOLS AND MATERIALS

- 3- to 4-inch-diameter **pots**
- **Propagating mix**
- **Pruning shears** or sharp scissors
- A **mother plant** (those listed above are easy choices)
- **Pencil**
- **Rooting hormone** (optional)
- **Propagation heat mat** (optional)
- Small **plastic cup**
- **Fertilizer**

DIRECTIONS

1. Fill pots with propagating mix; firm the soil. Water well.

2. Using shears, cut leaves with stems from the mother plant (remove no more than about 10 percent of the foliage), snipping as close to the bases of the leaf stalks as possible. Select only healthy, fully grown leaves. Trim the stems to 1 to 1½ inches long.

3. With the pencil, poke 1½-inch holes in the soil just off-center.

4. Dip the stems in rooting hormone **(A)**—knock off excess if it's the powdered kind.

5. Insert one-half to two-thirds of the stems into the soil, with the leaf tips pointing away from the pots' center. Gently firm the mix around the stems.

6. To speed up rooting and new growth, set the pots on a heating mat in bright, indirect light. Create a mini-greenhouse by inverting a plastic cup over the leaf as pictured **(B)**. Be sure to keep the soil moist.

7. When new leaves form, fertilize with a dilute solution of fertilizer.

8. When leaves cover most of the soil surface, move young plants into larger pots. African violets usually produce a cluster of new plantlets; gently tease them apart and repot into separate containers.

— Lauren Bonar Swezey

CLIPPINGS

• The Great Backyard Bird Count (note that the dates of this count will be different in 2002). Bird-watchers unite! At least from February 16 through 19. During this four-day period, researchers at the National Audubon Society and Cornell Lab of Ornithology are asking as many bird-watchers as possible to tally and report the number of bird species they have seen in backyards and neighborhood parks. Log on to the bird count website—www.birdsource.org—and feed your observations directly into the database. (Results will be updated hourly.) For alternative reporting instructions, call the Cornell Lab of Ornithology at (800) 843-2473.

• Certified organic seeds. Since 1856, Ferry-Morse Seed Company has been selling American gardeners seeds free of postharvest chemical treatments such as fungicides. Now Ferry-Morse has expanded its product lines to offer 86 varieties of certified organic flower, herb, and vegetable seeds. You can find these seeds at selected nurseries, garden centers, and health food markets, or you can order them on-line at www.ferry-morse.com.

Seed packets
identify contents
of cabinets.

Seed shopping in Denver, the old-fashioned way

■ At Rocky Mountain Seed Company in Denver's Lower Downtown, you can shop for seeds the way your grandparents might have. Kenneth A. Vetting is the third-generation owner of the family business founded by his grandfather F.C. Vetting. Established in 1920, the firm is quartered in a building that dates from the early 1900s. In the retail shop, antique wood cabinets lining the walls hold a plethora of seeds. Employees still use metal scoops to dip into bins of bulk seed. Seeds are then weighed on a 1930s scale. You can buy seeds by the pound, ounce, or packet.

Through its retail shop and mail-order catalog, the firm carries seeds of such heirloom vegetables as 'Early Golden Bantam' sweet corn (1902), as well as modern varieties of green beans, hybrid sweet corn, squash (nearly 60 varieties), peppers (50 varieties), and tomatoes (40 varieties). They also sell seeds of culinary herbs, wildflowers, and turf grasses. In fall, the shop stocks a large selection of spring-blooming bulbs.

Rocky Mountain Seed Company, at 1325 15th Street, is open from 8 to 5 Monday through Friday, until 11:30 A.M. Saturday. The catalog costs $2. To contact the company, write Box 5204, Denver, CO 80217; or call (303) 623-6223. — *C.S.*

Almost hedges

■ Agaves aren't usually lined up like Marines on parade. But designer Mark Bartos of Hortus GardenDesign in Pasadena had good reason for using them with strict formality in Marney Poxon's Pasadena garden. Since Poxon's pueblo revival residence was unquestionably Southwestern, Bartos preferred the garden to be too. But he also wanted it to look like it belonged in the neighborhood. "This is clipped hedge territory," Bartos says. So he juxtaposed natural plantings with areas of obvious order. Looser-textured plants such as acacia and artemisia were placed casually, as if they'd sprung up where they pleased. But he arranged the more architectural plants—like the double row of variegated agaves pictured here—in geometric patterns. "They're hedge substitutes," says Bartos.

For an even more formal look, agaves are mulched with pea gravel and framed in wood. The rest of the area is mulched with decomposed granite to resemble native desert soil. A combination of drip and spray irrigation is used to water the garden.

The balance between nature and order Bartos achieved pleases both the neighbors and Poxon. "The garden looks pretty," Poxon says, "and it smells as sweet as Arizona." — *Sharon Cohoon*

Water-wise landscaping on a small Las Vegas lot

■ When Liz and John Hartley moved from Denver to Las Vegas, they put the xeriscape techniques they'd already mastered into practice in a new setting.

For example, instead of installing a thirsty lawn in their 20- by 20-foot front yard, the Hartleys put in a rock garden. Apache plumes, mesquites, yuccas, and other natives are its foundation. Though they require an occasional watering during especially dry years, these tough plants get by almost entirely on rainfall. Perennials like gazanias and verbenas, which do need regular water, are used more sparingly. They're watered by drip irrigation.

Water harvesting is another xeriscape principle at work in this garden. Several miniwashes were sculpted into the terrain to collect rainwater and let it percolate into the soil instead of draining it into the street. (The sculpting also adds interest to what had been a pancake-flat yard.) A thick layer of mulch helps retain soil moisture, as does the shade provided by a mesquite tree.

In the Southern Nevada Water Authority Landscape Awards competition, the Hartleys' garden won first prize in a homeowner-designed and -installed category.— *S.C.*

STEVEN GUNTHER

Sunny gazanias bloom among the rocks in the foreground.

BACK TO BASICS

LINDA HOLT AYRISS

Apply dormant oil. To control aphids, caterpillars, mite eggs, and some common types of scale on deciduous trees, spray a dormant oil just before buds swell in late winter or early spring (mid- to late spring in cold climates). Using a horticultural (superior- or supreme-type) oil, thoroughly cover the branches **(A)**, crotches **(B),** and trunk **(C).**
— *L.B.S.*

ALLAN MANDELL

The Lenten rose

■ One of the earliest-flowering perennials, *Helleborus orientalis* is called the Lenten rose because it usually blooms during Lent. The flowers pictured here were grown by Elfi Rahr in her Bellevue, Washington, garden. For 25 years, Rahr has been cross-pollinating her favorite plants and collecting seeds of hybrid specimens that bear the largest, most vividly colored blossoms.

This evergreen perennial is hardy in all *Sunset* climate zones, forming 12- to 18-inch-tall clumps of glossy dark green leaves. The blossoms, about 2 inches wide, come in shades of rose, pink, purple, green, yellow, and white.

Around the first of the year, many gardeners cut the leaves off at ground level so that the flowers will be easier to see. Once the flowers have been pollinated, they fade to green, then handsome seed pods form and new bright green leaves emerge.

Many nurseries offer blooming plants for sale this month. A good source for mail-order plants is Gossler Farms Nursery (1200 Weaver Rd., Springfield, OR 97478; 541/746-3922); the catalog costs $2.

Hellebores do best in rich soil with good drainage. They flourish in the shade of high-branched trees or on the north or east side of buildings. In the Northwest's coastal climates, they can take full sun if the soil is constantly moist. — *Steven R. Lorton*

Brighten up February with stachyurus

■ Spilling from barren branches, the pendulous blossoms of *Stachyurus praecox* catch February's light like long crystals dangling from a chandelier.

Stachyurus praecox, a native of Japan, is a deciduous shrub that is hardy only in the mild coastal Northwest, where it does best in *Sunset* climate zones 4, 5, and 6.

Its limbs stretch out and up, growing slowly to a height of 10 feet or occasionally to 15 feet. In winter the naked shrub looks good in combination with broad-leafed evergreens and conifers. The flower stalks are 3 to 4 inches long, with stems that are a rich, purplish brown. On each stem, dozens of tiny bell-shaped blooms in yellowish white to pale greenish yellow appear. The flowers are followed by bright green, 3- to 7-inch-long toothed leaves that turn a subtle rosy red and yellow in fall, revealing small fruit to replace the flowers. The plant does best in the same loose, rich, well-drained soil that rhododendrons favor. It thrives under tall trees, which provide shade and protect its flowers from pelting rain.

Nurseries sell blooming *Stachyurus praecox* in containers this month. Water plants well in the containers and set them out as soon as the soil is workable. — *S.R.L.*

JANET LOUGHREY

pacific northwest • checklist

PLANTING

☐ **BARE-ROOT STOCK.** Zones 4–7: Plant ornamental and edible berries, roses, vines, trees, and shrubs this month. In colder zones, plant as soon as bare-root stock is available; do it on a day when the air temperature is above freezing and the soil is workable.

☐ **EARLY VEGETABLES.** Zones 4–7: Sow peas and spinach seed directly into the soil in mid- to late February.

☐ **HARDY ANNUALS.** Direct-sow seeds of calendulas, clarkias, English daisies, pansies, many kinds of poppies (including California and Iceland), snapdragons, and violas.

☐ **PRIMROSES.** Zones 1–3: Buy acaulis primroses for indoor display (they're perfect on windowsills). Zones 4–7: Grow acaulis primroses indoors or group them in outdoor containers. Plant slightly taller polyanthus primroses in garden beds.

☐ **SWEET PEAS.** Start seeds of flowering sweet peas indoors in 4-inch pots. Transplant seedlings into the garden in March or April.

☐ **WINTER-BLOOMING LANDSCAPE PLANTS.** Shop for trees and shrubs this month. Good choices include Chinese witch hazel, Cornelian cherry, daphnes, rhododendrons, sarcococca, Sasanqua camellias, *Stachyurus praecox* (see the facing page), viburnums, winter hazel, and wintersweet.

MAINTENANCE

☐ **ORDER SEEDS.** These firms offer seeds of plants that perform well in the Pacific Northwest. **Abundant Life Seed Foundation** of Port Townsend, WA (360/385-5660), specializes in heirloom vegetables. **Ed Hume Seeds** of Kent, WA (fax 253/859-0694), offers flowers and vegetables. **Nichols Garden Nursery** of Albany, OR (541/928-9280), offers culinary herbs and gourmet vegetables. **Territorial Seed Company** of Cottage Grove, OR (541/942-9547), offers vegetables and flowers. **West Coast Seeds** of Vancouver, B.C. (604/482-8800), sells herbs, vegetables, and flowers.

☐ **PRUNE HYBRID TEA ROSES.** Zones 4–7: Start by removing dead, injured, or diseased canes and any suckers sprouting from ground level. Then prune for shape. Select the three to five strongest canes and cut them back by about a third, leaving each cane with one outward-facing bud. The remaining canes should form a vase shape. In zones 1–3, prune after buds start to swell. ◆

WHAT TO DO IN YOUR GARDEN IN FEBRUARY

PLANTING

☐ **FLOWERING CHERRIES.** Zones 7–9, 14–17: For staggered bloom, plant several kinds. **Early blooming:** single pink *Prunus yedeonsis* 'Akebono'; double, dark pink *P. serrulata* 'Royal Burgundy' with purplish foliage; single rosy pink Taiwan flowering cherry (*P. campanulata*). **Midseason:** bright pink *P. s.* 'Beni Hoshi'; double, rose pink *P. s.* 'Kwanzan'. **Late:** semidouble, light pink *P. s.* 'Shogetsu'.

☐ **FLOWERING PLANTS.** Zones 7–9, 14–17: Nurseries should have a good selection of early spring–blooming shrubs and vines. Try azaleas, camellias, Carolina jessamines, daphnes, flowering quinces, forsythias, hardenbergias, heaths, primrose jasmines, or some viburnums.

☐ **GLADIOLUS.** Zones 7–9, 14–17: For flowers from spring through fall, begin planting gladiolus this month and make successive plantings every 15 to 25 days through July. An excellent selection of gladiolus is available from Dutch Gardens (800/818-3861 or www.dutchgardens.com).

☐ **LIVING VALENTINE.** Give your sweetheart a valentine that will live on long after February 14. Many blooming gift plants (azaleas, callas, camellias, carnations, gardenias, hydrangeas, miniature roses, and Oriental lilies) can be planted outdoors after blooming. Or tie a red ribbon around a citrus tree or bare-root rose for a gift that will go straight into the garden.

Sunset
CLIMATE ZONES

☐ Mountain (1-2)
☐ Valley (7-9)
☐ Inland (14)
☐ Coastal (15-17)

☐ **SPECIALTY TOMATOES.** Zones 7–9, 14–17: Some of the tastiest varieties for Northern California are 'Brandywine', 'Early Girl', 'Gardener's Delight', 'Green Grape', and 'Stupice' (available from Tomato Growers Supply; 888/478-7333 or www.tomatogrowers.com). Start seeds this month for planting out in late March or early April.

☐ **VEGETABLES.** Zones 7–9, 14–17: Set out roots of artichokes and asparagus and seedlings of broccoli, cabbage, cauliflower, celery (only in zones 15–17), green onions, kohlrabi, and lettuce. Plant beets, carrots, lettuce, peas, spinach, and Swiss chard. Sow seeds of eggplant, pepper, and tomato indoors using bottom heat to speed germination (try an easy-to-use seedling heat mat, $25 to $64 from Charley's Greenhouse Supply; 800/322-4707 or www.charleysgreenhouse.com); allow six to eight weeks to reach transplant size.

MAINTENANCE

☐ **FERTILIZE.** Zones 7–9, 14–17: Feed fall-planted annuals and perennials and established trees and shrubs. Wait to feed azaleas, camellias, and rhododendrons until after bloom. Later this month fertilize lawns.

☐ **HARVEST CITRUS.** Zones 7–9, 14–17: Most citrus should be at their peak flavor now (except 'Kinnow' mandarin oranges and 'Valencia' oranges, which ripen starting in April in coastal areas). Before harvesting the fruit, taste one to see if it's sweet, since ripening time can vary from year to year, depending on the weather. You can harvest as you need the fruit, but be sure to get it off the tree before it dries out or loses flavor, usually within two to three months. Lemons can be harvested year-round. ◆

southern california · checklist

PLANTING

☐ **SUMMER BULBS.** Plant achimenes, agapanthus, amaryllis, caladium, calla, crocosmia, dahlia, daylily, galtonia, gladiolus, tigridia, and tuberose bulbs. In shady areas, plant tuberous begonia tubers. 'Non-Stop' varieties, though with smaller flowers, will bloom well into fall. You can also continue to plant anemones, daffodils, and ranunculus.

☐ **WINTER-FLOWERING SHRUBS.** While they're in flower, select camellias and azaleas at nurseries, but resist planting them if the ground is rain-soaked. Wait until the soil dries out enough to be crumbly. Plant with the rootball at least an inch above soil level, then mulch to protect. Other shrubs to look for include Geraldton waxflower (*Chamelaucium uncinatum*), New Zealand tea tree (*Leptospermum scoparium*), and grevillea.

☐ **WINTER-FLOWERING VINES.** For a showy splash of color, try planting white- and pink-flowered *Jasminum polyanthum* or violet-flowered hardenbergia.

☐ **COOL-SEASON VEGETABLES.** In coastal (zones 22–24), inland (zones 18–21), and high-desert (zone 11) gardens, plant seeds of beets, carrots, chives, endive, fennel, kale, leeks, lettuce, mustard, green onions, parsley, peas, radishes, spinach, and Swiss chard, as well as bulb onion sets and seed potatoes. Sow herbs like chervil, cilantro, and dill. Set out seedlings of cabbage-family plants such as broccoli and cauliflower. Plant bare-root artichokes, asparagus, and rhubarb.

Sunset
CLIMATE ZONES

1-3 7-9 11 13 14-24

DEBRA LAMBERT

☐ **SUMMER VEGETABLES.** In the low desert (zone 13), plant eggplant, peppers, tomatoes, and other warm-season vegetables late this month. But be prepared to protect them with row covers or hot caps if a late frost threatens. In other zones, start seeds indoors for transplanting into the garden in six to eight weeks.

MAINTENANCE

☐ **DORMANT PRUNING.** Before new growth emerges, prune deciduous fruit and ornamental trees, grape and wisteria vines, roses, and summer-blooming shrubs. Wait to prune spring-flowering shrubs until after they bloom. You should also hold off on tropicals like hibiscus; it's too early to encourage growth.

☐ **SPRING FEEDING.** Feed ground covers, shrubs, perennials, and trees with a slow-release, organic fertilizer like well-rotted manure or cottonseed meal. Or use a complete granular fertilizer. If you're within 10 miles of the coast, also feed citrus and avocado this month, giving them a quarter of their yearly recommended nitrogen ration.

☐ **DRAIN STANDING WATER.** If plants are standing in pools of water, dig small, temporary trenches to let the water flow away.

WEED CONTROL

☐ **CONTROL LAWN WEEDS.** To prevent crabgrass and other annual weed seeds from germinating later in spring, apply a preemergent herbicide to lawns early this spring. If you prefer not to use a chemical herbicide, try one of the corn gluten–based products such as Wow! (order from Gardens Alive!; 812/537-8650). ◆

mountain • checklist

PLANNING AND PLANTING

☐ **PLANT BARE-ROOT STOCK.** As soon as your garden soil can be worked, plant bare-root stock. Many nurseries carry small-fruit plants such as blackberries, grapes, raspberries, and strawberries; all kinds of ornamental, fruit, and shade trees; and perennial vegetables such as asparagus and horseradish.

☐ **SHOP FOR SUMMER BULBS.** Garden centers start carrying lilies and other summer-blooming bulbs this month. Plant lilies as soon as your soil has thawed. Store bulbs and tubers of begonias, caladiums, cannas, dahlias, and gladiolas in a cool, dry place until March, when they can be started indoors. Or wait to plant them directly in the garden in May.

☐ **START COOL-SEASON CROPS.** Indoors or in a greenhouse, start seeds of cool-season vegetables, including broccoli, cabbage, cauliflower, kale, and onions, for transplanting outdoors four weeks before the average date of the last frost in your area.

MAINTENANCE

☐ **AVOID SNOW DAMAGE.** To prevent broken or permanently bent branches, remove heavy snow from trees and shrubs after each storm. Use a broom to gently lift and shake all branches within your reach.

☐ **CONTROL FUNGUS GNATS.** House plants are frequently infested with these annoying flying insects. Their numbers often become bothersome in winter and early spring. To control infestations use a soil drench of *Bacillus thuringiensis* (BT), specially formulated to kill gnats. Two mail-order sources are Gardens Alive! (812/537-8650) and Planet Natural (800/289-6656).

☐ **DEAL WITH ICE.** Instead of ice-melting salts, which can burn plants, spread sand or unscented nonclumping cat litter on icy driveways and sidewalks.

☐ **FEED WILD BIRDS.** When natural foods are scarce, wild birds seek out feeders. Seed-eating birds prefer millet, mixed birdseed, and sunflower seeds. Insect-eaters go for peanut butter and suet (hard beef fat available from butchers).

☐ **PREPARE PLANTING BEDS.** As soon as the ground can be worked, dig or till compost or other organic matter into the soil to prepare flower and vegetable beds for spring planting. If you live where spring comes late, you can dig in manure that's not yet fully rotted. By planting time it will have mellowed enough to feed plants without burning them.

☐ **PREVENT CROCUS DAMAGE.** Stop sparrows and finches from shredding crocus blossoms by placing foil pinwheels—the kind sold for children's Easter baskets—every few feet among the flowers. The flashing foil frightens away birds.

☐ **PRUNE SUCKERS.** It's easier to remove suckering stems from the bases of trees and shrubs while the ground is still frozen and before new foliage emerges. If needed, leave a few well-placed suckers to replace broken or old woody stems.

☐ **PULL WEEDS.** Freezing and thawing cycles create loose, friable soil that makes it easier to remove large-rooted weeds such as mallow and salsify by giving them a firm tug or popping them out of the ground with a trowel or weeder.

☐ **SPRAY DORMANT PLANTS.** Spray dormant oil on deciduous fruit and ornamental trees and shrubs to kill overwintering insect eggs, as shown on page 49. Thoroughly wet all surfaces including the undersides of branches. Dormant oil is not recommended for blue spruce because it may discolor the needles. To be on the safe side, test a small inconspicuous area of an evergreen before treating the entire plant. — *Marcia Tatroe* ◆

WHAT TO DO IN YOUR GARDEN IN FEBRUARY

PLANTING

☐ **BARE-ROOT PLANTS.** Zone 10 (Albuquerque): Plant deciduous trees, fruits (apples, blackberries, grapes, peaches, pears, raspberries, and strawberries), and roses.

☐ **PERENNIALS.** Zones 11–13 (Las Vegas, Tucson, Phoenix): For early spring color, plant blackfoot daisy (*Melampodium leucanthum*), brittlebush (*Encelia farinosa*), desert marigold (*Baileya multiradiata*), desert milkweed (*Asclepias subulata*), *Gaillardia aristata*, globemallow (*Sphaeralcea ambigua*), golden columbine, and moss verbena.

☐ **VEGETABLES.** Zones 10: Direct-sow peas by midmonth. After midmonth, start seeds of cool-season crops (broccoli, cabbage, cauliflower, and lettuce) indoors for transplanting in six to eight weeks. Zone 11: Sow seeds of root crops (beets, carrots, radishes, and turnips), Chinese cabbage, lettuce, spinach, and Swiss chard. Wait until the end of the month to plant potatoes. Zones 12–13: Set out transplants of tomatoes by midmonth. Try the prolific heirloom paste tomato 'Punta Banda' (available from Native Seeds/Search; 520/622-5561 or www.nativeseeds.org). Sow seeds of cucumber, eggplant, melon, pepper, and squash indoors for transplanting in six to eight weeks.

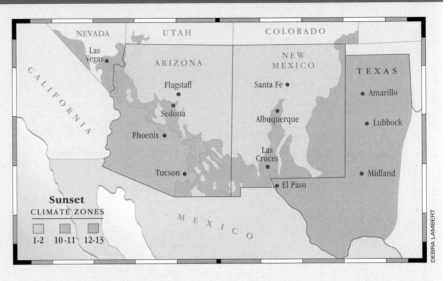

Sunset
CLIMATE ZONES
1-2   10-11   12-13

☐ **WOODY SHRUBS.** Zones 11–13: Plant Arizona rosewood (*Vauquelinia californica*), desert hackberry (*Celtis pallida*), hop bush, jojoba, plumbago (*P. scandens*), and Texas mountain laurel. Dig the planting hole as deep as the nursery container and three to five times wider. Water every seven to 10 days through the summer.

MAINTENANCE

☐ **CARE FOR ROSES.** When nighttime temperatures are forecast to remain above freezing, water established plants, apply a complete fertilizer, and water again.

☐ **FERTILIZE FRUIT AND NUT TREES.** Zone 10: Late in the month, spread granular fertilizer around the tree and scratch it into the soil. Water well before and after application.

☐ **INSPECT IRRIGATION SYSTEMS.** Clean or replace filters. Turn on the system and examine all emitters and connections, repairing or replacing those that leak or are clogged. Remove the end cap and flush out the entire system.

☐ **PREPARE PLANTING BEDS.** Zones 1–2, 10: Get ready for spring planting by digging compost, trimmings, and other organic matter into beds.

☐ **PRUNE PERENNIALS.** Zones 12–13: Cut back winter-flowering California fuchsia, chuparosa, red justicia (*Justicia candicans*), and salvia to promote late-spring bloom.
— *Mary Irish* ◆

2000–2001

Western Garden Design Awards

Twenty winners are among the most innovative home landscapes in the West

By Lauren Bonar Swezey

Sunset's Western Garden Design Awards program is back! Out of several hundred entries submitted by landscape architects and designers, seven jurors (see page 70) selected winning gardens based on their excellence in one of six categories—Colorful Beds and Borders, Garden Details, Garden Renovation, Outdoor Living, Regional, and Small Space. Each garden in this distinguished group contains a wealth of new ideas you can use in your own garden.

And the winners are ...

GARDEN DETAILS: PORTLAND

▮ Perfectly crafted

Visiting Joyce and Bill Furman's forested hillside garden in Portland is a calming experience. As you wander beneath the cool, lush tree canopy, you can hear the soothing sound of water running through creeks and cascading in waterfalls. Trees give the garden a sense of enclosure. • Remaking a bramble-covered, 3½-acre plot was a major undertaking. Because its steep slopes made it inaccessible to heavy equipment, designer John Pruden and his team cleared the site, planted the garden, and built its structures by hand. • Creating paths and water features took 1,000 tons of boulders, rock, and gravel. An intricate, Asian-inspired teahouse was meticulously constructed of cedar and copper shingles. Hand-hewn stairs and bridges connect pathways throughout the garden. Everywhere you turn there's something new to see—a bronze sculpture, a shapely specimen plant. "Stunning details," raved the jurors. "Beautifully crafted!"
DESIGNER: John Pruden, Portland International Garden & Design, St. Helens, OR (503/780-3687)

Ferns, hostas, and hydrangeas border a handmade rock waterfall. A Japanese maple (above) accents a staircase of wood poles. Red azaleas set off a stone fountain (left).

ALLAN MANDELL (3)

Curving steps (left) lead up to a clear blue pool surrounded by alternating ripples of fescue and bluegrass. Espaliered honeysuckle (above left) weaves above New Zealand flax–filled planters. A raised bed (above right) is bordered by a sleek slate water feature. Turf circles (below left) meander through a bamboo grove. Lantana and penstemon mingle (below right).

STEVEN GUNTHER (5)

OUTDOOR LIVING:

MALIBU, CALIFORNIA

▓ All that jazz

Vibrant colors and paving in bold, irregular patterns are the first clues that something's spectacularly different about Lee and Carmen Ritenours' coastal garden, designed by Mia Lehrer. Further investigation reveals a rhythmic row of Mexican fan palms contrasted by an irregular grouping of Queen palms, a series of turf circles skipping across a field of black Mexican pebbles, and fluid lines of turf waving in and around a blue pool. "Stunning!" agreed the jurors. "The garden has a beat of its own," said one. • That this garden is all about rhythm is no surprise—the owners are a jazz guitarist and a Brazilian native. Taking a cue from the owners' backgrounds, Lehrer used musical improvisation awash with vivid tropical colors to inspire her design. She describes the terrace paving—inspired by Brazilian landscape architect Roberto Burle Marx—as a "geometric pattern of colored concrete." With the dancing palms, the grass "notes," and the spicy orange, purple, and red foliage, the elements form an exceptionally lyrical landscape.

DESIGNER: Mia Lehrer, Mia Lehrer + Associates, Los Angeles (213/384-3844)

A broad flagstone patio, surrounded by a low stone wall, allows plenty of room for gatherings. Boulders and rock wall fragments (below) edge a decomposed-granite path that leads to the back patio.

REGIONAL: TUCSON

◼ In the heart of the desert

Nestled between two washes in the core of the Southwest desert, this natural garden, surrounded by saguaros, palo verdes, and thick native vegetation, takes full advantage of its impressive surroundings. • Using a minimalist approach, designer Jeffrey Trent developed a series of garden spaces that gently blend the house's architecture with the environment. To preserve and enhance the landscape required insight and careful planning, despite its deceptively casual appearance. "It's a simple, perfectly executed solution with some unexpected surprises," noted a juror. • Looking out from the back porch, an angular flagstone patio edged with a low wall for seating directs attention to the distant mountains. Broad steps lead visitors into the garden. Like archaeological ruins, fragments of rock walls built from stones excavated during house construction frame the patio and echo colors and forms in the adjacent hills.

• In keeping with the desert landscape, Trent used primarily native plants to enhance areas outside the patio. Closer to the house, he chose salvias, fairy dusters, and other more colorful desert-adapted varieties. Potted cactus accent the patio.

DESIGNER: Jeffrey Trent, Natural Order, Tucson (520/792-9274)

■ South of the border

It's 90° outside, the sun is blazing, and the sounds of splashing water fill the air. Against a rustic stucco wall, water trickles out of scalloped bowls into a colorful blue fountain bedecked with blazing bougainvillea. Although it seems like a scene from a remote Mexican village, this 430-square-foot townhouse garden is actually located at the base of the mountains west of Silicon Valley. "Enchanting!" exclaimed a juror. "The garden is a great achievement for such a small space."

• The remarkable transformation was no easy task. When owner Londa Patch moved into the townhouse, the 13- by 33-foot-long backyard was weed-infested and dilapidated. Since there was no access to the garden from the back, landscape designer Kathleen Shaeffer had to transfer every piece of concrete and slate and every bag of dirt through the house.

• A new, weathered-looking stucco wall accented with an aged wood-and-iron gate hides the old fence. Although the gate leads nowhere, it gives the impression that the garden continues and helps reduce the feeling of confinement. The colorful fountain, a focal point from most rooms in the house, immediately draws attention to the outdoor space. "During the day, it's a bright, sunny jewel," says Shaeffer. "At night, there's a magical quality to the light, shadows, and scent."

DESIGNER: Kathleen Shaeffer, Great Gardens, Santa Cruz, CA (831/423-7849)

The sound of trickling water in a Mexican-inspired fountain enlivens the courtyard. Raised beds are filled with a mix of shrubs and perennials.

THOMAS J. STORY (2)

GARDEN RENOVATION:
PARADISE VALLEY, ARIZONA

■ Desert oasis

As clean and crisp as a Philip Glass com-
position, the Sales family's minimalist garden designed by Greg Trutza is in complete
harmony with its surroundings. From the
angular, 90-foot lap pool accented by octopus agaves to the streamlined patio furniture and 4-foot grids of lawn, every detail
is, like the desert surroundings, purpose-
fully spare. • Before the remodel, the old
pool, glaring white pool deck, and haphaz-
ard plantings had little visual appeal or as-
sociation with the home. Now the spaces
are well integrated and perfectly connected. The tinted exposed aggregate pa-

tio links the indoor spaces with the pool, spa, and outdoor areas. Sculptural details are
repeated throughout the landscape. And mass plantings of ornamental grasses and
shrubs maintain the minimalist approach. "Very inventive," responded a juror.
DESIGNER: Greg Trutza, New Directions in Landscape Architecture, Phoenix
(480/998-4399)

An outdoor firepit in a stone bowl adds
nighttime drama to the garden. Bold
octopus agave scattered around the
patio create interest.

COLORFUL BEDS AND BORDERS: KENSINGTON, CALIFORNIA

■ A celebration of plants

Accented with boulders and urns,
these beds contain grasses,
perennials, and shrubs with foliage in
blue, gray, green, purple, and bronze.

Janet K. Anderson loves new and unusual plants. When she returned to her childhood home
in the East Bay hills, she began renovating the old gardens, originally created in the 1920s.
Anderson soon needed more help. That's when David McCrory and Roger Raiche began
working their magic. • During the next year, they added more than 500 different plants to her collection, including bamboos, cycads, geraniums, palms, 35 types of sages and roses, and hundreds of other perennials and shrubs—all arranged in borders accented with handsome
urns. "It's a remarkable collection of plants combined beautifully in the garden," declared a juror.
DESIGNERS: David McCrory and Roger Raiche, Planet Horticulture, Berkeley (510/849-4485)

An arbor leads to a stone fountain (left). Accessories decorate a copper-topped table (top). A vegetable garden yields a bountiful harvest (above). A raised swimming pool (below) glows at night.

■ Old World charm

Elegant urns filled with agaves, splashing lion's-head fountains, slate countertops: Although these could be details from a lavish Tuscan villa, they're actually in Kimberly Chamberlain's Italianate garden, designed by Terry Broussard. • Every inch of the pie-shaped lot is designed with outdoor living and entertaining in mind, with one twist: The garden is wheelchair-accessible. Chamberlain, who loves to garden, cook, swim, and entertain, has easy access to all outside areas, thanks to Broussard's creative design. "It's a remarkable use of an odd-shaped space," noted a juror. • In the back garden, a slate-tiled lap pool, raised for easy entry, is also a dramatic fountain and focal point. The stucco sides of a raised vegetable bed have a smooth top for more comfortable gardening. An elegant, vine-covered pergola and concrete paths link sections of the garden. A built-in barbecue, copper table, and outdoor shower make the garden unique.

DESIGNER: Terry Broussard, Broussard Associates Landscape Architects, Clovis, CA (559/325-7284)

PAUL MULLINS (4)

Perched above a canyon in Southern California, this boulder-edged pool is perfectly situated to take advantage of dramatic views.

GARDEN DETAILS:
TOPANGA, CALIFORNIA

■ Hilltop haven

Imagine: You're hiking in the Southern California hills above Topanga Canyon. The weather is hot and dry. Suddenly you come upon a pond you want to swim in, with a spectacular view of distant valleys and mountains. • For Ralph and Deborah Weiss, this isn't a fantasy, but a scene from their backyard swimming pool, designed by Nick Williams. Keeping the surrounding landscape in mind, Williams created a "natural watering hole" edged with boulders, flagstone, and native plants; a sandy beach entry adds to the illusion. On the canyon side of the pool, an infinity edge, or drop-off, offers bathers an unobstructed view. "The pool integrates perfectly into the landscape," observed a juror.

DESIGNER: Nick Williams, Nick Williams & Associates, Tarzana, CA (818/996-4010)

COLORFUL BEDS
AND BORDERS:
REDWOOD CITY, CALIFORNIA

■ Plant lover's paradise

Finally, Pamela Ryan was going to have her own garden. After years of waiting, she had a vision of the beds and borders she wanted. In fact, she had sketched a number of different possibilities when she met designer Bernard Trainor. Recognizing Ryan's love for unusual plants and her desire for a casual design, Trainor created exuberant borders filled with stunning displays of plants in various textures and colors. • Around an easy-care chamomile lawn, blowsy grasses (bronze-colored *Carex testacea* and *Miscanthus sinensis* 'Variegatus') contrast with bold foliage of angelica and *Verbascum bombyciferum* 'Arctic Summer'. Intermixed are orange-, purple-, and red-flowering perennials, including *Agastache aurantiaca* 'Apricot Sunrise', *Euphorbia griffithii* 'Fireglow', *Geum* 'Borisii', *Penstemon barrettial* 'Burgundy', and *Verbena bonariensis*. In keeping with the casual theme, Trainor bordered other beds with gravel and edged them with woven eucalyptus branches. Jurors were bowled over by the plant combinations.

DESIGNER: Bernard Trainor, Bernard Trainor Design Associates, Royal Oaks, CA (650/569-3163 or 831/786-9100)

Flowers of bright orange, purple, and yellow play off striking bronze, gray, and green foliage. Bordering the bed is a chamomile lawn that's mowed once or twice a year.

GARDEN RENOVATION: PHOENIX

■ Vision in red

Nothing is ordinary about this cheerful garden in one of Phoenix's oldest neighborhoods. What used to be a traditional front yard of lawn and foundation plants has been transformed into the focal point of the district.
• Owners Victor Vasquez and Scott Aycock wanted a garden where they could relax and socialize with their neighbors. In response, designer Carrie Nimmer turned the formerly flat, open landscape into an inviting courtyard garden to match the house's Spanish-Mediterranean architecture. Boldly colored red walls frame a courtyard filled with wildflowers, desert shrubs, cactus, and succulents. Inside the walls, colored concrete paving leads to built-in seating. Plant-filled containers add color and texture to patios and walls. "It's a wonderful example of how to turn a useless garden into a highly useable one," responded a juror.
DESIGNER: Carrie Nimmer, Landscape Designer, Phoenix (602/254-0300)

Penstemon, desert marigold, and verbena grow around a new courtyard surrounded by vivid red walls. Potted succulents and flowering shrubs accent the seating area.

GARDEN DETAILS:
CASTRO VALLEY, CALIFORNIA

■ Details make the difference

Excellent craftsmanship combined with a striking fusion of materials made jurors take note of Abe Rindal's Northern California garden, designed by Mathew Henning. On a flat suburban lot surrounded by looming homes, Henning created a garden filled with sophisticated details that draw the eye inward, away from unattractive views.
• Jurors were particularly impressed by the paving designs: Ribbons of black slate dissect larger bands of a multicolored African slate and exposed aggregate paving "to suggest the complexities of circuitry or programming in the high-tech world where the owner works," explains Henning. To soften the hard edges, Henning left planting strips between the paving and filled them with baby's tears. "It's truly original and beautifully executed," said one juror.
DESIGNER: Mathew Henning, Henning/Anderson, Oakland, CA (510/531-3095)

Puffs of green baby's tears soften bands of African slate. Long ribbons of black slate run through them.

Brick paving laid in geometric patterns is interplanted with ajuga and rupture wort. Bergenia, brunnera, and ferns soften the edges.

NORM PLATE

SMALL SPACE:
KENSINGTON, CALIFORNIA

■ Jigsaw puzzle

Modern art and landscape design meet head-to-head in this playful 25- by 30-foot entry garden, which gives new shape to paving. • Using geometric forms inspired by the functional and visual requirements of the small space, landscape architects Mathew Henning, Heather Anderson, and Emily Payne developed a jigsaw puzzle of irregularly shaped brick pads to greet visitors and lead them on an exciting journey to the front door. Around the bricks grows a patchwork of foliage textures. "Very innovative," observed one juror. "The geometric shapes create a dynamic tension but with harmony and balance." • Before the remodel, the front garden was fenced off from visitors, who were funneled directly to the front door along a stark concrete walk. Now, as guests step through the front gate, they're immediately welcomed by lush plantings and a striking brick pathway. Because the path is angled, it encourages visitors to experience the garden before arriving at the front door. "It's a three-dimensional entry that says 'Welcome; have fun; come in when you're ready,' " Henning explains.

DESIGNERS: Mathew Henning, Heather Anderson, and Emily Payne, Henning/Anderson, Oakland, CA (510/531-3095)

OUTDOOR LIVING: ALAMO, CALIFORNIA

■ Poolside pleasures

The concept of outdoor living attains new heights with the remodel of Craig and Cara Chases' Northern California ranch house garden. The previously humdrum yard has become the ultimate space for entertaining and family fun. • Jurors were wowed by the variety of gathering areas, numerous amenities for entertaining, and well-thought-out arrangement. "The integration of the house with the landscape is extremely effective," commented a juror. • Landscape architect Gary Orr's impressive attention to detail is evident throughout the garden. By setting the pool patio's grade a few feet below the grade of an existing Japanese maple, he opened up views beneath the tree's lowest limbs. A new concrete planter wall surrounding the maple was finished with board textures to suggest that the wall might have been constructed of wood recycled from an old ranch shed. The barbecue area is actually a fully equipped kitchen with sink, refrigerators, and electrical outlets. To connect the garden with the house's interiors, Orr used terra-cotta-like tile concrete pavement that reflects the interior tile floors. "This garden epitomizes the true concept of indoor/outdoor living," concluded one juror.

DESIGNER: Gary Orr, ORR Design Office, San Leandro/Sacramento (800/647-4781)

GARY ORR

A large terrace connects the patio dining area with the outdoor kitchen and spa. Raised planters border the geometric pool.

Extraordinary kangaroo paw flowers rise behind a row of 'Cream Delight' New Zealand flax (top). *Agave attenuata* and blue oat grass (left) mingle in front of *Senecio mandraliscae*. Multicolored bromeliads (center) edge a recycled-concrete patio. Coral bells (right) add a colorful touch in spring.

SMALL SPACE: SANTA MONICA

Textural treasures

"Contemporary, casual, and colorful" defines this Southern California garden filled with succulents and grasses. The textures are gorgeous, the foliage fabulous, noted one juror. • Designer Nicole Lopez, who owns the home with her partner, David Mota, turned what used to be a drab, lifeless front yard with a dying lawn into a horticultural wonder. For the front walk, she "splurged," purchasing 2- by 2-foot beige flagstone steppingstones. But for the patio off of the new bedroom door, she broke up her old concrete driveway and laid it out in a random pattern. Inset into the concrete on the edge of the patio is a plastic-lined pond now filled with fish and aquatic plants, thanks to surprise additions from neighbors. • Favoring a "high-style, low-maintenance garden," Lopez chose tough plants with interesting leaf color and foliage patterns. As a native Californian, she was particularly drawn to plants that define Southern California gardening, such as agaves, bush anemones, cycads, and New Zealand flax. Her neighbors are equally charmed by the handsome garden that reflects the area's easygoing lifestyle. "People often pull up in their cars and tell me how much they like the garden," says Lopez.

DESIGNER: Nicole Lopez, Nicole Lopez Landscape Design, Santa Monica (310/998-1975)

Native grasses, cactus, and wildflowers grow out of rock outcroppings. The stone edged swimming pool attracts more than just swimmers.

REGIONAL: PALO PINTO COUNTY, TEXAS

■ Touching the land lightly

Sometimes, what you don't do to a landscape is as important as what you do, particularly when it comes to gardening with native plants. This north-central Texas property, designed by Tary Arterburn and Mary Ellen Davidsson, sits among oaks and boulders. Its design is so unobtrusive that the house appears as if it landed in the middle of the natural landscape. But achieving this intentionally minimal design required painstaking care. Jurors were taken with Arterburn and Davidsson's simple yet exceptionally elegant landscape using prairie grasses, native plants that already existed on the property, and boulders.

DESIGNERS: Tary Arterburn, Mary Ellen Davidsson, MESA Design Group, Dallas (214/871-0568)

REGIONAL: SEATTLE

■ Falling waters

A devastating landslide on John and Julie Denney's hillside property turned a serious disaster into a fantastic opportunity. What once had been an unusable slope rising steeply out of Puget Sound has become a gorgeous garden filled with waterfalls, streams, granitelike outcroppings, and lush shade plants. • Using a combination of engineering skills, landscaping talent, and artistic sensibilities, designer Hendrikus Schraven stabilized the hillside and transformed unsightly structural retaining walls into manmade rock outcroppings and ledges that naturally blend into the hillside. A recirculating spring emerges from the granite rocks and tumbles down the hillside into a series of pools. New rock outcroppings also expanded the usable garden space next to the house, creating a level outdoor lawn and garden area. "Each detail was finished to perfection," noted a juror.

DESIGNER: Hendrikus Schraven, Hendrikus Schraven Landscape Construction & Design, Issaquah, WA (425/392-9977)

A dramatic waterfall (left) cascades down the newly stabilized steep slope and under a handbuilt wood bridge. Graceful wisteria clusters (right) frame the new lawn area created by the rock outcroppings. A small pond carved into the rock attracts wildlife.

A dreary backyard dominated by an old fiberglass pool was transformed into a lush, flower-filled garden and lily pond.

Gorgeous mountain views provide an impressive backdrop for this charming wildlife pond. The low wall in back obscures a fire buffer zone.

GARDEN RENOVATION: LAKEWOOD, WASHINGTON

New life for an old pool

What do you do with a leaky old pool surrounded by unattractive concrete decking that takes up half the backyard? Turn it into a colorful garden, of course. In a clever redesign, landscape architect Jeff Glander filled in the fiberglass swimming pool and transformed the area into a pond, verdant garden, and casual patio for outdoor living. • Instead of removing the entire pool, Glander demolished the concrete deck, cut off the top of the pool's shell, punched a hole in the bottom, and filled in the remaining shell with drain rock and high-quality soil. Then he built a new concrete-lined two-tier pond with a waterfall inside the old shell. Patio pavers and brightly colored flower beds replaced the concrete deck. "Suddenly, it looks like a place you want to spend lots of time," noted a juror.

DESIGNER: Jeff Glander, Jeffrey B. Glander & Associates, Olympia, WA (360/357-6972)

SMALL SPACE:
BOULDER CREEK, CALIFORNIA

Wildlife sanctuary

Birds and chipmunks feel right at home in this miniature oasis amid the dry chaparral of the Santa Cruz Mountains. A natural-looking pond surrounded by granite boulders, a low wall, and pockets of native and Mediterranean plants create a lush sanctuary for the wildlife. The design also addresses a very practical issue: the threat of wildfires. • Landscape architect Steve Sutherland needed to maintain a vegetation-free, 75-foot buffer zone for fire safety, but the space was a potential eyesore from the house. His solution was to edge the garden area with a dual-purpose wall to obscure the buffer zone from the house and provide a spot to sit and enjoy the views. An arched opening at the base of one wall ensures that quail continue to stop by. • To encourage visits from a wide variety of birds, a large portion of the garden area surrounding the pond was left unpaved. The colored concrete in the pond complements the golden sandy soil. Jurors applauded Sutherland's simple, yet highly creative design. "It's very original," remarked a juror.

DESIGNER: Steve Sutherland, SSA Landscape Architects, Santa Cruz, CA (831/459-0455)

GARDEN DETAILS:
SANTA ROSA, CALIFORNIA

▪ Bathing beauty

A relaxing morning soak in a large bathtub filled with steaming hot water is a great way to start the day. Or so thought designers and homeowners Anne-Marie and Jeff Allen. But their soaking tub is not indoors like most: It's outdoors—surrounded by a beautiful garden. • The tub has humble origins: It once served as a place to clean tools and keep drinks cold during parties before the Allens spruced it up to use as a bath. Hot and cold running water leads to a newly enameled green tub set on a thick stone slab. Surrounding the slab is a flagstone patio with Japanese black pebbles in the cracks. Screens made from bamboo and birch branches as well as plantings (golden currant, white abutilon, and New Zealand flax) create privacy. Gardenia, jasmine, sarcococca, and sweet olive fill the air with perfume. "Charming and playful!" noted an amused juror.
DESIGNERS: Anne-Marie and Jeff Allen, Allen Landscaping, Santa Rosa, CA (707/526-3177 or 433-3177)

A repurposed bathtub is the centerpiece for a new outdoor bathing oasis.

COLORFUL BEDS AND BORDERS:
KAILUA-KONA, HAWAII

▪ Tropical tapestry

High above the Pacific Ocean on the slopes of Mauna Hualalai is Fern and Larry Kanes' Hawaiian paradise created by designer Julie Ellison. The 165- by 60-foot garden, carefully carved out of a steep, rocky 4-acre parcel, glows in the tropical sun. • Three hundred feet of winding pathways covered with macadamia nut husk mulch lead through a kaleidoscope of more than 150 types of foliage and flowers. Gardenia, plumeria, and tuberose blooms fill the air with their heady scent. Bromeliads, creeping Charlie, dracaena, dumb cane, and philodendrons—plants that are familiar to most as indoor rather than outdoor specimens—tumble down hillsides and poke out of cracks and crevices. "It's like a Hawaiian English garden," observed one juror. "The garden is a wonderful juxtaposition of foliage colors," noted another.
DESIGNER: Julie Ellison, Art of Gardens, Kona/Hilo, Hawaii (808/965-6442)

Lush green, purple, and red foliage creates a tapestry of color. Angel's trumpet flowers at rear.

THIS YEAR'S JURY

Mary Rose Duffield, ASLA, Tucson
Lauren Bonar Swezey, Director WGDA, *Sunset*
Ronnie Siegel, ASLA, La Cañada–Flintridge, California

Kathleen N. Brenzel, *Sunset*
Nancy Hammer, Seattle
Chris Jacobson, San Francisco
Sharon Cohoon, *Sunset* ◆

Say it with nosegays

Lovely bouquets from your garden

By Kathleen N. Brenzel

■ These pretty bouquets, designed by Jill Slater for quick decorating or for gifts, have humble origins. Easy to assemble, each starts not with blooms from a florist but with flowers from cool-season bulbs and bedding plants—cyclamen, dianthus, narcissus, pansies, primroses, and stock.

To make one, gather about 10 flower stems (more for violets, below, and narcissus, right) from the garden or buy 4-inch plants at a nursery. Arrange the stems at the same height so the bouquet takes on a rounded shape. Around the flowers, add leaves with stems. Wrap a rubber band around all stems just under flower heads. Then cover the rubber band with tulle or wired ribbon.

Present the nosegay in a water-filled glass vase (about 4 inches tall with a 2-inch-diameter opening). Or prepare it as a simple bouquet to give as a gift: Wrap the stems with floral tape (available at craft or florist shops) and finish with a satin ribbon.

NORMAN A. PLATE (2)

Hello doily!

A nosegay of violets (30 stems) can be presented in a paper doily with a decorative bow. Cut a hole in the center of the doily and insert the bouquet stems through the hole. Wrap a length of floral wire around the center of the bow, then around the flower stems just under the doily. Wrap floral tape to close the doily's center hole around the stems and the bow wire, then wrap the stems down their entire length. Cut off excess tape.

Fairy primrose with sprigs of Douglas fir **(A)**; 25 stems of narcissus **(B)**; *Primula obconica* with foliage **(C)**; pale yellow stock **(D)**; fairy primrose with sprigs of grevillea, Geraldton waxflower, and eucalyptus **(E)**; cyclamen blooms with foliage and eucalyptus buds **(F)**; and pansies **(G).** Except where noted, each bouquet uses about 10 stems (or about two blooming stems each from five 4-inch nursery plants).

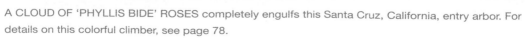

A CLOUD OF 'PHYLLIS BIDE' ROSES completely engulfs this Santa Cruz, California, entry arbor. For details on this colorful climber, see page 78.

March

THOMAS J. STORY

A water feature with a pair of falls

Cascades lace a lushly planted hillside

■ A steep bank rising behind the *Sunset* Northwest Idea House in Portland seemed like the perfect place for a waterfall. Better yet, why not two cascades so they could be seen from all rooms facing the garden? That was the thinking of Gerald Ouellette of G&O Landscaping in Sherwood, Oregon (503/625-6625), who specializes in building natural-looking waterfalls.

Using an excavator for rough work and shovels to finish, Ouellette sculpted the bank into a series of ledges. Starting from the bottom up, he laid a .45-mil rubber liner over the watercourse, then carefully placed boulders from the Columbia River Gorge on the liner. At the top of the watercourse, two streams converge from different directions, tumbling over flat ledges before pouring together into a pool next to the patio.

Two pumps hidden under rocks in the pool recirculate 150 gallons of water per minute from the pool to the falls. A biological filter beneath the stones keeps the water running clear.

Up on the hill, pinkish white blossoms of *Abelia chinensis* and purple-flowered verbena soften rock faces near a bright green tuft of 'Greek Spicy Globe' basil. The blue flowers of catmint and the silvery foliage of licorice plant (*Helichrysum petiolare*) spill out of nooks and crannies. Around the pool, a nicotiana bears starry white blooms, while hostas ('Krossa Regal' and 'Invincible') put out pale lavender flowers. In the crevices among the rocks, patches of brilliant green Irish moss (*Sagina subulata*) catch water droplets that sparkle in the sun.

— *Mary-Kate Mackey*

Southwest spirit

■ Joann Clark's house and garden in Yorba Linda would look right at home in Tucson. That's just what she wanted. Clark, owner of the interior designer firm Artistic Design & Company, fell in love with the desert while gathering ideas there for a client. Though she loved Southwestern style, it was the resource-respecting philosophy behind it that really sold her. "I admire the way Southwestern architecture and landscaping work with the climate instead of fighting it," she says, "and how nothing is wasted, especially water."

When it came time to renovate her home in Yorba Linda, she knew she wanted a pueblo style. When she turned to landscaping, a Southwestern motif was again her choice. That meant very little turf, lots of rock mulch, and a rainfall-collecting, dry creek bed that doubles as a design feature. The reservoir, which runs under the bridge leading to the entrance, also solved the problem of rainfall draining toward the house, which is 8 feet below street grade.

Southwestern landscaping also meant using tough, nondemanding plants such as palo verde and mesquite trees, prickly pear cactus, purple fountain grass, santolina, and red bougainvillea, another desert tradition. — *Sharon Cohoon*

STEVEN GUNTHER

TED STEFANSKI

HEIRLOOM TOMATOES
Take a bite of nostalgia

■ When asked why she grows 80 varieties of heirloom tomatoes, Maureen Moore, a retired history professor, recalls happy memories of her father's vegetable patch. "When I had my own garden," she says, "he and I competed to produce the biggest and earliest tomatoes."

Today Moore's 4,800-square-foot kitchen garden in the hills northeast of San Diego yields tomatoes ranging in size from marbles to baseballs and in every hue but blue. Moore opens the garden to visitors, sells young tomato plants at her home nursery (the Ginger Cat's Garden) in spring and early summer, and sells tomatoes at her informal farmer's market.

At the start of tomato-planting season, Moore hosts a backyard Tomato Festival, during which she lectures on tomato cultivation. (For more on tomatoes, see page 86.) *9–2 Sat or by appointment, Mar-Sep. 10149 Vista Montanoso, Escondido; (760) 749-8108.*

— *Debra Lee Baldwin*

Rustic arbor

■ Pat and Bob Morgan had a sitting area in their Maury Island, Washington, garden. But Vashon Island landscape designer T.M. Holtschlag noticed that it was often ignored: "Let me build you something you will use," he said. He built an arbor over it in a day.

The five-sided structure is made from downed branches of madrona, a rot-resistant wood. Holtschlag first cut five 8½-foot lengths for the vertical posts. Each post was sunk 18 inches into the ground. Then Holtschlag cut branches to span the uprights and attached them with 6-inch screws. Finally, he topped the arbor with smaller branches and twigs, wiring most of them in place to secure them from the wind.

The rustic arbor makes the deck an even more enchanting spot for sitting in good weather. — *Jim McCausland*

ANDREW DRAKE

JIM McCAUSLAND

The longest-blooming heath

■ Heaths are among the most impressive winter-flowering plants in some Western gardens. Many heaths bloom from January through March, but a few bloom from November through April or even May. One of the finest is pictured here flanking the walk in Jennifer Aflatooni's front yard in Port Orchard, Washington: pink-flowered *Erica darleyensis* 'Darley Dale'. Its white-flowered cousin *E. d.* 'Silberschmelze' (sometimes sold as *E. d.* 'Alba' or 'Mediterranean White') is another good choice. These tough, reliable plants thrive in *Sunset* climate zones 2–10, 14–24. Each plant will grow about 1 foot tall with a 2-foot spread in five years. Set out plants this month in well-drained soil on a site that gets full sun. — *J.M.*

CLIPPINGS

•**Apples, sweet or tart.** After sampling last fall's harvest, we found two new apples worth growing.

'Jubilee Fuji' is an extra-early sport of 'Fuji' with the same sweet flavor and crisp texture. This apple with blush red skin comes to harvest in late September west of the Cascades and in early October on the east side. If you prefer a tart apple, try 'Corail' (formerly called 'Pinova'), a new German variety with red-and-gold skin and spicy flavor.

Both 'Jubilee Fuji' and 'Corail' can pollinate each other and be pollinated by almost any other apple. Both are sold for about $14 per tree from C&O Nursery in Wenatchee, Washington (800/232-2636 or www.c-onursery.com).

'Comet Pink' daisy, left;
mimulus Jelly Bean White,
and Jelly Bean Apricot, above;
and 'Comet White' daisy.

CLAIRE CURRAN (4)

Pink fleece and friends

■ 'Comet Pink' and 'Comet White', two new marguerite daisies (*Argyranthemum frutescens*) distributed by the Flower Fields, share the same name. Beyond that, the similarities end. The pink version blooms so profusely its foliage is often totally hidden by flowers, making it a very showy bedding plant. 'Comet White' doesn't flower as freely, but it has wonderful blue-green, finely textured foliage and a nice mounded shape. Its overall grace makes it a great addition to a mixed perennial border. *A. frutescens* thrives in *Sunset* climate zones 14–24 and grows to about 3 feet tall by 4 feet wide. Give it full sun, good drainage, and regular water.

NEW FOR SPRING

Jelly Bean mimulus. Bush monkeyflower (*Mimulus aurantiacus*), a Pacific Coast wildflower, has a reputation

for being persnickety—difficult to propagate and intolerant of garden conditions, for example. But Rich Persoff, an Alameda-based hybridizer, has spent more than a decade correcting those flaws. In the process, he's also increased the flowering capacity of the plant, reduced its legginess, and introduced some great colors. Three of his elegant but hard-to-find hybrids have been picked up by the Flower Fields and are now in general distribution. Jelly Bean White and Jelly Bean Apricot are shown here; the third variety is pale yellow. *M. aurantiacus* grows best in zones 7–9 and 14–24, and reaches 2 to 3 feet tall and 1½ feet wide. Give it full sun (light shade in hot climates) and good drainage. Keep soil on the dry side and fertilize minimally. — *S.C.*

The perfect cottage garden rose

■ "It's a traffic stopper!" says landscape designer Lynn Robinson of the spectacular 'Phyllis Bide' rose in front of her Santa Cruz cottage. Each spring, clusters of dainty apricot to cream blooms open along the canes until the entry arbor is completely engulfed in a cloud of roses.

"I specifically sought out this rose after seeing it in a local garden," says Robinson. It's colorful, disease-resistant, and blooms all season long—even into December in Robinson's mild climate. It's also very casual-looking, she explains, because of the blowsy appearance of the flowers as they age. (You wouldn't want to choose this rose for a formal garden.)

The 10- to 12-foot-tall climber is easy to maintain. Robinson has no time for selective pruning, so she just shears it to the shape of the arbor in winter. The fertilizer regimen is equally simple. In late winter, she applies an organic mixture (usually alfalfa meal, compost, and epsom salts). After the first flush of bloom in spring, she sprays the foliage with a water-soluble fertilizer, such as Peters Professional Plant Food 20-20-20.

Since Robinson planted 'Phyllis Bide' seven years ago, she has made many new friends. "In spring when I see someone pulling over, I know they're stopping to look at the rose. I usually come out and say hi, because I know they want to know its name." 'Phyllis Bide' is available from Michael's Premier Roses (916/369-7673 or www.michaelsrose.com).

— *Lauren Bonar Swezey*

A toasty tepee for veggie seedlings

■ Planting tomatoes two months before the last frost date may seem like a dream. But a device sold variously as Wall O' Water and Wall-O-Water can help mountain gardeners get a head start on planting tomatoes, peppers, basil, and other warmth-loving summer crops. Essentially, the device is a collar composed of vinyl tubes that you fill with 3 gallons of water to form a self-standing, tepee-style cloche 18 inches tall. The tubes absorb solar heat by day then release it at night, keeping the temperature inside the cloche above freezing.

A week before planting, place the empty collar around a 5-gallon bucket on the soil. Then, using a hose, fill each tube three-quarters full with water. Remove the bucket, allowing the collar to close in upon itself. Let the soil inside warm for one week, then plant the seedling in the center of the cloche. Once plants begin to grow through the top, fill the tubes completely with water to expand the top of the cloche. After all danger of frost is past, remove the collar. Gently squeeze the water out of each tube, then dry and store for next year.

Wall O' Water is sold in many garden centers. Mail-order suppliers usually sell it in packages of three for about $9. Wall O' Water can be ordered through Irish Eyes Garden City Seeds in Thorp, Washington (877/733-3001 or www.gardencityseeds.com), and Seeds Trust in Hailey, Idaho (208/788-4363 or www.seedstrust.com).

— *Amy M. Hinman*

AMY M. HINMAN

If you like 'Bing', you'll love 'Lapins' cherry

DICK RIFKIND

Most cherry lovers would agree it's hard to improve on a good 'Bing', but that's precisely what the breeders have done at the Pacific Agri-Food Research Centre in Summerland, British Columbia. Breeders crossed 'Van' and 'Stella' cherries and came up with 'Lapins', a self-pollinating variety that produces large crops of delicious dark fruit that often measure almost 1 inch in width. The fruit resists splitting, and its texture is somewhat firmer than 'Bing'. 'Lapins' is a late-maturing cherry, with harvest time around late June and early July.

Growers have found 'Lapins' to be as hardy as 'Bing', down to -4°. On standard rootstock, this tree can reach 15 feet wide and 40 feet tall, but it should be pruned to keep it under 20 feet tall. If you want a smaller tree, look for one grafted on dwarf rootstock. Nurseries sell bare-root trees in early spring and in containers anytime. Also order from One Green World in Molala, Oregon (877/353-4028; www.onegreenworld.com) or Raintree Nursery in Morton, Washington (360/496-6400; www.raintreenursery.com). — *Dick Rifkind*

A happy meeting of native and nondesert plants

■ The owners of this new home in Paradise Valley, Arizona, wanted their landscape to reflect the surrounding desert. But they also wanted to incorporate some nondesert elements, including a vegetable garden and citrus trees. Landscape architect Steve Martino of Phoenix accommodated these seemingly disparate desires by using walls and well-placed plants to screen nonnative plantings and visually emphasize desert plants.

Along the house's south side, which faces a street, Martino created a series of 3- to 4-foot-tall curving walls that separate more lush plantings closer to the house from more natural plantings at the perimeter of the property. On the street side, where the site had been scraped bare during construction, Martino revegetated the ground by hydro-seeding with a mixture including brittlebush (*Encelia farinosa*), creosote bush, desert marigold (*Baileya multiradiata*), and globemallow (*Sphaeralcea ambigua*). The desert marigolds readily adapted to the sunny site.

CHARLES MANN (3)

Desert marigolds are predominant outside the perimeter wall (top and left), while artichokes and roses thrive inside (above).

Martino hid a small vegetable garden and citrus orchard behind curving walls. In this garden, which can't be seen from the street or from inside the house, the owners grow artichokes, Brussels sprouts, lettuce, and other crops in raised beds with waist-high railings that can be draped with shadecloth or frostproof blankets to protect plants as needed. Roses also grow in this enclosed space, along with grapefruit, lemon, and orange trees, which are shaded by several specimens of blue palo verde (*Cercidium floridum*). — *Nora Burba Trulsson*

pacific northwest • checklist

PLANTING

☐ **CAMELLIAS.** Zones 4–7: Spring-flowering japonica hybrids are coming on strong. Set out any of them right away or keep them in a container and enjoy them up close until blooms fade, then plant.

☐ **COOL-SEASON VEGETABLES.** Zones 4–7: Plant cole crops and leafy vegetables (broccoli, Brussels sprouts, cabbage, cauliflower, kale, kohlrabi, lettuce, mustard, spinach, Swiss chard); root crops (beets, carrots, radishes); alliums (chives, garlic, leeks, onions, shallots); peas; and potatoes. You can also plant bare-root asparagus, horseradish, and rhubarb, but do it right away.

☐ **LAWNS.** Start new lawns or patch worn ones this month, as grass growth begins. To start a lawn, save time by laying sod or save money by sowing seed. In either case, till the top 6 inches of soil, pick out roots and rocks, then till in a 2-inch layer of organic matter. Level the soil—a roller helps—then lay the sod or rake in seed and reroll. Don't let sod or the seeded area dry out until the grass is well established and growing strongly.

To patch a lawn, rough up the bare areas, rake in grass seed, cover with compost or peat moss, and water.

☐ **WARM-SEASON CROPS.** Start seeds of basil, cucumbers, eggplant, melons, peppers, and tomatoes indoors for transplanting into the garden in May, after danger of frost is past.

MAINTENANCE

☐ **CARE FOR CLEMATIS.** Zones 4–7: Cut back summer- and fall-flowering clematis to the strongest stems now, then scratch fertilizer into the soil around the bases of plants. Zones 1–3: Prune after danger of hard frost is past. In all zones, prune back spring-flowering varieties immediately after bloom.

☐ **CONTROL SLUGS.** When the weather is mild and damp, slugs come out in force. Control them while they're small. Iron phosphate bait is nontoxic to humans and pets, but it isn't the slug's favorite snack; metaldehyde-based poison baits still seem to be more attractive to slugs. If you prefer the direct approach, chop slugs in two whenever you see them (a machete is the perfect tool for this).

☐ **DIVIDE PERENNIALS.** Zones 4–7: Divide summer- and fall-flowering perennials like asters, chrysanthemums, and Shasta daisies to promote better bloom this year. Zones 1–3: Divide them in April. In all zones, wait until autumn to divide spring-flowering perennials.

☐ **FEED LAWNS.** Zones 4–7: Grass starts growing vigorously this month. Feed it with ½ pound actual nitrogen per 1,000 square feet. You can't go wrong by using a fertilizer formulated with a nitrogen-phosphorous-potassium ratio of 3-1-2. ◆

WHAT TO DO IN YOUR GARDEN IN MARCH

NURSERY SHOPPING

☐ **CITRUS.** Zones 8–9, 14–17: Choose young trees in 5-gallon cans—they'll establish faster than larger ones. Look for the new dwarf citrus on Flying Dragon (Hiryu) rootstock. Try 'Dwarf Lisbon' lemon, 'Dwarf Melogold' grapefruit-pummelo hybrid, 'Dwarf Mid-Knight' Valencia orange, 'Dwarf Star Ruby' grapefruit (requires less summer heat to ripen than most grapefruit), or 'Dwarf Washington' navel orange.

☐ **FRAGRANT ROSES.** For lovely, fragrant flowers, order one of the following 2001 introductions: From Heirloom Roses (503/538-1576 or www.heirloomroses.com), dusky pink 'Anne Hathaway' (floribunda/ shrub) and pink and amber 'The Oregon Trail' (shrub); from Jackson & Perkins (800/292-4769 or www. jacksonandperkins.com), light pink 'Pearl Essence' and deep apricot 'Sultry' (hybrid teas); and from Wayside Gardens (800/845-1124 or www.waysidegardens.com), fuchsia 'Peter Mayle' (hybrid tea).

☐ **PERENNIALS.** If you prefer to shop for perennials from home, several Northern California specialty nurseries offer perennials such as boltonia and *Nicotiana sylvestris* by mail. They include Canyon Creek Nursery (530/533-2166 or www. canyoncreeknursery.com), Digging Dog Nursery (707/937-1130 or www. diggingdog.com), Mountain Valley Growers (559/338-2775 or www. mountainvalleygrowers.com), and Weiss Brothers Nursery (530/272-7657 or www.plantperennials.com).

Sunset
CLIMATE ZONES
☐ Mountain (1-2)
☐ Valley (7-9)
☐ Inland (14)
☐ Coastal (15-17)

DEBRA LAMBERT

PLANTING

☐ **VEGETABLES.** Zones 7–9, 14–17: For a continuous crop of bush peas, beets, carrots, lettuce, radishes, spinach, Swiss chard, and turnips, sow seeds successively, two weeks apart. Set out seedlings of broccoli, cauliflower, and cabbage. If the last frost has passed, you can also start planting the first warm-season crops when they appear in nurseries. Most need warm soil (at least 60°) to thrive. To give plants a boost, plant through black plastic and use floating row covers.

MAINTENANCE

☐ **AMEND SOIL.** Zones 7–9, 14–17: Before planting, amend fast-draining or heavy clay soils with compost, ground bark, or other organic material to improve soil texture and water retention. If you use ground bark or another wood product, make sure it has been nitrogen-stabilized (read the label or ask the supplier), or add a nitrogen fertilizer at planting time so the mulch doesn't retard plant growth.

☐ **BEDDING PLANTS.** Replace fading cool-season annuals with heat lovers such as celosia, dahlias, marigolds, petunias, salvias, verbenas, and vincas. Plant from six-packs when you can; they're more economical and rapidly catch up to 4-inch plants. Cosmos, sunflowers, and zinnias are good choices too; they're great for cutting.

☐ **DIVIDE DAHLIAS.** About two weeks before planting, divide clumps of tubers that have been stored over the winter. Use a sharp knife to cut each clump into sections; include at least 1 inch of stem and an eye with each division. Discard soft or diseased tubers and cut off any dead roots. Allow tubers to air dry for a couple of weeks and then plant in well-prepared soil. ◆

southern california • checklist

PLANTING

☐ **PERMANENT PLANTS.** Early spring is one of the best times of year to plant ornamental trees, shrubs, ground covers, and perennials. The weather is mild and gentle on transplants, and nurseries are well stocked, providing plenty of choices.

☐ **SUMMER BULBS.** Continue to plant acidantheras, agapanthus, caladiums, calla lilies, cannas, crocosmias, dahlias, daylilies, gladiolus, tigridias, tuberose, tuberous begonias, and watsonias.

☐ **VEGETABLES.** If you have bare spots in your vegetable bed, your best bets to plant this month are beets, carrots, radishes, Swiss chard, and turnips. You can also squeeze in a few more cool-season vegetables such as kale, kohlrabi, leaf lettuces, mesclun mixes, and potatoes. Or start summer corn, beans, or squash.

MAINTENANCE

☐ **FERTILIZE MOST PLANTS.** If you can fertilize your garden only once a year, do it now. As the weather warms, plants are raring to grow, but rain may have leached most of the nitrogen from the soil. Give all your hardworking permanent plants a boost by sprinkling granulated high-nitrogen fertilizer around them. Annual and perennial flowers, all types of turf grass, container plants, house plants, and citrus and avocado trees will welcome food now too. Wait until after bloom to feed camellias and azaleas, then give them an acid-type fertilizer such as cottonseed meal.

Sunset
CLIMATE ZONES
1-3 7-9 11 13 14-24

DEBRA LAMBERT

☐ **PRUNE FUCHSIAS.** Trim trailing varieties to the edges of their containers. Cut upright types back by two-thirds so that only two or three nodes (buds or leaf scars) remain on the stems. Then feed to spur new growth.

☐ **PRUNE ORNAMENTALS.** Prune boxwood, pittosporum, and other evergreen shrubs to shape before spring growth surges. Wait until *after* bloom to prune spring-flowering ornamental fruit trees (peach, pear, and plum) and shrubs.

☐ **THIN FRUITS.** Begin thinning apples, pears, and stone fruit when they reach about ½ inch in diameter. Space fruit 4 to 6 inches apart or leave one fruit per spur. In general, the earlier the variety, the more heavily it needs to be thinned.

☐ **TURN HYDRANGEAS BLUE.** If you want blue hydrangeas to remain blue, apply aluminum sulfate to the soil before the flowers form. Follow package directions.

PEST CONTROL

☐ **CONTROL APHIDS.** New growth attracts these sucking pests. Dislodge with a strong blast of water from a hose. Or strip aphids from plants by hand. Wear thin disposable rubber gloves if you're squeamish.

☐ **MANAGE SNAILS.** To reduce their numbers for the rest of the year, handpick them, or trap them by allowing them to collect on the underside of a slightly elevated board, overturned grapefruit rinds, or lettuce leaves from which you can collect and dispatch the pests. Or set out commercial bait.

☐ **PREPARE FOR WHITEFLIES.** Set out yellow sticky cards (available at most nurseries) to trap whiteflies around susceptible plants like abutilons and fuchsias. ◆

mountain • checklist

PLANTING

☐ **BARE-ROOT ROSES.** Remove packaging material and soak the rose in a bucket of water for as long as 24 hours. Dig a hole 2 feet deep and 2 feet wide. Plant the roots so the bud union or graft is 2 inches below the ground. Mix a shovelful of compost and ½ cup of superphosphate into the backfill, refill the hole, then water. Mound soil over the canes to protect them from freezing. Later in the season, gradually remove the soil so that the canes are uncovered completely by the last frost date in your area.

☐ **EARLY SPRING COLOR.** Brighten up the garden by setting out frost-hardy English primroses and pansies in beds or frostproof containers. Before planting, harden off these greenhouse-grown flowers by placing them outdoors in a shady area for a few hours a day, gradually increasing their exposure to sunlight over a week; bring them indoors at night. After planting, cover the flowers with an old sheet or frost blanket (available at garden centers) if freezing temperatures threaten.

☐ **SOW COOL-SEASON VEGETABLES.** If you didn't amend vegetable beds last fall, dig in several inches of well-rotted manure or compost now. As soon as the soil is free of frost, sow seeds of beets, carrots, endive, kohlrabi, lettuce, onions, parsnips, peas, radishes, spinach, Swiss chard, and turnips.

☐ **SOW HARDY ANNUALS.** Scatter seeds of hardy annuals directly into the garden where you want them to grow. Among the flowers that germinate best in cold, moist soil are annual phlox (*P. drummondii*), bachelor's buttons, calendulas, California desert bluebells (*Phacelia campanularia*), California poppies, clarkias, Johnny-jump-ups, larkspurs, love-in-a-mist (*Nigella damascena*), moss roses, Shirley poppies, snapdragons, sweet alyssums, and wallflowers.

MAINTENANCE

☐ **CARE FOR LAWNS.** If your lawn is covered with gray snow mold, rake it off. Dehydrated turf grass attracts winter mites; to control them, keep the grass well watered, especially on south-facing slopes and along sidewalks.

☐ **FEED BULBS.** When early-flowering bulbs like crocuses and species tulips finish blooming, drench the leaves with a foliar fertilizer or manure tea. The nutrients absorbed through the foliage will feed the bulbs and nurture next year's flowers. Don't remove the leaves until they turn completely brown.

☐ **GROOM GRASSES, SHRUBS.** Trim ornamental grasses close to the ground before new growth starts. It helps to wrap an elastic cord around the whole clump and use a saw to cut the old stems below the cord. To keep shrubs compact, cut all stems of beautyberry, bluebeard, butterfly bush, dyer's greenweed (*Genista tinctoria*), rubber rabbitbrush, and snakeweed (*Gutierrezia sarothrae*) to within a few inches of the ground before they leaf out.

☐ **RELOCATE SEEDLINGS.** Bachelor's buttons, larkspur, poppies, and snapdragons often pop up in places you don't want them. Seedlings of these plants are easily moved to better locations. Choose stout, vigorous plants 2 to 3 inches tall and dig them up with a fist-sized clump of soil. Replant immediately and water thoroughly whenever the soil dries out until they get reestablished. Give extras to friends and neighbors.

☐ **TRANSPLANT SHRUBS.** Move shrubs while they are dormant to reduce the risk of transplant shock. Dig up as large a rootball as practical. Replant immediately and water thoroughly to keep the entire rootball moist until new growth appears.

— *Marcia Tatroe* ♦

southwest · checklist

PLANTING

☐ **CITRUS.** Zones 12–13 (Tucson, Phoenix): Try grapefruit ('Marsh Seedless' or 'Redblush'), lemon ('Eureka' or 'Lisbon'), mandarin or tangerine ('Daisy' or 'Fairchild'), sweet orange ('Trovita' or 'Valencia'), and tangelo ('Minneola' or 'Orlando').

☐ **GROUND COVERS.** Zones 12–13: Set out *Calylophus hartwegii,* dwarf periwinkle (*Vinca minor*), Mexican evening primrose, trailing indigo bush (*Dalea greggii*), and verbena.

☐ **PERENNIALS.** Zones 10–11 (Albuquerque, Las Vegas): Plant aster, chrysanthemum, coreopsis, feverfew, hollyhock, maximilian sunflower (*Helianthus maximilianii*), Shasta daisy, and statice. Zones 12–13: Plant blackfoot daisy (*Melampodium leucanthum*), California fuchsia, lantana, penstemon, and salvia.

☐ **SHRUBS.** Zones 12–13: Plant frost-tender shrubs like Baja fairy duster (*Calliandra californica*), hibiscus, red bird of paradise (*Caesalpinia pulcherrima*), ruellia, and yellow bells (*Tecoma stans*).

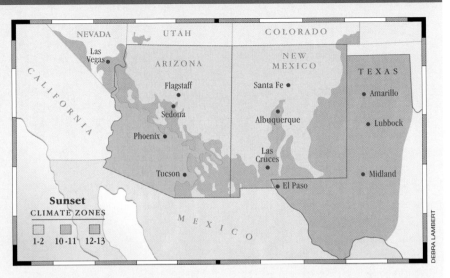

Sunset
CLIMATE ZONES
1-2   10-11   12-13

☐ **SUMMER BULBS.** Zone 10: Set out gladiolus corms when all danger of frost is past and the soil warms to 65°. Zones 11–13: Plant amaryllis, caladium, canna, crinum, hymenocallis, and zephyranthes.

☐ **VEGETABLES.** Zones 1–2 (Flagstaff, Santa Fe): Start seeds of celery and onion indoors for transplanting in six to eight weeks. Plant garlic. Zone 10: Plant onion sets. Sow seeds of broccoli, cabbage, carrots, cauliflower, kohlrabi, lettuce, radishes, and spinach in prepared beds. Start seeds of eggplant, peppers, and tomatoes indoors in six to eight weeks. Zones 11–13: Sow black-eyed peas, bush beans, cucumbers, lima beans, melons, okra, pumpkins, summer squash, and sweet corn. Set out basil, eggplant, and peppers.

☐ **VINES.** Zones 10–11. Plant Carolina jessamine, Lady Banks' rose, silver lace vine, trumpet creeper, and Virginia creeper. Zones 12–13: Plant any of the above, plus bougainvillea and coral vine.

MAINTENANCE

☐ **DIVIDE PERENNIALS.** Zones 10–13: Divide clumping perennials like chrysanthemum and daylily.

☐ **TEND PERENNIAL HERBS.** Zones 10–13: Cut back ratty-looking perennial herbs like mint and sage, then fertilize and water.

☐ **WATER.** Zones 10–13: As days lengthen and get warmer, adjust irrigation schedules. Citrus and fruit trees need water every 10 to 14 days.
— *Mary Irish* ◆

the great tomato taste-off

We prowl the West's tomato festivals to discover the most flavorful varieties you can grow

By Jim McCausland

There are hundreds of great tomatoes to choose from, so how can a thoughtful gardener possibly narrow the field to a promising half dozen or so? For answers, *Sunset* staffers queried tomato growers and chefs around the West, attended tomato festivals, and hobnobbed with growers at farmers' markets.

It didn't take long to discover that some tomatoes came up on winners' lists again and again, and that they fall into every possible category: big slicers; tomatoes for paste, sauce, and drying; cherry tomatoes; and even wild currant tomatoes.

A surprising number of favorite tomatoes are heirlooms—ones whose seed has been passed down from gardener to gardener for generations. Many have great stories attached. 'Brandywine', for example, was bred by the Amish more than a century ago. 'Paul Robeson' is a variety named for the African American singer and actor, but it was cultivated and named in Russia. 'Radiator Charlie's Mortgage Lifter' was bred by a West Virginia radiator repairman named M.C. Byles during the 1930s. He sold his seedlings for $1 each and paid off his $6,000 mortgage in six years.

But we don't grow tomatoes for stories. We grow them for that intense flavor you can only get from vine-ripened fruit—and for their amazing array of colors, shapes, and sizes.

ABOVE: Laid out for tasting, red tomatoes include 'Boondocks' and 'Brandywine'. RIGHT: Cornucopia of tomatoes shows an array of colors, shapes, and sizes.

the great **tomato** taste-off

CLOCKWISE FROM TOP LEFT: Ripe harvest of gold-striped tomatoes accented with chives. At the September Carmel TomatoFest in Carmel Valley, California, visitors sample chunks of ripe tomatoes in many colors. San Diego grower Tom Chino holds a lug of his prized crops. Once green gel disappears from around tomato seeds (as on top fruit), flavor diminishes.

Varieties

At the festivals we attended, everyone—from passionate vegetable gardeners to casual weekenders out for a good time—seemed intent on ferreting out the best-of-show tomato, something with flavors more rich and complex than the finest wine. Everyone, that is, except the chefs who were preparing tomato-based foods for festivalgoers to eat. Judged by the dishes they offered, these cooks were as interested in color and shape as in flavor, offering salads spangled with yellow, red, and orange cherry tomatoes, and basil-sprinkled, olive-oiled slabs of white, pink, green, and crimson tomatoes layered with thin slices of sweet onions.

It seems that presentation counts for a great deal more when tomatoes are prepared for eating, especially in light of the ways in which their flavors change when combined with other ingredients. A little salt can enliven a bland tomato, and seasonings such as basil flakes and salad dressings can completely alter the flavor of the tomatoes they dress. Cut up into salsa, a tomato's original flavor fades well into the background, overpowered by cilantro, garlic, onions, peppers, and salt.

With all these things in mind, we offer our spring list of great varieties. All have memorable flavors, a few are sculptural beauties, and some are downright ugly. But each one is worth growing.

Slicers

Every gardener needs at least one tomato variety that's big enough to slice onto hamburgers and sandwiches, and to fan out on deli trays.

'**Brandywine**' is a hands-down favorite. The original, a pink beefsteak type, can weigh 1½ pounds per fruit. It has big flavor to match, and a unique, melt-in-your-mouth softness to the flesh. It also grows in red, yellow, and black versions, but the original is still most favored. A wonderful lighter pink is '**Odoriko**', a Japanese hybrid with perfect balance between sweet and acid flavors.

'**Paul Robeson**' stands out among several great black tomatoes. Most appear tinged with black, brown, or purple, skin and flesh included. They tend to be richly flavored, sometimes with hints of spice or red wine, and they vary widely in size. 'Paul Robeson' weighs about 10 to 12 ounces. For an outstandingly rich black variety, try '**Cherokee Purple**', whose fruit often grows to 10 ounces or more. '**Black Prince**', from Siberia, is on the small end of the scale for black tomatoes; it's flavorful and juicy, and can be sweet when it gets enough summer heat.

Grow '**Earl of Edgecombe**' for its firm and meaty texture, superb flavor, and gold-orange skin and flesh. It is also remarkably disease-free. '**Flammé**', a French heirloom, is only half the diameter of 'Earl of Edgecombe' but has a deeper, persimmon orange skin and nicely balanced sweetness.

Among the classic reds, '**Dona**' is a medium-size French hybrid that was bred for the fresh market, where flavor is at a premium; plants produce liberally. '**Costoluto Genovese**' and '**Charlie Chaplin**' have fluted sides that make them tough to peel but great for stuffing or slicing. Of the two, the heat-loving 'Costoluto Genovese' has the most fluting and is probably better for eating, with a meaty, full-flavored, slightly tart interior. '**Stupice**', a Czech variety that's modest in size and cold-tolerant, does particularly well along the coast and in other mild-summer climates.

'**Green Zebra**' is an heirloom open-pollinated variety that comes true from seed. Its golden yellow base is covered with green stripes, and flavor is on the tart side, too green for some. '**Tigerella**' (also called 'Mr. Stripey') has met with better reviews for flavor. It's also on the small side, with yellowish stripes over a red base.

There are also a couple of great yellows worth noting: the huge (up to 2-pound) '**Pineapple**' (yellow with peach blush) and '**Nebraska Wedding**'. Though they aren't pictured here, they placed highly in tastings.

Cherries

Productive and easy, cherry tomatoes look great in salads, especially when colors are mixed. Beautifully bite-size, they make perfect appetizers to serve with dip.

If there was a consensus winner for flavor among all tomatoes, it was '**Sun Gold**'. In theory, the best tomato should have a good balance of sweetness and acidity, but nearly everyone who tasted this one simply lit up with delight. Forget the theories: This one's sweet as candy.

'**Isis Candy**' is a sweet red cherry that received almost as much praise as 'Sun Gold'. And if you'd like to drop a yellow into the mix, grow the mild, beautifully pear-shaped '**Yellow Pear**'. Some rated it highest among the cherries.

Paste tomatoes

Good paste tomatoes are seedless (or nearly so), meaty, and on the dry side—qualities that also tailor them perfectly to sauces and sun-drying. Some have good enough flavor to be used (and sold in supermarkets) as slicers.

'**Roma**' is the classic paste tomato, but in the tastings we attended, full-flavored '**San Marzano**' and sweet '**Viva Italia**' came out ahead. At 3½ inches long, 'San Marzano' is bigger than 'Roma' and has some resistance to late blight. 'Viva Italia' is a determinate type (it grows to a certain height, then stops), so all the fruit comes to harvest at about the same time. (That's a clear advantage for anyone who wants to do all their harvesting and canning on the same weekend.) And it's very sweet and disease-resistant. '**Principe Borghese**' is particularly favored as a drying tomato.

(Continued on page 90)

Growing tips

Tomatoes are generally heat-loving plants, some of which tend to grow tall, so give them full sun, rich soil, and a trellis or stake to grow on (see illustration, below right). Plant seedlings in the garden after all danger of frost is past, or plant a bit early and protect crops with row covers.

If your soil is rich and well amended with compost, you won't need to fertilize. But if it's nutrient-poor, apply controlled-release complete fertilizer once at planting time; if you need to feed the plants later to boost growth, use a relatively mild plant food like fish fertilizer. Too much nitrogen makes plants grow leaves at the expense of fruit.

There's one more thing to consider if you want really great tomatoes: water management.

The secret to growing the perfect tomato

Last summer at Gary Ibsen's Carmel TomatoFest in Carmel Valley, California, there were two plates of 'Early Girl' tomatoes on the tasting tables. One was among the sweetest, most intensely flavored fruits at the show, while the other—its genetic twin—was an unremarkable also-ran.

What made the difference? It all came down to culture. The unremarkable one was grown conventionally, while the sweet one was dry-farmed (a technique possible only where the ground retains enough moisture to support the plant all season long with no irrigation—like some areas near the Northern California coast, for example). Dry farming has several advantages. It keeps water off the leaves so plants aren't as susceptible to late blight, it concentrates sugar in the fruit, and it minimizes fruit splitting, which results when late-season irrigation pushes pressure inside the fruit past the breaking point. Among the disadvantages, dry-farmed plants produce fewer, smaller fruits than conventionally grown tomatoes.

Not every gardener can dry-farm, but the lesson is clear: If you can manage to water regularly but sparingly, you'll get sweeter, split-free fruit. Drip irrigation can help you achieve that.

Beating blight

Though tomato plants can (but don't usually) encounter many minor problems, there is one major problem that can cost you your whole crop: late blight. Caused by the same organism (*Phytophthora infestans*) that brought about the 19th-century Irish potato famine, it usually shows up around harvest time, transforming plants and fruit into disgusting blackened waste.

Tomatoes become infected when airborne spores land on wet plants, so your first line of defense is to keep leaves dry: Flood or drip-irrigate your tomatoes and never use an overhead sprinkler. To keep rain off leaves, some gardeners cover their rows with clear plastic tents. Fungicide prevents and controls late blight.

Lessons from the masters

The Chino family has been growing tomatoes near San Diego for decades and sells only directly to consumers and to a few choice (and choosy) restaurants. They grow scores of varieties through the year, all vine-ripened to perfection.

The Chinos find that indeterminate tomatoes (ones that grow and keep fruiting until stopped by frost or disease) are generally better flavored than determinate types, which come to harvest on smaller plants all at once. Virtually all the tomatoes listed in this article are indeterminate, but you'll encounter both determinate and indeterminate tomatoes in seed catalogs.

Here's the Chino system for growing tomatoes.

■ Prepare the soil by tilling 3 inches of well-aged manure into the top 6 inches of soil.

■ Plant seedlings in succession at three-week intervals from February through July. Cover earliest plants with sheet plastic stretched over hoops to boost warmth early in the season and prevent frost damage. Remove hoops after night temperatures stay above 50° to 55°.

■ Train indeterminate tomatoes up a trellis system like the one shown below (determinate varieties are best raised in cages). The trellis system keeps ripe fruit off the ground, so it's less susceptible to disease and is easier to harvest. The basic structure is made from 8-foot steel stakes pounded 18 inches into the ground at 4-foot intervals. Horizontal wires fastened to the stakes at 1-foot intervals give the tomato vines support as they grow; polypropylene string secures vines.

■ Harvest as soon as tomatoes color up fully. Look for green gel around the seeds. Once it turns clear, the tomato is overripe and flavor diminishes. Pick often: The Chinos harvest at least every other day. Cold degrades tomato flavor, so tear the plants out after nighttime temperatures start dropping below the mid 40s. (This is also a good argument for storing tomatoes on a kitchen counter instead of in your refrigerator's crisper).

■ Rotate your crops. This is the best crop insurance you can have, since many diseases survive in the soil, waiting for you to replant susceptible crops.

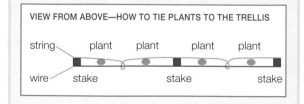

VIEW FROM ABOVE—HOW TO TIE PLANTS TO THE TRELLIS

12 winning tomatoes

'Stupice'

'Black Prince'

'Isis Candy'

'Costoluto Genovese'

'Charlie Chaplin'

'Sun Gold'

'Earl of Edgecombe'

'Brandywine'

'Flammé'

'Paul Robeson'

'Green Zebra'

'Dona'

Sources

An increasing number of tomato varieties are showing up as seedlings in nurseries. But if you can't find what you want locally, you can probably buy it through any of several mail-order nurseries that specialize in tomatoes. Some good ones include *Johnny's Selected Seeds* (207/437-9294 or www.johnnyseeds.com), *Natural Gardening* (707/766-9303 or www. naturalgardening.com), *Nichols Garden Nursery* (866/408-4851 or www. nicholsgardennursery.com), *Seeds of Change* (888/762-7333 or www.seedsofchange. com), *Shepherd's Garden Seeds* (860/482-3638 or www.shepherdseeds.com), *Territorial Seed* (541/942-9547 or www.territorial-seed.com), *Tomato Growers Supply* (888/478-7333 or www. tomatogrowers.com), and *Totally Tomatoes* (803/663-0016 or www.totallytomato.com). Two tomato books that can help you enormously are *The Great Tomato Book,* by Gary Ibsen (Ten Speed, Berkeley, 1999; $14.95; 800/841-2665), and Smith & Hawken's *100 Heirloom Tomatoes for the American Garden,* by Carolyn J. Male (Workman, New York, 1999; $17.95; 800/722-7202).

Tomato trials and growers

Growers, nurseries, and a winery have summer tomato festivals, trials, or tomatoes for sale. Find out more about these on our website, www. sunset.com. For more on the Carmel TomatoFest (or seeds of most winning varieties,) go to www.tomatofest.com. ◆

Best of the West 2001

A mail-order nursery for just about any plant, an expanded source for many old garden roses, and a daffodil display garden for springtime ordering. These are some of the things that make the West wonderful in 2001.

ROBIN CUSHMAN

Nonpareil nurserypeople

What's special about **Ray and Peg Prag** and their southern Oregon nursery, Forestfarm? Well, for 25 years, the Prags have produced a fantastic catalog of out-of-the-ordinary plants. They grow about 6,000 plants, of which 4,000 to 5,000 appear in their catalog. The Prags' nursery is to the West what Hillier's Nursery is to England: the go-to place for just about any plant. *$5 catalog. (541) 846-7269 or www.forestfarm.com.*

For the roses

Rose lovers long made pilgrimages to Limberlost Roses in Van Nuys, California, for Bob Edberg's selection of old garden roses. Now the formerly by-appointment-only establishment has been reorganized under a new owner, Amit Reichman, and renamed **Limberlost Nursery;** it offers 550 different cultivars—and is open Monday through Saturday. Meanwhile, Edberg hasn't abandoned the field: **Limberlost Roses** specializes in rose books new and old, including gems like a first-edition copy of William Paul's 1848 *The Rose Garden. Limberlost Nursery: 16152 Saticoy St.; (818) 997-6421. Limberlost Roses: 7304 Forbes Ave.; (818) 901-7798 or www.oldroses.com.*

Daffodil daze

Looking for a Wordsworthian crowd, a host of golden daffodils? Then make tracks for **Van Lierop Bulb Farms** in Puyallup, Washington. The company specializes in daffodils (along with tulips and irises), at their peak bloom in March. You can look over a small and perfect display garden to discover which daffodils you can't live without next year. Order bulbs on the spot, and they'll be on your doorstep in time for October planting. *13407 80th St. E; (253) 848-7272.*

NORMAN A. PLATE

Nursery gardens

What are *Sunset* readers' favorite nursery demonstration gardens? **Roger's Gardens** in Corona Del Mar, California (949/640-5800), earned much praise. Farther north in Aptos,

READER PICKS California, **Native Revival Nursery** (831/684-1811) won kudos for its selection of native California plants. And in Woodinville, Washington, **Molbak's Nursery** (425/483-5000) was described by a reader as "a wonder world of plants and flowers any season of the year."

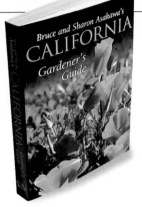

California here they come

A useful adjunct to *Sunset's* own *Western Garden Book* is *California Gardener's Guide,* by radio garden experts Bruce and Sharon Asakawa. It's a handsomely photographed primer to the best plants for gardens from Calexico to Crescent City. *Cool Springs Press, Franklin, TN, 2000; $25; (888) 591-5117.*

Most heroic tool

In August 1910, the West was burning from Montana to Oregon. Near Wallace, Idaho, ranger Ed Pulaski and his men were fighting one of the most savage blazes. Surrounded by flame, Pulaski ordered his men into a mine shaft and kept them inside at gunpoint. When a relief party found their motionless bodies, one rescuer called, "Come outside, boys, the boss is dead." Pulaski rose. "Like hell he is," he said.

As historian Stephen Pyne tells the tale in his new book, *Year of the Fires,* Pulaski emerged determined to perfect better tools for fighting forest fires. Tinkering in his blacksmith shop, he created a tool that's half ax, half mattock, and ideal for digging firebreaks. Even today, the **pulaski** is a preferred fire-fighting tool. Landscapers applaud the way it tears into brush and soil—its enduring popularity a tribute to the man who devised it. *U.S. Forest Service–approved pulaski, $57.95 from Forestry Suppliers; (800) 647-5368. Stephen Pyne's* Year of the Fires *will be published in May by Viking.*

Shogun

Broad-leafed evergreen trees that can withstand temperatures down into the low teens are extremely useful in the landscape—and about as rare as blue roses. That's why Monrovia's introduction of several new varieties in this category is such good news. The trees, part of Monrovia's **Shogun series,** are all indigenous to Japan. *Elaeocarpus decipiens* (Japanese blueberry tree), shown here, produces winter fruit attractive to birds. It is the first tree in the series available in wide distribution. *www.monrovia.com.*

LEFT: STEVEN GUNTHER ABOVE: THOMAS J. STORY (2)

Country charmers

Rambling over the ground or spilling from containers, nasturtiums are carefree creepers with a range of flower colors

By Kathleen N. Brenzel

Favorite faces in the nasturtium clan include Dwarf Jewel Mix (top), yellow double (center), and tangerine Whirlybird. Nasturtiums make beautiful bouquets (right).

■ To many gardeners, "neon" and "nasturtium" go together. That's because varieties with bright orange flowers glowing among green lily-pad leaves are the ones people remember the best. But not all of these casual plants that drape themselves gracefully over fences and trellises, spill from baskets, creep along path edges and around boulders, can be called neon. Nasturtiums now come in a rainbow of colors, from soft apricot and peach to pale yellow and creamy white, with mouthwatering names such as 'Creamsicle' and 'Vanilla Berry', or romantic names like 'Moonlight'. Old varieties with brilliant orange or gold flowers still remain garden favorites—'Empress of India' still reigns—but new dazzlers like fiery red 'Copper Sunset' are also coming on strong. And luxuriant foliage is no longer just apple green but ranges from purplish blue to green splashed with white.

Clearly, *Tropaeolum majus* is an annual (perennial in mild climates) with many virtues. "Nasturtiums are great for covering bare spots in the garden," says Renee Shepherd, who has grown many different varieties over the years. "They're easy enough for kids to grow from seed. They climb, they ramble, they spill. And the flowers are attractive to hummingbirds."

Nasturtiums are also at home in the kitchen. Leaves and flowers are edible, with a peppery, watercress flavor. As garnishes, they add bite to salads and color to open-faced sandwiches or vegetable dishes. Shepherd tosses chopped flowers and leaves into pasta along with chopped basil, chives, and parsley, then sprinkles the dish with parmesan cheese. Whirlybird mix is her favorite for this use because of all the color, though some cooks find 'Empress of India' more flavorful.

Blossoms are vibrant in bouquets too, especially when they're mixed in shades of deep orange-red, tangerine, and peach. They can last a week or more if you snip off the

Fresh colors include 'Moonlight' (top) and 'Peach Melba' (above). Mixed climbers ramble in Julie Heinsheimer's Palos Verdes, California, garden.

lower leaves before immersing stems in water.

What's more, these charmers are as easy to grow as they are versatile (see the facing page). We grew many varieties in *Sunset's* test garden—both mounding plants and climbers, spurred and spurless. Our favorite ones are listed at right.

For containers, low beds

Dwarf kinds form loose mounds about 10 to 15 inches tall—suitable for hanging baskets, patio containers, and low borders.

'ALASKA'. Rounded green leaves marbled with cream; flowers in a range of gold, salmon, orange, and mahogany.

'COPPER SUNSET'. Mounding plants with spurless, semidouble blooms of vibrant coppery red.

'CREAMSICLE'. Single-spurred flowers swirled orange and creamy white; deep blue-green leaves.

DWARF JEWEL MIX. Yellow, orange, and color blends; rich green leaves.

'EMPRESS OF INDIA'. Brilliant vermillion flowers; deep blue-green leaves. Plant grows in cascading mounds.

'PEACH MELBA'. Primrose yellow flowers with bright red throats.

'VANILLA BERRY'. Custard white blooms with paw-shaped, strawberry markings in the throat.

WHIRLYBIRD. Upward-facing blossoms of rich cherry-rose, cream, gold, mahogany, scarlet, tangerine, and a mix.

For rambling

Climbing types reach 6 feet tall and can gracefully twine up fences and arbors, or ramble over the ground.

'AMAZON JEWEL'. Spurred blossoms come in shades of pumpkin, peachy rose, gold, ruby, and pale lemon. Variegated foliage softly marbled in green and cream.

GLORIOUS GLEAM MIX. Lots of large, often fragrant, single and semidouble spurred flowers in shades of yellow, gold-orange, and scarlet.

'MOONLIGHT'. Soft primrose yellow flowers and bright green leaves.

Planting and care

• Plant nasturtiums in spring in mild-winter areas (fall in the low and intermediate deserts). If a freeze is predicted, cover seedlings with row covers. In cold-winter regions, wait until weather warms to plant.

• Plant from cell-packs, 4-inch pots, or seed, in a sunny spot (with afternoon shade inland) with well-drained soil. Set plants about 10 inches apart.

• Sow seeds ½ to 1 inch deep; keep soil moist until seeds emerge. Thin to 12 to 18 inches apart (half that distance in containers).

• Once established, plants do best with only moderate watering. Too much water and fertilizer prompts luxuriant foliage but fewer flowers.

Sources

Plants and seeds of many varieties, including Dwarf Jewel Mix, are widely sold in nurseries. Also try the follow-

THOMAS J. STORY (2)   BELOW: ROBIN CUSHMAN

Pale yellow 'Moonlight' (above) climbs a fence. 'Amazon Jewel' blooms (above left) in a more traditional deep tangerine color. Nasturtium petals (below) add color and bite to a mixed salad.

ing mail-order and on-line sources.

Cook's Garden, Box 5010, Hodges, SC 29653; (800) 457-9703 or www. cooksgarden.com. Eight varieties, including Glorious Gleam Mix and 'Peach Melba'.

Nichols Garden Nursery, Albany, OR; (541) 928-9280 or www. nicholsgardennursery.com. Nine varieties, including Alaska Mixed, 'Empress of India', and 'Moonlight'.

Park Seed Company, Greenwood, SC; (800) 845-3369 or www.parkseed. com. Six varieties, including 'Alaska', 'Empress of India', 'Moonlight', and Whirlybird.

Renee's Garden, (888) 880-7228 or www.reneesgarden.com for a source near you. Six varieties, including 'Copper Sunset' and 'Vanilla Berry'. ◆

Summer veggies in pots

Tips from *Sunset's* test garden help you grow your favorite crops in containers

By Jim McCausland

ABOVE: Cucumber vine is trained to a trellis.
RIGHT: Scarlet runner beans climb a wire obelisk.

THOMAS J. STORY (2)

If you have a sunny space for a pot on your patio or deck, you have enough room to grow summer vegetables. The trick to success with warm-season vegetables in containers is to choose compact varieties or to train vining crops like beans on vertical supports.

■ CONTAINERS. Large containers, ranging from 18 to 24 inches wide and 12 to 16 inches deep, provide plenty of room for roots and don't dry out as quickly as smaller containers. That translates into healthier plants that yield more produce. At *Sunset,* we've achieved good results with containers made of plastic, terracotta, and wood. Half-barrels work well too, as long as they have enough drainage holes.

■ POTTING SOIL. Start with a premium potting mix and supplement it with ½ cup of controlled-release fertilizer for each container. Or, if you prefer to use an organic fertilizer as we do in our test garden, blend three parts potting mix with one part aged chicken manure.

■ PLANTING TIPS. Press soil firmly around each seedling. When you're finished, the soil level should be 1 inch below the container's rim; if the soil settles after you water, add more.

At planting time, set trellises, tepees, or wire cages in containers to provide support for vining crops—pole beans, cucumbers, and tomatoes.

Water as often as needed to keep the soil as moist as a wrung-out sponge. In our test garden, we also fed plants with fish emulsion every 10 days and added a handful of complete organic fertilizer to each container every month.

Best summer vegetables for containers

You can plant 10 to 20 beans, three eggplants or peppers, or two cucumbers in a single large container. But don't plant more than one squash or tomato seedling per pot. Around the edges of the container, you can tuck in a few edible companions like basil.

BEANS. Both bush and pole types take well to containers. To support pole beans, put a trellis at the rear of the container or form a tepee with bamboo poles. Try bush- or pole-type 'Blue Lake'. We trained 'Dwarf Bees' runner beans up a wire obelisk (shown above).

CUCUMBERS. We grew 'Lemon' and 'Marketmore 86' (shown above) cukes up a trellis, tying the vines to the trellis as they grew. Neither variety produced as well as those grown in the ground.

EGGPLANT. We grew 'Ichiban', an Oriental type, in the same container as sweet peppers (see below); it bore beautiful small eggplants. Another one to try is 'Bambino', which produces walnut-size fruits.

PEPPERS. Try 'California Wonder' and 'Sun Bell' sweet peppers. Among the hot chilies, 'Habañero' does especially well in pots.

SUMMER SQUASH. Try a compact bush type like 'Eight Ball' or 'Spacemiser' zucchini, or train a climbing kind like 'Tromboncino' or 'Zucchetta Rampicante' on a trellis.

TOMATOES. Grow a tomato plant in a cage or train it up a trellis set in the container. Allow the plant to produce from one to three strong vertical leaders, tying them to the support as they climb. We've had good luck with the slicer type 'Black Krim', cherry types including 'Sun Gold' and 'Sweet Million', and the bush-type 'Roma' paste tomato. ◆

A landscape burglars hate

Strategies, plants, and devices that enhance security

By Jim McCausland • Illustration by Mary Chandler

A man strolls down your front walkway in broad daylight and knocks on the door. Although your neighbors notice him, they aren't suspicious. When nobody answers, he walks around to the side gate and lets himself into the enclosed rear garden, where he enters your house by way of a forced back door, window, or garage. Once inside, he heads for your bedroom to rifle through drawers, closets, and mattresses in search of jewelry, cash, and other valuables. A pro burglar will be out of there—with the loot—in less than 10 minutes.

This scenario is fairly typical for burglars, according to Ron Corbin, crime prevention specialist with the Las Vegas Metropolitan Police Department. Most burglaries are committed during daylight on weekdays, slightly less often at night, and most often when nobody is home.

According to national statistics, burglary and theft arc the two major crimes you're most likely to experience. Note: In most states, when anything is taken from inside your house, the crime is classified as a burglary (usually charged as a felony); when anything is taken from outside your house, it is a theft (often charged as a misdemeanor).

Fortunately, there are a number of steps you can take to make your yard a more formidable deterrent to criminal intentions. In evaluating security needs, it's helpful to think of your landscape in terms of public and private areas.

> *Fortunately, there are steps you can take to make your yard a more formidable deterrent to criminals.*

Protect the public part of your yard

Your main entry—and probably your whole front yard—is considered a semipublic area, if only because the law allows anyone free passage from the street to your front door unless you've posted your property with No Trespassing signs.

■ Keep the landscape open and park-like, with low shrubs (under 3 feet) and trees pruned high (7 feet or more off the ground). Intruders will have nowhere to hide if you, neighbors, or police show up unexpectedly to ask questions.

■ If you choose to have a fence in front, it should be a see-through type like a picket fence, so it won't give a burglar cover.

■ The area between the driveway and the house should also be open and well lighted so crooks can't prowl around parked cars and perhaps steal them or their contents.

■ Mount lights on eaves to wash light across the exterior walls of the house. At night this silhouettes intruders, making them visible from the street.

Safeguard the private areas

Your rear yard—or any part of the landscape that's cut off from public view by fences or walls—makes up the private area. While you want privacy so you can enjoy a peaceful nap in the sun, secluded spaces are also potential entry points for criminals. Here's how you can discourage them.

■ Grow thorny plants like agave, barberry, cactus, Natal plum, and yucca under rear windows. But keep them trimmed below the windowsills, so you could quickly jump over the plantings to escape a house fire.

■ Remove any tree branches that afford easy access over walls or to upper-story windows.

■ If your rear garden is fenced or walled, cover the barrier with a thorny plant like a climbing rose or bougainvillea. This gives you greenery and flowers to look at but provides a painful deterrent to would-be intruders.

■ If you don't have a fence but have the space, consider planting a hedge of dense, spiny shrubs like hedgehog or porcupine holly (*Ilex aquifolium* 'Ferox'), pyracantha, or one of the many shrub roses.

(Continued on page 100)

Front yard

1. If you want a fence in front, choose a picket or metal-rail type that you can see through.

2. Prune tree branches high for clear vision across yard. Remove limbs that act as ladders to upper windows.

3. Keep plantings low to reduce cover near the entry and driveway.

4. Install lamps that wash light across house walls to silhouette intruders.

5. Install path lights with motion or light sensors, or with timers to turn them on if you forget.

6. Mount motion sensor–activated floodlights on the garage.

7. Use manual or electronic locks on the garage door.

Backyard

8. Train thorny vines or climbing roses over fences or walls. Or plant a hedge of spiny shrubs.

9. Plant prickly shrubs beneath windows, but keep the windowsills clear for escape from fire.

10. Self-closing gates should have locks.

- Install self-closing gates and keep them locked. A padlocked gate in a hard-to-scale fence or wall makes it tougher for burglars and thieves to get in and get away with larger items like bicycles and computers.
- Lock up the garage or toolshed. You'd feel really silly if a burglar borrowed your ladder to break into an upstairs window. Garages are favorite entry points for intruders. Consider installing an automatic garage door opener, which effectively locks the door. Most new garage door openers have built-in security codes that are hard for crooks to crack electronically.
- Install floodlights to illuminate rear doors and windows.

Electronic security devices

Well-positioned floodlights activated by timers or motion or light sensors force criminals to do what they hate most: work in the light. Buy floodlights with built-in motion sensors ($20 to $62 at hardware stores) or hook up a motion sensor (about $16) to an existing light. When the sensor detects repeated motion within a preset radius (12 to 70 feet is common), it completes an electric circuit for 1 to 12 minutes, then turns it off again. That circuit can turn on a floodlight, activate a sprinkler system (which irritates burglars), or sound an alarm. But remember that stray cats and passing possums may also trigger the alarm (some sensors can be set to focus above the height of small animals). Mount sensors out of easy reach, so thieves can't easily turn them off.

The next line of defense

Think of landscaping and exterior security devices as your first line of defense. Your second line begins at the walls of your house and should include dead bolts on doors and secure window latches. Consider an alarm system monitored by security services or your local police department. ◆

11. Barking dogs attract attention that burglars prefer to avoid. Many breeds, from large rottweilers to miniature schnauzers, bark vigorously at intruders.

Around the house

12. Secure interior window latches. Consider a motion detector and a sensor that detects breaking window glass, linked to an alarm system. For sliding windows and patio doors, install track locks or use bars or rods to jam tracks.

13. Furnish all exterior doors with dead bolts.

14. Install a burglar/fire alarm system.

Aloe arborescens blooms behind bench. *Aloe thraskii* is the taller one in back of it, set against leafy green foliage of Chilean mesquite tree (*Prosopis chilensis*). Ground cover in front is *Dymondia margaretae*. RIGHT: *Aloe capitata* produces pompom blooms.

Made for California

Giant succulents blaze with bloom in Patrick Anderson's Fallbrook garden

By Debra Lee Baldwin • Photographs by Steven Gunther

■ When renowned British horticulturist Christopher Lloyd visited Southern California two years ago, he asked his hosts to show him gardens he wouldn't see back home. "How about a Japanese garden?" they suggested. Lloyd's response was polite but firm: "If I wanted that, I'd go to Japan." His opinion of some local landscapes, with their endless lawns bordered by evergreen shrubs, was equally withering: "It's astonishing you do so little with what you've got," he exclaimed.

His attitude changed dramatically when he and his hosts strolled through the Fallbrook garden pictured here, owned by succulent fancier Patrick Anderson and his partner, Les Olson. The ½ acre hillside garden is filled with aloes and agaves in soft hues and sculptural shapes. *Aeoniums,* euphorbias, and crassulas add texture and fill in the gaps between them, along with African daisies (*Arctotis* hybrids), Mexican blue palms (*Brahea armata*), golden barrel cactus (*Echinocactus grusonii*), organpipe cactus (*Lemaireocereus marginatus*), pindo palms (*Butia capitata*), blue-flowered pride of Madeira (*Echium fastuosum*), purple-flowered Mexican bush sage (*Salvia leucantha*), and brittlebush (*Encelia farinosa*), a native California shrub with silvery leaves and profuse sulfur-yellow flowers. In midwinter, when perennial gardens snooze, the 200-plus aloes in Anderson's collection blaze with candelabras of red, yellow, orange,

A: Pink-fringed echeveria hybrid resembles a crinkly cabbage. B: *Aloe grandidentata* flowers about to burst into yellow bloom. Flowers in background are *Aeonium arboreum*. C: Intimidating leaves frame stunning blooms of *Aloe marlothii*. D: Blue-green *Aeonium nierrense* offers a cool contrast.

BEAUTIFUL BRUTES

Following is a list of Patrick Anderson's favorite succulents. Large succulents do best in frost-free areas but may tolerate a few degrees below freezing. Inland, they like dappled shade during the summer months (keep them clean of leaf litter that might harbor snails, mealybugs, and other pests).

■ *Aeonium arboreum* 'Zwartkop'. Deep bronze, almost black rosettes, up to 6 inches wide. Grows to a 3-foot branched shrub. Good bedding plant; cut back every couple of years to keep it low and replant cuttings.

■ *Agave attenuata.* Forms huge rosettes of spineless, gray-green leaves. Very sculptural. 'Nova', a blue-gray variety, is more difficult to find but worth seeking for its striking color.

■ *Agave parryi huachucensis.* Spiny, symmetrical rosettes resemble foot-wide gray artichokes edged with black. Offsets freely; eventually forms attractive colonies. Good for smaller garden areas, but not where children play.

■ *Aloe arborescens* (tree aloe). Branches from the base to form a large shrub of overlapping gray-green, spiny leaves. Numerous deep orange flower spikes appear in early winter and stay six weeks or more. Attracts hummingbirds.

■ *Aloe brevifolia.* Small (6-inch) blue-gray rosettes have white teeth on leaf edges. Offsets can be transplanted to create an attractive ground cover, or left alongside the mother plant to form low-growing clumps. Salmon-orange flowers on 16-inch spikes in summer.

■ *Aloe cameronii.* Hard to find, but worth seeking. Produces bright scarlet flowers in midwinter. Leaves turn brilliant red in the summer sun. Branches freely to form a low, mounding shrub about 18 inches tall by 3 feet wide.

and cream. Clearly, it's a garden suited to the region's arid landscape and to the summer-dry climate; plants that grow here need little water once established.

All this beauty took preparation. Five years ago, Anderson and Olson sculpted the land—a former lime orchard—with a tractor. Then they amended the soil with decomposed granite to enhance drainage, fashioned dry streambeds, covered pathways with pea gravel, and added redwood bridges. At the top of the slope, they built a white stucco pavilion; its orange tile roof echoes the color of aloes in bloom. To provide shade, they planted lacy, drought-tolerant trees, such as *Acacia karroo, Cassia nemophila,* and mesquite (*Prosopis glandulosa* and *P. chilensis*).

They aimed for lushness. "You'd never see these plants growing so closely together in nature," Anderson says. Though the aloes and agaves started out small, by the time Lloyd visited, many had grown to human size and larger.

Anderson's admiration for giant succulents' form, texture, and quirkiness began at the Huntington Botanical Gardens in San Marino, where he works as a volunteer. Much of his collection came from Huntington plant sales, but he also shops in large nurseries and those that specialize in cactus and succulents.

Giant aloes and agaves are the stars of his collection, but they're also the thugs of the plant world. Their sprawling leaves menace with spikes, points, and serrated edges. "These are not plants for children," Anderson says as he examines a small

■ **Aloe ferox.** Large (2-foot-wide) solitary rosettes in gray or green with thorned leaves eventually form a single-trunk tree. Upright, multibranched stems bear yellow to deep orange flowers from December through February. A striking, if intimidating, specimen plant.

■ **Aloe striata** (coral aloe). Tapered pale green leaves bordered in red are smooth, fleshy, and thornless. Solitary ground-hugging rosettes rarely offset, but each produces brilliant orange flowers. Stunning when planted in groups.

■ **Crassula falcata** (propeller plant). Low, sprawling succulent with sickle-shaped, leathery gray leaves in opposite pairs. Fragrant flowers in late summer resemble scarlet heads of broccoli.

■ **Echinocactus grusonii** (golden barrel cactus). Magnificent, spherical cactus covered with bright yellow curved spines. Position where it will be illuminated by late-afternoon sun. Large specimens can be expensive and tend to be snapped up by professional landscapers. Plant small and be patient.

■ **Euphorbia ingens.** Valuable for large, vertical form. Bright green branching trunks eventually form a tree. Make sure you have room for it—cutting it back is dangerous because of its caustic sap.

■ **Euphorbia milii** (crown of thorns). A small woody shrub with branches covered by fierce-looking but fairly harmless spines. Blooms (technically, bracts) appear all year, in various shades of pink, yellow, or red.

■ **Euphorbia rigida.** Scaly gray leaves on branches up to 2 feet tall are topped by clusters of brilliant chartreuse bracts in late winter. Reseeds; weed out the ones you don't want. ◆

A: Coral tree (*Erythrina sykesii*) flowers appear before the tree produces leaves. B: Sunlight turns *Aloe cameronii's* leaves crimson. C: Golden barrel cactus (*Echinocactus grusonii*) march toward *Aloe arborescens*. D: *Aloe marlothii* flower.

puncture wound he got while weeding. "You're wise to approach them wearing goggles and leather gloves." So why on earth would anyone want to grow them? "Because they're otherworldly," he answers.

When gently squeezed, a sun-warmed, gel-filled *Aloe striata* feels like a human arm. The plant's gray-green skin is subtly striped with cream, its edges are translucent crimson, and its blooms resemble scarlet feather dusters. The plant looks stunning with a carpet of red lava rock around it. "That's just one plant," says Anderson, adding that a single aloe or agave may be all a patio garden needs.

When you buy one, just make sure you know how big it's going to get, he advises. Palm-size gray-blue rosettes of *Aloe brevifolia* make good ground covers. *Agave parryi huachucensis* (gray with black edges) looks like an oversize artichoke and grows to basketball size. *Aloe arborescens* (famous for rimming Laguna Beach's cliffs) reaches the size of a Volkswagen Beetle. *Aloe marlothii* is not for the faint of heart: Its brutish leaves are spiked like a giant cheese grater. Yet its blooms, which float horizontally above the plant, are worth the effort; they're several feet long and clustered with scorching orange florets. Less intimidating is *A. cameronii,* which forms a brick red mound of foliage that resembles overlapping starfish. "The more sun, the redder it gets," says Anderson.

And what about his British guest? When Lloyd returned home, he wrote Anderson: "I would love to have a garden of cactus and succulents, but as I can't, there's no use being envious. Whenever I come to Southern California, I can just enjoy yours."

Tulips in shades of pink and rose to deep coral echo the hues of crabapple blooms in La Conner, Washington.

MARK TURNER

The man who loves trees

Dick Rifkind is Idaho's champion (and a supplier) of oaks, maples, and more

By Jim McCausland

TORSTEN KJELLSTRAND

After Dick Rifkind finished talking about trees in a packed lecture hall at North Idaho College, an amazed student posed just one question: "Are you on pills?" Drugged, no. Animated, yes. It doesn't take much to get this trial lawyer turned nurseryman pumped up about his favorite subject.

"My dad was a federal judge who was nuts about horticulture," Rifkind says. "When I was about 8, he gave me my own pruning shears, and I was hooked." The gift showed the judge's prescience: Young Rifkind's horticultural tastes turned quickly to deciduous trees.

"I like working with hardwoods," he says. "I get excited about the seasonal changes, the flowers, the colors, and the stages of growth you see in trees like katsuras and sourwoods. Of course, I like evergreens too, but really, there's nothing like a deciduous tree."

His enthusiasm has changed his life in many ways. After practicing law in California and running a wholesale nursery on the side, Rifkind settled in northern Idaho, where chilly winters and warm summers are perfect for deciduous plants. He noticed that most nurseries carried the same limited stock, so he started his own nursery from scratch in 1992, offering a remarkably wide range of trees and shrubs.

"I was interested in *Stewartia pseudocamellia*, for example, but was told, 'No way—it's too cold here.' We tried it anyway, putting a test plant in a protected area, and had terrific luck. We've sold lots of them now." His

Crabapple, in fruit

White flowering crabapple (*Malus sargentii*)

Chinese scholar tree

Rifkind's top 10 trees for mountain gardens

1. Chinese scholar tree (*Sophora japonica*). Grows quickly into a massive tree with lacy foliage. Older trees are covered with spikes of pale yellow flowers in midsummer.

2. Flowering crabapple (*Malus* species and hybrids). The new varieties are disease-resistant and hold on to their small fruits.

3. Japanese stewartia (*S. pseudo-camellia*). In early summer it's covered with 2- to 3-inch single, white, camellia-like flowers. Fall color is a mix of reds, pumpkins, and purples, while winter bark shows a jigsaw pattern of cinnamon and silver.

4. Katsura (*Cercidiphyllum japonicum*). In spring this large tree is a heathery cloud of new growth. Foliage turns brilliant red or yellow in fall.

5. 'Nijisseiki' Asian pear (*Pyrus* 'Twentieth Century'). Its fruit gives you the crunch of an apple and the sweetness of a pear.

6. 'October Glory' red maple (*Acer rubrum*). This is the finest of the red maples, growing 18 inches per year into a full, rounded tree. Stays bright green all summer.

7. Red oak (*Quercus rubra*). Nothing says Halloween like the red oak's heavy, waxy leaves when they turn bright orange. This is a fast grower: 18 to 24 inches per year.

8. 'Satomi' dogwood (*Cornus kousa* 'Satomi'). This tree's pink flowers last from May until late June. Absolutely the best dogwood for cold areas.

9. Sourwood (*Oxydendrum arboreum*). In fall, when nothing much is in bloom, this 25-foot tree is covered with lily-of-the-valley-type flowers. Leaves often turn red then too.

10. Tupelo (*Nyssa sylvatica*). Shiny leaves turn brilliant scarlet, unmatched by even the reddest maple. Grows 18 inches a year in any soil, even standing water.

Katsura (*Cercidiphyllum japonicum*)

Bechtel crabapple (*Malus ioensis* 'Plena')

secret is to sell trees grown from seed instead of cuttings.

This led him to test other questionably hardy deciduous trees and shrubs, such as dawn redwood, 'Satomi' dogwood, and Tupelo. Customers drive to Rifkind's nursery from around the state and as far away as Spokane and even parts of western Montana.

Rifkind gets the word out about his trees in his newsletter (circulation 3,000), in a newspaper column he writes called "Gabby Gardener," and in the classes he teaches at the local college.

"I want to get people out of the rut," he says. "There's so much to grow here, so much that hasn't been widely used." ◆

Red oak (*Quercus rubra*)

Colorful discoveries for desert gardens

Five new plants with strong seasonal interest

By Lauren Bonar Swezey

Southwest gardeners can draw from an ever-expanding palette of desert-adapted plants, thanks to the efforts of devoted plant collectors and nurserymen like Ron Gass of Mountain States Wholesale Nursery in Glendale, Arizona, and Greg Starr of Starr Nursery in Tucson.

We asked Janet Rademacher, marketing director for Mountain States, to name her favorites among the newly introduced plants discovered by Gass and Starr. "There are so many good ones," says Rademacher, "but these plants are outstanding for their toughness and attractive bloom." Look for them at local retail nurseries or—by appointment only—at Starr Nursery (520/743-7052).

Spring through fall color

■ **Angelita daisy** (*Hymenoxys acaulis*). Native to Arizona and Texas. Perennial with bright green leaves grows 12 inches tall by 15 to 18 inches wide. Daisylike golden yellow flowers appear over a long season, but are heaviest in spring (for repeat bloom, shear off flowers before seeds form). "Tuck into tight places or use en masse," says Rademacher. Full sun, well-drained soil, moderate water. *Sunset* climate zones 10–13.

Spring and fall color

■ *Dalea capitata* **'Sierra Gold'.** Collected in Mexico by Gass and Starr. Lush-looking, semideciduous ground cover grows 8 to 12 inches tall by 3 to 4 feet wide. Yellow flowers are borne on 1-inch-long spikes. Cut back halfway in late winter. "One of the most durable ground covers for desert gardens," says Rademacher. Full sun, low to moderate water. Zones 10–13.

■ *Eupatorium greggii* **'Boothill'.** Collected by Gass in southeast Arizona. Herbaceous perennial with fuzzy light green leaves grows 2 feet tall by 2 to 3 feet wide. Fuzzy lavender-blue flowers appear on the ends of

Daintily poised on 1-foot stems, golden angelita daisy is backed by reddish orange penstemon in this Phoenix landscape.

branches in late spring and fall (also in summer in areas where temperatures stay below 100°). "Attracts clouds of butterflies," says Rademacher. Cut back nearly to the ground in late winter. Full sun or partial shade, moderate water. Zones 10–13; plants die back to the roots when temperatures fall to the mid-20s.

Fall color

■ *Dalea frutescens* '**Sierra Negra**'. Collected by Starr in west Texas. Partially deciduous shrub 4 feet tall by 6 feet wide, with 1-inch-wide compound leaves and nearly white branches. Brilliant rose-purple flowers are borne on 1½-inch spikes. "One of our best fall bloomers," says Rademacher. Prune severely in late winter to encourage bushiness and flowering. Full sun, low water. Zones 12–13.

■ *Muhlenbergia capillaris* '**Regal Mist**'. Native to southeast Texas; collected there by Benny Simpson, Lynn Lowrey, and Shannon Smith. Clumping grass 3 feet tall by 3 feet wide, with glossy dark green leaf blades. Deep pinkish red flower spikes rise 1 foot above the foliage. Prune in late winter to remove flower spikes and brown foliage. Tolerates a wide range of soils. Full or filtered sun, moderate water. Zones 10–13.

Clusters of rose-purple flowers cover *Dalea frutescens* 'Sierra Negra' for several weeks in fall. TOP: Backlit by afternoon sun, the wispy flower heads of *Muhlenbergia capillaris* 'Regal Mist' set a Tucson slope aglow. ◆

Designing with rhodies

Beautiful ways to use them in your garden

By Jim McCausland

When Sir Joseph Hooker was collecting rhododendron seed in the Himalayas 150 years ago, he remarked that above 12,000 feet in Darjeeling, about three-quarters of all plants were rhododendrons. If Hooker were to walk through some neighborhoods in the Northwest or coastal Northern California today, he might make a similar observation—that three-fourths of all the flowering shrubs are rhodies. There's good reason for that. As landscape designer Beatrix Jones Farrand once noted, no other shrub compares with them for grand effect.

The photographs on these pages show some of the beautiful ways rhododendrons can be situated in various landscapes. The design challenges come in giving these bold evergreens enough shoulder room and keeping their flower colors from clashing.

As you choose among nursery plants in 2-gallon cans, remember that, with time, most will grow taller than you. So before you buy, ask the nursery staff about the plant's size at maturity.

Rhodies for small spaces

Even if you only have a small space, it's usually possible to work a plant or two into the garden.

LOW BORDERS. Lower-growing rhododendrons (to 3 feet or less) are the ones to use in short borders along entry gardens or paths. These compact

ABOVE: Rhododendrons frame a stump beside a reflecting pool in John and Gael Dodd's garden in Langley, B.C.; from left to right are red 'Earl of Donoughmore', pale orchid 'Madame Jules Porges', and pink 'Mrs. Charles E. Pearson'. CENTER: *R. orbiculare,* a species with bell-shaped blooms. BOTTOM: A variegated Norway maple contrasts perfectly with 'Pink Walloper' and 'Lavender Queen' rhododendrons.

rhodies tend to have smaller leaves.

LIVING SCULPTURES. Place a small, shapely rhododendron as you would place a sculpture in your garden—at the ends of paths or in locations framed by larger plants.

ESPALIERS. Fortunately, most rhododendrons take well to pruning, so you can train them almost flat against a wall or fence. When you shop, try to find plants with a fan shape rather that a bush shape, so you'll have a head start on the training process.

ABOVE: Bordering a lawn are red 'Jean Marie de Montague', lavender-blue 'Fastuosum Flore Pleno', and pink 'Trude Webster'. LEFT: Plant *R. luteum* up close to enjoy its fragrance.

Rhodies for grander shows

TALL BORDERS. Broad pathways and winding grass corridors look especially inviting when they're lined with tall rhododendrons (to 6 feet or taller). Grow such rhodies in places where trees rise above or behind them to provide scale.

NEAR THE WATER. Mass rhododendrons on the far side of a pool or pond so their flowers will be reflected in the water, doubling their impact. Just make sure the rhododendrons are planted well above the waterline; otherwise, the roots will rot in the saturated soil.

IN THE WOODS. Most hybrid rhododendrons trace their lineage to plants of the open forest, which makes them natural choices for woodland gardens. In low-maintenance areas, you can use rhodies to create an evergreen cover that goes well with ferns, ocean spray, and other native woodland plants.

Consider color, texture, scent

COLORS. Choose rhododendrons as if you were assembling a wardrobe, thinking in terms of complementary and contrasting flower colors. If you buy plants in bloom, you'll be able to see how well a pink flower truss picks up the hue of a burgundy-leafed Japanese maple, for example. In mass plantings, group similar colors together (reds and pinks, for example),

but keep clashing colors apart or grow white-flowered rhodies as buffers between them.

LEAF TEXTURES. Whether you're planting rhododendrons together or mixing them with other plants, contrast is the key. Play large leaves against small ones, round leaves against narrow ones. Or use the classic technique of playing broadleaf rhodies off a contrasting background of conifers, as shown above.

FRAGRANCE. Plant fragrant varieties of rhododendrons by entries and patios, where you can enjoy their scent up close. Some good ones include 'Dora Amateis', 'Fragrantissimum', *R. fortunei*, and *R. luteum,* a deciduous azalea.

For further reading

The best new book about designing with rhododendrons is *Rhododendrons in the Landscape* by Sonja Nelson (Timber Press, Portland, OR, 2000; $29.95; 800/327-5680 or www.timberpress.com). Fifty-two pages of color photographs provide convincing examples. ◆

The Gardener Cook

By Renee Shepherd

Strawberries to treasure

Tiny alpine strawberries are flavorful and easy to grow

■ Among the choicest delicacies offered by my summer garden are the jewel-like fruits of alpine strawberries (*Fragaria vesca* 'Semperflorens'), also known by their romantic French name, *fraises des bois.* These berries, each no bigger than the tip of your little finger, have an intensely concentrated flavor I can describe only as ambrosial—reminiscent of strawberries, roses, and pineapples. Borne prolifically on charming, well-behaved perennial plants, they are much too perishable to be offered in markets in the United States. But in France, they are carefully hand-harvested and sold as a seasonal luxury to serve atop perfect individual custard tarts at Paris patisseries. At fine restaurants they are topped with crème fraîche and candied violets and served in exquisite stemware goblets.

Fruit and flowers often appear at the same time (left). Clusters ripen gradually from the base to the tips (below). For richest flavor, harvest all ripe fruit every two to three days. Plants grow into mounds about a foot tall and a foot wide.

Alpine strawberries are cultivated strains of wild or woodland strawberries. The berries are usually red, although varieties with cream or pale yellow fruit are also available.

In the garden, plants stay neater than standard strawberries because they don't form runners and their leaves are smaller. They make handsome edgings for flower beds and herb gardens, and are equally at home as rock garden plants, in window boxes, in patio containers, or cascading from strawberry pots.

I grow all my alpine strawberry plants in deep planters that line my kitchen patio; their little green serrated leaves, white flowers, and bright red berries complement the planters' red brick. Best of all, I can step outdoors in the morning to gather a handful of sweet, delicious fruit to sprinkle on my breakfast cereal—turning my simple meal into a fancy feast.

Originally I had only six plants. But last spring I planted a dozen more so I'd have enough berries to harvest for special occasions (a dozen well-fertilized and well-watered mature plants will yield about a cup of berries several times a week throughout the summer). I serve them in feather-light dessert crêpes or sprinkle them over freshly made Belgian waffles. If you have enough berries, you can also make little pots of sweet jam. The fruit contains more pectin than regular strawberries, so making jam is easy and quick.

Still, my favorite way to enjoy the richly seductive flavor of alpine strawberries is to eat them fresh from the plant, served in fancy cut-glass goblets with a sinful dollop of real whipped cream—a truly splendid indulgence. ◆

How to grow alpine strawberries

Plant in rich, well-drained soil in a site that gets full sun (filtered shade in very hot areas). Set them so crowns are 12 to 15 inches apart. Water regularly (about once a week, more often when weather is hot and windy) and fertilize occasionally. Mulch the plants to keep roots moist unless snails or slugs are menaces in your garden (they often hide in mulch). In mild areas plants begin to fruit in four months, with the heaviest crops in spring and fall. Plants produce the best fruit during the first two or three years.

ROBIN CUSHMAN (2)

Sources

Nurseries sell packaged seeds, as well as plants in 4-inch pots and 1-gallon containers. Or order potted divisions from *Raintree Nursery,* Morton, WA (360/496-6400 or www.raintreenursery.com), or from *Shepherd's Garden Seeds,* Torrington, CT (860/482-3638 or www.shepherdseeds.com).

THOMAS J. STORY (4)

Cherry tree branch bursts into bloom in a vase indoors. Prune off a branch when buds show color (A), then make a cut in the stem end (B) or lightly hammer it (C).

Flowering branches say spring

Indoor arrangements celebrate the season

By Lauren Bonar Swezey

Trim the branches from deciduous flowering trees or shrubs, arrange them in a vase, and watch the delicate buds unfurl. Pruning at this time of year is good for your tree too; it thins out the canopy so branches won't be overcrowded. Follow the steps below to create your own spectacular arrangement. If you don't have a flowering tree or shrub, you can buy blooming branches at many floral shops. DESIGN: Jill Slater

TIME: 15 to 20 minutes

COST: About $15 to 20 for a bunch of branches from a florist

MATERIALS
• **Pruning shears** or loppers
• **Ladder**
• **Vase**
• **Floral preservative**

DIRECTIONS

1. Prune your tree. When buds show color or a few flowers are beginning to open, choose a branch that's crowd

ing other branches or is expendable (make certain you don't cut a branch that will ruin the shape of the tree). Use pruning shears to cut small branches, or loppers (**A**) to remove branches larger than 1 inch in diameter. Cut one branch for a smaller vase and three to five branches for a large vase or floral bucket.

2. If necessary, trim the stem ends to fit the vase. Snip off dead or damaged twigs.

Choices for cutting

• Fruit trees such as apricot, cherry, crabapple, nectarine, peach, and plum
• Quince
• Forsythia
• Mimosa (*Acacia baileyana*)
• Saucer magnolia
• Witch hazel

3. On smaller stems, cut a slit in the bottom of the branch (**B**) to help the stem absorb water more easily. On larger branches (³⁄₄- to 1-inch diameter), lightly hammer the stem end (**C**) for the same effect.

4. Fill the vase with water and a packaged floral preservative or a solution of 1 tablespoon sugar and ¼ teaspoon bleach in 1 gallon of hot tap water. Arrange the branches.

A FOUNTAIN RINGED BY FLOWERS forms the centerpiece of this gracious and inviting entry courtyard in Arizona. For details on the annuals and perennials shown here, see page 121.

April

JIM McCAUSLAND

Euphorbias create a bright backdrop

These showy chartreuse plants set the stage for early spring color

■ Every spring, a new batch of Western gardeners is smitten with *Euphorbia characias wulfenii*. This evergreen perennial of Mediterranean origin bears striking clusters of chartreuse bracts that resemble flowers. In the entry court of Susan Stubblefield's Lake Oswego, Oregon, garden (shown above), it forms a perfect backdrop for orange tulips.

E. c. wulfenii grows in *Sunset* zones 4–24, thriving in well-drained soil and full sun. A dome-shaped shrubby perennial that grows to 4 feet tall, the plant has narrow blue-green leaves. After flowering, the blooming stalks die to the base. Just cut them out and leave the remaining stems for next spring's bloom. Wear gloves when you prune: *E. c. wulfenii* has milky sap that can irritate your skin.

Nurseries may also stock close relatives of *E. c. wulfenii*. The species *E. characias* has greener bracts; *E. c.* 'Goldbrook' produces chartreuse bracts. Heronswood Nursery (360/297-4172 or www.heronswood.com) offers these and other euphorbias in its catalog ($5). — *Jim McCausland*

A bunny of baby's tears

■ For the last three years, this charming Easter rabbit has nestled among spring bulbs and ajugas in Phyllis and Richard Null's garden in Eugene, Oregon.

To create a bunny like this, order an undivided flat of baby's tears (*Soleirolia soleirolii*) from your local nursery. Choose a site in full shade inland or in some sun if you're near the coast. Remove the entire "carpet" from the flat, taking care to keep it in one piece, and press the root mass lightly into prepared

ROBIN CUSHMAN

soil. To trace the bunny, make an outline with string or place a rabbit-shaped cake pan upside down on top of the baby's tears. With a sharp knife, trim away the excess baby's tears beyond the outline. Add back extra pieces to fill in any gaps (avoid using pieces too small to thrive).

When the baby's tears is established (look for new growth), use scissors to hollow out the rabbit's ear and form its three-dimensional haunch and neck. Clip it regularly to keep the bunny looking its best. When vigorous growth spreads beyond the design, cut it away and remove any roots.

The bunny will go dormant in cold winters, but will put on a new coat of tiny green leaves to greet the spring. — *Mary-Kate Mackey*

PVC pipe holds the stakes

■ Arne Reyier uses stakes to support plants and prop up fruit-laden branches in his Gig Harbor, Washington, garden. To keep stakes close at hand, he devised containers resembling the quivers that hold arrows. Reyier made the holders from lengths of 6- and 12-inch-diameter PVC pipe left over after a construction job. He drilled holes in the side of each pipe, then screwed them to a post sunk into the ground. — *J.M.*

JIM McCAUSLAND

RICK WETHERBEE

These radishes aren't root crops

■ With a large country garden, I have plenty of room to experiment with new and unusual vegetables. One of the most surprising crops I've tried recently is a podding radish, which you grow not for its roots but for its edible pods borne above the ground. Native to Southeast Asia are two types of podding radishes: 'Madras,' with short, mild-flavored pods; and 'Rat's Tail' (shown at left), with 12-inch-long spicy pods. The green or purple pods cover 4- to 5-foot-tall stems. Even my friends who don't relish radishes like the crispy texture of these pods and prefer their slightly milder bite. You can chop the pods, leave them whole to use fresh in salads, or toss them into stir-fry dishes.

Sow seeds in a sunny spot anytime from three weeks before the last spring frost through mid-August west of the Cascades (June east of the Cascades). Expect to harvest the first pods 50 days after sowing.

Seeds of podding radishes are available from Bountiful Gardens (707/459-6410 or www.bountifulgardens. org) and Pinetree Garden Seeds (207/926-3400). — *Kris Wetherbee*

Drumstick primroses beat the snow

■ April showers might bring May flowers in balmier locales, but April snows too often smash or freeze flowers in the West's frigid mountain regions. Frost-tolerant drumstick primrose (*Primula denticulata*) suffers no such indignities, blooming even in snowstorms. Regardless of the weather, these primroses keep producing flowers for several weeks from April into early May. Available now in full bloom at many garden centers, drumstick primroses come in shades of lilac, purple, rose, and white. Flowers the size of golf balls stand upright on stiff 8- to 10-inch stems.

This perennial is reliably hardy in *Sunset* climate zones 1–3, as long as it is protected by snow cover or a layer of winter mulch. It requires consistent moisture in spring and some protection from intense afternoon sunlight in summer. For dependable spring color, plant drumstick primroses among April-blooming daffodils and tulips or with Virginia bluebells (*Mertensia virginica*).

Container-grown plants are available from the Primrose Path (921 Scottdale-Dawson Rd., Scottdale, PA 15683; 724/887-6756 or www.theprimrosepath.com; catalog $2) and Shady Oaks Nursery (Box 708, Waseca, MN 56093; 800/504-8006 or www.shadyoaks.com; catalog free).

— *Marcia Tatroe*

Baskets that grow on you

■ Pretty baskets planted with annuals, ground covers, or succulents
make perfect tabletop decorations
for springtime parties, especially
when garnished with chocolate
eggs wrapped in foil. They're a
snap to put together.

TIME: About 35 minutes

COST: $15 to $20 (small basket) to
about $90 (planted trug)

**MATERIALS: Basket, black plas-
tic liner** (a garbage bag will do),
scissors, potting soil, plants

DIRECTIONS

1. Line a basket with black plastic;
trim off the excess with scissors.
2. Fill the basket to within 2 inches
of the rim with soil. **3.** Set in plants,
then add soil around them; press
to firm the soil. **4.** Because they
don't have drain holes, water the
baskets sparingly (test moisture
first by poking the soil with your
finger). **5.** Add finishing touches
such as candy eggs or ribbon.

— *Lauren Bonar Swezey*

THOMAS J. STORY (2)

ABOVE: The round white
basket (about 8 inches
wide) in front contains blue
star creeper and 10-inch-
tall *Chrysanthemum
paludosum.* The brown
basket (rear) is filled with
black mondo grass
(*Ophiopogon planiscapus*
'Nigrescens').

LEFT: Floral designer
Jill Slater planted this
20-inch-long English trug
with an array of handsome
succulents, including
aeoniums and sedums.
A twiggy bird's nest at one
end holds candy eggs.

Irises galore in Phoenix

■ Every April since 1965, Bobbie and Don Shepard have invited the public to visit their Phoenix nursery, Shepard Iris Garden, to see 2½ acres of blooming irises. Among the nearly 200 varieties of bearded iris varieties grown here are 30 that were developed and introduced by the Shepards, including 'Arizona Redhead' (which was introduced in 1998) and 'Splash Dance' (introduced in 1988).

After strolling through the garden, you can place an order on the spot or pick up a catalog. Iris orders are delivered in late summer, in time for fall planting in warm-winter climates.

Besides bearded irises, the Shepards grow nearly 150 varieties of spuria irises and more than 40 varieties of daylilies (*Hemerocallis*).

Shepard Iris Garden, located at 3342 W. Orangewood Ave., is open daily in April from 9 to 5. For more information about the nursery or to receive a free catalog, call (602) 841-1231.

— *Mary Irish.*

Bearded irises are 'Be Mine' (left), 'Arizona Redhead' (top), and 'Splash Dance'; they reach 36, 43, and 48 inches tall, respectively.

CHARLES MANN (3)

Heirloom roses in bloom

■ Old garden roses are the forerunners of modern hybrid teas. These heirloom types are valued for their fragrance, long life, resistance to disease and pests, and tolerance of soil types and temperature extremes. One of the best places to see how these plants perform in the low desert is at the Heritage Rose Garden, which was established in 1996 on the property of the University of Arizona's Maricopa County Cooperative Extension.

During April, most of the garden's 80 varieties are in bloom. One star performer is pictured here: 'Madame Isaac Pereire', a Bourbon rose dating to 1881. This small climber (to 10 feet) has deep magenta flowers with a rich fragrance. Like most heirloom roses, this one blooms extravagantly in spring, followed by intermittent blossoms in summer, and a final flourish in September and October.

Heritage Rose Garden, at 4341 E. Broadway Road in Phoenix, is open daily during daylight hours. Admission is free. For more information, call (602) 470-1556 ext. 831. For a wide assortment of heirloom roses, see the catalogs of the Antique Rose Emporium (800/441-0002 or www.weareroses.com) and Arena Rose (805/227-4094 or www.arenaroses.com). — *M.I.*

LINDA ENGER

Back to basics

Do away with wormy apples. Codling moth larvae love apples: They tunnel into fruits that are developing on a tree. To help control these pesky worms, hang a codling moth trap in the tree. These sticky-bottomed traps contain a nontoxic scent (pheromone) that attracts and traps the male moths so they can't mate. Set out two traps per standard tree or one per dwarf tree just before blossoms open. Replace them after nine or 10 weeks, depending on the traps. Moth traps are available from Peaceful Valley Farm Supply (888/784-1722 or www.groworganic.com).

LINDA HOLT AYRISS

CONNIE McLENNAN

Contain creeping bamboo. Running bamboo produces underground stems that will invade adjacent areas of the garden unless contained. Before planting it, form a barrier 1½ feet deep with strips of galvanized sheet metal or poured concrete. You can also plant bamboo in long flue tiles or bottomless metal drums. To limit the spread of existing bamboo, periodically plunge a spade to its full depth around the clump. New shoots break off easily and do not resprout. — *L.B.S.*

TERRENCE MOORE

Flowers ring the fountain

■ To rejuvenate the entry courtyard of their 1930s adobe, Murray and Sue DeArmond collaborated with landscape designer Jeffrey Trent of Tucson-based Natural Order. Together they transformed the space into a gracious and inviting garden centered around an existing fountain.

The fountain, a 6-foot-wide concrete basin topped by a statue of St. Francis of Assisi, exemplified the Southwestern garden style the DeArmonds envisioned. In the bed around it, Trent interplanted a few perennials for year-round interest, such as deer grass (*Muhlenbergia rigens*) and Mexican bush sage (*Salvia leucantha*), with annuals for seasonal color, including bedding begonias, *Chrysanthemum paludosum,* Iceland poppies, lobelias, sweet alyssums, and violas. The bed is irrigated by pop-up spray heads.

Elsewhere in the courtyard, flagstone walkways lead past lush perennial beds that include globemallows and penstemons. For added color in winter and spring, containers of cool-season annuals such as pansies, petunias, snapdragons, and stock sprout along the walkways.— *M.I*

Creeping thyme is accented with blooming erodium. In bed at left, lavender-flowered nemesias mingle with salvias. BELOW: Perennial bed contains nemesias, salvias, and purple heliotropes.

Friendly front garden

It's a hit with neighbors

■ Alison and Randy Barsh didn't set out to install a garden that would feel like a gift to their Huntington Beach neighborhood. It worked out that way. Alison had taken several classes at the Institute of the Gardens, at Roger's Gardens in Corona del Mar, California, and she was itching to get started. But her opportunities were limited—no backyard, a side yard that was all patio and pool, and a front yard with shady northern exposure. So she turned to landscape designer and institute instructor Cristin Fusano for help.

Fusano suggested concentrating most of the flowering plants along the fence line, the sunniest part of the front yard, then adding shade-tolerant evergreens near the house and leaving the center open. This design would give the Barshes a new outdoor room, and Alison the flower-filled garden she craved.

Climbing roses now weave their way through the metal bars of the front fence. Behind the fence are more roses, plus shrubby perennials such as salvias. Flagstones inter-

spersed with fragrant creeping thyme have replaced the lawn. This heavily planted perimeter gives the Barshes some privacy and is beautiful to look at from inside. But the arrangement is also unquestionably neighborly. Walkers, joggers, moms with strollers, teenagers, mail carriers—no one passes without stopping to smell the roses, Alison says. One neighbor even expressed her appreciation with a carton of ladybugs and this comment: "Thanks for bringing so much pleasure to the neighborhood." — *Sharon Coboon*

NORM PLATE (2)

A refreshing summer border

■ Last summer, visitors to Hudson Gardens in Littleton, Colorado, were greeted by a border composed of annual flowers and ornamental grasses in a range of fruity tones. Designed by Andrew Pierce, director of education and horticulture, the border featured Inca yellow marigolds, pink Splendor zinnias, cool-looking 'Rhea' salvias, and 'Homestead Purple' verbenas. Purple fountain grass (*Pennisetum setaceum* 'Rubrum'), bearing deep plum foliage and soft flower plumes, swayed in even the slightest breeze. Ruby grass (*Rhynchelytrum nerviglume*) bloomed in late summer, bearing reddish pink flower spikes over blue-green leaves.

This season, visitors will find a new annual border designed by Pierce. *Hudson Gardens is open year-round. 9–5 daily; free. 6115 S. Santa Fe Dr.; (303) 797-8565. — Colleen Smith*

A garden that welcomes guests

■ An entry garden ought to be inviting. To ensure that the front yard of their new home in Grand Junction, Colorado, possessed a welcoming quality, Bob and Nancy Hackett enlisted the aid of landscape architect Bob Arcieri.

Like open arms, colorful planting beds flank a wide walkway that leads to a covered front porch whose pillars are festooned with English ivy. The beds are filled with flowering ground covers such as *Ajuga reptans* and *Potentilla verna,* hardy shrubs like Japanese barberry and *Yucca filamentosa* (with creamy white blooms at far right), clumps of blue fescue, and long-blooming flowers like daylilies and pansies.

On one side of the garden, a small sliver of lawn is wedged between a flower bed and a dry creek bed edged by boulders. To accent the rear of the garden, Arcieri used upright and weeping varieties of flowering cherry trees that can tolerate the rela-

tively mild winters in Grand Junction.

For designing and installing the garden, Arcieri and Bookcliff Gardens of Grand Junction won a joint merit award in the 1999 Excellence in Landscape competition sponsored by the Associated Landscape Contractors of Colorado. —*J.M.*

Fresh use for an old ladder

■ Kathy Koehler turned her grandparents' old 6-foot-tall ladder into a cucumber trellis. "I didn't want to part with it," she says. The trellis keeps the cucumbers off the ground and helps air circulate; it also makes harvest a breeze.

To anchor the ladder firmly, Koehler dug two 6-inch-deep trenches parallel to the ladder's steps (for best exposure, the ladder is oriented to face east and west), then sunk its feet into the trenches. She draped a piece of plastic netting (about 13½ feet long) over the ladder so the ends hung 6 inches below the feet on each side. She mixed compost into the backfill, then refilled the trenches, burying the ladder's feet and the netting ends to secure them. Finally, she planted seeds around the ladder's base.

— *L.B.S.*

PAUL BOUSQUET

THOMAS J. STORY

New sweet corn is a winner

■ Every year, seed catalogs rave about "best ever" new corn varieties, the results of breeders' quests to improve flavor, texture, and growth habits. Once in a while, there's a real breakthrough. 'Sweet Symphony', a new type of corn known as a "sweet breed hybrid," is an example. Genetically, this new corn contains 50 percent standard (old-fashioned) corn, 25 percent supersweet corn, and 25 percent sugary enhanced corn.

Seeds of sweet breed hybrids germinate and grow well under cool conditions, says Mark Willis, vegetable seed manager for Harris Seeds in Rochester, New York. Plants are easy to grow and they produce tall, sturdy stalks. Yellow and white kernels are crisp and sweet.

Unlike other extrasweet corn varieties, though, 'Sweet Symphony' doesn't fully develop its sweetness until kernels have reached maturity. (Before harvest, test an ear by nicking a kernel with your thumbnail; if milky juice squirts out, the ear is ready to pick.)

At planting time, isolate 'Sweet Symphony' from supersweet varieties. Seeds are available from Harris Seeds (800/514-4441 or www.harrisseeds.com). — *L.B.S.*

WHAT TO DO IN YOUR GARDEN IN APRIL

PLANTING

☐ **ANNUALS.** Plant seedlings of cool-season annuals such as calendulas, English daisies, pansies, snapdragons, stock, sweet alyssums, and violas until danger of frost is past, then plant warm-season annuals like cosmos, marigolds, petunias, sunflowers, and zinnias.

☐ **COOL-SEASON VEGETABLES.** You can still plant seedlings of cool-season crops such as broccoli, cabbage, cauliflower, kale, kohlrabi, lettuce, spinach, and Swiss chard. Sow carrots, peas, and radishes, and plant seed potatoes and onion sets now.

☐ **FRUITS.** Zones 1–3: While bare-root stock is still available at nurseries, set out cane berries, grapes, kiwis, strawberries, and fruit trees. Zones 4–7: Bare-root stock is gone, so plant the fruits listed above from containers now.

☐ **HERBS.** Set out seedlings of chives, mint, oregano, parsley, rosemary, sage, and thyme. Sow seeds of basil after danger of frost is past.

☐ **LAWNS.** Zones 1–3: Plant lawns from sod or seed anytime this month unless (in the coldest areas) you're still contending with frozen soil or snow; if so, hold off until snow melts and the soil warms up. Zones 4–7, 17: Start lawns from sod or seed anytime this month.

☐ **PERENNIALS.** Nurseries are a sea of color now, featuring basket-of-gold, bleeding heart, columbines, Corsican hellebores, evergreen candytuft, forget-me-nots, primroses, rockcress, sweet woodruff, and wallflower. Plant immediately.

☐ **TREES, SHRUBS, VINES.** Zones 1–3: In cold-winter areas, you can still set out bare-root stock of many of the following plants. Zones 4–7: Container-grown flowering trees such as cherries, crabapples, dogwoods, and magnolias are in bloom; plant immediately. You can also plant roses (which are leafing out now), flowering shrubs (including azaleas), rhododendrons, lilacs, and many kinds of vines, from clematis to wisteria.

☐ **WARM-SEASON VEGETABLES.** Start seeds indoors for warm-season vegetables such as cucumbers, eggplants, melons, peppers, and tomatoes. Give seedlings bottom heat and plenty of light; they'll be ready for transplant into the garden in six to eight weeks, after danger of frost is past.

MAINTENANCE

☐ **CONTROL APHIDS.** Blast them off tender new growth with a jet of water; they're not very good at reorganizing and returning. Hose off subsequent generations as you see them.

☐ **CONTROL SLUGS.** Put out bait or handpick slugs before their populations explode.

☐ **FERTILIZE.** While soil is cool, use a liquid fertilizer on vegetable and flower beds to give plants a quick boost. ◆

WHAT TO DO IN YOUR GARDEN IN APRIL

PLANTING

☐ **BEDDING PLANTS.** Replace fading cool-season annuals with heat lovers like celosias, dahlias, marigolds, petunias, salvias, and verbenas. Plant from sixpacks when you can; they're more economical and rapidly catch up to 4-inch plants. Cosmos and zinnias are good choices too; they're great for cutting, and the old-fashioned annuals attract beneficial insects.

☐ **HARDY VEGETABLES.** Zones 1–2: As soon as soil can be worked, sow seeds of beets, broccoli, cabbage, carrots, cauliflower, endive, kohlrabi, lettuces, onions, parsley, parsnips, peas, potatoes, radishes, spinach, Swiss chard, and turnips.

☐ **TENDER PLANTS.** Zones 7–9, 14–17: It's hard to resist gorgeous tropicals and subtropicals such as bougainvillea, hibiscus, jacaranda, Mexican lime, mandevilla, pink trumpet vine, and plumeria, even if these tender plants are only marginally hardy in Northern California. Set them out now so they have the growing season to get established, and plant in protected sites—against a south-facing wall or under an overhang (but not under tall plants)—or in containers that can be moved to a protected area in winter.

Sunset
CLIMATE ZONES
☐ Mountain (1-2)
☐ Valley (7-9)
☐ Inland (14)
☐ Coastal (15-17)

☐ **SUMMER FLOWERS.** Zones 7–9, 14–17: All warm-season annuals can be planted now. For best buys, purchase sixpacks. Use 4-inch plants for instant color. Try ageratum, dwarf dahlia, globe amaranth, impatiens, lobelia, Madagascar periwinkle (vinca), marigold, statice, petunia, phlox, portulaca, salvia, sanvitalia, sunflower, sweet alyssum, verbena, and zinnia.

☐ **UNCOIL ROOTS.** When planting trees, shrubs, and vines, check their root systems after they come out of the container. If roots are starting to circle around the soil ball, score them with a knife and cut any circling roots (don't do this on plants with sensitive roots, such as bougainvillea or leptospermum).

☐ **HOTTEST PEPPERS.** For peppers with pizzazz, try growing 'Haba-ñero'—one of the hottest grown in the United States. Redwood City Seed Company (650/325-7333 or www.redwoodcityseed.com) sells orange, red, and yellow varieties (the red and yellow peppers are sold under the name 'Scotch Bonnet').

MAINTENANCE

☐ **PRUNE.** Zones 7–9, 14–17: After new growth appears, prune off frost-damaged wood on tender plants such as bougainvillea and citrus. Also prune to shape overgrown hedges and spring-flowering vines and shrubs after they bloom.

☐ **ROTATE VEGETABLE BEDS.** If you have room in your garden, rotate planting sites every year to avoid buildup of diseases and insects that can survive in the soil or on plant residue. Don't replant the same or closely related plants in the area where they grew the last two or three years.

PEST CONTROL

☐ **WATCH FOR INSECTS.** If aphids appear on plant foliage, buds, or stems, hose them off with a strong blast of water or spray with insecticidal soap or neem. For unfamiliar pest problems, contact a county extension agent. ◆

WHAT TO DO IN YOUR GARDEN IN APRIL

PLANTING

☐ **AZALEAS.** If you like to buy blooming plants, this is the month—while supply is good at nurseries—to shop for azaleas. Give these plants good drainage; plant them with rootballs slightly above soil level. A location with northern or eastern exposure is best. To protect the plants' surface roots, mulch after planting with pine needles, oak leaves, or redwood bark chips.

☐ **BEDDING PLANTS.** Replace fading cool-season annuals with heat lovers like celosias, dahlias, marigolds, petunias, salvias, and verbenas. Plant from sixpacks when you can; they're more economical and rapidly catch up to 4-inch plants. Also seed cleomes, cosmos, sunflowers, and zinnias for a cut-flower supply; these old-fashioned annuals also attract beneficial insects.

☐ **VEGETABLES.** Coastal gardeners (zones 21–24) can continue to plant quick-maturing, cool-season crops like leaf lettuces, radishes, spinach, and Swiss chard. Inland (zones 18–21), switch to warm-season crops like beans, corn, cucumbers, eggplant, melons, okra, peppers, pumpkins, squash, and tomatoes. In the high desert (zone 11), frost is still a possibility; wait two to four weeks before planting.

DEBRA LAMBERT

MAINTENANCE

☐ **FERTILIZE.** Feed any trees, shrubs, ground covers, perennials, turf grasses, and other ornamentals you didn't get to last month.

☐ **THIN FRUIT.** Begin thinning apples, pears, and stone fruits when they reach about ½ inch in diameter. Space fruits 4 to 6 inches apart or leave one fruit per spur.

☐ **SPRAY OLIVE TREES.** To prevent olive trees from bearing fruits that drop, staining driveways and sidewalks, spray with a fruit-control hormone like Florel as soon as small white flowers appear. Or knock off the blooms with strong blasts from a hose.

☐ **TIDY UP BULB FOLIAGE.** Because bulbs are gathering nourishment for next year's flowers, don't clip off their foliage until it has turned yellow. Tie the leaves in knots or braid for a neater look.

☐ **WATCH FOR IRON DEFICIENCY.** Camellias, citrus, gardenias, and other plants may exhibit yellowing leaves with green veins this time of year—symptoms of iron deficiency. To remedy, feed the plants with a fertilizer containing chelated iron.

PEST CONTROL

☐ **CONTROL APHIDS.** New growth attracts these sucking pests. Dislodge them with a strong blast of water from a hose. Or strip aphids from plants by hand. If you're squeamish, wear thin disposable rubber gloves.

☐ **CONTROL BUDWORMS.** Geranium budworms burrow into the buds of these plants and feed from the inside, ruining blossoms. Spray plants with *Bacillus thuringiensis* (BT) the day before the first full moon in April. That's when the parent moth usually lays eggs for the first time. Spray again 7 to 10 days after the full moon.

☐ **MANAGE ANTS.** If you see ants parading up the trunks of citrus or other plants, stop them with a sticky trap of Tanglefoot or set out traps containing boric acid. ◆

WHAT TO DO IN YOUR GARDEN IN APRIL

PLANNING AND PLANTING

☐ ANNUALS. Four to six weeks before the average date of the last frost in your area, start seeds indoors of warm-season annuals (ageratum, celosias, coleus, globe amaranths, and marigolds) and vegetables (eggplant, melons, peppers, squash, and tomatoes). In mountainous areas, start seeds of cool-season flowers and vegetables this month.

☐ HARDY VEGETABLES. Two to four weeks before the average date of the last frost in your area, it's safe to set out transplants of broccoli, brussels sprouts, cabbage, and cauliflower. Protect plants from late frost for the first few weeks with floating row covers.

☐ SUMMER BULBS. Start begonias, caladiums, callas, cannas, dahlias, gladiolus, and hardy gloxinias in pots indoors on a sunny windowsill. Wait to plant them outside until all danger of frost is past.

☐ SWEET CORN. Two weeks before last frost, sow seeds of sweet corn directly in the ground. In areas with short summers, try an early maturing, sugar-enhanced hybrid like 'Legend' (available from Park Seed, Greenwood, SC; 800/845-3369 or www.parkseed.com).

Sunset
CLIMATE ZONES

☐ 1-3 ☐ 10-11

DEBRA LAMBERT

MAINTENANCE

☐ CARE FOR LAWNS. Aerate lawns using a rental machine that removes plugs of soil; rake up the plugs and put them on the compost pile or leave them in place to decompose. To control crabgrass and dandelion seeds before they sprout, apply a corn gluten–meal preemergent herbicide (available from Planet Natural, Bozeman, MT; 800/289-6656 or www.planetnatural.com).

☐ CLEAN FLOWER BEDS. Gradually remove winter mulch and debris around perennials, then top-dress beds with 2 to 3 inches of compost.

☐ DIVIDE PERENNIALS. When new leaves appear, divide clumps of asters, bellflowers, chrysanthemums, daylilies, sedums, Shasta daisies, and yarrow. Dig a bucketful of compost into the soil before replanting divisions.

☐ ELIMINATE WEEDS. Hoe small weeds when the soil is dry; do it early in the day so the sun will dry the roots out. For larger weeds, water thoroughly, then use a hand weeder or trowel to pop them out of the ground.

☐ PRUNE ROSES. Toward month's end, after roses put out new foliage, cut off dead and blackened stems and canes. To prevent borer damage, seal each pruning cut with clear nail polish or white glue. As the weather warms up, remove last year's mulch and leave the soil bare until hot weather arrives.

☐ REMOVE TREE WRAP. If you wrapped tree trunks for winter protection, remove the wrap now; otherwise it can harbor destructive insects during the growing season.

☐ SPRAY FRUIT TREES. After pruning but before flowers and leaves appear, spray fruit trees with a mixture of dormant oil and lime sulfur or oil and fixed copper. If rain washes it off within 48 hours, reapply. — *M.T.* ◆

WHAT TO DO IN YOUR GARDEN IN APRIL

PLANTING

☐ **AGAVES AND CACTUS. Zones 11–13** (Las Vegas, Tucson, Phoenix): Set out container-grown agaves and cactus.

☐ **ANNUALS. Zones 1–2** (Flagstaff, Santa Fe): Set out pansies for early color. **Zone 10–13:** Plant ageratums, celosias, globe amaranths, lisianthus (*Eustoma*), Madagascar periwinkles, marigolds, Mexican sunflowers (*Tithonia*), portulacas, and zinnias.

☐ **CITRUS. Zones 12–13:** Set out container-grown trees in full sun. Dig the planting hole as deep as the rootball and at least twice as wide. Protect exposed trunks from sunburn with shadecloth or white latex paint. Water two or three times per week for the first month, then every five to seven days through summer.

☐ **LAWNS. Zones 1–2 and 10** (Albuquerque): Sow or reseed lawns with fine or tall fescue, perennial ryegrass, or a blend of these. In areas with long, warm summers, consider a blend of buffalo grass and blue grama grass. **Zone 11** (Las Vegas): In addition to tall fescue or perennial ryegrass, you can grow common or hybrid Bermuda grass. **Zones 12–13:** When night temperatures are warmer than 65°, sow common Bermuda grass or plant plugs or sprigs of hybrid Bermuda or zoysia.

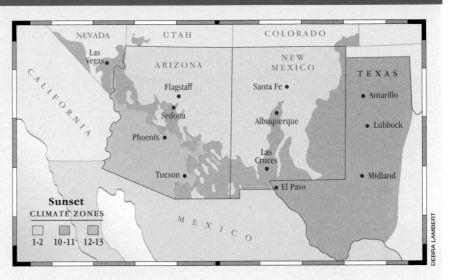

Sunset
CLIMATE ZONES
1-2 10-11 12-13

DEBRA LAMBERT

☐ **PERENNIALS. Zone 10:** Set out asters, chrysanthemums, columbines, daylilies, gazanias, geraniums, hollyhocks, and Shasta daisies. **Zones 11–13:** Plant coreopsis, gaillardias, and salvias.

☐ **SUMMER BULBS. Zones 10–12:** After the last frost, plant caladiums, cannas, crinums, dahlias, gladiolus, iris, and montbretias. **Zones 11–13:** Plant cannas, crinums, and zephyranthes.

☐ **VEGETABLES. Zones 10–11:** Sow seeds of beans, corn, cucumbers, melons, okra, pumpkins, squash, and watermelon; set out transplants of eggplants, peppers, and tomatoes after the last frost. **Zones 12–13:** Sow seeds of beans, black-eyed peas, cucumbers, melons, okra, and squash by mid-April; set out eggplant seedlings and sweet potato tubers anytime this month.

☐ **VINES. Zones 12–13:** Plant tender vines, including bougainvillea, *Mandevilla* 'Alice du Pont', pink trumpet vine (*Podranea ricasoliana*), and queen's wreath (*Antigonon leptopus*) in a warm spot with good winter protection.

MAINTENANCE

☐ **FERTILIZE PLANTS.** Almost everything in the garden can use fertilizer now. To avoid burning plants, water thoroughly the day before you fertilize and again immediately afterward. — *M.I.* ◆

summer

dazzlers

Five easy annuals for every garden

By Kathleen N. Brenzel and Jim McCausland

Photographs by Philippe Glade

Two summer annuals, magnified many times to show off their exquisite forms and colors, are Starfire mix marigold (left) and *Cosmos sulphureus* Sunny Orange-Red.

Among the stunners for summer gardens are (clockwise from top left): Sunflower, cosmos Psyche mix, 'Wheels' dahlia, and white tricolor daisy (*Chrysanthemum carinatum* Dunnettii Choice mix).

f you only had time and space to grow five summer flowers, which ones would you choose? We asked ourselves that question last year. Flowers in dazzling colors topped our list—ones whose vivid hues would stop passersby in their tracks and invite lingering looks. We'd toss in a few varieties with eye-catching frills, spots, or stripes. • Our next criterion: They would be annual (or behave that way), going from seed, tuber, or seedling to flower to seed again in one glorious spring-to-fall season. They would be easy to plant and easy to grow. We wanted nothing that needed fussing over, nothing temperamental or wimpy. The flowers had to be good for bouquets or good companions for cutting flowers. We wanted ones that would bloom over a long season (as long as we were faithful about deadheading, of course). • We made a list and pared it down. We browsed through nurseries and catalogs, choosing plants that piqued our interest. Finally we planted many varieties of five flower groups in *Sunset's* test garden in Menlo Park, California. • As they grew, we studied their backgrounds, noting that all of them hail from hot climates. Cosmos originated in tropical America. Dahlias come from Mexico and Central America, where they were first used as food (their tubers contain a nourishing starchy substance not unlike a potato), while improved varieties bloomed lustily at Montezuma's gardens in Huaxtepec. The marigold family, despite French and African names, is entirely American, found from New Mexico and Arizona south to Argentina. Summer mums are native to Morocco and have naturalized in sand dunes along Southern California's coast. Sunflowers grow wild from Minnesota to the Pacific Coast and south to Argentina. (Red sunflowers descend from *Helianthus annuus lenticularis,* a variety found in 1910 near Boulder, Colorado.) Together, these groups make up a colorful and sunny brotherhood. • By early summer, there was an abundance of blooms that we enjoyed as much in bouquets as in the garden. Our vases were always full. And those electric colors did more than caffeine to jump-start our days. We made note of the duds and the stars; our favorites are listed below. April is a splendid time to plant them all.

Annual chrysanthemums

Unlike the muted, mostly warm-toned perennials that sustain the autumn border, annual chrysanthemums are generally earlier and brighter, and flower longer. You're likely to encounter two kinds, both native to the Mediterranean region and both recently renamed by taxonomists (the new designation follows the old in these descriptions).

Tricolor daisy (*Chrysanthemum carinatum,* now *Glebionis carinatum*) is a 1- to 3-foot-tall annual whose flowers have bright bands of color around dark centers.

OUR FAVORITES: Court Jesters mix comes in orange, rose, salmon, scarlet, white, and yellow. White Carinatum Dunnettii Choice mix has white, yellow, bronze, and crimson flowers. In 'German Flag', scarlet rays and a golden yellow band surround the central disk. Merry mix has multicolored bull's-eye flowers on 2- to 3-foot-tall plants. Single Annual mixed comes in yellow, pink, purple, and rust.

It's a shame **crown daisy** (*Chrysanthemum coronarium,* now *Glebionis coronaria*) had its botanical name changed, since the word *chrysanthemum* combines the Greek for gold (*chrysos*) and for flower (*anthos*)—a perfect description for this lovely annual, which usually has yellow petal-like rays and a yellow central disk. Flowers can be single or double.

OUR FAVORITES: 'Primrose Gem' is a double yellow on a 3½- to 4-foot stem.

Cosmos

Cosmos (*C. bipinnatus*) must be one of the easiest annuals ever. Sow its seeds once, and pink or white flowers come back year after year from their own seeds. Flowers (mostly singles) start blooming in early summer and continue for months until the first hard frost. The wonderful Sensation strain is the best known of the clan, but cosmos come in many other flower forms—some have rolled or frilled petals—and in a range of solid colors and stripes.

OUR FAVORITES: 'Candy Stripe' produces white flowers with crimson borders or stripes and grows to 3 to 3½ feet tall. Three-foot-tall 'Daydream' has petals of rosy pink that fade to pale pink edges. Psyche mix bears semidouble blooms and grows to 3 feet tall. Seashell mix (to 3½ ft. tall) has rolled petals in creamy white and shades of red, rose, and pale seashell pink. Sonata mix, a 2-foot dwarf, bears many 3-inch single blooms in white, pink, and mixes. 'Versailles Tetra' (to 3 ft. tall) has 4-inch pink flowers and darker shading around a bright yellow eye.

Yellow cosmos (*C. sulfureus*) brings yellow and red flowers into the cosmos clan, but at a cost: Its seeds don't germinate as easily as common cosmos, and its flowers tend to be smaller (2 in. in diameter) than other cosmos. Many gardeners find it easiest to grow from nursery seedlings.

summerdazzlers

Eye-catching colors or unique forms define these brilliant blooms (left to right): tricolor daisy with bronze and gold markings, Seashell mix cosmos, 'Anatole' dahlia, and 'Candy Stripe' cosmos.

OUR FAVORITES: Bright Lights mix has large (2½-in.) flowers of yellow, gold, orange, or scarlet on 3- to 4-foot plants. 'Lemon Twist' bears clear lemon yellow flowers on stems to 2½ feet tall. Ladybird mix grows to only 1 foot in height. Sunny Orange-Red and Sunny Gold top out at 15 inches.

Dahlias

During the 19th century in England, winning dahlias fetched hefty cash prizes in competitions, motivating breeders to produce a steady stream of larger, increasingly exotic varieties. In *The English Flower Garden* (1883), English landscape designer William Robinson called the large-flowered varieties "monstrosities," prompting breeders to work on smaller single-flowering types to be used as bedding plants. Today, Westerners grow both. Named varieties, many of them magnificent in bouquets, number in the tens of thousands.

OUR FAVORITES: 'Anatole' has white flowers streaked with crimson and grows to 3½ feet tall. 'Bashful' (2½ ft. tall) bears deep purple blooms with lavender tips and golden yellow centers. The flowers of 5-foot-tall 'Chilson's Pride' are pure pink with white centers. 'Pink Gingham' (to 4½ ft. tall) has petals of bright lavender-pink with white tips. 'Siemen Doornbosch' bears lilac blossoms with creamy pincushion centers on stems to 1½ feet tall. On 'Wheels' (to 3½ ft. tall), red petals and a yellow fringe surround the center disk.

Marigolds

The vast array of garden marigolds traces back to three ancestors: African marigolds, French marigolds, and signet marigolds, all of which originated in the Americas.

In the 16th century, the Spanish took seeds of *Tagetes erecta* to Africa, where it naturalized so quickly that botanists thought it must have been native there. When *T. erecta* finally reached England, the Brits named it **African marigold.** The name still sticks—especially in the craws of growers who would like to see it renamed American marigold. These 1- to 3-foot-tall plants do well in heat and produce huge flowers.

OUR FAVORITES: 'French Vanilla' and 'Snowball' are creamy white 2-footers. Inca mix and 'Perfection', both with gold, orange, and yellow flowers, are excellent midsize varieties. 'First Lady' (to 20 in.) has yellow flowers. 'Deep Orange Lady' (to 20 in.) blooms in orange. Plants of Sugar and Spice mix bear 3½-inch flowers of orange, yellow, and white on 20-inch-tall stems.

French marigold (*T. patula*) came to England via France, so it, too, wound up with a logical but inaccurate moniker. These marigolds are shorter and more refined, usually

Plant our fiesta flower bed

This dazzling combination glows in the summer sun. Many of these flowers—especially the cosmos—attract butterflies and hummingbirds. In late summer and early fall, flocks of tiny finches and other seed-eating birds swoop in to graze among the spent blooms. Mass the taller-growing cosmos in the rear, with a clump of sunflowers behind (optional) and dahlias, marigolds, and midsize cosmos in the middle row. Plant lower-growing marigolds and yellow cosmos in front.

A. Ladybird mix dwarf cosmos; **B.** 'Mr. Majestic' marigold; **C.** 'Tangerine Gem' or Starfire mix marigold; **D.** 'Bashful' dahlia; **E.** Ladies mix marigold; **F.** Sonata mix cosmos; **G.** Sonata White cosmos; **H.** Seashell mix cosmos; **I.** Bright Lights mix cosmos; **J.** 'Candy Stripe' cosmos; **K.** Cosmos Sensation strain.

staying below 1 foot tall.

OUR FAVORITES: Disco mix has single 2¼-inch flowers of clear yellow, orange, or red on compact 10-inch plants. 'Gypsy Sunshine' (frilly butter yellow blooms) and 'Honeycomb' (frilly reddish petals edged with gold) are floriferous 6- to 10-inch-tall plants. 'Jaguar' bears single golden yellow flowers dabbed with maroon spots over neat, mounding 10-inch plants. 'Mr. Majestic' produces single bright yellow blooms with mahogany stripes on a 1- to 2-foot plant. The single flowers of 'Striped Marvel' (2 ft.) are striped red and gold like a pinwheel.

Signet marigolds (*T. tenuifolia*) produce many yellow flowers on 8- to 16-inch plants with fine foliage.

OUR FAVORITES: 'Lemon Gem' and 'Golden Gem' both have dainty single flowers on 8-inch plants. Starfire mix has miniature single flowers in shades of red to gold and reaches 12 to 14 inches in height.

Sunflowers

In 1888, while living in southern France, Vincent van Gogh made a remarkable series of sunflower paintings. Done to decorate his house for a visit from fellow artist Paul Gauguin, the works show sunflowers with dark and light centers, long and short petals, and blooms of many sizes. These oils hint at the wonderful variety of these large, sunny flowers. Today the color range is even greater, with red, mahogany, and white forms in many sizes.

Sunflowers grow quickly and are easy to tend—that's why they're favorites with children. If you want to use them for cut flowers, as van Gogh did, choose varieties with long stems and smaller flowers. It helps if they're pollenless, so they don't shed on your furniture and carpet.

OUR FAVORITES: Pollenless 'Dorado' bears golden yellow flowers with dark centers on 5-foot stems. 'Sunrich Lemon' is pollenless and has 3- to 8-inch flowers with lemon yellow petals and black disks on 4- to 6-foot-tall plants. 'Strawberry Blonde' is pollenless and bears 5-inch straw-colored flowers overlaid with light red on 6-foot-tall stems. Multiflowering branching types such as creamy yellow 'Valentine' (5 to 6 ft. tall with 5- to 6-in. blooms) look better in the garden longer than single-stemmed sunflowers like 'Sunrich Lemon'.

Planting and care

Except where noted, these annuals prefer mostly sunny locations. Keep old flowers picked off to prolong bloom.

• **Annual mums.** In hot climates, choose a spot that gets some afternoon shade. Sow seeds outdoors after weather warms for blooms in summer and fall. (If you live in a mild-winter climate, you can also sow in fall for spring and summer bloom.) You may also plant from nursery containers. Summer mums aren't fussy about soil. Space plants about 8 inches apart. Water deeply and frequently where soils are porous, less in heavy soils. Feed mums two to three times during the growing season.

• **Cosmos.** Sow seeds in open ground from spring to summer, or set out transplants from cell-packs, 4-inch pots, or 1-gallon cans. (Yellow cosmos are easiest to start from nursery-grown plants.) Cosmos will flower best in poor, sandy soil; heavily amended soils and lots of fertilizer result in fewer flowers. Space plants about 12 to 18 inches apart. They can tolerate some aridity, but for best bloom, water them regularly (once a week or so), especially in hot inland valleys.

• **Dahlias.** Provide light afternoon shade in hottest areas. Plant tubers in spring after soil has warmed and danger of frost is past. Dig holes 1 foot deep in loose loam high in organic matter. Space largest kinds 4 to 5 feet apart and smallest ones only 1 to 2 feet apart. Drive a stake into the hole; place the tuber horizontally, 2 inches from the stake, with the eye pointing toward it. Cover tuber with 3 inches of soil and water thoroughly. As shoots grow, gradually fill the hole with soil. Start watering regularly after shoots are above the ground. Dahlias planted in soil enriched with compost rarely, if ever, need supplemental fertilizer.

• **Marigolds.** Plant in full sun. Marigolds are easy to grow from seed and sprout in a few days in warm soil. Or set out plants from nursery flats, cell-packs, or 4-inch pots. Slugs and snails are especially fond of young marigold foliage; use traps or ring the planting with horticultural diatomaceous earth (available at nurseries).

• **Sunflowers.** Sow seeds in spring. If you use young nursery plants, space them 8 to 12 inches apart in soil well amended with compost. After true leaves appear, water plants deeply once a week. Fertilize once when plants are actively growing, using a controlled-release fertilizer. Large-flowered kinds need rich soil and lots of water.

SOURCES. Nurseries sell many kinds of annual mums, cosmos, dahlias, marigolds, and sunflowers. The varieties shown in this article came from the following sources: • Connell's Dahlias: (253) 531-0292 or www.connells-dahlias.com. • Park Seed Co.: (800) 845-3369 or www.parkseed.com. • Shepherd's Garden Seeds: (860) 482-3638 or www.shepherdseeds.com. • Stokes Seeds: (800) 396-9238 or www.stokeseeds.com. • Swan Island Dahlias: (800) 410-6540 or www.dahlias.com; catalog $4. • Thompson & Morgan: (800) 274-7333 or www.thompson-morgan.com. • W. Atlee Burpee & Co.: (800) 888-1447 or www.burpee.com. ◆

THOMAS J. STORY

Many different flowers in sunny south-of-the-border hues give this bouquet a casual country garden look.
DESIGN: Jill Slater

Chinese wisteria 'Cooke's Special' mingles with 'Rêve d'Or' roses in designer Michael Bates's Sonoma County, California, garden.

Wonderful wisterias

A shopper's guide to this clan of showy spring-flowering vines

By Lauren Bonar Swezey

In the western China province of Hubei, the much-loved vine that westerners know simply by the scientific name *Wisteria* is called *chiao teng* (beautiful vine). In Japan, it's called *Fuji*. By any name, this rambunctious climber with lacy green foliage is an exceptional beauty in bloom. Dramatic clusters of flowers in blue, pink, purple, and white can dangle from 1 to 3 feet in length.

You can train these twining woody vines as climbers, ground covers, or trees (tree wisterias are often sold already trained). Plants will thrive in any soil that drains well and in every climate zone in the West. Make sure, though, that you have room to grow them: Wisterias are vigorous, even rampant growers.

Chinese and Japanese wisterias are the most widely sold types. Silky wis-

terias, also from Japan, deserve equal attention. These three types have surpassed the southeastern American species (*W. frutescens* and *W. machrostachya*), introduced in the 18th century but now seldom planted here.

Choosing a wisteria

Go for named varieties that are propagated from cuttings, buds, or grafts; they'll start blooming within the first couple of years after planting. Avoid buying seedlings (often sold as floribunda white or floribunda blue), cautions wisteria grower Guy Meacham of Rippingale Nursery in Oregon. "They may take 10 to 15 years to bloom, and one has no idea of the quality and quantity of the flowers," he says. Below we list varieties recommended by Guy Meacham or by Peter Valder in his book *Wisterias:*

A Comprehensive Guide (Timber Press, Portland, 1995; $32.95; 800/327-5680).

CHINESE VARIETIES (*W. sinensis*) produce 1-foot-long flower clusters in midspring before foliage expands. Leaves are divided into 9 to 13 leaflets. Chinese wisterias bloom in sun or partial shade. Vines twine counterclockwise.

■ **'Cooke's Special'.** Clusters of fragrant blue-purple flowers are 20 inches long. The variety can rebloom. It was introduced by a California nursery, L.E. Cooke.

■ **'Prolific'.** Cloaked in dense, blue flower clusters. 'Prolific' blooms at a very early age; it flowers sporadically throughout the summer.

JAPANESE VARIETIES (*W. floribunda*) produce dramatic 1½- to 3-foot-long flower clusters, usually in midspring before or while foliage is expanding.

Leaves are divided into 15 to 19 leaflets and turn yellow in fall (except where noted). Flowers of most varieties are scented. Vines twine clockwise. Japanese wisterias are most effective when grown on pergolas so the long flower clusters can hang freely. They bloom best in full sun.

- **'Caroline'** (most likely *W. floribunda* 'Caroline', but sometimes sold as *W. sinensis* 'Caroline'). Mauve flowers come out in early spring. The variety is fast growing and early flowering.
- **'Macrobotrys'** (also known as 'Longissima'). Grows exceptionally long clusters (sometimes as long as 3 feet) of moderately scented violet-purple flowers.
- **'Royal Purple'** (also known as 'Black Dragon'). Sweetly scented dark purple flowers emerge in midspring.
- **'Shiro Noda'** (also sold as 'Alba', 'Longissima Alba', and 'Snow Showers'). Blooms in long clusters of densely packed white flowers. In *Wisterias,* Valder calls the late-flowering 'Shiro Noda' "one of the most beautiful of all," although it has poor autumn color.
- **'Violacea Plena'** (also sold as 'Black Dragon'). Bears double deep purple flowers. It is the only known double.

SILKY VARIETIES (*W. brachybotrys,* also known as *W. venusta*) produce a profusion of short (6-inch), fat clusters of large, strongly scented flowers that open all at once, usually in midspring when leaves are just opening. Broad leaves with 9 to 13 leaflets have silky hairs. Most vines twine counterclockwise (an exception is noted). Silky wisterias have velvety seed pods and bloom best in full sun.

- **'Murasaki Kapitan'** (also sold as

A 75-year-old Japanese wisteria spreads over a metal arbor at Bishop's Close at Elk Rock Garden in Portland. Nearby, a twice-blooming 85-year-old Chinese wisteria 'Alba' (right) is espaliered over a window.

JANET LOUGHREY (2)

ANDREW DRAKE

This tough, vigorous Japanese wisteria was brought 80 years ago from England to Seattle, then transplanted to Susan Russak's garden in Mercer Island, Washington. It now reaches three stories tall. A close-up of a Japanese wisteria bloom shows the delicate two-toned flowers.

'Murasaki' and 'Violacea'). Profuse blue-violet blooms in early spring. Twines clockwise.

- **'Shiro Kapitan'** (also sold as 'Alba'). 'Shiro Kapitan' has white flowers with yellow markings. "Superior in color to the white cultivars of *W. sinensis*," notes Valder.

Care

Choose a location that allows shoots room to spread. Water newly planted wisterias regularly for the first year or two, until the plant is well established. While plants are young, fertilize twice a year, in early spring and midsummer. Once it is established, water infrequently (more frequently in hot climates). In coastal areas, old vines need little to no supplemental water.

Sources

Look for named varieties at local nurseries or order by mail from one of the suppliers below.

Forestfarm, 990 Tetherow Rd., Williams, OR 97544; (541) 846-7269 or www.forestfarm.com; catalog $5. Sells 19 kinds.

Greer Gardens, 1280 Goodpasture Island Rd., Eugene, OR 97401; (800) 548-0111 or www.greergardens.com; catalog free. Sells about 20 kinds.

Pruning

Unless grown as a ground cover or trained as a tree, wisteria needs the strong support of a sturdy pergola or trellis. Pruning is also critical to maintain this vigorous grower.

THOMAS J. STORY (2)

Late winter

1. Once the vine has developed its structure, cut back side shoots to two or three buds (count from where shoot originates). Shorten the flower-producing spurs that grow from side shoots to just beyond the last flower bud (flower buds are fatter than leaf buds).
2. Thin any excess shoots by cutting them back to the main stem.
3. Cut back the growing tips to limit length.
4. Remove seed pods.

Summer

Cut long, whippy shoots back to three leaves. Do not cut shoots that are needed to extend the vine or fill in gaps. ◆

Antique wood doors open Calvo's studio to garden beds filled with fragrant lavender and edged with boxwood. RIGHT: Calvo pauses in her water garden, where she's painting water lilies. Joan Irvine Smith, founder of the Irvine Museum and a Calvo collector, describes the artist's style as a melding of "European impressionism with the traditions of the California plein air artists."

Art lessons

Artist Maria del Carmen Calvo shares
the secrets of her glorious garden

By Sharon Cohoon • Photographs by Claire Curran

Artists, you can't help but notice, have more interesting gardens than the rest of us. That's because they're so suffused with talent, everything they touch blossoms into self-expression. Isn't that what, in our heart of hearts, we all believe? And isn't it a demoralizing thought? Well, it's also dead wrong, says Maria del Carmen Calvo, a painter shown here in her garden in Capistrano Beach, California. "Artists don't live in beautiful spaces *because* they are artists," says Calvo. "They live in beautiful spaces so that they *can be* artists." They believe that a stimulating, nurturing environment is a necessity, not a luxury, and they go to great lengths to create it. "Beauty feeds our souls," she continues. "We need

Flanked by pots of purple fountain grass (*Pennisetum setaceum* 'Rubrum'), the entry gate opens onto one of Calvo's many garden rooms. The cherub fountain inside is a focal point. TOP LEFT: Calvo made this container of concrete, using an old carving to make the pattern. Artfully dappled dalmatians pause by an aged wood door.

it in order to function at full capacity." And that "we," insists Calvo, includes all of us.

What is beautiful and soul-nourishing to Calvo is a garden that reminds her of the ones with which she grew up in northern Spain. That means familiar plants grown in a timeless manner—rows of olive trees, parallel hedges of lavender, citrus in pots in the front courtyard, and a pair of overturned *ollas* (earthenware jugs) planted with ivy geraniums at the gate. "You see ollas in front of most gardens in Spain," she says, "and mostly planted in geraniums." In addition to giving the garden color, texture, and fragrance, says Calvo, for her these plants also evoke memories and provide comfort.

What else makes a garden magical?

Water is an essential element of a garden, says Calvo. The Moors occupied Spain for 700 years, and their gardening style, she says, permanently changed the country. Water is always central to a Moorish garden. "I've created a garden where I'm never far from its sound," she says. Though Calvo's garden is not large, she has included seven fountains, most of her own design.

Garden rooms with pleasing human proportions are something else this artist strives to achieve. ("You can't help but feel good when you're in them.") Calvo's garden is divided into many rooms, some big enough to be shared by the family, others cozy enough for a tête-à-tête or solitary retreat. But Calvo isn't quite satisfied. "I've got a few more improvements in mind," she says, smiling.

The **patina of age** adds charm to a garden. And it's the most difficult element to achieve in the West, where everything looks like it was just taken out of its wrapper five minutes ago. Calvo achieves it by collecting antiques—large architec-

tural pieces such as gates, windows, and doors, which she stores until she finds inspiration for their use. Or she'll commission a new piece that replicates something older.

The things that make Calvo feel centered in her own garden may not be yours. But we can all find what we need to fashion our own beauty. "All you have to do," Calvo says, "is think with your soul."

LEFT: Concrete squares trimmed with rock are a classic patio treatment throughout southern Europe, says Calvo: "So this floor really reminds me of home." Rocks and marble chips were pressed into the wet concrete. ABOVE: Water trickles through a rusty pipe—set into the top of a concrete wall backed with iron—onto a stone basin in this fountain. Grasses growing in front add to the rustic setting. Pavers (foreground) are studded with bits of glass, which sparkle in moonlight.

Thinking like an artist

- **GATHER IDEAS.** In order to create beauty in your garden, says Calvo, you need ideas. Gather images to draw from. "Visit museums, walk through gardens, take a hike," she says. "Beauty is everywhere." Also collect books, clippings, and photos of gardens and accessories you like.

- **LOSE FEAR; LEARN TRUST.** "Most people know what they like," says Calvo, "and they have good instincts. But they block them out of fear. Let the fear go. It's your worst enemy." Say, for instance, you always wanted to plant an all-red border, including foliage. What's stopping you? Try it. It could be the most exciting flower garden you ever planted. If not, refine it until it is.

- **"ENJOY THE PROCESS."** Artists accept that things never turn out the way they imagined them the very first time, says Calvo. They're willing to make second, third, and fourth attempts. The fountain she designed for the courtyard just outside her studio, shown above, is a good example. What Calvo originally pictured for this space was a weeping wall—a monolith with a constant trickle of water running down its face. During the construction process, however, she found her original idea too plain and kept embellishing the design until she reached the finished product shown here. "Don't invest so much in the outcome," she advises. "Enjoy the process." ◆

Garden magic in baskets

Ground covers create living liners for baskets and hayracks

By Lauren Bonar Swezey
Photographs by Thomas J. Story
Designs by Bud Stuckey and Jim McCann

■ For years *Sunset's* garden staff lined hanging baskets with dry sphagnum moss. When coco-fiber inserts became available, we switched to those. Then last spring, Bud Stuckey, our test garden coordinator, began experimenting with living plant materials. He used a variety of ground covers to form leafy liners for wire basket frames. Then he filled the baskets with potting soil and planted seasonal flowers, ferns, and succulents. He discovered that the living liners worked instant magic on hanging baskets, freestanding baskets, half baskets, and hayrack planters.

The ground cover–lined baskets are very easy to assemble. The secret is to start with a mudflat (a nursery flat with no dividers) of one of the ground covers from our list below, left. The roots of these plants form well-knit carpets that fill the flat. Carefully cut to fit baskets, they make nearly seamless liners. Hang the baskets in partial shade. With regular water and minimal care, they will last for months.

7 LIVING LINERS

- Baby's tears (*Soleirolia soleirolii*)
- Blue star creeper (*Laurentia fluviatilis*)
- Chamomile (*Chamaemelum nobile*)
- Creeping thyme (*Thymus praecox articus* 'Elfin')
- Irish moss (*Arenaria verna* or *Sagina subulata*)
- Scotch moss (*A. verna* 'Aurea' or *S. subulata* 'Aurea')
- *Sedum spurium*

Easter parade

LEFT FRONT: Blooming blue star creeper lines a wire mesh box filled with lavender violas and creamy yellow nemesias. **RIGHT REAR:** Scotch moss covers a wicker basket filled with purple lobelias. **RIGHT FRONT:** Chamomile cloaks a wire basket spilling with white violas and blades of bluegrass grown from seeds planted in the potting soil.

Tropical basket

Lined with baby's tears, a half basket features a bird's nest fern flanked by two mother ferns and pink polka-dot plants.

Victorian cage

'Elfin' creeping thyme carpets a wire basket with variegated 'Tricolor' sweet potato vine planted on top.

Tropical basket

TIME: 30 minutes

COST: About $60

MATERIALS

- Knife
- One piece of cardboard or coco-fiber liner
- One 16-inch-wide wire half basket
- One mudflat (at least 16 by 16 inches) of baby's tears (shown) or other ground cover
- 1 cubic foot potting soil
- ¼ cup organic fertilizer
- One 6-inch bird's nest fern (*Asplenium nidus*)
- Two 4-inch mother ferns (*Asplenium bulbiferum*)
- One sixpack pink polka-dot plant (*Hypoestes phyllostachya*)
- One sixpack violas

DIRECTIONS

1. Cut a piece of cardboard or coco-fiber liner to fit inside the flat back of a half basket (it will hang against a wall or other surface).

2. Set the flat back of the basket diagonally on the mudflat. With a knife, trim a top corner of the ground cover flush with the top of the basket (photo A).

3. Remove the ground cover from the flat (B) and set it inside the front of the basket with the leafy side facing out (C). The top edge of the ground cover should be flush with the top of the basket, and the bottom corner should fit into the bottom. Press the rest of the ground cover around the front of the basket.

4. Fill the basket ¾ full with potting soil (D). Mix in ¼ cup organic fertilizer.

5. Set the largest plant in the center of the basket (E), 4-inch plants on either side of it, and the sixpack-size plants around the edges. Fill around the plants with soil and water thoroughly.

6. Hang the basket in partial shade. Make sure the ground cover and the soil around the companion plants stay moist. Baby's tears and chamomile can be sheared if they get too bushy. The others don't take to shearing, but they can be patched or replanted if necessary.

FOR A ROUND BASKET, omit step 1 and work the ground cover all around the wire frame. Once the basket is hanging, rotate it regularly so light reaches all sides and foliage grows evenly.

FOR A HAYRACK, construction is similar to that of a half basket, but you'll need to place cardboard or coco-fiber liner against the back and very bottom of the hayrack (it will not get enough light to support lush growth). If the hayrack is more than 16 inches long, you'll need at least two mud-flats of the same ground cover and will have to cut pieces to fit.

Southwest style

Sedum spurium lines a half basket spilling with donkey tail (*S. morganianum*) and rosettes of purplish and light green echeveria.

NORMAN A. PLATE

Hot pink hayrack

Blue star creeper (out of flower) covers a wall-mounted hayrack featuring impatiens and caladiums with heart-shaped leaves.

SOURCES
Most local nurseries or garden centers stock wire basket frames, but you may have to ask them to order mudflats of ground covers. For a wide selection of wire baskets and hayracks, call Kinsman Company; (800) 733-4146 or www.kinsmangarden.com. ◆

How to win the war against weeds

Attack both annuals and perennials as soon as you can

By Sharon Cohoon • Illustrations by Claudia Stevens

If you were to compress all the advice written on weed control to a single maxim, it would be: Attack early in the game. Getting weeds out of the garden at the start of the season, when they're most vulnerable, is a smart strategy for two reasons: It keeps annual weeds from forming seed heads and it keeps perennial weeds from developing deeper roots.

The most important thing you can do is to prevent more seeds from developing. Here's why: Most weeds in your garden are annuals, and annual weeds are phenomenally prodigious seed producers. A single crabgrass plant, for example, can produce 100,000 seeds, according to Barbara Pleasant, author of *The Gardener's Weed Book: Earth-Safe Controls* (Storey Communications, North Adams, MA, 1996, $12.95; 800/441-5700).

If you don't get rid of these intruders before they develop viable seeds, the number of foes you'll have to battle will increase every year, and you'll always be playing catch-up.

With perennial weeds, seeds aren't the only problem, since they produce fewer of them. Instead, perennials ensure their own survival by developing extensive underground root systems and/or sending out runners aboveground. If you catch them young, perennial weeds can usually be pulled out of the ground easily. But once established, they can be next to impossible to get rid of, as anyone who has battled Bermuda grass or yellow nutsedge in flower beds will attest.

annuals

Annuals: Off with their heads

To keep annuals from setting seed, weed early and often. Slicing off the top of the plant is all you have to do; there's no need to remove the roots. Many gardeners find that the most efficient tool for this task is some type of scuffle hoe, which cuts weeds at or just below the soil surface.

You can use the same off-with-their-heads approach to reduce the amount of annual weeds in a lawn. Simply mow high (3 inches or so) and often (weekly or biweekly). This keeps new seeds from forming, and the taller grass shades the ground, preventing the germination of weed seeds already in the soil.

What about all the seeds already lurking in the soil, waiting to sprout? The easiest way to control them is by never letting them see

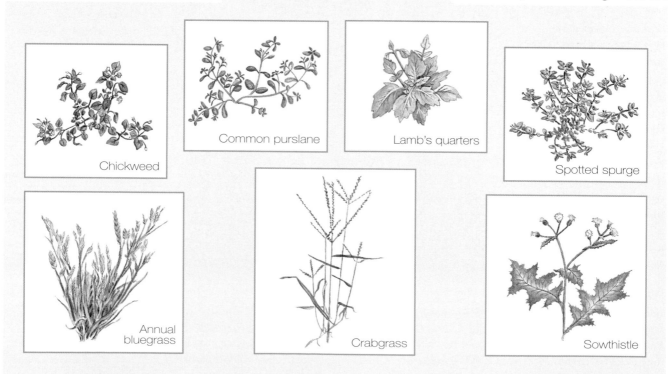

Chickweed

Common purslane

Lamb's quarters

Spotted spurge

Annual bluegrass

Crabgrass

Sowthistle

the light of day. If sunlight doesn't reach them, they don't germinate. Plant closely so that most of the soil is shaded by foliage, and mulch thickly so sunlight won't reach the soil. Avoid excessive cultivation, which brings weed seeds closer to the surface. In vegetable beds, don't leave the earth bare between crops: Put down a temporary mulch or plant a cover crop like clover that you can dig under later.

If you're preparing a new flower or vegetable bed, try another approach: forcing out the enemy. Till and amend the soil as you normally would prior to planting. Then keep the prepared soil moist for a few days to encourage weed seeds to sprout. When they do, hoe them off and water again. Repeat this process until there are few weed seeds left to sprout, leaving little weeding thereafter.

Perennials: Yank 'em out young—roots and all

With perennials, it is essential to get all of the plant out of the ground. When perennial weeds are tender seedlings, they can usually be pulled up by hand with ease, especially when the soil is moist. But the more time you allow these weeds to take hold, the harder they are to eradicate. The least bit of Bermuda grass rhizome left behind can sprout into a new plant.

The best time to weed is shortly after a rain or an irrigation cycle. Hand-pulling is the quickest method. If the weeds don't yield easily or if they detach from the roots when you pull, switch to a trowel or dandelion weeder and dig or pry them out. ◆

perennials

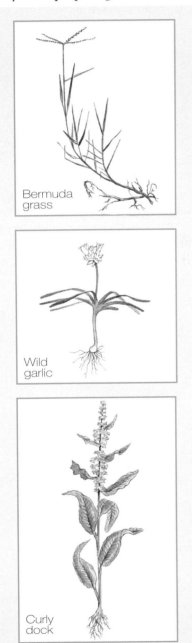

Bermuda grass

Wild garlic

Curly dock

Fountain grass

Field bindweed

Dandelion

Oxalis

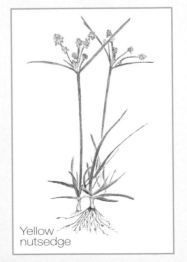

Yellow nutsedge

Spectacular succulents

Robert Cohen has the magic touch with these obliging plants

By Sharon Cohoon
Photographs by Claire Curran

Maybe you think you know as much as you want to about succulents. I know I did. They're the sculptural little plants, usually shunted off to the side in nurseries, that you dash past without a glance on your way to check out the newest perennials. Right? Okay, now take a look at the dreamy concoctions on these pages. They're made with the same plants we've been ignoring. Could it be we've overlooked some of nature's choicest plants?

Robert Cohen, the maestro responsible for the compositions shown here, isn't guilty of that: He's been madly in love with succulents for at least 15 years. There's hardly a container in his Newport Beach, California, garden that doesn't have donkey tail (*Sedum morganianum*) cascading from it or at least one big green *Aeonium* rosette tucked in somewhere. Cohen admires succulents for their sculptural perfection, seductive textures, subtle colors, substance, drama, and remarkably forgiving, flexible natures.

But he doesn't like to show them off alone. He prefers combining a half-dozen kinds in pots, blending tone-on-tone patterns reminiscent of brocades. He mixes succulents with plants that have foliage of an entirely different nature, such as asparagus fern, coleus, or curly parsley. Succulents also look great in primarily floral arrangements.

Blame his passion on roots, he says. Though Cohen is now the co-owner

of the Four Seasons Hotel in Beverly Hills, much of his life has revolved around the florist trade. His father was a florist, and Cohen himself owned the Windsor Florist. These experiences shaped his approach to gardening. "Everything I touch seems to turn into a bouquet," he says. Few of his plantings are without his favorite succulents. "They

TOP: Garland is made up of small *Aeonium, Sedum rubrotinctum* (pork and beans), and other succulents. Gray-blue plant in top is *Echeveria elegans.* Donkey tail cascades over the side. All are inserted into mesh cylinders filled with moss. ABOVE LEFT: Mixed succulents fill a birdbath. ABOVE RIGHT: Donkey tail with Myers asparagus fern in hanging basket.

ABOVE: Robert Cohen and his wife, Beverly. "Warty" plant closest to front is *Kalanchoe beharensis* 'Fang', also known as feltbush. *Kalanchoe tomentosa* (panda plant) grows to its right. LEFT: Cohen's lathhouse.

are wonderful," he says. "No bouquet should be without them."

Cohen's succulent bouquets

- **Select wide, shallow containers.** Since many succulents are wider than they are tall, planters of the same proportions are usually the most aesthetically pleasing. Terracotta dishes aren't the only options. For instance, with drainage holes added, the concrete birdbath on page 150 makes a splendid container.
- **Start with the accent piece.** "Look for a plant that will give the finished arrangement some drama," says Cohen. "You don't want all short, round pieces." He usually selects something sharply vertical. Sansevieria (snake plant) is one of his favorites, but he also uses asparagus fern, euphorbias, and even ivy trained up small trellises.

- **Plant contrasting companions in small groves.** "You rarely find individual plants alone in nature," says Cohen. "Usually things grow in clumps, and that's how I like to arrange them."
- **Set plants close together.** "I don't have the patience to wait for things to fill in, and with succulents you don't have to," he says. If there are gaps in a pot's planting, he fills them with cuttings from succulents elsewhere in the garden. They invariably take root. If one succulent overtakes its companions in a container, Cohen simply cuts it back and lets the others catch up.

Planting tips

- **Use succulents appropriate for your climate.** The *Aeoniums* and echeverias that Cohen favors flourish in his mild, coastal garden but are too tender for mountain gardens

and don't like harsh desert summers. Sempervivums are cold-hardy in all zones, as are many sedums and some *Delosperma* (ice plant). In the desert, gasteria, haworthia, and agaves are better choices.

- **Provide good drainage.** Succulents will forgive most failures—too much or not enough water or lack of fertilizer—but they *do* like their roots in quick-draining soil. Use a cactus potting mix that is 50 percent pumice. If you live in a particularly wet climate, you might want to use an even grittier mix. For extra protection from winter root rot, move containers under the eaves during prolonged rainy stretches.
- **Water frequently when the weather warms.** Succulents can survive considerable neglect, especially in mild climates, but they look better with regular irrigation in the desert and elsewhere when temperatures climb. In fact, it's hard to overwater them in summer.
- **Feed infrequently.** Though succulents could probably get by without any fertilizer, to keep them in peak condition most succulent fanciers feed them two or three times a year with a liquid fertilizer (20-20-20, for instance) diluted to half strength. ◆

MIDAS HIMSELF WOULD ADMIRE these gilded trees at VanDusen Botanical Gardens in Vancouver, B.C.
For more on the spectacular goldenchain tree *(Laburnum* x *watereri* 'Vossii'), see page 159.

May

DAVID WINGER

Wildflowers replace a lawn in Denver

Unthirsty native plants reveal their colorful nature in May

■ When the city of Denver changed the street designation of their corner lot, Jim and Dorothy Borland's overgrown side yard became their official front yard. The Borlands, both professional horticulturists, decided a landscape renovation was in order. They tore out aging shade trees and junipers and built a porch along the new front of their home. They replaced a bluegrass lawn with a planting of wildflowers and native shrubs that reflects their philosophy of using native plants in urban landscapes while conserving water.

Throughout the growing season, whenever rain was forecast, Jim set out small plants that he grew from seed, ultimately planting 10,000 seedlings representing 1,500 species of annual and perennial wildflowers, shrubs, and small trees. In February, he sowed Indian paint-brush by scattering seeds into frost cracks.

The Borlands' new front yard is bursting with color in May. Drifts of Indian paintbrush in shades of yellow, orange, and red join dozens of species of penstemon, including the prominent blue spikes of *P. glaber*. Prickly poppy, with its huge crinkled white flowers, provides a stately elegance from early summer to first frost. Spires of yellow prince's plume (*Stanleya pinnata*) tower over the left side of the scene.

Eventually the small trees and shrubs, including piñon, rabbitbrush, and Western sand cherry, will mature and play a larger role in the water-thrifty landscape. But for now, the Borlands' yard proves that gardening with unthirsty native plants is anything but dull.

— *Marcia Tatroe*

Star-spangled pathway

■ A well-designed path meanders through the garden like a creek flowing through the countryside, with calm stretches that invite visitors to slow down and admire the scenery. Redmond-based Jerzy Radka of Greenwood International Landscape Design and Installation designed such a path in a large back garden for Margo Paddock and Paul Osborne in Woodinville, Washington.

Along one swath, steppingstones tiptoe through a lush carpet of blue star creeper (*Pratia pedunculata,* formerly known as *Laurentia fluviatilis*). Its tiny star-shaped flowers appear from spring through summer. Margo Paddock planted plugs of this ground cover at 6-inch intervals one spring. By the end of the third summer, the plugs had filled in. Blue star creeper can take light foot traffic but produces fewer flowers the more it gets stepped on.

This part of the path is framed by orange-flowered daylilies and lady's-mantle (*Alchemilla mollis*), with airy chartreuse blooms. — *Jim McCausland*

NORM PLATE

Irises are perfect mixers

■ This month, as tall bearded irises go into bloom, it's easy to see why they enjoy their reputation as one of the choicest perennials. You can see how well they mix with other perennials in the display beds at Schreiner's Iris Gardens near Salem, Oregon. In the bed shown at left, for instance, the variety 'Pallida Variegata' (often sold as 'Zebra'), with cream-striped leaves and blue-lavender flowers, is paired with Iceland poppies, peonies, and Russell hybrid lupines.

Tall bearded types reach heights from at least 28 inches to more than 40 inches. Their flowers are distinguished by beards, which are the tufts of fine hairs down the top center of each lower petal (called a fall). Irises like full sun and well-drained soil.

Schreiner's display gardens are open from 8 to dusk daily during May and the first week in June. For driving directions or a mail-order catalog ($5), call (503) 393-3232 or visit www.schreinersgardens.com. — *J.M.*

JANET LOUGHREY

THOMAS J. STORY (4)

Paint a pot

■ Paint in cheerful colors can transform a humble clay pot into a work of art like the ones pictured here. You don't need artistic talent to create simple designs; for the blue-and-white pot pictured at right, follow the guidelines below. DESIGN: Jennifer Cobble Willhoite

TIME: 20 to 30 minutes, plus drying time
COST: $20 for several pots, including paint and materials. Container prices vary widely, depending on size.

TOOLS AND MATERIALS
• Clear **acrylic sealer**
• One 8-inch **terra-cotta pot**
• White, cobalt blue, and yellow **acrylic paints**
• One **1-inch-wide paintbrush**
• One high-quality **fine-tipped paintbrush**

DIRECTIONS
1. Spray the inside of the pot with two to three coats of clear acrylic sealer to prevent water from seeping through the pot. Allow sealer to dry, about 30 minutes for each coat.
2. Hold the pot upside down over your hand with your fingers gripping the small hole on the bottom. Paint the entire pot with two thin coats of white paint; the paint dries quickly, so there's little or no drying time needed between applications.
3. Using the fine-tipped brush, paint blue stripes horizontally around the pot's rim. Next, paint vertical stripes in varying thicknesses (**A**).
4. Turn the pot sideways and paint large S's around the body of the pot (**B**).
5. To make the small flowers, hold the pot upside down as shown; paint an X for each flower (**C**). Then paint a plus sign on top of the X. Once the paint is dry, dab a small dot of yellow paint in the center.
6. Allow the pot to dry 20 to 30 minutes (or until dry to the touch), then spray the outside with two to three coats of acrylic sealer (allow to dry between sprays).
To create other designs: Paint half circles, thin and narrow stripes, and small and large dots. — *Lauren Bonar Swezey*

A

B

C

Irises in Boulder

■ Just off Iris Avenue on Broadway in Boulder, Colorado, Long's Gardens has been a landmark since 1905. Each spring during May and June, thousands of irises bloom in a breathtaking spectrum of colors on the 7-acre site. The gardens are overseen today by Catherine Long Gates, a third-generation member of the founding family. Among her favorite irises, Gates cites these six; all are tall bearded types, unless noted.

'Flopsy'. Pure white flowers have sweet fragrance.

'Firenze Frolic' (top photo). Bred by Catherine Long Gates, this iris has a yellow background bordered in garnet.

'I Love Lace' (photo at right). Orange beards look striking on pale lavender flowers.

'Pallida Variegata' (often listed as 'Zebra'). One of Long's Gardens' all-time favorites, it features pale purple, grape-scented flowers and cream-striped foliage.

'Red Rooster'. A border bearded iris with deep red-brown flowers, it reaches about 26 inches high.

PAUL BOUSQUET (2)

'Sunpolka'. Bright yellow-and-white-ruffled petals seem to dance in the breeze.

If you visit Long's Gardens, at 3240 Broadway, in May and June, you can dig iris rhizomes directly from designated fields. Hours are 9 to 5 daily; digging forks and bags are provided. Iris plants cost $3.50 each.

If you can't visit in person, the Long's Gardens catalog lists about 400 iris varieties. Rhizomes are shipped in July and August. For a free copy, call (303) 442-2353 or go to www.longsgardens.com. — *Colleen Smith*

BACK TO BASICS

Planting lingo. Gardening books and periodicals often use specific terms to describe the process of setting out plants from nursery pots. Here's what those terms mean. *Rootball:* The root system of a plant grown in a container. *Score a rootball:* To make four to six cuts around a rootball and across the bottom with a sharp knife so roots will grow out into the surrounding soil rather than continue to twine around the rootball. *Scarify a planting hole:* To roughen the sides of a planting hole with a shovel or spade. *Backfill:* The soil removed in the process of digging a planting hole that is put back in around a plant's rootball. — *L.B.S.*

LINDA HOLT AYRISS

Terrific trailers

■ Bacopa (*Sutera cordata*) is now one of the most popular annuals (perennial in mild climates) for containers. Its trailing habit, long bloom season, and copious small flowers make it a choice plant for cascading over the edges of patio pots, window boxes, and hanging baskets. New flower colors, including lavender and brick red, have joined the more familiar white 'Snowflake'.

This year there's also a delightful blue-flowered variety, called 'Blue Showers', from Paul Ecke Ranch; it's sold under the Flower Fields label. In the container pictured below, it pairs with Swan River daisies (*Brachyscome* 'Mauve Delight' and 'Jumbo Misty Pink') and *Salvia* x *sylvestris* 'May Night'.

Bacopa is a thirsty plant. Keep it well watered, especially during hot weather, and give it partial shade. Feed every two weeks with an acid-type fertilizer.

— *Sharon Coboon*

CLAIRE CURRAN

A carpet of sun-catchers

In Pasadena, succulents and grasses go for bold

■ "Give us anything but a lawn." That's what Kira and Brian Deputy asked of Woodland Hills–based landscape architect Steven Ormenyi when they set about landscaping their front yard in Pasadena. The couple had just acquired property with a house that Kira describes as a midcentury modern, with a mess of Algerian ivy out front. They knew they had to get rid of the deeply thatched ivy. The question was, what should replace it? "We wanted the design to be drought-tolerant and low-maintenance," says Kira. "But the most important thing was that it be bold enough to go with the very simple lines of the house."

Ormenyi focused on succulents—mostly aloes and agaves—which add a dense, architectural feel to the garden. The tawny plumes of Mexican feather grass (*Stipa tenuissima*), the silvery leaves of snow-in-summer (*Cerastium tomentosum*), and the metallic-blue fingers of *Senecio mandraliscae,* when hit by sunlight, bounce it back, adding sheen and shimmer to the cool and bold

look of the succulents.

The planting is drought-tolerant, although perhaps not as low-maintenance as anticipated; wayward seedlings of Mexican feather grass have to be plucked out frequently, and the snow-in-summer needs periodic trimming to keep it from engulfing the aloes. But there's something interesting happening in the yard throughout the year, says Kira. And squadrons of hummingbirds zoom in when the aloes are in bloom. — *Sharon Cohoon*

CLAIRE CURRAN (2)

JANET LOUGHREY

Chains of gold

■ Few garden plants can rival the spectacular flower show put on by goldenchain tree (*Laburnum* x *watereri* 'Vossii'). From mid-May to early June, the trees pictured here at Van-Dusen Botanical Gardens in Vancouver, B.C., dangle 10- to 20-inch-long clusters of pea-shaped yellow flowers. Gold-enchain tree grows especially well in the temperate climate of the Pacific Northwest. This deciduous tree, with green bark and bright green leaves resembling clover, eventually reaches a height of 15 to 30 feet and 10 to 20 feet wide.

To complement the overhanging chains of gold, these trees are underplanted with bulbs and perennials in shades of lavender and pink. Blooming along the path are the tall, elegant spikes of *Allium hollandicum* 'Purple Sensation' and ornamental chives (*A. schoenoprasum* 'Forescate').

VanDusen Botanical Garden is at 5251 Oak Street. Hours vary seasonally. Make plans to attend the VanDusen Flower & Garden Show in late May and early June; it features more than 250 special displays, theme gardens, and commercial exhibitors. For more information, call (604) 878-9274 or visit www.vandusengarden.org.

— *Janet Loughrey*

A watering hole for birds and bees

■ If birds, bees, and other wildlife know there's a steady supply of fresh water in your garden, they'll visit regularly. That's a sure thing, says Carrie Nimmer, a Phoenix-based landscape designer who specializes in creating animal-friendly gardens. So when Fred and Marion Emerson asked her to create a garden that would attract Sonoran Desert wildlife, Nimmer knew a water feature was paramount.

She designed a feature that consists of a 2- by 4-foot galvanized steel trough meant for watering horses (available at feed stores), an iron grate, a recirculating pump, a feeder tube (disguised with a length of bamboo), and a big rock with a bowl-shaped depression.

The trough is buried in the ground and covered with the grate. The rock rests atop the grate and is tilted slightly so that water spills off it; the water then flows down through the grate into the trough and is pumped back up again. Surrounding grasses and flowering perennials, which include yellow-flowered Mexican poppies, add to the impression that this is a natural water hole.

Birds drink from the depression in the rock, and butterflies, bees, and other pollinating insects sip water from the lichen that grows on the rock.

— *S.C.*

Cast-bronze bees rest on the lichen-encrusted rock.

CHARLES MANN

An arbor draped by Lady Banks' rose

■ When Bill and Mary Lou Piatkiewicz were planning their new backyard in Tucson, the first item on their wish list was a secluded area where they could read and relax. To fulfill their wish, they enlisted the aid of John Harlow Jr. of Harlow Gardens. Harlow's solution? An arbor that would be shrouded by that grande dame of climbing roses, Lady Banks' (*Rosa banksiae*).

Because this vigorous rose needs sturdy support, Harlow designed a circular arbor—about 8 feet high, with a diameter of 16½ feet—composed of tubular steel panels. The rose canes arch over the arbor's open top. A 4½-foot-wide gap creates an entrance to the brick-floored room, which is outfitted with wicker furniture.

Around the foot of the arbor, Harlow set out 14 plants from 5-gallon containers, alternating the two forms of the rose: yellow-flowered 'Lutea' and white-flowered *R. b. banksiae* 'Alba Plena'. The roses quickly covered the panels, creating an enclosed outdoor room.

Throughout the year, the Piatkiewiczes enjoy the shade cast by the dense canopy of evergreen foliage. Masses of blooms cover the outside of the arbor from late February through April. Low-voltage lights at the base of the arbor create a dramatic effect at night. — *Mary Irish*

TERRENCE MOORE

THOMAS J. STORY

Green soybeans: Eat them like peanuts

■ In Japanese snack bars, *edamame*—green soybeans—are as popular as salted peanuts are in beer pubs around the West. You crack open the plump green shells and pop the cooked beans right into your mouth. Not only are they tasty, but edamame are loaded with nutrients—vitamins, protein, and calcium. You can buy podded soybeans at supermarkets, but seeds are easy to grow.

Choose a warm, sunny location protected from frost and wind. Amend the soil with compost. Then plant seeds 1 inch deep and 3 inches apart in rows 12 to 14 inches apart. (Green soybeans grow only about 2 feet tall and are naturally upright, so they can be planted closely.) When seedlings have about five leaves, pile soil into a mound a few inches high around the stems to give them a bit of support. Keep soil moist but not soggy. Don't fertilize: It reduces yields.

When pods are plump and still green, in 75 to 90 days (depending on variety), pull up the whole plant, then pluck off pods. (They all ripen at the same time, so you won't be losing any crop.)

To prepare edamame, boil pods whole in lightly salted water until tender, about 10 minutes. Or add soy sauce to the water (about 1 tablespoon per quart of water) instead of salt, as does Ralph Crane, garden instructor at the Arboretum of Los Angeles County. Pop the beans out of their shells to eat. Shelled beans can also be mixed into a stir-fry or added to salads.

SOURCES: Johnny's Selected Seeds, Albion, ME (207/437-4301 or www.johnnyseeds.com), and Territorial Seed Company, Cottage Grove, OR (541/942-9547 or www.territorialseed.com). — *S.C.*

pacific northwest · checklist

PLANTING

☐ **ANNUALS.** Sow seeds of almost any kind of annual after the average date of last frost in your area. Good candidates for sun include cosmos, geraniums, marigolds, petunias, sunflowers, and zinnias; for light shade, try begonias, coleus, and impatiens.

☐ **FUCHSIAS.** Give all kinds partial shade (full sun near the coast). As plants grow, pinch them back to make them bushy; feed and water regularly through the summer to promote bloom.

☐ **HERBS.** When the soil warms up, plant basil, dill, fennel, lovage, oregano, rosemary, sage, and thyme. Plant mint where it will get plenty of water. Edge beds with chives and parsley.

☐ **SUMMER BULBS.** Callas, cannas, dahlias, and gladiolus are among the bulbs that can go in now.

☐ **VEGETABLES.** Set out all warm-season crops as soon as danger of frost is past. Sow seeds of beans and corn; set out seedlings of eggplant, pepper, and tomato. Start cucumber, melon, pumpkin, and squash from seed if you have a long, warm growing season; otherwise set out transplants.

MAINTENANCE

☐ **CONTROL APHIDS.** Spray them off tender new growth with a jet of water whenever you see them, and you won't need to treat them with pesticides. In bad cases, use an insecticidal soap for control.

☐ **CONTROL SLUGS.** Go on slug patrol at night with a flashlight and pruning shears, cutting them in half as you see them, or put out a pet-safe bait such as iron phosphate. If you prefer a more effective, metaldehyde-based bait, put it where pets and birds can't get to it, since it can sicken or kill them.

☐ **FEED PLANTS.** Dig controlled-release organic fertilizer into the backfill of everything you plant this month; or apply liquid fertilizer two weeks after planting; or scatter complete granular fertilizer over the root zone two weeks after planting and scratch it in with a rake. Then water well.

☐ **FERTILIZE LAWNS.** Early this month, apply 1 pound of actual nitrogen per 1,000 square feet of turf and water it in well.

☐ **MAINTAIN SPRING BULBS.** When flowers fade on daffodils, grape hyacinths, and tulips, fertilize lightly and keep watering until leaves start to die back; this helps the plant prepare for bloom next spring.

☐ **PRUNE SPRING-BLOOMING SHRUBS, VINES.** As soon as bloom is finished, prune plants for shape.

☐ **SHEAR HEDGES.** To keep the base of the hedge from becoming light-starved and sparse, clip so that the hedge's bottom is wider than its top. ◆

WHAT TO DO IN YOUR GARDEN IN MAY

PLANTING

☐ **BULBS ON SALE.** To get the best prices, order your fall bulbs during preseason sales, starting about now and lasting until early to mid-July. Try Breck's (800/722-9069 or www.myseasons.com), Brent and Becky's Bulbs (877/661-2852 or www.brentandbeckysbulbs.com), and the latest White Flower Farm Bulb Book (800/503-9624 or www. whiteflowerfarm.com).

☐ **FLOWERS FOR CUTTING.** Long-blooming perennials provide a good source of cut flowers. Try alstroemeria, coreopsis, gaillardia, gloriosa daisy, lavender, *Limonium perezii,* purple coneflower, scabiosa, Shasta daisy, and yarrow.

☐ **HERBS.** Fresh-picked herbs add a special zest to recipes. Good choices to plant now are basil, chives, cilantro, oregano, parsley, rosemary, sage, and thyme. Plant successive crops of cilantro, since it goes to seed fairly quickly in warm weather. To keep woody herbs (such as oregano and rosemary) producing fresh green growth, prune regularly once the plants are established.

Sunset
CLIMATE ZONES
☐ Mountain (1-2)
☐ Valley (7-9)
☐ Inland (14)
☐ Coastal (15-17)

☐ **TOMATOES.** Zones 7–9, 14–17: It's too late to start from seed, so look for seedlings at nurseries. Upstarts Organic Seedlings supplies a line of organic tomato (and other) plants to nurseries throughout the Bay Area. Several seed catalogs also offer plants of tomatoes and other vegetables by mail. One newer mail-order source of organic seedlings is Seeds of Change (888/762-7333 or www.seedsofchange.com).

MAINTENANCE

☐ **APPLY IRON CHELATE.** If foliage of azaleas, camellias, citrus, gardenias, and others is yellowish with green veins, the plants need iron. If the plants also need nitrogen and other nutrients, use iron chelate powder (according to label directions) or apply a complete fertilizer containing iron.

☐ **CARE FOR BULBS.** Zones 7–9, 14–17: When spring-blooming bulb foliage has turned yellow, cut it off with shears or wait until it turns completely brown and pull it off. If bulbs are crowded and didn't bloom well, mark locations and divide in summer. Zones 1–2: Pick spent flowers from daffodils, tulips, and other spring-blooming bulbs.

☐ **CHECK DRIP SYSTEMS.** Before the weather turns hot, check your drip-irrigation system to make sure it's operating properly. Clean filters, check emitters and spray heads to see that they're working (replace ones that aren't), inspect lines for leaks, and adjust the automatic controller for warmer weather, if necessary. After making any repairs, open end caps and flush out lines before running the system.

☐ **HARDEN OFF SEEDLINGS.** Zones 1–2: Move seedlings of warm-season flowers and vegetables to a coldframe or other protected area. Or gradually expose them to the outdoors, giving them longer periods of stronger sunlight. Cut back slightly on water and fertilizer as the planting date grows nearer to prepare seedlings for transplanting.

PEST CONTROL

☐ **CONTROL WEEDS.** Pull or hoe weeds whenever possible, or spray with a fatty acid–derived herbicide (Safer SuperFast Weed and Grass Killer) that won't harm humans or animals. ◆

WHAT TO DO IN YOUR GARDEN IN MAY

PLANTING

☐ **LATE-BLOOMING PERENNIALS.** Fill bare spots in the garden with summer bedding plants. Choices include dahlia, marigold, petunia, portulaca, salvia, scabiosa, vinca, verbena, and zinnia. In shadier areas, try begonia, caladium, coleus, impatiens, and lobelia.

☐ **SUBTROPICALS.** Midspring is the ideal time to plant avocados, bananas, cherimoyas, citrus, guavas, mangoes, and other tropical and subtropical fruit in areas where they are appropriate. Planting now gives them a long season of growth before hardening off for the winter. Bougainvillea, ginger, mandevilla, palms, thunbergia, and other subtropical ornamentals can also be planted now.

☐ **VEGETABLES.** Set out basil, cucumber, eggplant, melon, okra, pumpkin, and squash. In the low desert (zone 13), plant Jerusalem artichoke, okra, pepper, and sweet potato.

MAINTENANCE

☐ **PRUNE.** If hibiscus, princess flower, and other subtropicals have become leggy and awkward, cut them back by as much as half. This is also a good time to cut back lavender, rosemary, santolina, and other Mediterranean perennials, which tend to fall apart and die out at the center after a few seasons. Hard pruning postpones the inevitable.

Bishop
NEVADA
CALIFORNIA
San Luis Obispo
Bakersfield
Tehachapi
Santa Barbara
Lancaster
Los Angeles
Palm Springs
Sunset
CLIMATE ZONES
San Diego
1-3 7-9 11 13 14-24
MEXICO
DEBRA LAMBERT

☐ **RENEW MULCH.** Renew mulch around trees, shrubs, and established perennials to keep roots cool, preserve soil moisture, and discourage weeds. Homemade compost is ideal—partially decomposed is fine. Or use shredded bark or wood chips.

☐ **STOP IRRIGATING ONIONS.** When foliage on garlic, shallots, and bulb onions begins to dry out, stop watering. After about half the foliage slumps to the ground, bend the rest downward to initiate maturing. Harvest the bulbs when foliage is yellow and thoroughly dry.

☐ **STEP UP WATERING.** As temperatures warm, plants need water more often. Monitor new plantings closely to be sure soil around them doesn't dry out. Also check container plants frequently. To rejuvenate a dry rootball, set the entire pot in a large bucket of water. When the soil is thoroughly wet, lift out the pot and drain.

PEST CONTROL

☐ **MANAGE ANTS.** Ants parading up the trunks of citrus or other plants are likely feeding on the honeydew secreted by aphids or scale insects. Stop the parade with a sticky trap of Tanglefoot or set out traps containing boric acid.

☐ **PROTECT TOMATOES.** Watch for hornworms and pick them off leaves by hand. To prevent blossom-end rot—a calcium deficiency that can be triggered by sudden heat or overfertilizing—mulch plants heavily to keep soil moist, and be stingy about feeding. In the desert, to protect against sunburn, cover plants with shadecloth or screening.

☐ **CONTROL APHIDS, SPIDER MITES, AND WHITEFLIES.** To keep these pests under control, direct a strong stream of water from a hose to the susceptible plants, concentrating on the undersides of the leaves, where these pests tend to hide. If the problem is severe, try insecticidal soap or horticultural oil. ◆

WHAT TO DO IN YOUR GARDEN IN MAY

PLANTING

☐ ANNUALS. At high elevations, start annuals indoors after May 1 for transplanting outside after June 1.

☐ CHRYSANTHEMUMS. Set out small pots of blooming chrysanthemums so they will grow into large plants and rebloom this fall. Spring-planted chrysanthemums are better able to survive the winter cold. For added insurance, look for extra-hardy varieties, including 'Bronze Elegance' (bronze), 'Emperor of China' (rose pink), and 'Penelope Pease' (white and pale pink).

☐ FLOWERS. This month, nurseries are filled with annuals for summer color. Shop early to get the best selection. Cover the new transplants with floating row covers for frost protection on cold nights. Remove covers when danger of late frost is past. Don't put tender annuals out until a week or two after the last frost date for your area.

☐ ORNAMENTALS. Evergreens, perennials, roses, shrubs, trees, and vines can go into the garden now. To help prevent transplant shock, use floating row covers or evergreen boughs to shade plants for the first two weeks. Keep plants well watered.

☐ SUMMER BULBS. When the soil starts to warm up, plant bulbs of acidanthera, calla, canna, crocosmia, dahlia, freesia, gladiolus, and ixia. It's not too late to set out bulbs of hardy lilies.

MAINTENANCE

☐ CARE FOR LAWNS. Begin watering and mowing lawns as needed. Mow using the highest setting, ideally 2 to 3 inches. Never cut off more than a third of the grass blade at one time or the lawn may scorch. Leave grass clippings on the lawn to provide extra nutrients and organic matter. To prevent matting, use a mulching mower or mow frequently.

☐ CONTROL APHIDS. Pay particular attention to tender new growth. If you notice that an infestation of aphids is starting to develop, blast them off with a strong spray of water or spray them with insecticidal soap.

☐ DIVIDE SPRING BULBS. After the leaves turn brown, dig up crowded clumps of daffodils, tulips, and other spring bulbs and gently pull the bulbs apart. Before replanting, till 2 inches of compost and a handful of complete fertilizer into the soil.

☐ FERTILIZE. Feed spring-flowering shrubs after they bloom and start a monthly fertilizing program for long-blooming annuals, perennials, and container plants. Apply fertilizer to bluegrass lawns by mid-month. Fertilize roses this month and then once a month through mid-August.

☐ GUARD AGAINST WILDFIRE. In fire-prone areas, create a defensible zone around the house by removing brush and dead vegetation, trimming overhanging branches, and keeping plantings well watered. Clear dead leaves and pine needles from your roof and gutters. Don't store firewood next to structures.

☐ HARVEST ASPARAGUS. From the third spring onward, you can harvest asparagus spears for a few weeks by cutting or snapping them off at ground level. When the spears no longer grow larger than $3/8$ inch in diameter, refrain from picking them. This will allow them to develop into ferns to replenish plants for next year.

☐ SUPPORT PERENNIALS. When asters, Oriental poppies, peonies, Shasta daisies, and summer phlox reach about 6 to 8 inches tall, encircle them with stakes or place hoops over them so the plants will grow up through the supports.

— M.T. ◆

WHAT TO DO IN YOUR GARDEN IN MAY

PLANTING

☐ **FLOWERS.** Zones 1–2 (Flagstaff): Set out transplants of ageratum, celosia, coreopsis, cosmos, four o'-clock, gaillardia, globe amaranth, gloriosa daisy, lisianthus, Madagascar periwinkle, nicotiana, portulaca, salvia, strawflower, and zinnia after all danger of frost is past. Zones 10–13 (Albuquerque, Las Vegas, Tucson, Phoenix): Early in the month, set out ageratum, coreopsis, cosmos, four o'clock, gaillardia, salvia, and zinnia.

☐ **LAWNS.** Zones 1–2, 10: Plant or overseed with bluegrass, fescue, ryegrass, or a mixture of these. Zones 12–13: Plant or seed Bermuda or improved buffalo grass.

☐ **PALMS.** Zones 12–13: Plant palms when soil temperatures are over 75°. Dig the planting hole the same depth as the rootball and twice as wide. Use twine to tie the fronds up over the bud to protect it. When new growth occurs, cut the twine.

☐ **PERMANENT PLANTS.** Zones 1–2, 10: Plant trees, shrubs, vines, and ground covers from containers. Zones 11–13: Plant heat-loving black dalea, lantana, and red bird of paradise to attract butterflies.

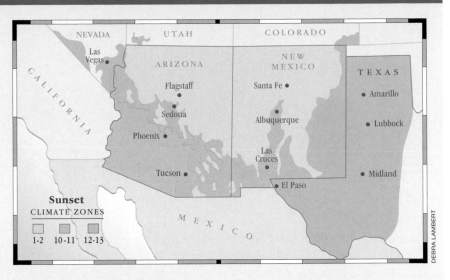

Sunset
CLIMATE ZONES
☐ 1-2 ☐ 10-11 ☐ 12-13

DEBRA LAMBERT

☐ **SUMMER BULBS.** Zones 1–2: Plant caladium, dahlia, and elephant's ear (*Colocasia esculenta*). Zones 10–11: Plant acidanthera (*Gladiolus callianthus*), canna, gladiolus, montbretia, and tiger flower (*Tigridia*) as well as those listed above. Zones 12–13: Plant crinum, habranthus, and zephyranthes.

☐ **VEGETABLES.** Zones 1–2: When soil temperatures are above 60°, sow seeds of beans, corn, cucumber, okra, pumpkin, and watermelon. Set out plants of sweet potato. Start seeds of eggplant, pepper, squash, and tomato indoors for transplanting outdoors in six to eight weeks. Zone 10: Sow seeds of beans, black-eyed pea, corn, cucumber, melon, pumpkin, radish, and tomato. Zone 11: Plant the above vegetables early in the month and okra and sweet potato through midmonth. Zones 12–13: Sow seeds of okra, summer squash, and watermelon. Set out transplants of eggplant, pepper, and sweet potato early in the month.

MAINTENANCE

☐ **CARE FOR ROSES.** Zones 11–13: Water plants deeply, fertilize, and spread mulch around the root zones.

☐ **MULCH.** Spread mulch around plants to keep roots cool, hold weeds down, and save soil moisture.

☐ **SHADE TOMATOES.** Zones 11–13: Place shadecloth or old white sheets on a frame over plants to shield tomatoes from sunburn and extend fruit set. — *M.I.* ◆

spots of sunshine

Yellow flowers and foliage can wake up quiet corners of your garden

By Steven R. Lorton

ave you ever looked skyward to see a break in the clouds with sunlight streaming through, then followed that stream with your eyes to find its golden light bathing a spot in your garden? Sunlight makes plants shimmer and shine, and seeing a sunlit garden all dewy, fresh, and golden brightens your day. • A patch of yellow flowers or foliage is like a spot of sunshine: It draws your attention while warming and illuminating a quiet corner. After the sun goes down, pale yellow flowers don't disappear into dark shadows. Instead, they linger in twilight and glow by moonlight. • Almost any color, including green, red, and orange, combines well with yellow. Blue and yellow are a classic pairing. If you've been schooled in the haughty old aphorism "yellow with pink will always stink," just thumb your nose at stuffiness and give it a try. The combination, especially in spring, is as cheerful as a picket fence skirted with primroses. Throw in some foliage of soft blue, white, and green for color that sparkles with the freshness of a new season. (Remove yellow from that mix and the palette of pastels would go flat.) • This month, nurseries throughout the West are flaunting plants whose yellow flowers or foliage can brighten your garden in spring, summer, fall, or winter. The photographs on these pages show some ways to use them. There's still enough time to plant before the summer heat sets in. As the plants grow, you can bask in your own spot of sunshine.

Yellow flowers brighten this perennial planting in the Santa Fe garden owned by Elspeth Bobbs. They include (clockwise from left) feathery plumes of goldenrod (*Solidago*), lemon yellow daylily (*Hemerocallis*), and yarrow (*Achillea*). Their companions are orange daylily, pink-flowered yarrow, and lavender German statice (*Goniolimon tataricum*).

Daylily (*Hemerocallis*)

Asteriscus maritimus

Lantana

Strawflower

'Valentine' sunflower

21 sunshine plants

Thousands of great plants have yellow flowers or foliage. Here we list 21 of our favorites. But don't limit yourself to our choices—half the fun is making your own discoveries!

Flowers

• *Asteriscus maritimus,* sometimes called gold coin. Perennial. A tough, reliable plant, loaded with yellow flowers; great in Mediterranean gardens. Blooms over a long summer season. Grows 1 foot tall, spreads to 4 feet. Full sun. *Sunset* climate zones 9, 15–24.

• *Coreopsis grandiflora.* Perennial. Produces bright yellow blooms over a long summer season. Very tough and drought resistant. For large semidouble blooms, look for 'Sunburst' and 'Early Sunrise'. Grows 1 to 2 feet tall. Full sun. Zones 2–24, H1–H2.

• *Coreopsis verticillata.* Perennial. A prolific summer bloomer—stops traffic in late spring and summer gardens. 'Moonbeam' has pale yellow flowers; 'Zagreb' has golden yellow blooms. Grows 2½ to 3 feet tall. Full sun. Zones 1–24.

• *Crocosmia* 'Solfatare'. Corm. Bladelike leaves are bronze, with pale orange-yellow flowers appearing on spikes. Grows to 2 feet tall. Full sun to partial shade. Zones 4–24.

• Crown imperial (*Fritillaria imperialis*). Bulb. Produces a startling spire of bell-shaped flowers in mid- to late spring. Grows 3½ to 4 feet tall. Full sun or light shade. Zones 1–7, 14–17.

• Daylily (*Hemerocallis*). Perennial. Blooms over a long summer season. Many varieties have yellow flowers—'Buttered Popcorn' and 'Jen Melon', for instance. Tiny 'Stella d'Oro' is a star for the corners of beds or the front of a border. Named hybrids grow 1 to 6 feet tall. Full sun to light shade. All zones.

• Fernleaf yarrow (*Achillea filipendulina*). Perennial. Blooms mid- to late summer. For richest yellow flowers, look for 'Gold Plate' and 'Coronation Gold'. Both are beautiful in borders with blue delphiniums, red-hot pokers (*Kniphofia uvaria*), and Shasta daisies. Grows 3 to 5 feet tall. Sun. Zones 1–24, A1–A3.

• Goldenrod (*Solidago*). Perennial. Flowers are large plumes of gold in midsummer. Happiest in not-too-rich soil. Good meadow planting with Michaelmas daisies and black-eyed Susans. Grows 1 to 3 feet tall, sometimes more. Full sun to light shade. Zones 1–11, 14–23.

• *Helianthus multiflorus.* Perennial. From midsummer to frost, plant is filled with rich yellow 3-inch flowers, good for cutting. Grows in a clump to 5 feet. Full sun. Zones 1–24.

• Jerusalem sage (*Phlomis fruticosa*). Shrubby perennial. Holds its yellow flowers for a long spell in mid- to late summer. Grows to 4 feet. Full sun, but will tolerate light shade. Zones 3b–24.

• Kangaroo paws (*Anigozanthos flavidus*). Evergreen perennial. Blooms from late spring to fall if spent flower spikes are cut down. A strong plant for vertical structure in the garden. Grassy leaves reach 3 feet, flower spikes go to 5 feet. Full sun. Zones 15–24.

• Lantana (*L. montevidensis*). Evergreen shrub grown as an annual in cold climates. Blooms throughout summer. 'Sunburst', 'Spreading Sunshine', and 'Gold Rush' are strong yellows. Creeping branches spread 3 to 6 feet over ground. Full sun. Zones 8–10, 12–24, H1–H2.

• *Ligularia stenocephala* 'The Rocket'. Perennial. Robust flower spike shoots up 5 feet or more in early summer. Flowers last longest when plants get afternoon shade. Zones 1–9, 14–17, A2–A3.

• Moneywort, creeping Jenny (*Lysimachia nummularia* 'Aurea'). Perennial ground cover. Forms ground-hugging mat with runners up to 2 feet long; makes a handsome golden carpet under perennials and shrubs. Leaves stay yellowish gold unless knocked back by frost. At its best in strong indirect light (direct sun scorches leaves). Zones 1–9, 14–24.

• Strawflower (*Helichrysum bracteatum*). Summer annual. Yellow varieties are 'Cockatoo', 'Dargan Hill Monarch', and 'Diamond Head'. All have grayish

Yellow-flowered kangaroo paws (*Anigozanthos*) edge these raised beds in Southern California, where they mingle with lavender-flowered society garlic, chocolate-colored New Zealand flax, and grasses. DESIGN: Judy Kameon, Elysian Landscape, Los Angeles.

green foliage. Flowers dry beautifully and keep well. Grows 2 to 3 feet tall. Full sun. All zones.

• Sunflower (*Helianthus annuus*). Annual. Flowers come in a range of sunny colors, from pale yellow to deep golden yellow to mahogany. Plants range from 2 to 10 feet tall. Full sun. All zones.

Foliage

• *Acorus gramineus* 'Ogon'. Grassy perennial. Foliage is bright yellow until cut down by frost. Grows well in boggy soil. Clumps reach 10 inches tall. Full sun. Zones 3b–10, 14–24.

• *Carex elata* 'Aurea' ('Bowles Golden'). Sedge. Bright yellow foliage all year. Grassy clumps are 2 feet tall. A bright, glowing yellow grass for sun or partial shade. Zones 2–9, 14–24.

• Golden oregano (*Origanum vulgare* 'Aureum'). Bright golden foliage in spring turns to green by late summer and fall. Grows about 1 foot tall, sometimes more. Full sun to part shade. Zones 1–24.

• Golden sage (*Salvia officinalis* 'Icterina'). Perennial herb. To 2½ feet. Full sun. Zones 2–24, H1–H2.

• New Zealand flax (*Phormium tenax* 'Yellow Wave'). Big, bold perennial. Swordlike leaves can reach 5 feet tall. Full sun or light shade. Zones 7–9, 14–24, H1–H2 (regrows after freezes in zones 5–6). ◆

'Yellow Wave' *Phormium*

Golden oregano

kitchen garden
wreaths

Edible and easy to make, they'll last for months

By Lauren Bonar Swezey
Photographs by Claire Curran

■ "The wreath speaks to everyone," explains Teddy Colbert, who created her first living wreath 25 years ago. "Love without end; honor and victory. Today it's primarily a sign of hospitality."

Colbert's early wreaths were sensational living tapestries— succulents of different colors, sizes, and shapes growing in wire frames wrapped with sphagnum moss and filled with potting soil. She built a business around them. But eventually she longed to branch out, using other kinds of plants.

Salad greens, for instance. In the fields near her home in Somis, California, she discovered the beauty of lime green and red baby lettuces beside frisée (curly endive). Lettuce seedlings made her salad greens wreath a stunning success.

"Then I asked myself, if lettuces work, why not herbs or even strawberries?" says Colbert.

On page 173, we give basic instructions for constructing any of Colbert's wreaths. You can buy frames at a craft or floral supply store. Colbert also sells wreath frame kits (800/833-3981 or www.livingwreath.com), as does Kinsman Company (800/733-4146 or www.kinsmangarden.com). Other supplies are available at nurseries and home centers.

Herbs galore

"The herb wreath has delivered us from many dull meals," says Colbert. It needs regular trimming—use the snippets as garnishes or chop them to put in soups, salads, and herb butters.

FAVORITES: Chocolate mint, cilantro, dill, English thyme, garlic chives, Italian parsley, oregano, sage, salad burnet, sweet basil, and sweet marjoram.

PLANTING AND GROWING TIPS
• Use a 14- or 18-inch-diameter frame.
• Start with young plants (especially basil, which, preferably, should only have its first set of true leaves). If you can't find young ones, start from seed.

• In planting, alternate types of herbs. Position dill (which grows tall) and sage (which likes drier conditions) on the flanks of the wreath.
• Plant mints at the bottom, where they get extra moisture.
• Grow in a sunny spot just outside the kitchen.
• Use fish emulsion, diluted to half-strength, every time you water.

Simply strawberries

"A strawberry wreath is so easy to make," says Colbert. "Just start with young plants and don't bury the plants' crowns."

Use everbearing strawberries, which produce from early summer through fall.

PLANTING AND GROWING TIPS

• In spring and summer, start with six-packs of young seedlings. In winter, use bareroot plants (soak before planting).

• Use 28 plants for a 14-inch-diameter frame and 36 plants for an 18-inch-diameter frame.

• Plant the first set of strawberries toward the outside of the wreath, placing them 4 inches apart; angle the foliage outward. Plant another set of plants between the first ones; direct the foliage upward.

• Give the wreath a half turn periodically so the bottom plants don't stay wet.

• Use a dilute (quarter-strength) solution of a balanced fertilizer (such as 14-14-14) every time you water.

Mixed lettuces

"Set a salad wreath on the table and the guests can harvest their own greens," says Colbert. There are dozens of different lettuces and greens available. Choose at least five colors and textures; alternate them when you plant.

Start varieties from seed and transplant them when they have only two or three sets of leaves, or buy sixpacks of frisée and lettuces at a local nursery with a good selection (buy only young seedlings that aren't rootbound).

FAVORITES: 'Oak Leaf', 'Lollo Rossa', 'Red Oak Leaf', and 'Red Sails' lettuces; 'Neos' chicory frisée.

PLANTING AND GROWING TIPS

• Use a 14- or 18-inch-diameter frame.

• Let the wreath grow on a fence, gate, or table in full sun.

• Give hanging wreaths a half turn periodically so the plants at the bottom don't stay too wet.

• To harvest, snip off just the outer leaves, so the small plants will continue growing for up to several months.

Build your own living wreath

How to make your own, in nine easy steps

TIME: One to two hours each

COST: $50 to $60 for a 14-inch wreath; $55 to $65 for an 18-inch wreath

TOOLS AND MATERIALS

- One 2-cubic-foot bag (or bale) **sphagnum moss**
- **Bucket**
- **Thin rubber gloves**
- **Screen** or perforated nursery tray
- 30-gallon **trash bags**
- **Controlled-release fertilizer** (high nitrogen for herbs and lettuces, a balanced fertilizer for strawberries)
- **Water-absorbing polymers** (such as Broadleaf P-4)
- One 1-cubic-foot bag **potting soil**
- One 14- or 18-inch **living-wreath frame** (or three floral box-wire frames of the same size)
- 80 to 95 feet of **#24 copper wire** (buy the larger amount if making your own frame), wound onto a spool or dowel
- **Wire cutters**
- Four **skewers** and four **corks** (for 14-inch wreaths with candleholders); or nine of each for an 18-inch wreath
- One **chopstick** or pair of long tweezers
- **Seedlings**

DIRECTIONS

1. Soak the moss in a bucket of water until thoroughly wet (wear gloves when handling moss, which can irritate skin). Let moss drain for several hours on a screen or nursery tray, covered with plastic to prevent it from drying out.

2. While moss drains, cover a worktable with plastic. Mix fertilizers and polymers into the potting soil and set aside.

3. Place the moist moss in the center of the work area with the greener (top) side down. Spread the moss out to form a round mat about 2½ times the diameter of the frame and 1½ inches deep. Try to spread it out in one piece. Add moss to thin areas. Set aside extra moss.

4. Place the frame upside down in the middle of the moss mat. (If you are using frames without feet, fasten two together with wire to form a tube.) If you plan to hang the wreath, attach a loop of wire to a cross support at the top of the frame; for the lettuce or strawberry wreaths, which benefit from occasional rotations, add another hanger at the bottom.

5. If your frame has candleholders, mark their locations with skewers. Scoop the prepared soil mix into the frame so that no wire is exposed, and gently firm it down.

6. Lift the outside edges of the moss mat over the frame toward the center of the wreath. Start with a side flap, then pull over the opposite side, top, and bottom flaps (**A**). Make a hole in the center of the moss mat; lift the inside edges of the moss over the soil and frame without stretching it. Patch exposed areas with extra moss.

7. Leaving a 6- to 8-inch tail of wire at wreath top, wrap the moss-covered frame tightly with a continuous length of wire at ¾-inch intervals (**B**). (If possible, ask a friend to help hold the moss in place while you wrap.) Along the way, patch any thin or broken spots in the lining with extra moss. If you need to take a break from wrapping, use an extra skewer to mark the wire's position. When you are back at the top, go one more time around the frame, then twist running

wire and the tail together tightly. Cut the wire and curl the ends into the moss.

8. Turn the wreath right side up. If your frame has built-in candleholders, replace the skewers with corks. Using a chopstick or tweezers, make a hole through the moss into the soil on the inside edge. Remove a plant from its container and shake excess soil from around the roots or gently swirl the rootball in a bucket of water. Insert the roots deeply into the hole in the frame (**C**) and push the surrounding soil and moss around the roots and stem. Continue planting around the inside edge, then work outward, covering the frame with plants (**D**); see planting tips for each type of wreath. Remove the corks from candleholders.

9. Water the wreath well and set it in bright, indirect light for several days. Once the plants have acclimated, hang the wreath. If your frame does not have feet to distance it from the wall, add the third frame behind your wreath.

Wreath care

- Display your wreath in full sun (light afternoon shade in hot inland areas).
- Keep the soil moist but not soggy. Soak the wreath in the top of a clean trash can lid filled with water, letting it sit for 10 to 20 minutes or until it is thoroughly moist.
- Cut off spent plants as needed, leaving their roots to hold the moss in place.
- Replace plants as necessary. Make a ball of moist soil mixed with polymers and fertilizer; cover the ball with moss. Poke it into the empty spot; secure it in the wreath base with copper wire. Replant entire wreath when plants fade. ◆

The Botanic Gardens undergo a breathtaking 50th-anniversary makeover

By Marcia Tatroe
Photographs by Charles Mann

nstead of slipping complacently into middle age, Denver Botanic Gardens is celebrating its 50th anniversary this year with a dramatic face-lift. Since the fall of 1999, when Rob Proctor was named director of horticulture, more than 20 gardens have been added or renovated. Proctor, a popular garden writer and botanical artist, has been guided by his belief that a public garden should engage and challenge visitors by "examining different genres" and reinterpreting garden trends and traditional themes with a "Colorado twist." That twist means choosing plants that thrive in the unique geography and climates of the mountain West. • Proctor tapped the talents of like-minded designers and staff members, turning them loose to rethink stagnant parts of the garden. What's emerging is a bold new look seldom seen before in Colorado gardens. Hundreds of new plants have been introduced. Existing plant collections have been reorganized. Familiar plants have been arranged in new and unexpected ways to create startling juxtapositions of color and texture. • Meanwhile, visitors have a rare opportunity to witness the garden's ongoing renovation as it unfolds. And perhaps be motivated to try some revamping of their own at home.

In the Romantic Garden (above), a bench is flanked by chartreuse coleus with magenta-flowered *Salvia greggii* 'Lipstick' on its right; behind, red plumes of *Amaranthus hypochondriacus* sweep over silvery *Artemisia* 'Powis Castle'. Nearby, orange cannas (at left, near gazebo), purple fountain grass, blue spikes of Russian sage, and purple coneflowers thrive. In the foreground, purple *Verbena bonariensis*, lavender 'Cut Wonder' ageratum, and purple-leafed perilla mingle. DESIGN: Lauren Springer (beds), Tom Peace (containers).

denver's garden showcase

denver's garden showcase

The Hildreth Fountain is circled by chartreuse coleus, orange-red cigar plant (*Cuphea ignea*), 'Indigo Spires' and 'Lady in Red' salvias, and scarlet ivy geraniums. DESIGN: Rob Proctor. The Drop-Dead Red Border (right) features 'Scarlet Splendor' zinnia, 'Blaze' verbena, and rosy pink *Sedum* 'Vera Jameson'. DESIGN: Rob Proctor. In the French Kitchen Garden (top right), rosettes of ornamental kale front *Artemisia* 'Powis Castle', purple basil, artichokes, and more. DESIGN: David Macke.

Major new gardens

ROMANTIC GARDEN. Divided into three distinct areas, this garden reflects the many moods of romance. Schlessman Plaza, designed by Tom Peace of Denver and Lauren Springer of Masonville, Colorado, is lush and lusty. Smoldering reds and oranges burn alongside passionate purples enlivened by chartreuse and silver foliage. The fragrance garden, also designed by Springer, is filled with seductively scented flowers and aromatic foliage, making this a favorite site for weddings. The Colorado Springs Waterway Garden, designed by Environmental Planning & Design of Pittsburgh, is modeled after the water canal and wall creations of noted Mexican architect Luis Barragán.

MEDITERRANEAN PLAZA. After years of service as a soil-filled planter, the Hildreth Fountain was restored as the centerpiece of the new Mediter-

arches crosses the central walk and leads the visitor into a vivid display of bulbs, annuals, and perennials representing the favorite flowers of artist Claude Monet. The garden looks out over a water lily pond spanned by a bridge fashioned after the one that Monet painted so often in his renderings of his garden in Giverny, France.

More fresh features

CHILDREN'S SECRET PATH. Almost uncomfortably narrow for adults, this path gives kids a chance to do what they like best—to creep, crawl, climb, and explore.

CUTTING GARDEN. This rainbow-themed garden is filled with fresh and everlasting flowers, ornamental seed pods, and berries for bouquets.

MORRISON CENTER SENSORY GARDEN. All five physical senses are stimulated in this garden with an emphasis on taste, smell, hearing, and touch, as part of the gardens' Horticultural Therapy Program.

SACRED EARTH. A plaza, a cultivated area for vegetables, an aquatic plant pond, and an ethnobotanical exhibit focus on Native Americans of the Four Corners region and their relationship with plants, including those grown for medicinal and spiritual purposes.

SHADY LANE. Beneath the crabapples along the East-West Path, this border of shade-loving perennials meets the challenges of shade gardening.

WESTERN PANORAMAS. Surrounding the central amphitheater, large borders represent three of Colorado's most significant ecosystems: Montane, Plains, and Subalpine.

WILDFLOWER TREASURES. Rare and endangered species are displayed in large hypertufa troughs on a flagstone plaza inside borders portraying Colorado's diverse floristic zones.

WOODLAND MOSAIC. Mature trees over a large wood deck offer visitors a shady retreat suggestive of a tranquil mountain meadow. ◆

ranean garden. In the sun-drenched plaza, blue water and cobalt pots contrast with the primary reds and yellows of flowers and foliage.

FRENCH KITCHEN GARDEN. This nod to the potager gardening tradition demonstrates that the vegetable garden doesn't have to be a strictly practical patch with plants lined up in straight rows like soldiers standing at attention. Here, vegetables are arrayed in a geometric pattern outlined by red bricks and traversed by gravel paths. In this culinary mosaic, vegetables, herbs, and edible flowers are grown in containers as well as in beds. Designed by David Macke of Denver to evoke the romance of a French country garden, this visual feast is garnished with herbal topiaries and decorative trellises laden with peas and runner beans.

MILE-HIGH GARDEN. The new entrance garden, designed by Tom Peace, acts like a shop window, enticing visitors inside and giving them a taste of what lies beyond the gates. Formerly a large expanse of bluegrass lawn, the garden now features a medley of shrubs, perennials, and ornamental grasses whose good looks in all four seasons belie their rugged natures. This water-thrifty garden showcases some of the best performers for high-elevation Western gardens

MONET GARDEN. Hints of this garden begin just inside the main gate. A progression of vine-covered metal

A well-placed strawberry tree (*Arbutus unedo*) gives Billy Spratlin and Alex Kochnuk's front courtyard in Newport Beach, California, just the right amount of screening from the street.

Privacy without walls

How to create neighborly seclusion

By Sharon Cohoon • Photographs by Steven Gunther

"I might have been a goldfish in a glass bowl for all the privacy I got." — Saki

Saki [Hector Hugh Munro] wrote those words in 1904 in his book *Reginald,* but they hit home with considerable force in 2001. Growing populations that crowd today's cities and housing developments make many of us feel like overexposed goldfish every time we walk out into our yards. For better or worse, many of our homes take up most of their lots. What's left, typically, are narrow strips of ground in front, side yards barely wide enough to walk through, and backyards that feel like the stage in an amphitheater because neighbors on both sides can peer down from their second-story windows. No wonder, despite our coveted Western weather, we're reluctant to venture into such gardens. In settings like these, even lighting the barbecue feels like a performance.

It doesn't have to be that way. The goldfish bowl suggests the solution. If fish have a few retreats within their glass bowls where they can go to escape the public eye, they're happy; you don't have to build a wall around the whole aquarium. Humans are the same: We don't need to be totally enclosed to enjoy privacy. In fact, in a small yard, total enclosure can seem like imprisonment. And the chance to peek out at the world from a veiled hideout makes you feel like a kid in a treehouse again. You can see them, but they can't see you. Delightful.

Here are some ways to create private hideouts within a "fishbowl" garden.

Front-yard screening

When Billy Spratlin and Alex Kochnuk created a semihidden dining alcove in their front yard nine years ago, they started a trend in Bayshores, their Newport Beach, California, neighborhood. As is typical in properties close to the beach, lots in this community are tiny. Yet, with the help of Tustin, California–based landscape architect Dale Waldo, they were able to carve out a delicious retreat in a pocket-size space (shown on page 178). The curved wall-planter that wraps around the dining area is only waist-high. But the judicious placement of plants—a strawberry tree in the planter and several liquidambars screening a corner—makes the space surprisingly private. "It feels sheltered without seeming unfriendly," says Spratlin. Other Bayshores homeowners have copied the front courtyard idea since, he says.

Linda and Russell Jacques, who also live in Bayshores, took a differ-

Privacy solutions

A. Screen of clipped hedge blocks neighbor's view.

B. Vine-covered arbor blocks views from second-story windows next door.

C. Layers of plants—pillowy perennials, shrubs, and small trees—create privacy and soften a fence or wall.

D. Low-level shrubs can conceal the trunks of mature trees.

E. Fence shields you from view when it is slightly higher than eye level, or approximately 6 feet tall. To add privacy without extending a fence, mount a trellis on top.

F. Single tree placed at the front corner of a driveway blocks views of an entry.

G. Berm, a mound of soil planted with ground covers, low-growing shrubs, and perhaps a small tree, provides privacy from the street.

CONNIE MCLENNAN

Before you begin, some tips

- Determine what you want to block out or be shielded from.
- Evaluate how plantings and additional structures will affect your neighbors, patterns of sun and shade in your garden, and any views you want to preserve.
- Find out exactly where the boundaries of your property are, so you don't end up building or planting on your neighbor's property.
- Check local ordinances and easements that could affect your plans. Many communities have guidelines to protect solar access or views.
- Any structures or plantings on the property line belong to you and your neighbor. So before you begin, discuss changes you want to make with your neighbor. If construction or planting you do on your property affects the health of plants on your neighbor's property, you could be liable for damages.

ent approach with their front yard. Linda's main concern was making the shallow space feel more like a garden. The Jacques have a corner dining nook and a side patio (see photos at right) that overlook this area. They wanted to see greenery and flowers from these vantage points, not pavement and cars. "But this is a neighborly community," says Linda, "and we didn't want to look unwelcoming." Jay Rodriquez of Upper Crust Landscaping solved the problem through strategically placed berms and multitrunked pink melaleuca trees. The Jacques have the screening they want now but haven't walled themselves off from their neighbors—and they have a prettier view, says Linda.

TOP: A low berm, planted with a pink melaleuca tree, screens the corner of Linda and Russell Jacques' property, as well as their courtyard gate, from the street.
ABOVE: View from the gate shows how the tree, and the low berm it grows on, help block out the street and the houses beyond it.

King palms in large pots provide leafy screening where it's needed most—above the fence—in this Newport Beach courtyard patio. DESIGN: Linda Jacques.

Backyard retreats

Often, the easiest way to create a retreat in the backyard is to extend the living space immediately outside the house with hardscaping, then screen off the resulting outdoor room with a vertical structure. A pergola topped with vines to block overhead views is a typical solution; a framework of planter boxes topped with a trellis might be another. The illustration on page 179 shows others.

Side-yard solutions

The side yards in many new tracts aren't yards at all—they're barely walkways. But even if they aren't usable as garden space, they can't be ignored because, from some rooms, they constitute the entire view. Find some way to "green up" these areas. At the Jacques home, for instance, Rodriquez suggested a row of king palms in large pots be placed in front of the fence.

Creating privacy within confined spaces is a challenge. But if a goldfish can find escape from the public eye within its tiny glass globe, we can create privacy in a garden. ◆

Standards:
Small worlds of color

Patio trees are best-sellers in Western nurseries

By Sharon Cohoon

Trained as a standard, this 40-year-old bougainvillea graces a patio at Sherman Library & Gardens in Corona del Mar, California.

STEVEN GUNTHER

interest in patio trees, says Barron, is the ever-shrinking size of Western gardens. The yards of newer homes, in particular, are often too small to accommodate a full-size tree, he says. But even the smallest courtyard has room for a patio tree, some of which can be maintained at 4 to 5 feet tall by pruning. Another contributing factor to their popularity is versatility: Patio trees grow equally well in a large container as they do in the ground.

At the same time, gardeners are learning to blend standards into their landscapes. Tree roses, for instance, don't have to look like isolated exclamation points, says Tom Carruth, hybridizer and horticulturist for Weeks Roses. They can serve as vertical elements in mixed borders or mingle in beds with shrub roses.

For all these reasons, patio trees are available in greater quantity and variety than ever (see "15 Standard Choices" on the facing page).

Prune to promote bloom

"Often and lightly" is the best pruning policy for all standards, according to Barron. Tree roses are no exception. "Hard pruning just encourages long shoots to form," says Carruth. Plants that flower almost continuously, like Paraguay nightshade (*Lycianthes ranton-netii*), benefit from trimming as often as once a week. With shrubs that set buds once a year, like azaleas, wait until after bloom to shape.

Vigorous plants like bougainvillea occasionally need to be pruned hard. The nearly 40-year-old bougainvillea standard pictured above at Sherman Library & Gardens in Corona del Mar, California, is cut back by one-half to two-thirds every three to five years, according to John Bishop,

Standards—flowering shrubs or woody vines trained to look like small trees—have never been in greater demand. Patio trees in which the plant's crown is at least 30 inches above the top of the container are especially popular. The demand is so great, in fact, that some wholesale nurseries have shifted

their production emphasis to meet it. At Hines Nurseries in Irvine, California, 10 acres are now devoted to growing patio trees versus just 2 acres for full-size trees, reports Felix Barron, field operations manager at Hines. Twenty years ago, that ratio was exactly reversed, he says.

The main reason for the surging

manager of horticulture. The rest of the time, it is pruned lightly for shape. "If you want flowers, you have to keep pruning standards or your flower production will gradually decline," says Bishop.

Stake young plants

Standards are naturally top-heavy, especially when young. To keep their delicate trunks from snapping in the wind, support them with a sturdy wood stake or ½-inch-diameter galvanized pipe. As they mature, some plants develop trunks strong enough to support crowns. But if you live in an area with gusty winds, you might want to keep them staked indefinitely.

15 standard choices

You'll find many standards sold in 2- and 5-gallon containers. Tree roses usually come in 36- and 60-inch-high sizes.

- *Alyogyne huegelii*
- *Azalea,* Southern Indica varieties
- *Bougainvillea*
- *Camellia japonica*
- Cape mallow (*Anisodontea hypomandarum*)
- *Euryops pectinatus* 'Viridis'
- Flowering maple (*Abutilon* hybrids)
- *Fuchsia* hybrids
- *Gardenia jasminoides* 'August Beauty', 'Mystery', 'Veitchii'
- *Hibiscus rosa-sinensis*
- *Lantana* hybrids
- New Zealand tea tree (*Leptospermum scoparium*)
- Paraguay nightshade (*Lycianthes rantonnetii* 'Royal Robe')
- *Rhaphiolepis indica*
- Roses (floribunda, ground cover, shrub, and hybrid tea) ◆

CLAIRE CURRAN (2)

TOP: 'Gartenmeister Bonstedt' fuchsia standard thrives in a glazed pot. This plant blooms nearly year-round in mild climates.
LEFT: New Zealand tea tree is now commonly available as a standard.

Matchmaking for roses

Shrub roses make surprisingly good partners
for many perennials and annuals in pots

By Jim McCausland

Roses and perennials fill these pots on Karen Steeb's patio in Woodinville,
Washington. Blooms include red 'Prince Palace', pink 'Romantic Palace',
and white 'Hampton Palace' roses. White petunias add accents.

Container designers are always on the hunt for new flower combinations to try. But they usually pass on roses, which can grow too large for pots and suffer from too much disease. Now, a spate of newer, tougher, smaller roses has started to change all that. Often sold as landscaping or ground cover roses, they come in nearly every color, bloom nonstop, and many have excellent disease resistance.

We asked landscape designer Karen Steeb of Woodinville, Washington, to combine roses with perennials, annuals, herbs, and landscape shrubs. Her efforts are pictured here.

After growing these combinations of roses and perennials in pots for a season, Steeb pronounced the exper-iment a success; almost all of the roses thrived.

Plant combinations

Steeb used roses in the Palace series—Danish-bred types that are easy to find in nurseries and garden centers, and by mail from Arena Rose Company (free catalog; 888/544-9943 or www.arenaroses.com). Roses in this series were bred with container culture in mind. About two feet tall at maturity, they produce fragrant double flowers from June through frost and beyond. Red 'Prince Palace', pink 'Romantic Palace,' and yellow 'Sundance Palace' were some of Steeb's picks for pots.

Planted alone, any of these roses would have been bushy enough to fill

How to plant a rose-perennial combo

The principles for planting these containers are the same; only the plant combinations change.

Choose a pot that's 18 to 24 inches in diameter and at least as deep. Steeb favors thick-walled plastic ones, which hold moisture better than terra-cotta, provide good insulation against heat and cold, and weigh less than terra-cotta, ceramic, or cement. If you buy containers without drain holes, drill two or three 1-inch holes in the bottom of the container.

Also buy a bag of rich, fast-draining potting soil. Since potting soil quality varies so much from brand to brand, and brands vary from state to state, ask your nursery for a recommenda-tion. If they say they're all the same, find a better nursery.

For a finished look from planting day forward, use only perennials from 4-inch and 1-gallon nursery containers.

Pour potting soil into each con-tainer until it comes to within 4 inches of the rim, then firm it; Steeb steps into the pot and stamps the soil with

her feet. Sprinkle timed-release fertilizer onto the potting soil. Use an extended release formula: Six or nine months is good.

Wearing gloves to protect your arms from thorns, arrange the plants—still in their nursery pots—on the soil; experiment with different combinations to see which foliage textures and colors work best together. Place taller plants at the back or—if the finished pot is meant to be seen from all sides—in the center. Put trailing plants along the edges and use intermediate plants as fillers.

Once you have the plant combinations worked out, remove each plant from its pot, rough up the rootball, and plant, packing the soil around the plant. Water well; add more soil if rootball settles (soil level should be about ½ inch below the container's rim).

out a container, but mixed with other plants, they stretched and twined together with their pot-mates. Because the yellow 'Sundance Palace' in Steeb's pots was plagued with black spot, yellow roses that are more disease-resistant might make better choices. See "Yellow roses tat are resistant to black spot," above right.

In addition to the plants that Steeb used to blend with roses, including geraniums, lavender, nandina, and petunias, there are a number of other excellent companions, such as catmint, diascia, fleabane, forget-me-nots, hardy geraniums, *Heuchera* 'Palace Purple', hostas, lady's-mantle, Shirley poppies, sweet alyssum, and violas.

How to keep plants looking good

Plants grown in containers need more care than those growing in the garden, since they're planted more densely, tend to dry out faster, and exhaust the soil nutrients quickly. Apply a granular organic fertilizer (4-6-2) every six weeks throughout the growing season; water whenever the top couple of inches of soil dries out. Groom plants frequently by pinching, pruning, and cutting off spent blooms.

Yellow roses that are resistant to black spot

The black spot that plagued Steeb's 'Sundance Palace' yellow roses is a fungal disease that results in black spots and yellowing on leaves. It's ubiquitous among roses, especially on many yellow-flowered types.

Some yellow roses, however, have good resistance to black spot. These include 'Aspen', a compact spreading or trailing yellow, 'Lexington', a soft yellow 2-foot upright, and 'Atlantis Palace'. ◆

Sizzling combo in a cool blue container includes bronzy canna 'Tropicana', yellow 'Sundance Palace' rose, and lime green sweet potato vine. Gray-green *Helichrysum petiolare* cascades over pot edges at left.

Ivy geraniums spill from rooftop planters in Manhattan Beach, California. At right are 'Sunset Magazine' (top), a regal type, and 'Mr. Henry Cox', a zonal type.

Summer darlings

Geraniums are easy, forgiving, versatile

By Sharon Cohoon
Photographs by Steven Gunther

Like your best pals, geraniums are cheerful, easygoing, and non-temperamental. They let you enjoy their company without making outrageous demands. Like true friends, they hang in there, even if you neglect them.

Many geraniums bear showy flowers. Some flaunt exceptionally colorful foliage. And the leaves of scented types delight our noses with aromas of lemon, mint, and rose.

Geraniums are also very versatile plants. Most kinds look good in pots. Cascading types, like ivy geraniums, are especially attractive trailing from hanging baskets and window boxes. Scented geraniums make fine summer guests in herb gardens.

Before we go any further, let's clear up the botanical confusion. The plants we're discussing here are properly called pelargoniums. When Dutch and English explorers came across these plants in South Africa in the 1700s and introduced them to Europe, botanists originally classified them as geraniums. Later, they were moved to the genus *Pelargonium*. But to most of us, they will always be geraniums.

Here's an overview of the major types you'll find at nurseries.

Common or zonal geraniums

Zonal types, with round leaves topped by umbrella-shaped flowerheads, are the plants most commonly thought of as geraniums. "Zonal" refers to a zone or ring of deeper color just inside the leaf margin (the zone isn't always conspicuous). There are single-flowering types, but doubles are the big sellers. Colors include red, magenta, salmon, orange, pink, lavender, and white; some flowers have a second color.

A subgroup of zonals, called fancy-leafed geraniums, are grown primarily for their variegated leaves. A good example is 'Mr. Henry Cox' (shown above), which has yellow leaves with a red zone and splashes of green and purple-brown.

Standard zonals like full sun; variegated fancy-leafed types do best in partial shade. Use them as bedding plants or grow them in pots.

Two showy regal types are 'Lord Bute' (top) and 'South American Bronze'.

Ivy geraniums

Their succulent, glossy leaves resemble those of ivy. They produce single or double flowers in a range of colors—red, pink, lavender, white, and bicolors—over an extended period. Because of their trailing habit, floriferous nature, and tolerance of tough conditions, ivy geraniums are one of the most popular summer annuals for containers. The Balcon series is particularly carefree—they're self-cleaning. In frost-free climates, ivy geraniums are also used as a ground cover. Ivy types normally perform best in full sun; in very hot climates, like the deserts, they appreciate afternoon shade.

Scented geraniums

This group is prized for the delightful fragrances its leaves release when brushed or rubbed. Rose, lemon, and mint are the predominant scents, but there are many more, including apple, coconut, ginger, nutmeg, and other herbal aromas. Leaves vary greatly in size and shape; some look more like leaves of oaks, grapes, or ferns than geraniums. Leaf textures can be coarse or smooth as velvet. White or soft yellow variegation is common; a few kinds have brown splotches.

All scented types are attractive in containers, but the trailing kinds like chocolate mint, peppermint, and 'Snowflake Rose' are ideal in hanging baskets or window boxes.

In frost-free climates, pelargoniums make great landscaping plants. Try apple or nutmeg as edgers, advises Kathryn Jennings of Katie's Scenteds, a geranium specialist in Lakewood, California.

Most scented types look their best when given some shade "at least in the afternoon, and especially in hot climates," says Jennings.

Regal types

These are grown for their flowers. Regal geraniums (also known as Martha Washington geraniums or Lady Washington pelargoniums) are big, shrubby plants with stiff dark green leaves and showy 2- to 3-inch-wide blooms in rounded clusters. Colors include red, orange, pink, purple, mauve, and white. Most have darker markings of some sort, sometimes in dramatic, near-black shades. The regals have a shorter bloom period than ivy and zonal types, but hybridizers are working on that. In the meantime, try longer-blooming 'Georgia Peach' or 'White Champion', says Jack Tipich, a San Pedro hobbyist known for his prizewinning regals. Regals love sun, and they're usually grown in pots.

Sources

For unusual scented, fancy-leaf zonals, and other geraniums rarely found in nurseries, try these mail-order sources.

Geraniaceae. *(415) 461-4168 or www.geraniaceae.com.*

Goodwin Creek Gardens. *(800) 846-7359 or www.goodwincreekgardens. com.*

Katie's Scenteds. *(562) 619-6266 or www.katiesscenteds.com.*

Growing tips

SOIL. Geraniums tolerate most garden soils, as long as they provide good drainage. If your soil is particularly heavy, amend it with compost or pumice. To improve the drainage of potting soil, mix in some additional perlite.

WATER. Irrigate bedding plants when the top inch of the soil is dry. Water container plants when the soil surface is dry to the touch. Regals are a little thirstier; irrigate whenever soil approaches dryness.

FERTILIZER. Add a balanced slow-release fertilizer to the potting soil or bed area at planting time. Then supplement periodically with a liquid fertilizer at half or quarter strength.

PESTS AND DISEASES. As a group, geraniums are fairly trouble-free. Ivy geraniums have virtually no pest problems or diseases wherever they are grown. The same is true of scented types in most areas.

Rust can be a problem with zonal types. If it occurs, pick off afflicted leaves or spray with a fungicide labeled for rust control.

Various budworms are an annoyance in mild-winter areas. They nibble holes in leaves and drill into flower buds, spoiling the blooms. Their favorite targets are zonal and scented types with soft leaves. At the first sign of damage, spray with *Bacillus thuringiensis* (BT). Repeat every seven days until the problem dissipates. Or grow ivy or scented types that aren't bothered by budworms. ◆

Silvery *Plecostachys serpyllifolia,* golden breath of heaven, lobelia, and penstemons surround peach tree.

The abundant garden

Escondido "farmer" Maureen Moore shows how to reap
the richest harvests by combining edibles with ornamentals

By Sharon Cohoon • Photographs by Bob Wigand

Maureen Moore, owner of the Ginger Cat's Kitchen Garden, a farm stand and nursery in Escondido, California, has learned what it takes to keep a garden as productive as possible: Make everything work double duty. Her vegetable beds, for instance, contain a surprising number of ornamentals. But they're not just there for aesthetic purposes. The flowers attract beneficial insects, which control crop pests, and also provide cut flowers for her table.

Her flower garden is the reverse. Though it is mostly ornamental, Moore tucks in plenty of culinary herbs and other attractive edibles like leafy greens. Because everything in the garden does more than one job—including Maureen—her 2½-acre property is astonishingly productive. Yet, as the photographs show, it's also very beautiful.

The secret, says Moore, is the same as for a successful yet busy life: "Build in plenty of structure." Here are some of Moore's organizational tips.

Divide the garden into separate rooms, each with a primary purpose. Moore's original kitchen garden, for example, is a 55- by 88-foot plot subdivided into neat, rectangular beds. It's an "enclosed kitchen garden, according to classic principles," says Moore with satisfaction. The well-defined beds provide leeway for mixing in flowers, garden art, and other ornamentation while maintaining a sense of order.

A vine-draped fence frames the garden; just inside it grows an informal row of sunflowers, cosmos, and tithonia.

Where necessary, crops grow against supporting structures—tepees, bamboo accordions, trellises—so the garden looks neater and crops fare better than when plants sprawl on the ground. "There's no reason a kitchen garden can't also be pretty," says Moore. "It doesn't make it any less productive."

Use edibles as ornamentals. Moore's ornamental garden contains sage, basil, thyme, and other "harvestables," as well as flowering perennials. The fence that defines this space is draped with wine grapes. ("If we don't like the wine, we'll convert it into gourmet vinegar," says the ever-practical Moore.)

Attract beneficials. The entry arch that leads into the kitchen garden is covered with a purely-for-pleasure climbing rose. The Guinea gold vine and honeysuckle that cloak the fence adjoining the kitchen garden are also strictly ornamental. But the hummingbirds and other useful pollinators that frequent the area might beg to differ. The sunflowers and tithonia provide shelter and food for beneficial insects; they furnish cut flowers for the farm stand and Moore's own table, and their sunny colors gladden the heart of every visitor.

Moore's garden is a reflection of her lifestyle with its many roles.

•**Farm stand owner.** Much of the kitchen garden's yield is sold at an informal neighborhood farmer's market held at the Ginger Cat every Saturday during the growing season, March through September.

•**Plant propagator.** Tomatoes are one of her passions: She grows 130 varieties, which she sells at her informal nursery. Perennials, mostly old-fashioned types like cottage pinks, monarda, and verbascum, are another specialty.

•**Avocado grower.** Moore grows some 76 trees, which produce 10,000 to 12,000 pounds of fruit.

•**Poultry keeper.** A chicken coop houses 20 or so hens. The eggs Moore and her husband, Richard, don't use are sold to neighbors.

The more ideas Moore dreams up to make her garden increasingly productive and self-sustaining, the richer her life becomes. No day at the farmette is the same, she says. But "for someone with a huge need for variety—and that's me—it's the perfect job."

Ginger Cat's Kitchen Garden: 9–2 Sat Mar–Sep; otherwise by appointment. 10149 Vista Montanoso, Escondido, CA; (760) 749-8108. ◆

ABOVE: Golden feverfew and breath of heaven, gray *Westringia* 'Morning Light', and pink-flowered *Ajuga* 'Rosea' grow in front of wine grapes.
LEFT: Giant sunflowers and gray dusty miller mingle with 'Bright Lights' Swiss chard.

LOCAL ARTISTS FIND INSPIRATION in Larry and Joanie Petersen's flowerful garden in Bozeman, Montana. For details on the colorful plantings, see page 197.

June

English garden style in Bellevue

Choice perennials give a lush look to this entry

■ A beguiling flower garden lines both sides of the front entry to Beth McCann's house in Bellevue, Washington. Essentially a Northwest adaptation of an English cottage garden, it packs a large number of flowering perennials into a fairly small space. Some, like the white-flowered astilbe on the left side of the garden, thrive in the shade of a 'Bradford' ornamental pear. Others, including the hardy geraniums 'Johnson's Blue' and 'Wargrave Pink', are happy in either sun or shade. Along the entry path, tall purple delphiniums, rosy pink Russell lupines, and white *Sidalcea candida* flower best in full sun.

At the front of the bed, English boxwoods form an evergreen screen that hides the bases of the perennials growing behind. Along the eaves, an evergreen clematis vine (*C. armandii*) displays glossy leaves year-round and fragrant white flowers in spring.

McCann isn't afraid to move or remove plants. "If they don't work in one place, I try them somewhere else or get rid of them." Such rigorous editing has culled her perennial collection down to reliable performers that don't need much attention. She fertilizes once in May and again in June with liquid fertilizer. —*Jim McCausland*

A butterfly bush with fountains of bloom

■ Prized for its splashy color in late spring, fountain butterfly bush (*Buddleja alternifolia*) also attracts butterflies and hummingbirds to mountain gardens. For two weeks in June, each arching branch is flocked with clusters of sweetly fragrant lavender flowers.

Fountain butterfly bush is not finicky but prefers well-drained soil and a sunny spot in the garden. Although drought-tolerant once established, occasional deep irrigation promotes bloom. This deciduous shrub can get quite large, reaching 12 feet tall with an equal spread. To keep it more compact or to improve its shape, prune after flowering stops. For a dynamite spring duo, plant tall bearded irises in front of fountain butterfly bush.

Of the two forms available, silvery gray–leafed 'Argentea' is hardy in *Sunset* climate zones 2B (Denver) and 3A–3B (Grand Junction, CO, and Salt Lake City). Dark green–leafed form matures faster and is hardy in zones 3A–3B. Both forms are spectacular in flower. Plants are available from High Country Gardens (800/925-9387 or www.highcountrygardens.com) and Wayside Gardens (800/845-1124 or www.waysidegardens.com). — *Marcia Tatroe*

Working on the railway

■ Tom Speer has been working on his Hard Rock and Dynamite Railroad for the last decade. His industriousness is apparent in the magical garden railway that dominates his backyard in Littleton, Colorado.

In Speer's layout, G-gauge model trains chug around 500 feet of track surrounded by dozens of miniature structures. Plants are carefully chosen to create a landscape perfectly scaled to the train—each car is roughly the size of a loaf of bread. A tuft of sweet alyssum looks like a wildflower meadow; patches of Irish moss simulate expansive lawns. Dwarf Alberta spruce (*Picea glauca albertiana* 'Conica') only 12 inches tall take on the dimensions of forest giants. Elfin, lemon, and woolly thymes drape 24-inch-high flagstone cliffs. In autumn, Virginia creeper turns scarlet on the trellis behind the trestle. And in the winter, Speer runs a locomotive equipped with a snowplow to clear the tracks.

Speer's layout is one of about 90 in the metro Denver area, according to the Denver Garden Railway Society. For more information about the hobby, pick up *Garden Railways* magazine (www.gardenrailways.com) or call (877) 547-2253 for the free booklet "Beginning Garden Railroading."

— *Colleen Smith*

Hummingbirds can't resist it

■ When it comes to plants favored by hummingbirds, *Agastache* 'Desert Sunrise' ranks high on Ross Hawkins's list. Hawkins, founder of the Hummingbird Society, has visited Santa Fe Greenhouses/High Country Gardens in New Mexico during the last three summers to photograph migrating hummingbirds. He always knows where to set up his camera. "There are salvias, penstemon, and other hummingbird plants in the garden, but 'Desert Sunrise'

gets the most visitors by far. The birds fight over it," he says.

The high nectar content of the flowers could account for this plant's appeal with hummers, Hawkins speculates. "Even last summer, when Santa Fe was on strict water rationing, the plant looked nice and juicy," he says. Maybe the quantity of flowers on each stalk attracts them too. "The birds start at the bottom and work their way up. They get lots of fuel from one stop."

A hybrid between *A. cana* and *A. rupestris,* 'Desert Sunrise' bears large flower spikes in a blend of orange, pink, and lavender shades. Bloom is nonstop from midsummer through fall. Both flowers and foliage are pleasantly aromatic. This perennial grows about 40 to 48 inches tall and 2 feet wide. It likes well-drained soil and will tolerate heat and drought.

You can buy 'Desert Sunrise' at Santa Fe Greenhouses or mail-order plants from High Country Gardens (800/925-9387 or www.highcountrygardens.com). For information on the Hummingbird Society, call (800) 529-3699 or visit www.hummingbird.org.

— Sharon Cohoon

Discover the Chihuahuan Desert in El Paso

■ The pungent scents of chocolate flower, Mexican oregano, and creosote bush wash over you as you walk the paths of the Chihuahuan Desert Gardens on the campus of the University of Texas at El Paso. Opened in 1999, this is the first public garden to showcase the native plants of the high-elevation Chihuahuan Desert, the largest desert in North America.

In the United States, the Chihuahuan Desert (shown in green on the map at right) extends from southwest Texas to the southeast corner of Arizona near Tombstone, where it merges with the Sonoran Desert. Hot summers, moderated by monsoon rains, see at least 100 days above 90°. Winters are cold, with occasional snowfall and an average of

100 nights below freezing.

The Chihuahuan Desert Gardens in El Paso display more than 100 plant species in a series of 15 theme gardens that mimic desert ecosystems. Theme gardens include a mountain spring lush with evening primroses and a sand garden sweetly fragrant with catclaw acacia. You'll find many ideas for adding a touch of the high desert to your garden.

The gardens are open to visitors daily year-round. Daylight hours from March through October are best for wildflowers in bloom. On summer evenings you might

spot hawkmoths at work. From Interstate 10, take the Sun Bowl Dr. exit and go one block to University Ave. Parking is a block farther on University.

— Judith Phillips

THOMAS J. STORY

Plant a pesto pot

■ Most good cooks agree: Basil is a must-have herb—it's wonderful in marinades, salads, and soups, and the key ingredient in pesto sauce.

The pot pictured above combines several types—'Sweet' and 'Profuma di Genova' in back (these mild-tasting green basils make the best pesto), 'Red Rubin' (a spicier, more pungent basil that's striking in salads and vinegar), and 'Windowbox' (a flavorful, compact, 6- to 9-inch-tall basil; good on fish or for sprinkling into sauces or salads).

Specialty basils are available at many local nurseries or they can be ordered by mail. Renee's Garden (888/880-7228 for store locator or www.reneesgarden.com) sells 'Profuma di Genova' and 'Windowbox'. Territorial Seed Company (541/942-9547 or www.territorial-seed.com) sells 'Sweet' and 'Red Rubin'.

TIME: 10 to 15 minutes

COST: $35 to $50

MATERIALS

- 23-inch-wide container, at least 9 inches deep
- 2-cubic-foot bag of potting soil
- Organic granular fertilizer
- Three green basil plants, two purple basil plants, three dwarf basil plants, from 2- or 4-inch pots

DIRECTIONS

1. Put the container in a spot that gets full sun. Fill it to within about 2 inches of the pot rim with potting soil. Mix in a granular fertilizer.
2. Gently remove the basil seedlings from their nursery containers, then set them in the big pot so the tops of their rootballs sit about an inch below the pot lip. (If you start basils from seed, allow four weeks for the seedlings to reach transplant size.) Plant three large green basils toward the rear, two purple basils toward the center, and three dwarf basils in front. Fill in around the plants with soil.
3. Water well. Harvest by pinching growing tips or leaves. — *L.B.S.*

TERRENCE MOORE (2)

Artful garden walls in Tucson

■ John and Nancy Alegret of Tucson have found some graceful ways to incorporate concrete block walls into the patio gardens that wrap around their hillside home.

At the rear of the house, the Alegrets painted a 13-foot-tall retaining wall to complement the exterior color of their house. They added decorative features to the wall, including a terracotta sculpture in a niche, a wrought-iron gate leading to a staircase, and a tiled corner seat, to visually tie the wall to the house. They planted an espaliered pomegranate in a narrow strip of soil at the base of the wall. As the tree grew, the Alegrets attached a thin metal bar near the top of the wall to serve as a support collar for the upper limbs.

The pomegranate is festooned with brilliant red flowers in summer, followed by delicious ruby red fruit and blazing yellow leaves in fall. To maintain the espaliered shape, Nancy Alegret prunes unwanted growth twice a month.

In front of the house, the Alegrets erected another concrete block wall to reduce traffic noise and increase privacy. Borrowing an idea they had seen at a pottery factory in Puebla, Mexico, the Alegrets set small slabs of stone between the blocks during construction. The slabs serve as platforms to display pots of cactus and succulents. — *Mary Irish*

Joanie Petersen (above) invites artists to paint in her garden (right).

A painterly garden in Montana

■ Artists find visual inspiration in the flowerful gardens of Larry and Joanie Petersen in Bozeman, Montana. During the summer, the Petersens invite members of Bozeman Artists to visit their gardens for painting sessions that run from morning to midafternoon. The artists usually focus on the floral combinations in the beds, but Anna Goins recently painted a portrait, shown above, of Joanie Petersen in her garden.

The highlight of the season comes between mid-June and early July, when the big crepe-papery blossoms of Oriental poppy (*Papaver orientale*) open in shades of red, salmon, and pink. Four years ago, the Petersens started the poppy seeds indoors during the spring and transplanted the seedlings into beds in the fall.

Many of the other flowering plants, chosen for their hardiness in Montana's harsh winter climate, were purchased at local nurseries. Tall bearded irises in shades of purple and pink add splashes of color and foliage texture. Blooming just beneath the poppies and irises, dame's rocket (*Hesperis matronalis*) sends up clusters of tiny purple flowers resembling summer phlox. The flowers are underplanted with variegated bishop's weed (*Aegopodium podagraria* 'Variegatum'), a shade-loving ground cover with white-edged leaves that play off the surrounding lawn.

To promote lush blooms and foliage, the Petersens dig llama manure from a friend's farm into the beds in fall and give plants a biweekly dose of liquid fertilizer during the growing season. — *Amy Hinman*

LYNN DONALDSON FAR LEFT: SHELLY SAUNDERS; PAINTING: ANNA GOINS

The tropics, in Riverside

■ When Julia Romo visited Mexico City some years ago, she had a love-at-first-sight reaction to the most beautiful tree she'd ever seen—royal poinciana *(Delonix regia)*. She found the scarlet, azalea-like flowers that covered the ferny foliage captivating. She brought home a few seeds to try, and placed them directly into the soil. After several years passed, she removed one seedling to prevent it from crowding the other. Ten years after planting, the tree finally bloomed, spectacularly.

Madagascar native *D. regia* grows in many tropical and subtropical climates around the world, including Hawaii. So why don't we see more of them in Southern California? Mature trees can tolerate temperatures as low as 25°

without harm when they are dormant, says horticulturist Steve Brigham, owner of Buena Creek Gardens in San Marcos. However, if they remain in full leaf during winter, as they can along the coast, they can freeze at 40°, so many growers consider raising the tree here nearly impossible.

Riverside, on the other hand, is an ideal climate for *D. regia*, says Brigham, due to hot summers and relatively dry, cold winters. The trees need plenty of water during the warm months.

Seeds are available from Green-Dealer Exotic Seeds, Box 37328, Louisville, KY 40233; (502) 458-7201 or www.greendealer-exotic-seeds.com.

— *Judy Wigand*

Garden lessons in Big Sur

■ Children thrive on new discoveries: digging in the dirt, hunting for earthworms, catching insects. At the Captain Cooper School in Big Sur, these and other gardening activities are now part of the school's kindergarten-through-fifth-grade curriculum, thanks to the new Children's Garden created by Merrie Potter and partially funded by Chez Panisse, the Packard Foundation, the Doris Parker Fee Foundation, and other grants obtained through the Big Sur Arts Initiative.

Potter designed the garden to be both educational and inspirational. There are raised beds and a greenhouse, as well as a butterfly garden, a pizza garden (full of herbs used to make pizza), a pond with tadpoles, and a touch, taste, and smell garden.

Potter also converted the school's old jungle gym into a hideaway by covering it with chicken wire (leaving an opening) and planting potato vine and jasmine around it.

The children learn to plant, weed, use garden tools, and introduce beneficial insects. But Potter also allows time for them to just be in the garden. "There needs to be a balance between work and having fun," says Potter. "Part of the joy of gardening is having time to enjoy what you've accomplished." — *L.B.S.*

JANET LOUGHERY

Cream bush for sprays of summer flowers

■ When the cream bush or ocean spray (*Holodiscus discolor*) goes into bloom in Kate Bryant's Portland garden, it's apparent why she likes this Western native. In June and July, when few other shrubs are flowering, it bears nodding foot-long clusters of creamy white blossoms that turn tannish gold as they age. Bryant underplanted her cream bush (shown at left) with coral bells (*Heuchera sanguinea*).

This deciduous shrub is at its best near the coast. A good choice for low-maintenance gardens, it requires little summer water once established. West of the Cascades, most plants don't grow taller than 10 feet, but they can reach 20 feet tall and 15 feet wide in moist, rich soil. In dry, sunny locations east of the Cascades, they usually stay under 3 feet tall and 4 feet wide.

Look for cream bush at nurseries that specialize in native plants. One good mail-order source is Forestfarm (541/846-7269 or www.forestfarm.com). — *J.M.*

BACK TO BASICS

LINDA HOLT AYRISS

It's time to thin apples. To keep apple trees from producing too much small fruit, remove some of the excess after June drop (when trees spontaneously abort unpollinated fruit). Thin triple clusters to doubles, and double clusters to singles. However, don't thin at all if your tree is bearing lightly this year. Other kinds of fruit—especially Asian and European pears—need heavy thinning in order to produce large fruit.   — *Steven R. Lorton*

The right way to deadhead rhodies

JIM McCAUSLAND

■ After rhododendrons bloom and flowers fall off, the spiky base of each truss still remains. Snap off each of these just above the emerging leaf buds, as shown here. The process, called deadheading, makes the shrub look better and allows the plant to channel its energy into new growth instead of seed production.— *J.M.*

Minimal space, maximum effects

Good backbone plantings anchor
this garden in Huntington Beach

■ Every successful border starts with the right foundation
plants, insists Sandy Atherton of the garden design team,
Atherton and Lewis. So no exceptions were made for the
border pictured above, in the small yard in Huntington
Beach, California, owned by Margo Cormier and Nesip
Tarcan. "It's natural to want to dive right into color," says
Atherton, "but you need to establish the background first,
even when you're working with a garden this small."

Since the bed shown at top was only 3 feet wide, the designers chose slender shrubs that would still provide
enough height to give the homeowners privacy inside their
courtyard—*Ilex vomitoria* 'Will Fleming' (which grows to
10 feet tall) and *Pittosporum tenuifolium* (to 15 feet).

For more foliage interest, the designers added 'Tuscan
Blue' rosemary and bronze flax (both mostly vertical),
plus lavender, thyme, helichrysum, lamb's ears, and other
plants with mounding habits. Only then did they turn to
color, using the purples of heliotrope and verbena to
complement the flax, and soft apricots, such as 'Terra
Cotta' million bells and 'Sunset Celebration' rose, for
gentle contrast.

For continuity in the courtyard (above), Atherton and
Lewis used many of the same foundation plants. For vari-
ety, they added different secondary plants— *Loropetalum*
'Razzleberri', purple-leafed heuchera, and 'Vancouver
Centennial' geraniums, for instance.

Cormier and Tarcan are delighted with the results, and
the designers are pretty pleased too. "The textures are
very pleasing," says Sherry Lewis, "and so are the subtle
colors. This is one of our favorite gardens."

— *S.C.*

WHAT TO DO IN YOUR GARDEN IN JUNE

PLANTING

☐ **ANNUALS.** Sow seeds of cosmos, marigold, portulaca, sunflower, sweet alyssum, and zinnia early in the month, or set out nursery seedlings of all the above, plus coleus, geranium, impatiens, Madagascar periwinkle, and petunia.

☐ **BULBS.** For late-summer color, plant canna, dahlia, gladiolus, montbretia, tigridia, and tuberous begonia.

☐ **PERENNIALS.** Plant aster, baby's breath, basket-of-gold, campanula, columbine, coreopsis, delphinium, erigeron, feverfew, foxglove, gaillardia, gilia, heuchera, Oriental poppy, penstemon, potentilla, purple coneflower, salvia, Shirley poppy, and Siberian wallflower. For foliage, try artemisia, dusty miller, and lamb's ears.

☐ **PERMANENT PLANTS.** Plant trees, vines, ground covers, and shrubs.

☐ **VEGETABLES, HERBS.** Sow seeds of cucumber and squash immediately, plus successive crops of beets, bush beans, carrots, kohlrabi, lettuce, onions, parsnips, peas, radishes, spinach, Swiss chard, and turnips. Set out nursery seedlings of eggplant, peppers, and tomatoes. All herbs can go in this month.

MAINTENANCE

☐ **CONSERVE WATER.** Irrigate on still mornings or evenings so more water soaks into the soil and less is lost to evaporation. Consider installing a drip-irrigation system. Cut back on watering the lawn: Apply about 1 inch of water every 10 days; the grass will turn straw brown (in this semidormant state, it is easily damaged by heavy traffic), but it will recover in fall when cooler weather and rains come. To retain soil moisture, spread a 2-inch layer of organic mulch over the root zones of permanent plants (trees, shrubs, vines, perennials); put a 1-inch layer of mulch around annual flowers and vegetables.

☐ **CONTROL SLUGS.** Bait for them or handpick in the evening or on a rainy day.

☐ **DEADHEAD FLOWERING PLANTS.** Pick faded flowers to keep bloom coming for as long as possible.

☐ **DIVIDE PERENNIALS.** When perennials become overcrowded, dig plants and divide them. Some, like Oriental poppies, can be separated root by root; others, like iris, have to be cut apart with a knife or sharp spade. Discard dead or woody old roots.

☐ **FERTILIZE.** After bloom, feed spring-flowering plants.

☐ **PRUNE SPRING-BLOOMING SHRUBS.** Thin and shape them now, before they set next spring's flower buds.

☐ **TREAT APHIDS.** Blast them off new growth with a hose. Follow up with a spray of insecticidal soap, if necessary. ◆

WHAT TO DO IN YOUR GARDEN IN JUNE

PLANTING

☐ **BULBS, CORMS, TUBERS.** Zones 1–2: For late-summer color, plant begonias, dahlias, gladiolus, montbretia, and tigridia.

☐ **CILANTRO.** To make sure you have plenty of cilantro for cooking through the summer and fall, plant successive crops of seeds, every six to eight weeks. Look for a variety that takes longer to go to seed, such as 'Slow-Bolt' (from Renee's Garden, available at local nurseries or online at www.reneesgarden.com).

☐ **LOW-MAINTENANCE SHRUBS.** Zones 7–9, 14–17: For attractive color and form with minimal watering, try blue hibiscus, cape mallow, ceanothus, euphorbia, feathery cassia, Jerusalem sage, lavender, New Zealand flax hybrids, plumbago, rockrose, Russian sage, and tree mallow.

☐ **MELONS.** Now that soil is thoroughly warm, newly planted melon seedlings should thrive. In cooler climates choose short-season varieties that ripen in 65 to 75 days. Also, plant through holes in black plastic, and cover seedlings with fabric row covers (available at nurseries) to build up heat. Hot, inland climates are ideal for any kind of melon; a particularly tasty one is 'Ambrosia' cantaloupe.

Sunset
CLIMATE ZONES
☐ Mountain (1-2)
☐ Valley (7-9)
☐ Inland (14)
☐ Coastal (15-17)

DEBRA LAMBERT

☐ **NATIVE GRASSES.** Zones 1–2: At month's end, sow seed of blue grama, buffalo grass, and crested wheat grass. For the first year, water between summer showers and pull weeds around plants.

☐ **SUMMER BLOOMERS.** For annuals, try garden verbena, globe amaranth, Madagascar periwinkle (vinca), portulaca, scarlet sage, sunflower, and zinnias. For perennials, try coreopsis, gaillardia, gentian sage, 'Homestead Purple' verbena, penstemon, rudbeckia, Russian sage, statice, salvia, summer phlox, and 'Victoria' mealycup sage. Good foliage plants for fillers are low-growing artemisias, dusty miller, and golden, purple, or tricolor sage.

MAINTENANCE

☐ **GROOM ROSES.** On hybrid teas and grandifloras, snip off faded blooms ¼ inch above the first leaf (from top) with five leaflets. For a long-stemmed rose, cut just above the second leaf with five leaflets.

☐ **MULCH.** To help control weeds, minimize water evaporation, and keep roots cooler, apply a 2- to 4-inch-thick layer of organic material (use the larger amount for taller plants) under shrubs, trees, and vines and on flower and vegetable beds. To prevent crown rot, keep mulch several inches away from stems and trunks.

☐ **PROTECT FRUIT CROPS.** To keep birds from raiding sweet cherries and other fruits, cover trees with plastic bird netting or fabric row covers (available at nurseries). To keep the cover from blowing off, fasten it around the trunk and to the branches with wire or twine.

☐ **SHAPE PLANTS.** On young or fast-growing trees, shrubs, and vines, pinch or prune off poorly placed growth and any stems that are growing at an awkward angle. Cut back vigorous shoots to give the plant the shape and size you desire. ◆

southern california · checklist

PLANTING

☐ **FRAGRANT PLANTS.** Summer evenings and sweet-smelling flowers were made for each other. Some plants to consider are angel's trumpet (*Brugmansia*), gardenia, *Nicotiana sylvestris,* night jessamine, *Stephanotis floribunda,* summer phlox, tuberose, and white heliotrope.

☐ **SUBTROPICALS.** They are widely available in nurseries now. Choices include flowering trees (bauhinia, crape myrtle, tabebuia), fruit trees (avocado, citrus, sapote), shrubs (bird of paradise, hibiscus, princess flower), and vines (bougainvillea, mandevilla, trumpet). This is also a good time to plant all kinds of palms.

☐ **SUMMER COLOR.** It's not too late to plant summer annuals. Choices include ageratums, celosias, dahlias, gomphrena, marigolds, petunias, portulaca, salvia, sunflowers, verbena, vinca, and zinnias. In the shade, plant begonias, coleus, impatiens, and mimulus. Also look for summer-blooming perennials such as daylilies, gaillardia, lion's tail, penstemons, rudbeckias, Russian sage (*Perovskia atriplicifolia*), salvia, and Shasta daisies.

Sunset
CLIMATE ZONES

1-3 7-9 11 13 14-24

DEBRA LAMBERT

☐ **SUMMER VEGETABLES.** Set out seedlings of cucumbers, eggplant, peppers, squash, and tomatoes. Sow seeds of beans, corn, cucumbers, New Zealand spinach, pumpkins, and summer and winter squash. In California's high desert (zone 11), sow seeds of corn, cucumber, melon, okra, squash, and watermelon.

MAINTENANCE

☐ **CUT BACK DELPHINIUMS.** For a second bloom by summer's end, cut back plants after flowers are spent, leaving only a pair or two of leaves at the bottom of each spike.

☐ **FERTILIZE.** Roses, annual flowers and vegetables, container plants, lawn, and other actively growing plants will benefit from fertilizing now. Don't feed native or drought-tolerant Mediterranean plants, though; they are summer dormant.

PEST AND DISEASE CONTROL

☐ **CONTROL CATERPILLARS.** Spray or dust plants that have pest caterpillars (such as cabbage worm, tomato hornworm, or geranium budworm) with *Bacillus thuringiensis* (BT). Since BT kills all caterpillars, use it only on problem plants to prevent harming the larvae of monarch, swallowtail, painted lady, and other welcome butterflies.

☐ **CONTROL GIANT WHITEFLY.** Examine the undersides of leaves of target plants—banana, hibiscus, plumeria—for white waxy spirals, where eggs are deposited. Wash away with jets of water. Pick off and discard leaves that have long, waxy filaments hanging from them.

☐ **MANAGE ROSE PROBLEMS.** Along the coast, "June gloom" creates ideal conditions for powdery mildew. Combat the problem by hosing down foliage early in the morning to wash off spores. Or spray with 1 tablespoon each baking soda and fine-grade horticultural oil diluted in a gallon of water; avoid spraying when temperatures exceed 85°. Inland, watch for spider mites. To hold mite population in check, keep foliage clean by spraying often with water, particularly the undersides of leaves. ◆

WHAT TO DO IN YOUR GARDEN IN JUNE

PLANTING

☐ **PERENNIALS FOR FALL COLOR.** Plant fall-blooming perennials now, including asters, chrysanthemums, *Gaura lindheimeri, Helenium autumnale, Helianthus maximilianii,* Japanese anemones, rudbeckias, *Salvia pitcheri, Sedum* 'Autumn Joy', sunset hyssop (*Agastache rupestris*), and zauschnerias.

☐ **SUMMER FLOWERS.** When the weather warms up, sow seeds of cosmos, marigold, morning glory, portulaca, sunflower, and zinnia. For instant impact, set out nursery seedlings of ageratum, amaranth, celosia, China aster, coleus, gazania, geranium, heliotrope, impatiens, Madagascar periwinkle, nierembergia, petunia, and scarlet sage.

☐ **VEGETABLES.** After the last frost date for your area, set out transplants of warm-season vegetables, including cucumbers, eggplants, gourds, melons, peppers, pumpkins, squash, and tomatoes. Sow seeds of beans, corn, and tender herbs directly in the ground. To garnish salads, sow edible flowers such as calendulas and nasturtiums between vegetable rows.

☐ **WATER GARDENS.** Put tropical water lilies and other frost-tender aquatic plants into outdoor ponds when the water temperature reaches 70°. Fertilize at planting time and monthly through September to encourage bloom.

MAINTENANCE

☐ **HOUSEPLANTS.** Take houseplants outside for the summer after all risk of frost is past. Cut back leggy growth and put the plants in a protected location out of wind and direct sunlight—a covered porch or patio is ideal. Houseplants outside need more water than when grown indoors—check the pots daily and fertilize every other week.

☐ **PINCH ASTERS, MUMS.** To encourage branching, compact growth, and extra flowers, pinch or shear fall-blooming asters and chrysanthemums until mid-July. Remove the top few inches of each stem whenever the plant reaches 1 foot tall.

☐ **PRUNE SPRING-BLOOMING PERENNIALS.** To promote rebloom later in the season, cut perennials back by half when they've finished blooming. These include aethionema, *Alyssum montanum,* basket-of-gold, blue flax, campanula, candytuft, catmint, dianthus, hardy geranium, moss phlox, pansy, thyme, and viola.

☐ **PRUNE SPRING-BLOOMING SHRUBS.** If needed, prune beauty bush, bridal veil spiraea, forsythia, kerria, lilac, mock orange, quince, and weigela immediately after flowering.

☐ **TREAT CHLOROSIS.** When leaves turn yellow while veins remain green, it's a sign of chlorosis, a condition caused by an iron deficiency in the soil. Correct chlorosis by applying a chelated iron product to the foliage and to the soil around the root zone, following the package instructions.

PEST CONTROL

☐ **COLORADO POTATO BEETLE.** This striped beetle and its red larvae can kill potato, eggplant, and tomato seedlings. Hand-pick adults and larvae you find on plants, and squash any orange-yellow egg masses on the underside of leaves. Treat heavy infestations with *Bacillus thuringiensis,* a biological control, or pyola, an insecticide that combines pyrethrins with canola oil (from Gardens Alive; 812/537-8650 or www.gardensalive.com).

☐ **JUNIPER SPITTLE BUG.** This insect leaves deposits of white foam on some junipers. Although unsightly, the foam is relatively harmless to the plant. If deposits are numerous, blast the bugs and foam off with a strong spray of water.

— M.T. ◆

WHAT TO DO IN YOUR GARDEN IN JUNE

PLANTING

☐ **SUMMER COLOR.** Zones 1–2 (Flagstaff, Santa Fe): Plant calendula, marigold, and zinnia early in the month. Zones 10–12 (Albuquerque, Las Vegas, Tucson): Plant celosia, four o'clock, globe amaranth, kochia, Madagascar periwinkle, portulaca, and zinnia early in the month in a place that gets only filtered sun.

☐ **VEGETABLES.** Zones 1–2, 10: Sow seeds of brussels sprouts, cabbage, and carrots anytime this month. Zones 10–11: Plant corn early in the month; plant cucumbers, melons, and summer squash by midmonth. Wait until midmonth to sow broccoli and cauliflower. Zone 12: You can still sow seeds of Armenian cucumbers, black-eyed peas, corn, melons, okra, and yard-long beans. Set out transplants of sweet potatoes early in the month.

MAINTENANCE

☐ **CARE FOR ROSES.** Zones 11–13: Cut off faded flowers, then build a moat around each plant to concentrate water in the root zone. Mulch each plant well. Zone 10: After first bloom, wet the soil, fertilize, and water again.

☐ **MOW LAWNS.** Mow Bermuda, St. Augustine, and zoysia grass 1 to 1½ inches tall. Keep hybrid Bermuda at about 1 inch.

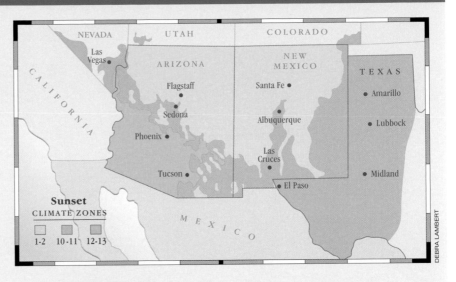

Sunset
CLIMATE ZONES
1-2 10-11 12-13

DEBRA LAMBERT

☐ **MULCH PLANTS.** Zones 10–13: Put a 2- to 4-inch-thick layer of organic or gravel mulch over the root zones of trees, shrubs, vines, flowers, and vegetables.

☐ **PROTECT FRUIT.** To keep birds away from ripening apples, grapes, peaches, and other fruits, cover plants with bird netting or enclose fruits in brown paper bags and staple them shut.

☐ **TREAT CHLOROSIS.** Zones 10–13: Iron deficiency (chlorosis) causes plants to develop yellow leaves with contrasting green veins. Apply a chelated iron product to the soil around the root zone, following package instructions.

☐ **WATCH SUCCULENTS.** Zones 11–13: Cactus and other succulents may show symptoms of heat stress, including sudden wilting and skin that turns yellow or pale green or becomes wrinkled. If these symptoms occur, water plants deeply every one to two weeks and provide afternoon shade until temperatures moderate.

☐ **WATER.** Zones 12–13: Irrigate fruit trees every 7 to 10 days. If you use a drip-irrigation system, flood-irrigate monthly to wash accumulated salts out of the root zone.

PEST CONTROL

☐ **BEET LEAFHOPPERS.** These greenish yellow, inch-long insects spread curly top virus to cucumber, melon, and tomato plants. Protect crops by covering them with shade cloth. Remove and destroy infested plants. — *M.I.* ◆

CLAIRE CURRAN   RIGHT: ROBIN CUSHMAN

Country gardens

They're casual, colorful, and as at home in the city as in the country

By Steven R. Lorton

■ A country garden isn't just a plot of ground outside the city limits. It's a style, a way of growing plants in informal arrangements and accenting them with homespun accessories that exude the spirit of country. You can find it on the prairies of Wyoming or in the middle of Los Angeles, Seattle, or Denver. • Abundant and free-flowing, a country garden is filled with flowers of different colors and heights, all mingling together. Big cabbage roses might bloom among white daisies, with a sprinkling of poppies in front. Delphiniums and hollyhocks create a spatterpaint effect behind them. Sunflowers might rise up like torches from a tangle of nasturtiums. Perennials grow in sweeps. Bulbs pop up in colonies, then scatter out to dot the gar-

den here and there as they expand their territory. Ferns snuggle next to logs and stumps. Grasses tuft up next to rocks, then march into meadowlike plantings, where they rustle and nod in the breeze. Trees grow singly or in groves, pruned to enhance their natural shapes, to clear out dead or damaged branches, or to open the lower levels of the garden to more light. Boughs of lofty evergreens

RIGHT: Yarrow, purple coneflower, monarda, cosmos, delphiniums, and dahlias ramble together in front of Leanna Olson's garden shed in Coos Bay, Oregon. Birdbath in foreground is made from painted and stacked terra-cotta pots. ABOVE: Different varieties of sunflowers bloom together.

ALL THAT IN THIS DELIGHTFUL GARDEN GROWS
SHOULD HAPPY BE AND HAVE IMMORTAL BLISS.

LEFT: Exuberant collection of flowers brings a country look to this garden in Mission Viejo, California, created by Sue Alderton and her son Devin. In front of the fence, roses mingle with pansies, petunias, Iceland poppies, cranesbill, marguerite daisies, and *Salvia* 'Indigo Spires'. Foxgloves grow behind the fence. **ABOVE:** *Gaura lindheimeri* shows butterfly-shaped flowers on wispy stems.

wave and sway with a cheerful abandon that eludes their sophisticated and sheared cousins.

Structures are tucked unobtrusively among the plantings, so they don't interfere with the garden's natural rhythm. Benches and swings invite lingering; trellises support vines.

Little surprises abound, hidden amid curving trunks, dangling vines, obscuring shrubs, and tall grasses. Look among the meadow flowers—purple coneflower and yarrow, for example—and you might find a gaily painted birdbath. Follow a crook in a pathway and you come upon an old chair, its seat planted with tiny mosses or succulents, or a pair of well-used garden boots enjoying new life as containers filled with flowers. There are always birdhouses—as many as their inhabitants' territorial nesting needs will allow.

A country garden is relaxed, because the gardener's spirit can have full play, with little thought given to compatible colors and repetition of form and texture. (After all, does anything in nature truly clash?) Vegetables and flowers grow together, and self-sowing plants are considered blessings, not irritants. The country garden is something of a paradox: It is delightfully jumbled, but as you walk through it you sense that it is one of the very best manifestations of a well-ordered universe.

Country garden flowers

Some plants are better than others at delivering the casual look. Take *Gaura lindheimeri*, for example. This tough perennial (shown above right) grows in all but the West's coldest zones 1 and 2A and bears clusters of small white or pink flow-

ers resembling butterflies that have alighted on airy 2½- to 4-foot spikes. The effect is billowy, soft, and delicate. Other plants for the country garden look, grouped by role, are listed below. Most can be planted now; wait until fall to plant poppies.

Confetti. Small-flowered plants are the support cast to larger-flowered ones. California poppies (*Eschscholzia californica*) bear orange to cream blooms, while Shirley poppies (*Papaver rhoeas*) bear flowers in many shades of white, pink, red, and violet. Salvias have flowers in many colors, from cobalt blue (*S. guaranitica*) to hot pink (*S. chiapensis*), depending on species.

Sun-catchers. Perennials with white, yellow, or pink daisylike flowers practically glow in sunlight. They combine beautifully with ornamental grasses to create an old-fashioned

Here are ideas you can use, from country gardens around the West

1. Colorful chair nestles among California poppies in Mary Gey-McCulloch's garden in Friday Harbor, Washington. **2.** Rustic birdhouse adds down-home charm to a flower border. **3.** Handmade sign peers out between gloriosa daisies and zinnias. **4.** Outdoor bouquet of peonies, roses, delphinium, fennel, and grasses fills enamelware coffee pot in Washington's Skagit Valley. **5.** Artful arrangement of pots, fresh apples, and antique tools covers this outdoor potting bench at Debbie and Doug Thomsen's Orchard Hill Farm in Paso Robles, California. **6.** Well-used chair and basket find new life as planters.

meadow look. *Coreopsis verticillata* has bright yellow 2-inch flowers, *Rudbeckia fulgida* and *R. hirta* sport golden yellow blooms, purple coneflower (*Echinacea purpurea*) has white or pink flowers, and the blooms of Shasta daisy are snowy white. Sunflowers are especially at home in a country garden; flowers come in yellow, red, and rust.

Eulalia grass (*Miscanthus sinensis*), feather reed grass (*Calamagrostis* × *acutiflora*), and purple fountain grass (*Pennisetum setaceum* 'Rubrum') capture sunlight in their seed heads, while the woolly gray leaves of lamb's ears (*Stachys byzantina*) sparkle like silver.

Reachers. Tall candles of bloom make beautiful backdrops or living exclamation points among lower-growing perennials. Our favorites are delphiniums, in shades of blue and lavender to pink and white; hollyhocks (*Alcea rosea*), with single, semidouble, or double blooms in many colors including white, pink, rose, red, yellow, and apricot; common foxgloves (*Digitalis purpurea*), in shades of purple, pink, cream, and apricot; and *Ligularia stenocephala* 'The Rocket', with spikes of yellow daisies that can grow as tall as 5 feet.

Climbers. Few casual gardens are ever without nasturtiums. Their lily-pad leaves and bright orange, yellow, or red flowers ramble over picket fences and along the ground. Climbing roses add color and softness to trellises and fences. 'Climbing Cécile Brunner', with pale pink flowers, is a stunner against a weathered wood shed. 'Fourth of July' has single flowers with white and red stripes; it is dazzling when draped over a split-rail fence.

(Continued on page 210)

Postcard from a country garden

t all began one day when my son, 11 at the time, walked into our Seattle house and announced that he was going to "go hang out at the mall with some friends."

"Uh, I don't think so," I replied.

Within six months, my wife, Anna Lou, and I had purchased 10 acres of land near the village of Birdsview in the Skagit River Valley, about an hour's drive north of Seattle. There we built a weekend-summer house, surrounded on three sides by meadow and on the fourth by stands of alders and conifers. And from that point on, we spent all of our free days there, surrounded by kids who joyously splashed in our pond, ran through the woods, petted the neighbor's cows, and piled up in sleeping bags each night like a pack of puppies, happy and exhausted. Hanging out in malls no longer even entered their heads.

But I needed a project. I started by cultivating and planting around the foundation of the house; gradually I moved outward, eventually covering about 3 acres.

First I mowed an irregular island out of the native grasses and another along the woods surrounding the house. In these beds, I planted sword ferns and vine maples, like those growing wild nearby. Then I added perennials, chosen as much for their foliage as for their bloom. Some of my favorites: astilbe, bugbane (*Cimicifuga*), columbine (*Aquilegia*), daylilies (*Hemerocallis*), euphorbias, filipendula, geraniums, meadow rue (*Thalictrum*), and peonies, and, in the wooded areas, hellebores by the hundreds.

I planted trees in groves to block, frame, or give depth to views—including glorious vistas of the Cascades. Where the garden blends into the wild land, I planted small trees and shrubs that flower and others that offer autumn color. I set

out bulbs like daffodils and camas, which have naturalized with gusto.

As my foray into "Tarzan gardening" deepened, I planted a *Clematis montana* 'Grandiflora' near an ancient cedar. It now crawls high and mightily through the tree, and when cloaked with white blossoms in spring, it looks like a nation of doves has roosted in the old cedar.

I once complained that there was nothing worse than slugs. God was listening, I know, and sent me wild blackberries. We whack on these monsters constantly to keep them at bay. But no matter the challenges, if I'm not working in my country garden, I'm thinking about it. It is a deep and abiding love affair that makes me hope for reincarnation: I want to come back, several times at least, as a bird to nest in my favorite trees!

— *S.R.L.* ◆

'Small Sugar' pumpkins reach 7 inches in diameter. This one rests on plastic foam.

Grow your own pumpkin pie

Plant this summer, and when fall comes, you'll have pumpkin for pie

By Steven R. Lorton

Can anything beat homemade pumpkin pie for Thanksgiving dessert? Not if the pie is made from homegrown pumpkins. Growing and baking your pies from scratch is a fine family project, and if the rich pumpkin flavor doesn't surpass any pie you ever tasted, your sense of accomplishment will.

This is the time to start growing your pumpkins from seeds. Check catalogs and seed packets for varieties recommended for pies.

Last year, we grew several kinds in *Sunset's* test garden, then sent the harvest to our test kitchen, where cooks used the puréed pumpkin flesh in scratch pies. In the tasting that followed, 'Cinderella' won top honors and 'Small Sugar' came in a close second. Both varieties have a rich, sweet pumpkin flavor and flesh that bakes well into a firm but creamy filling.

Growing tips

Choose a site in full sun. After the danger of frost is past and the soil is warm, create mounds of soil about 6 inches high, 1 foot in diameter, and 6 to 8 feet apart (remember, one pumpkin vine can eventually occupy up to 500 square feet of space). Sow seeds 1 inch deep, planting five or six per hill.

After the seeds sprout, thin to the two strongest seedlings. As they grow, steer new shoots in the direction you want them to crawl.

When you water, try not to splash the leaves, since this encourages mildew. Feed plants regularly with a balanced granular fertilizer or liquid plant food.

As the pumpkins mature, slip a sheet of plastic foam, a piece of plywood, or a shingle under each fruit. This will keep the pumpkin's shell from touching the ground and developing rot.

Pumpkins mature three to four months after planting. When the shell has hardened and has a strong, even yellow color, harvest is close. In cold areas, after the first frost kills the leaves, cut the fruit from the vine, leaving at least an inch of stem. Elsewhere, harvest after the leaves and vines turn brown and brittle.

Store pumpkins in a cool, dry place until you are ready to prepare them for pie.

Seed sources

'Cinderella' (also sold as 'Rouge Vif d'Etampes') and 'Small Sugar' are available from Nichols Garden Nursery (866/408-4851 or www. nicholsgardennursery.com) and Territorial Seed Co. (541/942-9547 or www.territorial-seed.com). ◆

'Florida Sun Jade'

'Florida Sun Rose'

'Florida
Sun Splash'

'Sunlover
Cranberry Salad'

'Florida Sun Lava'

'Ducksfoot Red'

'Sunlover Red Ruffles'

Coleus is back in style

Splashy leaf colors and forms
add tropical flair to garden beds
and containers

By Lauren Bonar Swezey

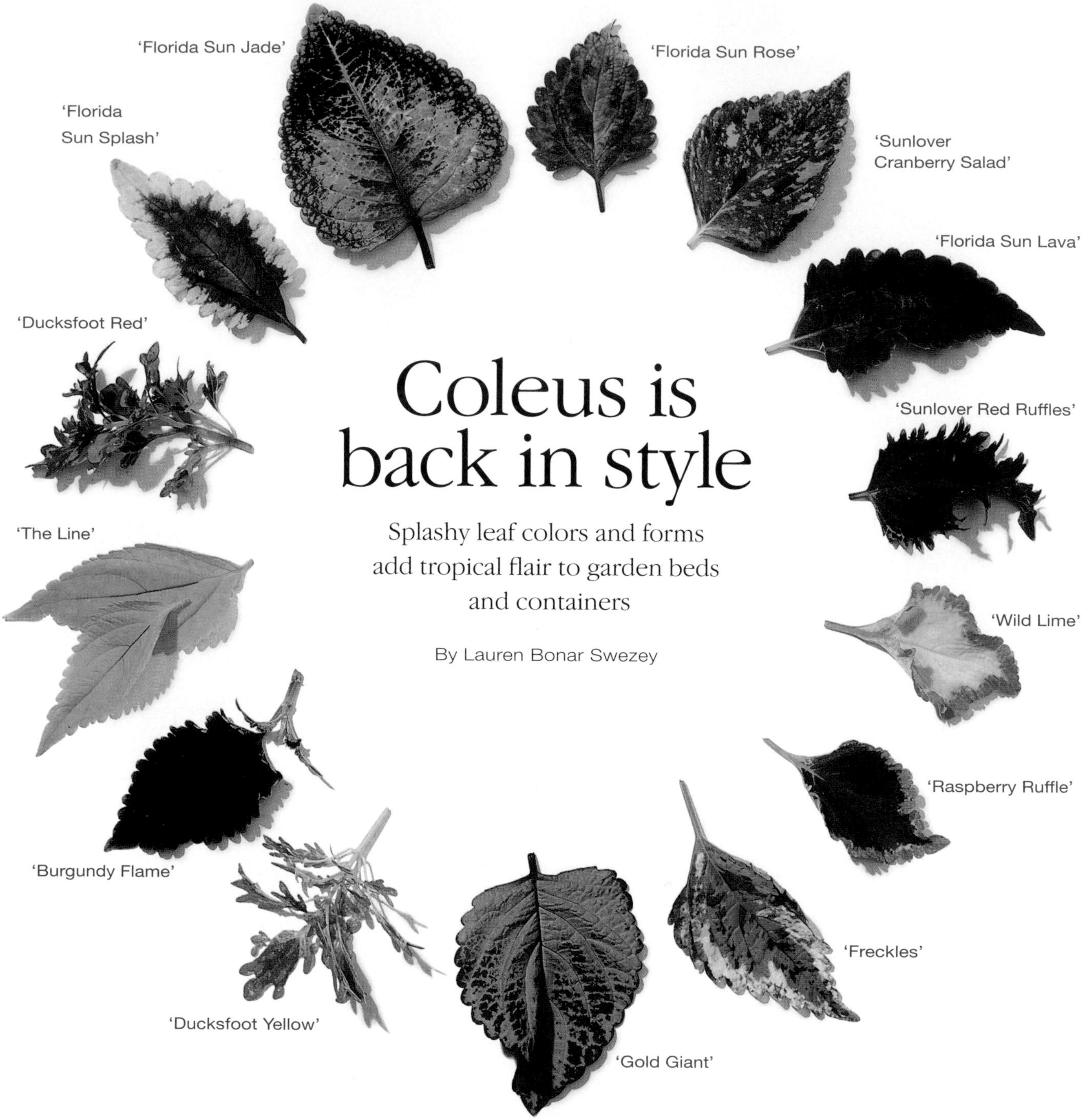

'Wild Lime'

'The Line'

'Raspberry Ruffle'

'Burgundy Flame'

'Freckles'

'Ducksfoot Yellow'

'Gold Giant'

D uring the English cottage garden fad of the
1980s, many gardeners avoided coleus because
its brash foliage just didn't fit with their purple-
and-pink color schemes. But in recent years, as tropical
plants and bolder color schemes have become popular,
gardeners have rediscovered the value of coleus in beds
and containers.

The growing popularity of this plant has encouraged
breeders to develop hybrids in a dazzling array of leaf
shapes, colors, and patterns. One specialist, Glasshouse
Works, offers around 125 varieties of coleus.

Native to tropical Africa and Asia, coleus (recently re-

classified as *Solenostemon scutellarioides*) is a tender
perennial; grow it as an annual in all but the mildest climates. Coleus thrive in warm air and soil temperatures,
so June is the perfect time to plant. Look for plants in
nurseries or order from one of the mail-order specialists
listed on the facing page.

Choose among leaf shapes
and color variegations

Coleus come in an intriguing range of leaf shapes and
markings. Spade-shaped leaves are the most common
form; they can be broad like 'Florida Sun Jade' or fairly

Growing tips

Exposure. In coastal climates, coleus thrive in shade or sun, but pinks and other vivid shades become more intense in brighter light. Farther inland, coleus with darker leaves (burgundy or plum) can tolerate full sun, but chartreuse types may become bleached out. In hot climates, it's best to plant coleus in filtered sun or where they will get afternoon shade. Don't plant coleus in windy areas or where they'll get reflected heat off a building.

Soil. Plant in well-drained garden soil or in raised beds. Amend soil with plenty of compost.

Watering. Water regularly to keep the soil moist, but not wet. Roots rot in soggy soil.

Feeding. Feed with a high-nitrogen fertilizer to promote foliage growth. Avoid fertilizers high in potassium.

Pinching. Some varieties are naturally compact, but others benefit from pinching. If young plants are leggy, pinch off new growth to encourage bushiness. To promote lush, healthy foliage, discourage coleus from blooming by pinching off flower buds as they appear. Many of the newer cutting-grown varieties flower late in the season or not at all. Older seed-grown types usually start flowering earlier.

narrow like 'The Line'. There are kinds with ruffled leaves, such as 'Sunlover Red Ruffles'. For varieties with highly lobed leaves, try the frilly 'Ducksfoot Red' and 'Ducksfoot Yellow'.

Leaf markings range from flecks and splotches such as those on 'Freckles' and 'Sunlover Cranberry Salad' to nearly solid shades of burgundy and chartreuse.

Use a single kind to highlight a bed or container of flowers. You can also create a kaleidoscopic effect in a mass planting of several kinds with complementary leaf colors and patterns.

Mail-order sources

Avant Gardens, 710 High Hill Rd., Dartmouth, MA 02747; (508) 998-8819 or www.avantgardensne.com. Catalog $3 (refundable with first order).

Glasshouse Works, Box 97, Stewart, OH 45778; (740) 662-2142 or www. glasshouseworks.com. Free catalog. ◆

Coleus with pink, burgundy, and green markings mingle with shade-loving impatiens and begonias in large terra-cotta pots. DESIGN: Jean Manocchio
TOP: Vibrant 'Wizard Mixed' coleus fill a bed beneath cycads and fan palms at Sherman Library & Gardens, Corona del Mar, California.

Lay a path in just one day

A quick way to make a weed-free path with
a natural-looking surface

By Sharon Cohoon with Judy Wigand • Photographs by Bob Wigand

LEFT: All-purpose sand
covers concrete-based path.
ABOVE: To create steps,
position railroad ties, then
spread dry concrete mix
between them.

When you spend most of your gardening time pulling weeds out of your path, you're doing something wrong, concluded garden designer Judy Wigand of San Marcos, California. The path that weaves through her flower-filled landscape used to be made of decomposed granite, or DG, as professional landscapers call it. Wigand loved the natural look of DG but unfortunately, weeds loved it too—more weed seeds germinated in the permeable material than anywhere else in the garden.

Wigand decided it was time for a new path. But what kind? Poured concrete would look too austere.

Brick and flagstone were too expensive. Wigand's solution: A path with a surface that looks like decomposed granite but has a durable, weedproof base.

To accomplish this, she deepened the existing pathway, then spread dry concrete mix right out of the bag in the excavated area. Next she moistened the mix and, while the concrete was still wet, sprinkled all-purpose sand over the surface so it would adhere to the wet concrete.

"Spreading the concrete while it is still dry makes this a quick project. We did ours in a day," says Wigand. See her directions on the facing page.

Since it was installed more than two years ago, the path has required almost no care. Wigand adds loose sand each year to replace what is washed away by winter rains.

Materials
- **Flat-edge shovel**
- **Concrete mix** sufficient to cover path (a 90-pound bag will cover 600 square inches of path, 2 inches deep)
- **Metal-toothed rake**
- 2-foot length of **2-by-4** for leveling
- **Garden hose** with adjustable nozzle
- **All-purpose sand** (approximately one 80-pound bag for fifteen 90-pound bags of concrete)

5 steps to a garden path

2 Pour dry concrete mix directly from the bag into the excavated path. Using a metal-toothed rake, spread the concrete mix evenly until it forms a 2-inch layer.

1 Lower the existing path 2 inches, using a flat-edge shovel to remove the soil. Or dig a new path 2 inches below garden grade.

3 With the 2-foot length of 2-by-4, level the concrete mix and smooth the surface with a side-to-side motion.

4 Using a garden hose with the nozzle set for fine misting, moisten the concrete mix gently but thoroughly until water begins to puddle on the surface.

5 While the concrete is still wet, sprinkle with all-purpose sand until it covers the surface lightly, like powdered sugar on a pancake. Allow the concrete to harden for 12 to 24 hours. After the concrete is dry, sprinkle on loose sand if you want a thicker coating. ◆

COLORFUL AND FRAGRANT PLANTINGS line this flagstone path connecting home and office. For more on this walkway garden in Santa Fe, see page 222.

July

sunset garden guide

Redesigning a steep Seattle slope

ABOVE: Pink astilbe accents a knot garden.
RIGHT: An entertainment patio reposes at
the base of the relandscaped hill.

■ It's hard to believe, but three years ago this courtyard garden was a steep, ivy-covered slope held loosely in place by large granite rocks. Torrential rains had caused the hill to slip, and Seattle city engineers told Don and Robyn Cannon that the whole slope would have to be re-engineered for stability.

The Cannons hired Nakano Associates (206/292-9392) to handle the project. To stabilize the slope, the landscape architects built three retaining walls. The two upper walls, which are made from interlocking concrete blocks (sold as Pisa Stone), are anchored by a reinforcing geotextile set deep in the hillside. The lowest wall is made from brick that matches a walkway that continues around much of the house. The brick wall and the first of the concrete walls are backed by hedges of boxwood; yews border the top concrete wall. One end of the walkway flares out to form an entertainment patio big enough for a table, chairs, and a small fountain.

At the end of the graveled, 5- by 13-foot terrace pictured above left, Robyn placed a cast-concrete sculpture of winged Nike as a focal point. To steer the eye to the statue, she designed a modified knot garden consisting of bands of dwarf boxwood that twist around clumps of pink astilbe.

Was the engineering work successful? Well, the slope was unharmed by the 6.8-magnitude earthquake that shook Puget Sound on February 28. —*Jim McCausland*

impromptu bouquets

■ For *Sunset* test garden coordinator Bud Stuckey, bouquet making is effortless—something to accomplish between daily chores such as weeding, watering, planting, and picking spent blooms. His secret: A weathered table is nestled among the plants to serve as an instant work surface, and a collection of rugged vases sits by a hose bibb, ready to fill. Bud always has clippers with him, usually tucked in a pocket.

Before starting to work, he fills a vase with water and sets it on the table. Then as he moves from one chore to another, he clips whatever materials look interesting that day, whether ornamental grasses, vines, shrubs, or perennials, dropping them a bunch at a time into the vase. By the time he's done with his chores, so is his bouquet—for a patio table (or some lucky editor's desk).

Easy garden bouquet contains red and apricot dahlias, blue delphiniums, and sunflowers, all fringed with lacy 'Plum Passion' nandina foliage, feathery purple fountain grass, and sprays of white-flowered potato vine.

organic bounty in Sedona

■ While thumbing through a beautiful book titled *A Window on Sedona: Living in the Land of the Red Rocks* (Cinnamon Stone Publishing, 2000; $35.95; 520/282-8513), we spotted a photo of our friend Ludmila Loisy harvesting vegetables in her garden. Originally from Czechoslovakia, Loisy has lived in Sedona with her husband, Don, since 1988. She has devoted herself to organic gardening, which can be a challenge here in Arizona's high-desert country (*Sunset* climate zone 10). Loisy grows almost all of her vegetables from seed, preferably of heirloom varieties. Here is a list of her favorites, along with a source for seeds in parentheses (addresses below).

- **Beets:** 'Detroit Dark Red' (R, S, W), 'Yellow Intermediate Mangel' (S)
- **Cucumber:** 'Poinsett 76' (R)
- **Green beans** (bush types): 'Bountiful Stringless', 'Contender', 'Slenderette' (all R)
- **Lettuce:** 'Four Seasons' (S)
- **Muskmelons:** 'Hale's Best Jumbo' (R, S), 'Shumway's Giant' (R)

- **Peppers:** 'California Wonder' (R, S), 'Jalapeño' (R, S, W), 'Red Peter Pepper' (R), 'Sweet Banana' (R)
- **Tomatoes:** 'Amish Paste', 'Caspian Pink', 'Red Brandywine', 'Yellow Brandywine' (all R)
- **Watermelon:** 'Black Diamond' (R)
- **Winter squash:** 'Lakota' (W), 'Waltham Butternut' (R)

R R.H. Shumway Seedsman, Box 1, Graniteville, SC 29829; (803) 663-9771 or www.rhshumway.com.
S Seeds of Change, Box 15700, Santa Fe, NM 87506; (888) 762-7333 or www.seedsofchange.com.
W W. Atlee Burpee & Co., Warminster, PA 18974; (800) 888-1447 or www.burpee.com. — *Dick Bushnell*

PAULA JANSEN; ABOVE: THOMAS J. STORY

Great plants for the Northwest

"If you're building a garden, it's great to have a little direction from the experts," says Richard Hartlage, director of the Elisabeth C. Miller Botanical Garden in Seattle. Now, thanks to the new Great Plant Picks program sponsored by Miller Botanical Garden, Northwest gardeners can get guidance from a group of 30 regional horticultural experts. The panel has selected plants that are easy to grow, vigorous, long-lived, reasonably resistant to diseases and pests, and readily available from mail-order sources or specialty nurseries (look for tags designating the picks).

The 2001 lineup includes 15 top trees, shrubs, and perennials for gardens west of the Cascades. Here are three of the winners.

Cornus kousa chinensis '**Milky Way**'. This dogwood is a four-season beauty that produces white starlike flowers in late spring, a lush canopy of medium green leaves in summer,

Helenium 'Moerheim Beauty' has brown-centered blossoms.

red fruits and crimson foliage in autumn, and showy winter bark. The tree grows to about 10 feet tall in a decade, reaching 30 feet or more at maturity.

Helenium '**Moerheim Beauty**'. In late summer when other perennials are waning, this sneezeweed puts on a glorious show of bronzy orange daisies. It grows to about 3 feet tall.

Hydrangea quercifolia '**Snow Queen**'. This oak-leafed hydrangea bears large conical clusters of white flowers in late spring and early summer. The leaves turn plum purple in fall. The shrub grows to 6 feet tall and 8 feet wide.

You can view all 15 selections on the Web at www.greatplantpicks.org, or obtain a complete list by writing to Great Plant Picks, Box 77377, Seattle, WA 98177. — *Debra Prinzing*

Celebrate lavender in Sequim

■ This month, visitors to Sequim (pronounced *squim*), at the north end of Washington's Olympic Peninsula, can gaze over rolling fields of lavender like the one pictured at left. Locals talk about lavender varieties as if they were fine wines—as one grower told us, "'Provence' has the sweetest fragrance, but English lavender has the sweetest taste. 'Grosso' has the purest lavender scent."

Many growers here sell nursery plants of almost any kind of lavender you can name. Visitors can also sample foods flavored with lavender and lotions that carry the scent. In late July, there's even a lavender event, the annual Celebrate Lavender Festival (800/500-8401 or go to www.lavenderfestival.com).

Start your self-guided driving tour of local lavender growers at Cedarbrook Herb Farm (360/683-7733). From U.S. 101, exit on Sequim Avenue and head south just ¹⁄₁₀ mile to the entrance. After you've ambled through the extensive herb garden, of which lavender is only a part, pick up a map that will lead you to other lavender farms. Read each listing carefully: Many farms welcome drop-in visitors, but some are open by appointment only. — *J.M.*

Outdoor living— French style

■ Gravel terraces have been a fixture in domestic landscapes in the south of France for many centuries. For Lucinda Lester, an interior designer in Southern California with a passion for all things French, that was excuse enough for wanting such a terrace of her own.

Although she chose it for its romantic associations, gravel has proven to be a very practical hardscaping, she says. (The driveway and garden paths at her home are also covered with gravel.)

To begin with, gravel is very economical compared to other paving materials. It's also blissfully easy to clean and to maintain—there's no reglazing, regrouting, revarnishing, patching up, or scrubbing down. True, you can't walk barefoot on it. "But I love the sound it makes underfoot," says Lester. "There's something very tranquilizing about that crunch."

The canopy of trees shading the terrace is another quintessentially French idea. Lester wanted London plane trees, a French tradition, but they don't fare well in her area, so she substituted fruitless mulberry.

Like plane trees, the mulberries are deciduous. They provide an umbrella of shade in the summer, when that's welcome, then allow in more sun in the winter, when that's what is needed. When they are more ma-

ture, the trees will be pollarded (the main branches are trimmed back to the trunk) regularly to keep them shapely and compact. Then this gravel terrace—the perfect cover for the trees' heavy surface roots—will be so convincingly provençal, Lester may never have to leave home to feel that she is in France.

— *Sharon Cohoon*

STEVEN GUNTHER

Crystal-clear water for koi

■ A gorgeous pond filled with colorful fish can add serenity to a garden. But keeping it clean and free of algae takes careful planning. Sharon and Fred Andres of Saratoga, California, found the ideal solution for keeping their pond—4 feet deep, 20 feet wide, and 32 feet long—crystal clear and their 40 koi healthy: a biological filtering tank (see drawing below).

The tank, hidden from view by foliage and a pavilion, has a side trough that traps heavy debris such as fallen leaves; gravel filters out smaller particles. The trough needs cleaning only four times a year, which takes about 5 minutes. Filtered water is recirculated from the tank to the pond by a hidden ¾-horsepower pump.

— Lauren Bonar Swezey

A. Removable **drainpipe**

B. **24-inch cutout** in tank partition

C. Fine-mesh stainless steel **screen**

D. **Aquarium gravel,** about 18 inches deep

E. **Bricks** to support screen

F. 6-inch **concrete** with ¾-inch reinforcing rods

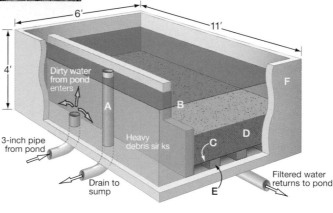

BACK TO BASICS

Keep pests in check. One easy, effective way to control aphids, spider mites, thrips, and whiteflies is to blast them from stems and the tops and undersides of leaves with a strong jet of water from the hose. The device pictured at left, called a Pest Blaster, can help. The curved head, fitted with a brass nozzle, attaches to the end of a hose to deliver a small stream of high-pressure water strong enough to dislodge pests without damaging foliage. Pest Blaster ($15) is available from Denman & Company, Orange, CA (714/639-8106).

— J.M.

Surprises in the path

■ The flagstone path in the Santa Fe garden pictured on page 216 connects the residence of Catherine and Jess Clemens with the office of their landscape design firm, Clemens & Associates, at the back of the property.

Catherine decided to concentrate most of the garden near the path where she, her husband, and the office staff could best appreciate it as they go back and forth all day long. She began by placing a focal point—a potted purple verbena—in a 2-foot-diameter circle of bare earth at the point where three segments of the path meet (the third segment leads to a gate that opens onto a parking area). She planted aromatic thyme in some of the 1- to 2-inch gaps between the stones. Other plants, including 'May Knight' salvia, with its indigo flower spikes, are volunteers that took root in the gaps. Catherine observes, "Seedlings seem to love it near flagstone. It shades their roots better than mulch, and they don't have to compete for water with as many other plants."

"We all love the sensory feedback along the path: watching things come into bloom, brushing against fragrant plants like catmint, even hearing seed pods rattle as you walk by," she says.— *S.C.*

big pots
of summer

■ When summer finally heats up in the Pacific Northwest, container designer Tina Dixon of Bothell, Washington, fills pots with tropical (and tropical-looking) plants that flaunt their lush foliage and flowers through fall. Her pots go together quickly, and they look great from the moment they're planted. To duplicate her efforts, start with a large ceramic or terra-cotta pot—at least 24 inches in diameter and 17 to 20 inches deep. For more tips, see "Great Gardens with Potted Plants" on page 238.

— *J.M.*

UPPER LEFT: Sago palm *(Cycas revoluta), Carex elata* 'Aurea', *Pelargonium* 'Crystal Palace Gem', *Anagallis monelli, Lantana* 'Professor Raoux'.
ABOVE: Elephant's ear *(Alocasia macrorrhiza), Crocosmia* 'Norwich Canary', pelargonium, *Lantana* 'Professor Raoux', *Anagallis monelli.*

1. Using a drill with a ½-inch glass-and-tile bit, drill three or four additional drainage holes around the existing center drain hole in the bottom of the pot.

2. Fill the pot with premium planting mix to about 6 inches below the rim. Add water, blending it in well to completely moisten the mix. Tamp the soil down slightly with your hands.

3. Arrange plants in their nursery containers atop the soil; adjust design as desired. Remove the tallest plant from its nursery container, rough up its rootball, and plant it.

4. Repeat the process with lower-growing plants; place trailers around the edge. Add soil to raise the level to 1 to 2 inches below the rim. Scatter controlled-release fertilizer over the soil. Water.

Grand prize staircase in Vail

PAUL BOUSQUET

Pink-flowered woolly thyme softens stairs made of sandstone slabs.

Located on a mountainside overlooking the town of Vail, Colorado, this steeply inclined site presented a challenge to landscape designer John Rosenfeld, of Johnie's Garden in Minturn, Colorado. The homeowners wanted a landscape with a touch of formality that would also complement the natural beauty of the site. Rosenfeld's resulting design not only accomplished those goals, but it won a grand award in a statewide competition sponsored by the Associated Landscape Contractors of Colorado.

To stabilize the slope, Rosenfeld built a retaining wall with locally gathered boulders. The stairway, which provides access from a second-story deck to lower terraces, was constructed without mortar. Its large, buff-colored sandstone slabs were set well back into the slope in pairs, so that only a small part of each one remains exposed as a tread. A wrought-iron lantern on a stone pedestal illuminates the stairs after dark.

Every crevice along the staircase is planted with aromatic woolly thyme (*Thymus pseudolanuginosus*), which is allowed to grow over the steps anywhere that it doesn't impede foot traffic. In July, the thyme's pink flowers cascade down the steps.

Pink bleeding hearts dangle over the left side of the staircase. Higher up the slope, an informal mix of perennials creates a meadowlike transition between the boulders above the staircase and the blue spruce forest behind the home. The mix includes blue delphiniums, white *Gypsophila repens*, rosy pink Himalayan fleeceflower (*Persicaria affinis*), and yellow potentilla.

— *Marcia Tatroe*

tough plants for the coast

■ Creating a lush-looking but easy-care landscape right on the shoreline can be a challenge. But Lew Whitney of Roger's Gardens in Corona del Mar, who designed the landscape around this putting green for Marilyn Hester-Gianulias, understands coastal conditions thoroughly and knew just which plants would tolerate the heavy salt spray. For turf, his choice was hybrid fescue: "It always does well at the coast." The blond grass that looks like sea foam rolling onto the shore is Mexican feather grass (*Nassella tenuissima*). The small shrubs are natal plum (*Carissa macrocarpa*). And the festive fringe of pink? That's 'Siskiyou Pink' gaura, one of the toughest, longest-blooming perennials around.

Though it is a pretty convincing imitation, the putting green is not natural grass. It's a synthetic look-alike from OnePutt Greens (www.1puttgreens.com). Its nonuniform tufting pattern makes it look more grasslike than most turf. "Plays like the real thing, too," says Hester-Gianulias. — *S.C.*

STEVEN GUNTHER

CLIPPINGS

• Red imported fire ant alert. If you suspect red imported fire ants (RIFA) are on your property, don't attempt to eliminate these pests yourself. The California Department of Food and Agriculture has an active eradication program in effect. To report suspicious nests (small, dome-shaped mounds or nests around trees, pipes, or other structures) call their hotline (800/491-1899).

•Herbal recipes and remedies. Do lavender crème brulée, chamomile under-eye oil, or rose hip chili sound like recipes or remedies you'd like to make? If so, *The Herbal Epicure,* by Carole Ottesen (Ballantine Wellspring, New York, 2001; $16) is for you.

DAVID WINGER

A golden elderberry

■ It is a rare shrub that is as pretty out of flower as in full bloom, but *Sambucus canadensis* 'Aurea', an ornamental variety of American elderberry, can make this claim. All season long, its golden leaves glow in the sun. In early summer, it bears large, loose clusters of creamy white flowers. Later in the season come red berries that make tasty jelly and wine—if you can keep the birds from gobbling them all up.

American elderberry is hardy in *Sunset* climate zones 1–7 and can be grown at elevations up to 8,000 feet. This vigorous shrub spreads by suckers and needs plenty of room: It can reach 10 to 12 feet tall and as wide. The shrub prefers damp soil, though established plants can tolerate drier conditions. Planting in full sun ensures richer golden foliage color (in shade the foliage fades to lime green by midsummer).

Sambucus canadensis 'Aurea' is available at local nurseries and from mail-order growers including Forestfarm (541/846-7269 or www.forestfarm.com) and Heronswood Nursery (360/297-4172 or www.heronswood.com). — *M.T.*

STEVEN GUNTHER (8)

grow your own
pineapples in pots

■ Remember how sweet pineapple tastes in Hawaii? Southern California gardeners can enjoy that taste by growing crops in containers to harvest fruit when it is perfectly ripe. That's what Paul Quong of Villa Park, California, has been doing the last 15 years. The process calls for patience—plants can take up to 24 months to produce ripe fruit—but is otherwise easy, he says. Here's his method.

Pots of pineapple plants line Quong's patio year-round. The fruits take longer to ripen in Southern California than they would in Hawaii, but winter chill does not damage the plants. In colder areas, move plants indoors next to a sunny window before frost, or under grow lights. — *S.C.*

1. Buy a supermarket pineapple with healthy green leaves. Cut off the crown (**A**), leaving several inches of fruit (**B**). Soak crown in water for a day or two to absorb moisture (**C**).

2. Fill a 1-gallon plastic pot about three-quarters full with lava rock (**D**). Add 2 to 3 inches of redwood compost (**E**). Set the crown on top (**F**). To make it easier to gauge soil moisture, cover half the crown with additional compost. Place plant in sunny, warm location.

3. Water frequently, especially during the summer. When pineapple leaves start to grow, begin fertilizing. Quong uses a dry, citrus-type fertilizer three to four times a year, in addition to a liquid fertilizer once a month.

4. Transplant pineapple to a 5-gallon pot when it outgrows its original container, then to a 15-gallon size.

WHAT TO DO IN YOUR GARDEN IN JULY

PLANTING

☐ **ANNUALS.** There's still time to plant annuals that will give you a great summer show until frost. Get seedlings at your local nursery or garden center.

☐ **CROPS.** For fall harvest, sow seeds of beets, broccoli, bush beans, carrots, Chinese cabbage, kohlrabi, lettuce, peas, radishes, scallions, spinach, Swiss chard, and turnips. Plant potatoes by July 4, also for fall harvest.

MAINTENANCE

☐ **BATTLE SLUGS.** Both rain and irrigation bring out slugs. A little bait and evening raids with a machete will help. If you have pets and use a metaldehyde-based slug poison, put the bait in petproof slug traps or under boards propped up by bricks.

☐ **COMPOST.** Keep adding organic matter and turning the pile at least weekly. To keep bacteria working, soak the pile before it dries out completely.

☐ **DIVIDE BEARDED IRISES.** As foliage starts to turn brown, stop watering. When leaves are mostly withered, trim them back to fans, then dig and divide the rhizomes (thick horizontal roots) with a sharp knife or spade. Let the rhizomes cure in the shade for a few days, then replant in amended soil.

☐ **FEED CHRYSANTHEMUMS.** For best bloom this fall, feed plants with a low-nitrogen liquid fertilizer (often called a bloom formula) every three weeks until buds start to show color. When the first blooms open, feed weekly.

☐ **MAINTAIN FUCHSIAS.** Snip or pick off blooms as they fade to keep flowers coming—but expect bloom to slow in hot weather. Feed plants monthly with a complete liquid plant fertilizer (do it every two weeks if plants are in containers).

☐ **MAINTAIN GROUND COVERS.** To keep them neat and compact, shear ground covers back after bloom. If the cover is low, use a lawn mower. With the top gone, it's also a good time to bait for slugs, which often use ground covers as hideouts.

☐ **MONITOR HOUSEPLANTS.** Be on the alert for aphids and other critters. Check daily to make sure plants have enough water. Hose off dusty leaves (or better, rinse them in a lukewarm shower).

☐ **MULCH SHRUBS.** Spread a 3-inch layer of organic mulch under shrubs, especially azaleas, camellias, and rhododendrons, to conserve moisture.

☐ **WATER WISELY.** For irrigation advice, see "Gardening in a Dry Year" on page 242.

☐ **WEED.** Hoe young weeds on a warm, sunny morning and let their exposed roots bake in the sun until evening. Water before you pull mature weeds, whose taproots come out of damp soil most easily. ◆

WHAT TO DO IN YOUR GARDEN IN JULY

PLANTING

☐ IRIS. Plant new rhizomes. If you have overcrowded clumps in the ground, dig them up six weeks after flowers fade. Discard dried-out or mushy rhizomes; cut apart healthy ones and trim leaves back to 6 inches. Plant new or just-divided irises in full sun and fast-draining soil. Maryott's Gardens in Corralitos, California, offers about 500 varieties of irises by mail (877/937-4747 or www.irisgarden.com).

☐ PATRIOTIC POT. For a floral display on the Fourth of July, create a container of nursery plants with red, white, and blue flowers. Red-flowered choices include annual phlox, celosia, nicotiana, geranium, petunia, *Salvia coccinea,* and scarlet sage. For white, try annual phlox, dahlia, dwarf cosmos, nicotiana, geranium, heliotrope, petunia, a white variety of scarlet sage, or sweet alyssum. For blue, choose gentian sage, lobelia, mealycup sage, petunia, or verbena.

MAINTENANCE

☐ CLEAN UP FALLEN FRUIT. Diseases, worms, and other pests may be living in fallen fruit. Pick up the fruit as soon as you notice it; discard it in the trash.

☐ ENCOURAGE BOUGAINVILLEA BLOOMS. Zones 7–9, 14–17: Bougainvillea flowers best if kept on the dry side. Allow the top several inches of soil to dry out between waterings.

Sunset
CLIMATE ZONES
☐ Mountain (1-2)
☐ Valley (7-9)
☐ Inland (14)
☐ Coastal (15-17)

DEBRA LAMBERT

☐ DEEP-WATER MATURE TREES. If you haven't watered mature trees, they may be suffering from drought stress. Deeply water fruit trees, citrus, and flowering trees once every week or two (use the higher frequency in hot climates). Water drought-tolerant trees about once a month or so.

☐ FERTILIZE CYMBIDIUMS. To encourage flower formation for next winter's bloom, fertilize cymbidiums every time you water. Use liquid fertilizer, such as 20-20-20, diluted to half strength.

☐ STAKE FLOPPY PLANTS. If you haven't already done so, stake beans, delphiniums, gladiolus, peonies, and tomatoes, especially in windy areas. Drive stakes at least a foot into the ground; tie plants securely. Stake-Ups are a new kind of plant support from Garden Works (425/455-0568); they have flexible arms that wrap around the plant, allowing you to stake even a mature one.

PEST CONTROL

☐ CONTROL BUDWORMS. Zones 7–9, 14–17: If your geraniums, nicotiana, penstemons, and petunias appear healthy but have no flowers, budworms may be eating the buds. Look for holes in buds and black droppings on the leaves. Spray affected plants every 7 to 10 days with *Bacillus thuringiensis* (Bt), available at most local nurseries or by mail from Harmony Farm Supply & Nursery (707/823-9125 or www.harmonyfarm.com).

☐ CONTROL YELLOW JACKETS. These stinging wasps are nuisances during outdoor barbecues. A simple method of controlling them is with a yellow jacket trap containing an attractant that lures wasps in. The traps are available at nurseries or by mail from Peaceful Valley Farm Supply (888/784-1722 or www.groworganic.com). ◆

WHAT TO DO IN YOUR GARDEN IN JULY

PLANTING

☐ **SUBTROPICALS.** Flowering tropical shrubs—angel's trumpet, cestrum, hibiscus, princess flower—are plentiful in nurseries, as are bougainvillea, passion flower, thunbergia, and trumpet vine. This is also the time to plant avocado, cherimoya, mango, and other exotic fruit trees, as well as tropical evergreens like palms and tree ferns.

☐ **SUMMER VEGETABLES.** Coastal (zone 22–24) and inland (18–21) gardeners can continue to plant summer vegetables. Set out cucumber, eggplant, pepper, squash, and tomato plants. Sow snap beans and corn. Or plant the year-round crops—beets, carrots, and Swiss chard. In the low desert (zone 13), start pumpkins and winter squash.

☐ **SUMMER COLOR.** It's not too late to plant summer annuals, especially heat lovers like celosia, creeping zinnias (sanvitalia), marigolds, portulaca, salvia, and zinnias.

MAINTENANCE

☐ **WATER CAREFULLY.** Give shade trees a slow, deep soak monthly to ensure good health. Water established shrubs and perennials deeply, too. Container plants need to be watered frequently; daily soakings may be necessary.

Bishop
NEVADA
CALIFORNIA
San Luis Obispo
Bakersfield
Santa Barbara
Tehachapi
Lancaster
Los Angeles
Palm Springs
Sunset
CLIMATE ZONES
San Diego
1-3 7-9 11 13 14-24
MEXICO

DEBRA LAMBERT

☐ **TIME LAWN WATERINGS.** If your lawn has brown patches despite regular watering, it may not be able to absorb water as quickly as your sprinkler system delivers it, says Gary Matsuoka, of Laguna Hills Nursery in Lake Forest. Instead of watering for a steady 15 to 20 minutes—the way most sprinklers are set—break up the irrigation into 3 to 4 intervals of 4 to 5 minutes, about an hour apart, he suggests.

☐ **HARVEST.** To encourage further production, pick beans, cucumbers, peppers, squash, and tomatoes often. Pinch back herbs to encourage branching; use clippings fresh or dried. Harvest early in the day before heat dissipates volatile oils.

☐ **FERTILIZE SELECTIVELY.** Feed annual flowers and vegetables, cymbidium orchids, ferns, fuchsias, roses, tropicals, and warm-season lawns. Also fertilize citrus and avocados that you didn't get to last month.

PEST CONTROL

☐ **CONTROL CATERPILLARS.** Spray or dust plants that have pest caterpillars (such as cabbage worm, geranium budworm, or tomato hornworm) with *Bacillus thuringiensis* (Bt). Since Bt kills *all* caterpillars, use only on problem plants so as not to harm the larvae of monarch, swallowtail, painted lady, and other welcome butterflies.

☐ **CONTROL GIANT WHITEFLY.** Examine the undersides of leaves of target plants—banana, hibiscus, plumeria—for white, waxy spirals where eggs are deposited. Wash away with jets of water. Pick off and discard leaves that have long, waxy filaments hanging from them.

☐ **BAKE AWAY FUNGUS AND NEMATODES.** Use the power of the sun to destroy fungus, bacteria, and nematodes in troublesome sections of the garden. Level the area, thoroughly moisten the soil, then cover it with a thick, transparent plastic tarp. Use rocks or soil to weigh down the edges. Leave the tarp in place 4 to 6 weeks, then remove it. Replant in fall in healthy soil. This technique works best in full sun and warm inland locations. ◆

WHAT TO DO IN YOUR GARDEN IN JULY

PLANTING

☐ DRESS UP PERENNIAL BEDS. When spring-blooming perennials, such as bleeding heart, fernleaf peony, and Oriental poppy, go dormant in summer, cut off their yellowed foliage and fill the gaps with container-grown annuals. Dig the planting holes for the annuals to the side of the perennials, being careful not to disturb their roots.

☐ REPLACE COOL-SEASON ANNUALS. Clarkia, Iceland poppy, pansy, and stock can't stand intense summer heat. When they start looking ragged, pull them out and replant beds and containers with heat-tolerant annuals, such as gazania, globe amaranth, gloriosa daisy, Madagascar periwinkle, marigold, petunia, portulaca, sunflower, and zinnia.

MAINTENANCE

☐ BE KIND TO BLUEGRASS. When temperatures regularly exceed 90°, bluegrass goes dormant; it will turn brown if it does not receive adequate moisture. During heat waves, water every other day to prevent stress to the lawn. Mow grass blades 3 to 3½ inches high so they'll shade the roots and help retain soil moisture.

Sunset
CLIMATE ZONES
☐ 1-3   ☐ 10-11

DEBRA LAMBERT

☐ CARE FOR CONTAINER PLANTS. In really hot weather, check containers daily and water when they start to dry out. Feed weekly with a liquid fertilizer. If annuals become leggy, cut their stems back by half to renew their vigor and restore their shape.

☐ DIVIDE TALL BEARDED IRIS. The best time to divide overcrowded clumps of tall bearded iris is six weeks after they finish blooming. Toss out old and leafless rhizomes and replant only healthy new fans. Irises are heavy feeders, so before replanting dig in a bucketful of compost or well-rotted manure and a handful of balanced fertilizer.

PEST CONTROL

☐ CORN EARWORM. This striped black, green, or pink caterpillar damages sweet corn by chewing through the silk tassels and into the kernels. To protect against this pest, put a drop of mineral oil on the silk of each ear of corn just after the silk starts to turn brown. The biological control *Bacillus thuringiensis* is also effective against corn earworm if sprayed every two weeks after the corn stalks reach 18 inches tall.

☐ SLUGS. Often the only sign that slugs have been eating plants is their telltale shiny slime trails. Slugs are night feeders that hide out of sight in the mulch during the day. Trap slugs by placing damp, loosely rolled-up newspapers in the garden at night. The next morning, dispose of the newspapers and the slugs hiding inside.

☐ SQUASH BUGS. These angular, ⅝-inch-long, black and gray beetles can destroy both foliage and developing fruits on all types of squash. They are particularly fond of winter squash. Check the undersides of leaves for shiny brown egg masses and crush them. Squash bugs are resistant to chemical insecticides, but Pyola, a product combining pyrethrin with canola oil, is effective at eliminating both adult and immature squash bugs. — *M.T.* ◆

WHAT TO DO IN YOUR GARDEN IN JULY

PLANTING

☐ CROPS. Zones 1–2: Plant pumpkins early in the month to ensure maturity before frost; plant second crops of beans, cabbage, lettuce, and spinach. Zone 10 (Albuquerque): Plant cantaloupe, eggplant, okra, peppers, pumpkins, tomatoes, watermelons, and winter squash. Potatoes go in at month's end. Zone 11 (Las Vegas): Plant bush beans, corn, cucumbers, and squash. Zones 12–13: Plant black-eyed peas, corn, pumpkins, and winter squash.

☐ PERENNIALS. Zones 1–2: Plant perennials through the end of the month so plants can get established before winter.

☐ SUBTROPICALS, SUCCULENTS. Zones 11–13: Plant hibiscus, lantanas, and palms. If you plant succulents, including agaves, aloes, and cactus, provide shade to reduce transplanting stress.

MAINTENANCE

☐ CARE FOR ROSES. Zones 1–2, 10: After each bloom cycle, remove faded flowers, cutting them off just above a leaf node with five leaflets (nodes closest to the flower have three leaflets). Then fertilize and water plants deeply in preparation for the next round of bloom. Zone 11: Apply fertilizer at half strength monthly. Zones 12–13: Do not fertilize this month since plants are not actively growing at this time, but keep them well watered.

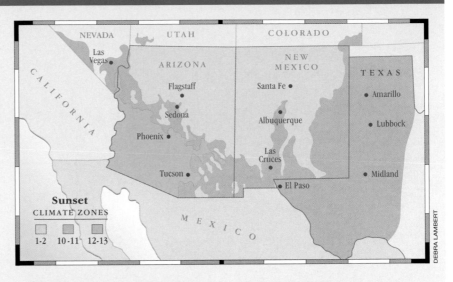

☐ COMPOST. Water the compost pile weekly and turn it often to keep it working. Zones 11–13: Compost piles need afternoon shade to prevent their drying out. Build the pile under a large tree or provide a cover such as shadecloth.

☐ FERTILIZE. Feed annuals and vegetables with high-nitrogen fertilizer and water it in well. Zones 11–13: Fertilize lawns monthly. Feed established palms with a balanced fertilizer and an iron chelate formulation.

☐ MULCH. Apply a 3-inch layer of organic mulch to conserve soil moisture, keep down weeds, and give plants a cool root zone.

☐ SOLARIZE SOIL. Trapping radiant energy from the sun beneath plastic causes soil temperatures to rise to levels that are lethal to many weed seeds, nematodes, and other harmful organisms. First cultivate the soil and water well; then cover the area with a thin sheet of clear plastic. Leave the plastic four weeks if temperatures are over 90° or up to eight weeks in cooler climates.

☐ WATER. Irrigate early in the morning to maximize water uptake by plants. Water annual vegetables and flowers when the top inch of soil has dried out. Deep-water large cactus this month to prevent wilting. Agaves should be watered every other week. — *Mary Irish* ◆

■ Nostalgic charm

Despite the genteel appearance of her English-style landscape, garden design consultant Laurie Connable of Poway, California, considers herself a bit of a rebel. "I don't necessarily follow the rules," she says. "When I go to a nursery, sometimes I buy one of everything I like, instead of the rec-

ommended threes, fives, and sevens. I might mix bright colors and pastels—another no-no. And sometimes I like to put the tall things in the front—or at least in the middle." Her garden is her playground, she says, and the fewer restrictions she places on herself, the more fun she has.

Of course, Connable does have a few guiding principles. First, she plants some areas en masse. When she finds perennials that perform well—like 'Butterfly Blue' scabiosa—she uses them in quantity for impact. And she finds one color to use throughout the garden for continuity. For Connable,

enchanted gardens

By Sharon Cohoon

An inspired marriage of plants, furnishings, and accessories makes these gardens magical

What makes a garden enchanting? Quite simply, beautiful details. Take the pair of crisp white wicker chairs nestled (at left) in a curve of flowers. With their plump pillows, aren't they an invitation to plop down, settle in, and sniff the roses? Or, in the garden pictured on the next page, can't you almost smell the perfume of the angel's trumpet or hear the splash of the fountain? If you could stroll through the shady Asian garden (page 236), wouldn't you love to linger, letting your eyes wander over the Japanese stone cat, the softly glowing lantern, the miniature Thai spirit house that seems to float over exotic foliage? Wouldn't you want to know what else this coolly mysterious garden hides?

In these three gardens, the details mirror their owners' interests and histories. Laurie Connable, whose garden is pictured here, is crazy about plants. "Nurseries are my candy store," she says. She finds ways to present living bouquets with panache—in massed containers, atop antique iron carts. Charles Eglee wanted a garden (page 234) that reflected his passion for Bauer pottery and Malibu-style tile. Artists Wayne and Barbara Chapman (page 236) can't resist art objects, either; they've woven their collection into their garden in refreshing ways.

These are deeply personal environments—"little worlds unto themselves," says Eglee. Therein lies the secret of enchantment.

LEFT: Coral, provided by the 'Joseph's Coat' rose and kalanchoe in pots, sets the tone for this charming seating area near a lily pond. Yellow 'Climbing Peace' rose and a sea of blue scabiosa contribute complementary hues. BELOW LEFT: 'Lucille Ball', a hybrid tea, echoes the coral tones. BELOW RIGHT: An antique wrought-iron cart, sprayed white, holds zonal geraniums, kalanchoe, and a grinning cat.

BOB WIGAND (3)

that's white, which might be in the form of flowers (such as white sweet alyssum) or furniture. "Even my chicken coop has white trim," she says. She also makes sure every major area has a focus: "When you use a rainbow of color, a few well-placed focal points help anchor it."

■ Mission magic

When Charles Eglee approached Los Angeles landscape architect Rob Steiner for help with his Pacific Palisades, California, garden, he knew what he was after: "I wanted to move the inside out." A collection of Bauer pottery from the '20s sets the tone for the interior of the mission revival–style house Eglee shares with his wife, Ninkey Dalton. He wanted the pottery to inspire the garden.

Steiner made a bright orange jardiniere the focal point of a large koi pond encircled by a ribbon of bog plants (below right). "Basically, we made most of the backyard a water garden," he says. The jardiniere also inspired plant choices, such as orange-flowered cannas. And it provided the tie-in for more clay art—a plaque of San Jose tile hangs on one wall, and the table is topped with mosaic.

When an 80-year-old front-yard tree died, Eglee asked Steiner to turn the newly sunny space into "a hacienda courtyard." Naturally, they started with a fountain. And, just as naturally, its centerpiece was another Bauer work— this one, a cool blue oil jar. Again, the jar inspired plant choices. The blue foliage of the agaves, for example, seems dyed to match, and the yellows and red oranges of aloes, nasturtiums, and daylily blooms are a delicious contrast.

As Steiner says, the Eglee-Dalton garden, although quite small, is amazingly rich.

STEVEN GUNTHER (4)

ABOVE: The earthy oranges and Pacific blue tones of the San Jose tile plaque on the wall are repeated in paint, table surface, and flower colors. The painting by Nancy Kintisch was waterproofed for outdoors. LEFT: Orange jardiniere and koi pond are surrounded with acorus, brilliant orange cannas, and other bog lovers. TOP LEFT: The owners' dalmatian, Bongo, surveys her domain. Fragrant brugmansia (angel's trumpet) and blue morning glories frame the entrance. BOTTOM LEFT: Water spills from a turquoise Bauer oil jar. The glass balls are Japanese fishing-net floats.

ABOVE LEFT: Potted plants and intriguing objects cluster together on either side of the entry stairs. A Japanese-style structure, designed by the homeowner, houses a light. ABOVE: Antique Chinese bed is the focal point of the garden, but many other objects are partially hidden in the foliage. RIGHT: A Thai spirit house and the owner's own ceramic pieces keep company with ferns, a philodendron, and a cast-iron plant. BELOW RIGHT: An antique Japanese lantern houses another light. BELOW LEFT: A beckoning cat, a Japanese good luck symbol, greets visitors beside a water-filled ceramic pot.

◼ Asian Pacific allure

Though Wayne Chapman has always loved to putter with plants, the garden he shares with his wife, Barbara, in Solana Beach, California, didn't really feel pulled together until he began adding inanimate objects. "When I started incorporating some of the things we love, the garden really started to take shape," he says. The first item he added was a huge Japanese storage jar, which he turned into a fountain. More transformed objects soon followed. Now they're everywhere—an antique Chinese bed acts as a backdrop for an assembly of pots and plants, for instance, and a Thai spirit house protects the front entrance to the home.

Though the garden contains items from non-Asian countries, too, a feeling of the Far East dominates. Chapman created the temple structure that houses a light near the stairs, the massive gate at the side entrance, and the cobblestone and beach-pebble pathways—all with a Japanese flavor. "When

you're a potter," says Chapman, "it's hard not to be influenced by the Japanese. Their aesthetic is so strong." He also made the numerous clay bird feeders and wind chimes throughout the garden.

Since the garden is mostly green, it provides a simple background for Chapman's ever expanding collection of artifacts that, in this deeply shaded garden, seem to emerge from the shadows one by one. ◆

great gardens with
potted
plants

It's easy to have a garden almost anywhere

By Sharon Cohoon

■ Potted plants are magicians: They can turn hardscape into landscape. Take a look at the spaces—entries, a courtyard, a deck—on these pages. There's hardly an inch of bare ground in any of them. All the plants are growing in containers—lots of them. Yet is there any doubt that these spaces look like gardens?

Pots filled with greenery and flowers soften the hard edges of a patio or deck. They also create the feel of a garden where there's no earth to plant one. Plants in pots contribute gentle textures, graceful movement, delicious scents, and seasonal changes. They lure butterflies, hummingbirds, and other welcome visitors. In short, they can add life to urban outdoor spaces. Best of all, because container plantings are portable, you can make little changes at any time without disturbing the whole scene.

Don't these examples make you want to start a little garden? It's easy. All you need is potting soil, containers, and plants, and a place to display them.

Entries

Your first opportunity to create a contained garden is by your front door. In this important space, visitors form their initial impression of your home, so this is the area you'd most like to appear welcoming. The simple addition of a few potted plants is all it takes to change the picture from austerity to hospitality.

The trio of containers at the entrance to Billy Spratlin and Alex Kochnuk's home in Newport Beach, California (page 240), planted with coleus and purple fountain grass, is a good example. Spratlin, the gardener in the family, chose bisque-colored pots to coordinate

Edging wide steps in a San Clemente, California, garden, terra-cotta pots display angel-wing begonias, pink and red semperflorens begonias, lime and rust coleus, purple heliotrope, and tuberous begonias.
DESIGN: Lew Whitney

Container gardening tips

- Give potted plants the conditions they need. Assess the site for your contained garden as you would for an in-ground planting. Does the area get full sun, filtered shade, or deep shade? Choose plants accordingly. Is the area sheltered or exposed to lots of wind? If it's exposed, you'll need to install a trellis, windbreak, or other protection before putting your pots there.

- Use foliage plants lavishly. They add structure and form to the garden and are a good foil for flower displays. They also create a point of interest in shade, especially when you use glossy leaves that catch the light, or ones with white and yellow markings.

- Choose containers to match the style of your house. A rusty enamel pot or other junk-shop find may look sweet beside a Cape Cod–style cottage, but ill at ease on a Mediterranean terrace. Also, don't mix pots of too many styles. Stick to a theme.

- Pay attention to watering—the single most important element of container gardening. (Containers dry out fast—especially in hot, windy weather.) If you have many pots, make it easy by trying some of the following devices. A *hose-end nozzle* with an on-off lever allows you to turn off the water between containers. Choose one with an adjustable spray head so you can select a flow gentle enough to avoid washing soil from the pot or disturbing plant roots. *Long-handled watering wands* attach to garden hoses to extend your reach; they're perfect for irrigating hanging baskets or pots in the middle of large groupings. *Garden coils*—self-retracting hoses—also extend your reach and take up little storage space. *Drip irrigation,* a micro-irrigation system that delivers water to individual containers through a network of thin tubes and emitters, is the ultimate time-saver; install an automatic timer to make it even easier to operate.

STEVEN GUNTHER

Dressing up a front entry, coleus and purple fountain grass fill these pots in Billy Spratlin's garden in Newport Beach, California.

with the flagstone paving. The simple plant combination looks fresh and contemporary against a sleek glass-brick backdrop. He also created a contained garden at the alley entrance, shown on the facing page. The rich combination of leaf textures is the story here; flowers are secondary. (The more gardenlike you want a potted-plant space to appear, the more important it is to focus on foliage plants.) Spratlin also used vertical space to help create a convincing garden by mounting pots of staghorn ferns and donkey tails on the wall near the gate.

Stairs

If outdoor stairs are wide enough, line them with potted plants. Nothing looks more cheerful. In most cases, simplicity is best—one red geranium in a terra-cotta pot per step, for instance. At the San Clemente, California, garden shown on page 238, however, the stairs were broad enough to accommodate a whole symphony of seasonal flowers.

Courtyards, patios, and decks

Like entries, outdoor living areas ought to be warm and welcoming. But because they're often paved, bricked, or tiled, they have a tendency to look cold and uninviting. Potted plants soften such spaces. You don't need many: A few splashes of flower color can make a patio feel like a garden.

Containers also define the boundaries of a space—where a patio edges up to a lawn, for instance.

STEVEN GUNTHER

LEFT: Clustered pots filled with scented geraniums, ornamental grasses, and succulents create the look of a garden bed on a paved surface. Design: Billy Spratlin.

BELOW: A single pot brings colorful blooms—purple heliotrope, red 'Dark Eyes' fuchsias, red and yellow tuberous begonias, red impatiens, and lobelias—to an entry.

DESIGN: Tina Dixon.

Side yards

A narrow walkway along the side of a house is often highly visible from indoors. "Green up" such an area with potted plants, and you can raise your shades to a pretty view. If space is really tight, hanging baskets are a good option.

Windows

Window boxes decorate outdoor spaces while framing the view from indoors. Many kinds—including wood, plastic, wrought iron, terracotta, and fiberglass—are available at garden and home supply stores. In all cases, make sure they are properly supported from the bottom, and anchor them to the wall as well. ◆

Pots on a lakeside deck near Seattle contain red geraniums, white marguerites, yellow euryops, purple and white petunias, feathery green parrot's beaks, deep blue lobelias, gray dusty millers, and ivy. DESIGN: Tina Dixon

In this water-wise garden, tomatoes are planted with delphiniums and roses, which have similar water needs. Mulch covers the root zones, and berms around the plants focus water over the roots.

Gardening in a dry year

How to plant—and keep existing plants healthy—if water is rationed this summer

By Jim McCausland • Illustrations by Linda Holt Ayriss

In much of the Northwest, last winter was the second driest in 100 years (only 1976–77 was worse), with rainfall running about half to two-thirds the normal amount. This past March, while standing in a lake bed that's drying out, Washington Governor Gary Locke declared a drought emergency; the state's Department of Ecology started gearing up for water-management programs this summer. Oregon was affected too; by mid-May, Portland had received only 18.77 inches of rain—far less than the nearly 30.54 inches considered normal for that time of year.

What does this insufficient rainfall really mean for Northwestern gardeners? Simply this: Though water supplies may be limited this summer, smart gardening practices will allow you have a great garden.

How to make your garden water-efficient

1. Group plants according to their water needs. Some plants need regular water to look their best; others, once established, do fine with irrigation every two to three weeks. Clustering plants that have the same water requirements allows you to apply sufficient water without waste.

2. When planting, water first and amend the soil. Dig the planting hole no deeper than the rootball, but make it two to three times as wide. Fill it with water and let it drain once before planting; otherwise, the adjacent soil will suck moisture from the rootball and the backfill soil around the plant. Amend the backfill with an equal amount of aged compost before refilling the hole. Such organic matter improves the soil's water-holding capacity.

3. Build berms around plants. Build a berm around the drip line of shrubs and perennials so that hose water soaks in directly over the root zone rather than spreading into the surrounding soil.

4. Mulch. Spread a 2- to 4-inch layer of organic mulch such as bark chips over the root zones of permanent plants. Take care not to pile mulch against the main stems, which can cause crown rot.

5. Eliminate weeds, which can compete with edibles and ornamentals for water and nutrients. Especially around annual flowers and vegetables, smother them beneath black plastic or landscape fabric and hoe them or handpick them regularly.

6. Reduce lawn watering. To stay green all summer, lawns need about

1 inch of water per week. If you apply the water faster than the soil can absorb it, runoff and waste result. Instead, irrigate at intervals, especially in heavy soils or on slopes: Turn on the sprinklers for about 10 minutes once a week, turn them off to let moisture soak in, then turn them on again for another few minutes.

Some gardeners cut back to 1 inch of water every two weeks; under this regime, lawns turn straw-colored and go semidormant but bounce back quickly after the weather cools in fall. A semidormant lawn is easily damaged by roughhousing kids, dogs, and traffic, though, so go easy on it until the grass greens up in autumn.

Also, mow high—about 2 to 2½ inches for bluegrass, 2½ to 3 inches for tall fescue. Keep mower blades sharp, since grass that gets shredded by dull blades uses more water. Don't overfertilize; too much nitrogen encourages the production of thirsty new growth.

7. Water when temperatures are cool. Irrigate in the early morning or evening when air is cool and still keeps evaporation to a minimum.

8. Be sure the sprinkler system is working properly. To make sure your sprinkler system is operating efficiently, watch it run. Check for wet spots or a constantly running water meter, which are signs of problems. Replace broken sprinklers or risers, and adjust sprinklers so they apply water only to lawns and not to

To keep a potted plant from drying out too quickly, nest the pot in a larger one. Fill the gap with sand.

adjacent paths or sidewalks. Unclog heads with a knife or piece of wire. While you're at it, repair leaky outdoor faucets; all those drips add up to buckets of wasted water.

9. Pay attention to container plantings. If you garden in containers, use glazed terra-cotta or plastic ones; unglazed terra-cotta loses moisture through its sides. Or nest smaller pots inside larger ones, as shown above.

10. Consider installing a drip-irrigation system. This is especially effective with potted plants, since

one drip emitter per pot usually supplies all the water the plant needs. For a simpler, less expensive solution for plants on flat ground, use soaker hoses—flat hoses perforated on the side—or porous ooze types. Run them among flowers and shrubs such as roses and along rows of vegetables or hedges, or coil them around trees.

Water-saving tips from a Northwest grower

Kristi O'Donnell, manager of Meerkerk Rhododendron Gardens, maintains 10 acres of ornamental trees, shrubs, bulbs, and perennials on Whidbey Island, Washington. The gardens usually get about the same amount of annual precipitation (25 inches) as California's Napa Valley—about one third less than Seattle gardens receive.

Although most rhododendrons are anything but drought-tolerant, O'Donnell has found ways to make them—and everything else in the garden—thrive with little water. She starts by using many of the planting principles outlined above.

In addition, the first summer after planting, she thoroughly soaks plant roots once every three weeks; however, if the garden has had at least ½ inch of rainfall per week, she provides no extra water. The second summer after planting, she irrigates plants only once a month or as needed when rainfall drops below ½ inch per week.

From the third summer on, the plants are not irrigated unless they show signs of water stress. O'Donnell checks the plants in the morning. If the leaves have lost their luster, (a sign on most plants that foliage will soon wilt), she applies water slowly to the root zone with an old-fashioned, hose-end rosette sprinkler.

Finally, O'Donnell never feeds rhododendrons with high-nitrogen fertilizer between the Fourth of July and winter because nitrogen promotes thirsty top growth, which may not harden off before winter. ◆

A dry year in a wet cycle?

Oregon State climatologist George Taylor thinks it's a mistake to worry too much about one dry winter. "Climates have wet and dry cycles," he told us, "and though such cycles typically last many years, each always includes years that don't fit the pattern. There are dry years in wet cycles, and wet years in dry cycles. I think this past winter is an example of a dry year in a wet cycle. Show me three dry years in a row, and I'll start wondering whether the pattern is changing."

This summer, the Northwest's aquifers seem "in pretty good shape," Taylor says. Northwesterners may have to endure some water rationing and a fire season that is pushed up by several weeks, but in a year or two, we could easily resume the wet cycle that makes gardening here so easy.

Falling waters

These three fountains start with great pots

By Sharon Cohoon

Pleasure isn't complicated. Omar Khayyám celebrated that fact in *The Rubáiyát* in his famous lines: "A Jug of Wine, a Loaf of Bread—and Thou / Beside me singing in the Wilderness." Softly burbling fountains, which bring so much pleasure to gardens, need not look complicated, either. Tons of boulders, miles of pipes, and truckloads of statuary are not necessary to create a beautiful fountain for a patio or courtyard. The timeless fountains pictured here all can be reduced to a few elements— a great pot, a pump, some pipe, and a spout to splash the water back into a reservoir. Their look is simple but elegant.

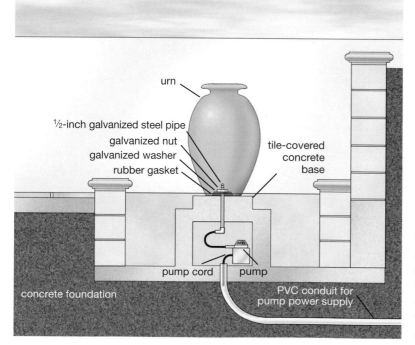

- urn
- ½-inch galvanized steel pipe
- galvanized nut
- galvanized washer
- rubber gasket
- tile-covered concrete base
- pump cord
- pump
- concrete foundation
- PVC conduit for pump power supply

Oil jar classic

This glazed blue oil-jar fountain sits on a tile-covered concrete pedestal framed by a 20-inch-deep pool in the Hollywood, California, garden of Laura Smith and Michael Doret. A submersible, recirculating pump housed within the pedestal (see drawing) pushes water through a galvanized pipe, which fits through a hole in the jar's bottom; the water then trickles over the jar's rim into the 3½-foot-square, concrete-lined pool. A rubber gasket and galvanized washer and nut hold the pipe in place and seal the hole. The pump runs on standard household current (120 volts) with a ground fault circuit interrupter (GFCI) outlet for safety. DESIGN: Frank Perrino, Woodland Hills, CA, and Laura Smith, Hollywood. Jar from Gladding, McBean (916/645-3341, ext. 202). Tiles from Los Angeles–based California Pottery and Tile Works (323/235-4151).

Urn of stone

Water spills from an antique French stone urn into a rectangular pool and a narrow, 18-inch-deep channel in this San Clemente, California, garden. A pump recirculates the water. The design, a joint effort of Larry Steinle, a Laguna Beach landscape architect, and Lew Whitney, chairman of Roger's Gardens in Corona del Mar, is the focal point of a garden corner that invites quiet contemplation. Scented geraniums and other foliage plants grow nearby.

STEVEN GUNTHER (2)

Big bowl fountain

This rough-textured pot would look as appropriate in an ancient village square in Italy, Greece, or Spain as it does in this garden owned by Robert and Carolyn Volk of San Marino, California. Water recirculates through a pump placed in a fiberglass pond liner beneath the pot; stones cover the liner. The pot is from Al's Garden Art in South El Monte, California. DESIGN: Mark Bartos, BEM Design Group, South Pasadena. ◆

PAUL BOUSQUET

IN THIS BRECKENRIDGE, COLORADO, plaster box, cherry red painted tongue, multicolored pansies, and hot pink sweet William thrive in the high-mountain sunshine. For more on these colorful but tough annuals, see page 252.

August

CHARLES MANN

the late-summer show
in Santa Fe

■ At higher elevations of New Mexico, perennial flower color doesn't reach its peak until late summer, but there's a big reward for the wait: The plants that bloom late often put on a long show. Santa Fe–based landscape designer Julia Berman (505/820-3314) combined a number of pretty but summer-tough perennials in this garden overlooking the Sangre de Cristo Mountains.

In the bed shown above, the tall lavender-blue flower sprays of Russian sage (*Perovskia*) appear in July and hang on until October. White coneflower (*Echinacea purpurea* 'White Lustre' and 'White Swan' are widely available) lasts just as long. Wine cups (*Callirhoe involucrata*), the small purplish red flowers spilling over the

brick edge, keep on blooming until frost stops them. Just behind the wine cups is magenta-flowered *Origanum laevigatum* 'Herrenhausen', an ornamental oregano; its colorful bracts last until frost, then the foliage turns burgundy. 'Herrenhausen' is not common; one source is Carroll Gardens in Maryland (800/638-6334 or www. carrollgardens.com).

All these perennials appreciate good drainage, which is why Berman planted them in a raised bed. Since the native soil is heavy in clay, she amended it by blending 1 part perlite, 1 part compost, and 4 parts soil. The lawn fronting the bed is blue grama—"the best of the warm-season native grasses," says Berman. — *Sharon Cohoon*

instant water gardens in pots

■ "Water, water everywhere" seems to be one of the new themes at Denver Botanic Gardens. Last year, Joe Tomocik, curator of aquatic plants, added 51 water gardens in containers, including the trio shown here. In front is white trumpet pitcher plant (*Sarracenia leucophylla*). In the large container behind, the yellow-and-red-flowered blooms of *Canna* 'Cleopatra' rise above blue flag iris (*I. versicolor*). Variegated common reed (*Phragmites australis*) thrives at left.

To follow Tomocik's lead, choose a container of 1- to 7-gallon capacity that has no drainage holes. Arrange plants (still in their nursery pots) in the container. Check the water level regularly and add water as needed. Plants will need occasional feeding with an aquatic plant fertilizer.

— *Colleen Smith*

PAUL BOUSQUET

shady island bed in Colorado Springs

■ Shaded by a canopy of stately old trees, this island bed is as refreshing as an iced latte on a hot August afternoon. The Green & White Garden, as it's called, is one of more than a dozen theme plantings in the Horticultural Art Society Demonstration

RANDY TATROE

Gardens in Colorado Springs. In this bed, the focus is on foliage. Hostas with chartreuse, bluish green, and green-and-white-variegated leaves are the mainstay. In contrast to the hostas' bold, broad-leafed forms are the lacy textures of ostrich fern (*Matteuccia struthiopteris*). The centerpiece of this bed is a concrete birdbath poised on a redwood pedestal, handcrafted by Timothy Spear of ForestEdge Gardens (719/495-9175 or www.forestedgegardens.org).

Elsewhere on the grounds, plantings devoted to annuals, perennials, herbs, roses, native plants, and other themes acquaint visitors with gardening opportunities in the Colorado Springs area. The Horticultural Art Society Demonstration Gardens are at the corner of Cache La Poudre Street and Glen Avenue in Monument Valley Park. Admission is free. The grounds are open daily during daylight hours in summer. For information on garden tours and classes, call (719) 475-0250.

—*Marcia Tatroe*

deerproof country garden

■ When you garden in deer country, growing vegetables can be a real challenge. To keep out high-jumping deer, many gardeners surround their crops with tall fences that have the look of a maximum-security prison. That's not the case in this enclosed garden in rural Redmond, Washington—it's surrounded by a graceful fence built by Harry Beal of Castle-n-Grounds, based in Duval, Washington.

The design of the 10-foot-tall fence is adapted from a pattern the owner saw in a past issue of *Sunset*. Along the bottom of the fence, closely spaced pickets keep out small animals. A grid of squares made of 1-by-1s forms a deer-proof barrier above the pickets. The fence is capped by 2-by-8s and beveled 2-by-6s. All wood is cedar, except for

the pressure-treated corner posts topped by finials. Deer have never jumped over the swinging picket gates at the front and back of the enclosure, says Beal.

Inside the 50-foot-square enclosure, vegetables that deer would otherwise devour grow along with flowers in raised mounds of compost and sand. — *Jim McCausland*

PLANT PROFILE

'Red Lake' currant

■ From mid-August well into September, clusters of glistening ruby berries dangle from the 'Red Lake' currant shrubs in Brigitte Suter's Homer, Alaska, garden. Suter eats the tart fruits fresh, bakes them into pies and muffins, and uses them to make jelly and a sweet dessert wine.

This hardy shrub is an exceptional performer in most of Alaska, and it also produces well throughout the Pacific Northwest and Rocky Mountains (*Sunset* climate zones 1–6). The plant reaches 5 feet high and as wide. Like other currants, it prefers full sun and evenly moist soil with good drainage. In early spring, Suter spreads compost and well-rotted cow manure around the plants. Two- and three-year-old stems tend to bear the most fruit, so cut stems older than three years to the ground during dormant season.

— *Steven R. Lorton*

a bountiful grape arbor
in Eugene

■ Each summer, four different varieties of table grapes bear a generous harvest of fruits on a rustic arbor in my Eugene, Oregon, garden. The bounty starts in mid-August, when 'Himrod' yields seedless golden grapes, which are crisp and amazingly sweet. Two weeks later, 'Lakemont' (the most prolific of my four vines in cool summers) bears clusters of seedless green grapes. Next comes 'Flame' (right) with large bunches of small, tasty red grapes. In mid-September, blue 'Concord' grapes ripen; these seeded fruits make excellent jam and juice, but I prefer to eat mine right off the vine.

Using salvaged Douglas fir trees that had fallen in a winter storm, landscape carpenter Art Peck built the 10- by 18-foot arbor over an existing patio. The 10-foot upright posts are strapped to 12-inch con-crete footings buried 9 inches in the ground. The cross-pieces are notched and bolted together.

At each corner of the arbor, I planted one bare-root vine in soil amended with compost and organic fertilizer. In their first summer, I allowed the vines to sprawl on the structure to encourage as much leaf growth as possible. The following winter, after pruning, I tied the main stems to the upright posts with hemp twine. By the third summer, the vines had formed a leafy canopy.

In January when the grapes are dormant, I prune each vine back to its own quadrant on the top of the structure. By the end of June, vigorous new growth covers the whole arbor, making a sun-dappled area for dining and entertaining.

— *Mary-Kate Mackey*

DEIDRA WALPOLE

urban eden

■ Though Freddie and Judy Schwartz live just a few blocks off Wilshire Boulevard in ultra-urban West Los Angeles, the nervous energy of the city disappears the minute you walk into their backyard. There, Asian serenity rules. "Exactly the mood we wanted," says Judy with satisfaction.

Encino-based garden designer Mark David Levine designed the garden. He started with trees—lots of them. Their sizes vary from dainty through midsize to stately—mayten, acacia, and blue Atlas cedar, for example. Their silhouettes range from soft and spilling, like Australian willow, to stiff and sharply outlined, like Japanese black pine. Foliage colors run the gamut of greens, with some plums and blues as well; leaf shapes also vary greatly.

Next, Levine repeated the shapes and colors of the trees in evergreen shrubs and ornamental grasses. The burgundy leaves of 'Little John' azaleas, for instance, are a miniature version of those on the 'Krauter Vesuvius' plum trees. Billowy *Miscanthus sinensis* 'Variegata' recalls the fountain shape of the willows.

Finally, Levine placed groups of these plants to make them look as if they had been planted by nature—one 8 feet up the slope, for instance, then another 10 feet up, on the opposite side of the stairs. "As if the same things had all reseeded several different places, as they tend to do in the wild," he says.

All these trees make this garden quiet, sheltered, and serene. "I feel very protected in this space," says Judy. "When I'm out here, the world is gone." — S.C.

cool summer beauties in Breckenridge

■ In the planter box pictured on page 246, cherry red painted tongue (*Salpiglossis sinuata*), multicolored pansies, and hot pink sweet William (*Dianthus barbatus*) thrive in the high-mountain sunshine of Breckenridge, Colorado, a resort town perched at 9,600 feet. These and other colorful but tough annuals dress up Main Street from June through September, tended by a small crew of city gardeners. On June 1, seedlings started in a greenhouse are planted, in high-quality potting soil, in the boxes and hanging baskets that line the central plaza, municipal parking lots, and storefronts. The flowers are fertilized weekly, watered if rain does not fall (baskets daily, boxes every other day), and deadheaded throughout the growing season. More annuals are tucked into median strips to beef up perennial plantings.

In mountain climates like that of Breckenridge, cool-season annuals such as Iceland poppies, pansies, petunias, snapdragons, and sweet William bloom all summer long, and they can even withstand an occasional frost or snow. Begonias, clarkias, cosmos, lobelias, nasturtiums, painted tongue, and schizanthus also enjoy mountain living, but they need to be covered if untimely freezes threaten. —*M.T.*

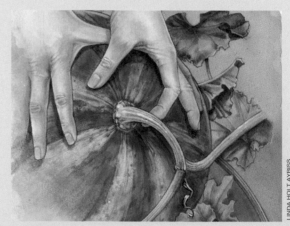

BACK TO BASICS

LINDA HOLT AYRISS

When to harvest melons.
Muskmelons *(cantaloupes):* After the skin has become netted, check vines daily. When the fruit is ready, it will "slip" (separate) from the vine with a gentle tug. ***Watermelons:*** Look for a withered tendril where the vine meets the melon, a creamy white belly (yellowish on seedless kinds), and dull skin. Listen for a hollow sound when you thump the fruit. — *J.M.*

PLANT PROFILE

a **rose-scented** apple

■ Eat a rose apple and kiss your lover, and your kisses will taste like roses—so say devotees of this East Indies fruit. *Syzygium jambos,* commonly known as rose apple, is a crisp-textured fruit like an apple with a distinct rose flavor. It can be eaten raw, diced into salads, used for jams and jellies, or distilled into rosewater.

Its best use, though, is as an ornamental tree. It stays small—about 20 feet—but has a wide, dense canopy of leathery, glossy, dark green leaves. New growth is mahogany red. Greenish white flowers have stamens that look like little shaving brushes; they're followed in late summer by ivory, egg-shaped fruits. Use single-trunk specimens as lawn trees and multi-trunk ones as hedges or screens.

Rose apple tolerates heavy clay and sandy soils. Despite its tropical origins, it can survive temperatures as cold as 28° for short periods. It prefers ample summer water, but once established is surprisingly resistant to drought. It is a light feeder. Eunice Messner (below), the Anaheim gardener whose crop we harvested for this photo,

CLAIRE CURRAN (2)

feeds her plant twice a year with steer manure topped with compost. Controlled-release granular fertilizer would also work.

Rose apple trees are sold at Atkins Nursery, Fallbrook (760/728-1610); Exotica Rare Fruit Nursery, Vista (760/724-9093); Mimosa Nursery, Los Angeles (323/722-4543); Pacific Tree Farms, Chula Vista (mail order also; 619/422-2400); and Papaya Tree Nursery, Granada Hills (818/363-3680). — *S.C.*

ARTHUR GRAY; TOP: THOMAS J. STORY

sugar kettle water garden

■ This tranquil setting in Scott Daigre's California garden is a mirror image of scenes he grew up with in Lafayette, Louisiana, where sugar mills dotted the landscape. Kettles used in the mills make great containers for water plants. "Every oak tree in Lafayette had one underneath it," he says. "And every kettle contained the same plants—water hyacinth and Louisiana iris, with a ring of cast-iron plants (*Aspidistra elatior*) around the outside."

"This is the easiest water garden imaginable," says Daigre. Just fill a large pot of glazed ceramic or metal (without a drain hole) with water, then add a pot or two of water plants. To set the plants at the proper water level, place them on bricks or overturned pots inside the kettle. — *S.C.*

THOMAS J. STORY

hand tool garage

■ You're out in the garden and you forgot to bring your trowel with you. So you stop what you're doing and dash back to the garage or tool shed to find it. Here's a better solution: Keep your hand tools in the garden where you need them, but store them in a converted mailbox.

The wooden mailbox pictured at left, which was purchased at a nursery, is mounted atop a 6-foot-tall 4-by-4 redwood post and secured with 3-inch-long lag screws. Tucked in a perennial bed within easy reach of a path, it keeps tools close by when spent blooms need clipping. (Another good place to put a tool garage is just outside the back door.)

Drill a hole in the top center of the post and in the bottom center of the mailbox of your choice. Set the mailbox on the post and screw it in place.

Anchoring the post in sand (you'll need a 10-pound bag) allows you to move it easily at season's end. Dig a hole 2 feet deep and 6 to 8 inches wide, pour a 6-inch layer of sand into the hole, position the post in the hole, then fill in around it with sand and tamp it down firmly. Otherwise, you can set the post in concrete.

— *Lauren Bonar Swezey*

STEVEN GUNTHER (2)

umbrella with a **view**

■ Roxy Engle liked the designs on the painted umbrellas Ken Parker sold at the Palm Springs street fair, but she had a better idea: Why not have him paint her umbrella with a mirror image of what she sees from the patio

of her home in the Coachella Valley? Fortunately, Parker is used to such requests.

In addition to the 30 standard designs he produces, he does lots of custom work, painting umbrella tops and bottoms with fade-proof billboard paint (guaranteed for three years). Prices range from $250 for a 4-foot-diameter umbrella to $500 for an 11-footer; prices also vary with detail of design. Smaller sizes are machine-washable. *Ken Parker Collection: (760) 320-6322.* — *S.C.*

CHARLES MANN

sculpture in the grass

■ Sometimes it's more fun when garden art takes you by surprise. In the sculpture garden at the Zaplin-Lampert Gallery in Santa Fe, for example, visitors round a curve in the path before they spot this jackrabbit by artist Mark Rossi; the cast-bronze sculpture is half hidden behind a clump of silver banner grass (*Miscanthus sac-* *chariflorus*). There are at least a dozen other sculptures in this garden, all placed with the same subtlety. Besides demonstrating how to display outdoor art effectively, the garden makes beautiful use of ornamental grasses. During the summer, the gallery, at 651 Canyon Road, is open daily. *(505) 982-6100.*

— *S.C.*

pacific northwest • checklist

PLANTING

☐ **COOL-SEASON CROPS.** Zones 4–7: Early in the month, set out beets, cabbage and other cole crops, carrots, lettuce, onions, peas, radishes, and spinach. Carrots, lettuce, peas, radishes, and spinach will be ready for harvest this fall. Beets, broccoli, cabbage, collards, kale, kohlrabi, leeks, and mustard can be harvested through winter and into spring.

☐ **LATE-SUMMER COLOR.** Zones 4–7: With a couple of months of warm weather ahead, you can still plant annual flowers for a good, long show—and you can take advantage of end-of-season prices at nurseries and garden centers. Impatiens, marigolds, and pelargoniums are good candidates. Also plant perennial asters and chrysanthemums.

MAINTENANCE

☐ **CARPENTER ANTS.** Watch for carpenter ant trails that lead to your house, especially if you use logs or other pieces of dead wood as natural garden sculptures. If you have an infestation, call a professional exterminating service for help.

☐ **DIVIDE PERENNIALS.** Dig up crowded clumps of perennials such as bearded irises and Oriental poppies. Use a spade to cut small clumps in half and large clumps into quarters. Immediately replant the divisions in amended soil.

☐ **HARVEST HERBS FOR DRYING.** Pick in the morning, after dew has evaporated, and dry herb leaves on a clean, horizontal piece of window screen. It should be in a cool, dry spot out of direct sunlight and where wind won't blow leaves away. When herbs are completely dry, store them in jars.

☐ **PROPAGATE SHRUBS.** Growing plants from cuttings gives you more plants just like their parents. Possibilities include azaleas, camellias, daphne, euonymus, holly, hydrangeas, magnolias, and rhododendrons. Snip 4- to 6-inch cuttings in the morning, strip off all but the top three or four leaves, and dip the cut ends into rooting hormone. Then insert cuttings into 4-inch pots filled with sterile soil; water well. Place the cuttings in bright light, out of direct sun, and keep them constantly moist. Before frost hits, move them into a greenhouse or sunroom. Next spring, you'll have rooted plants to transplant into 1-gallon cans or set out in the garden.

☐ **PRUNE CANE BERRIES.** On June-bearing plants (those that give you a single, large summer crop), remove all canes that produced fruit this season. On ever-bearing plants, cut back by half any canes that have already borne fruit. The part that has fruited will look withered.

☐ **WATER.** Deeply irrigate moisture-loving plants like rhododendrons twice a week. Spray the foliage too; it washes dust off leaves and helps stressed plants absorb water quickly. ◆

WHAT TO DO IN YOUR GARDEN IN AUGUST

PLANTING

☐ **BABY LETTUCE. Zones 7–9, 14–17:** Grow a miniature version of romaine or bibb lettuce that's just the right size for an individual salad. Heads grow quickly, so you can sow seeds successively a couple of weeks apart. 'Little Gem' romaine reaches 5 to 6 inches tall. 'Tom Thumb', an English heirloom bibb lettuce with tight, solid heads, grows 4 to 6 inches tall. Both are available from Shepherd's Garden Seeds (860/482-3638 or www.shepherdseeds.com).

☐ **SELECT PLANTS CAREFULLY.** Most nurseries pay careful attention to keeping plants moist, but even one missed watering can severely stress plants in summer. When shopping, check plants carefully. Unless a particular variety is going through summer dormancy, foliage should look perky and lush, without wilted or burned leaf edges. Don't buy leggy plants or ones that are overgrown and rootbound.

☐ **SHRUBS FOR SUMMER-TO-FALL BLOOM. Zones 7–9, 14–17:** For a show of flowers that lasts well into fall, try one of the following long-blooming shrubs or shrubby perennials: blue hibiscus, Brazilian plume flower, butterfly bush, Cape fuchsia, lavatera, oleander, plumbago, princess flower, and many of the salvias (check hardiness before shopping; not all plants are hardy in every zone).

Sunset
CLIMATE ZONES
☐ Mountain (1-2)
☐ Valley (7-9)
☐ Inland (14)
☐ Coastal (15-17)

DEBRA LAMBERT

☐ **SWEET PEAS. Zones 7–9, 14–17:** To get an early crop of flowers next spring, sow an early-flowering variety—such as knee-high 'Explorer' (crimson, light pink, navy blue, purple, rose, scarlet, and white) or 'Winter Elegance' (cream, lavender, pink, salmon, and white)—now. These types bloom when days are short. Seeds can be found at nurseries that sell seeds from Renee's Garden, or go to www.reneesgarden.com. Protect new growth from slugs and snails, and provide support for the tall vines.

MAINTENANCE

☐ **CUT FLOWERS.** Enjoy your homegrown cut flowers as long as possible by supplying them with a clean vase and a cut-flower food. Before arranging flowers, wash the vase in hot soapy water to eliminate bacteria and fungus. Then combine 1 cup lemon-lime soda (do not use diet drinks) with 3 cups water and ¼ teaspoon of household bleach. Fill the vase partway with the mix. Remove lower leaves from flower stems, recut stems under water, and arrange in the vase.

☐ **DEEP-WATER LARGE TREES AND SHRUBS.** Trees and shrubs may need a deep soaking now, even if they're watered by a sprinkler system (some systems don't run long enough for water to penetrate the soil deeply). Use a deep-root irrigator or a regular hose set to deliver water slowly into a basin around the plant. Or lay a soaker hose—one that emits low-flow water though holes (or through porous sides) along its length—around the plant within its drip line. Run the water until the soil is soaked to a depth of 12 to 18 inches (use the deeper amount for larger shrubs and trees) under the drip line of the plant. Check moisture penetration by digging down with a trowel.

☐ **PROTECT HOUSEPLANTS.** Treat infestations of spider mites and scale with insecticidal soap or horticultural oil. ◆

southern california · checklist

PLANTING

☐ **ANNUALS AND BIENNIALS.** Sow seeds of Iceland poppies, snapdragons, stock, sweet peas, and other annuals in flats. Canterbury bells, foxglove, hollyhocks, verbascum, and other biennials should be started now too.

☐ **BULBS.** Freesia, ixia, sparaxis, watsonia, and other South African bulbs, which naturalize beautifully in our climate, start showing up in nurseries this month. Shop early for best selection; plant immediately. Rhizomes of bearded iris, another great naturalizer, will show up soon too, and should also be planted immediately.

☐ **FINAL SUMMER CROPS.** Coastal (zones 22–24), inland (zones 18–21), and low-desert (zone 13) gardeners can sow a final crop of beans and corn. Coastal gardeners can also set out transplants of eggplant, pepper, squash, and tomatoes for a fall harvest.

☐ **WINTER CROPS.** Coastal, inland, and high-desert (zone 11) gardeners can start cool-season vegetable seeds in flats. In six to eight weeks, the seedlings will be ready to transplant into the garden. Possibilities include broccoli, brussels sprouts, cabbage, cauliflower, collards, kale, Oriental greens, peas, spinach, and Swiss chard. Direct-sow beet, carrot, and turnip seeds, or start them in peat pots to transplant later into garden soil, pot and all.

Sunset
CLIMATE ZONES
1-3 7-9 11 13 14-24

DEBRA LAMBERT

MAINTENANCE

☐ **FERTILIZE.** Continue feeding warm-season annuals and vegetables every two to four weeks. Feed warm-season lawns like Bermuda, St. Augustine, and zoysia.

☐ **PRUNE TO SHAPE.** Tidy up any plants with branches that are diseased, leggy, tangled, or out of balance, but avoid severe pruning.

☐ **REMOVE WATERSPROUTS AND SUCKERS.** Stone-fruit trees and citrus may put out watersprouts—rampantly growing shoots—this time of year. Prune shoots flush with branch or part of trunk where they sprouted. Wisteria may put out suckers below the graft. Pull them off to keep them from overgrowing grafted plant.

☐ **WATER.** By late summer, shade trees appreciate a slow, deep soak. Repeat irrigation monthly as long as weather remains warm. Also give established shrubs and perennials a deep soak. Shallow-rooted citrus and avocado need water more frequently—once a week inland, every other week along the coast. Container plants dry out rapidly now; daily soakings may be necessary.

DISEASE CONTROL

☐ **CONTROL FIREBLIGHT.** This bacterial disease makes the foliage of cotoneaster, evergreen pear, pyracanthas, toyon, and other susceptible plants look as if it has been scorched by fire. To control it, prune out and discard diseased twigs and branches. Make cuts 4 to 6 inches below any visible damage on small branches and 12 or more inches below on large branches. To keep the disease from spreading, disinfect tools between cuts with a solution of 1 part bleach to 9 parts water.

☐ **CONTROL LAWN PROBLEMS.** Brown patches in cool-season lawns could indicate a fungal disease. Treat affected areas with fungicide, following label directions carefully. ◆

WHAT TO DO IN YOUR GARDEN IN AUGUST

PLANTING

☐ GROUND COVERS. Consider replacing heat-stressed lawns on south-facing hillsides and along sidewalks and driveways with heat-tolerant ground covers. Creeping junipers, daylilies, *Persicaria affinis,* rock cotoneasters, 'Silver Carpet' lamb's ears, snow-in-summer, woolly thyme, and yarrows are good candidates for hot spots where grass does poorly.

☐ LAWNS. New lawns of cool-season grasses (bluegrass, creeping bent, crested wheatgrass, and fescues) should be seeded in mid- to late August (July at higher elevations). Prepare the site by tilling into the soil 1 to 3 cubic yards of compost per 1,000 square feet and raking the surface smooth. After seeding, water frequently until the seeds germinate.

MAINTENANCE

☐ CARE FOR ANNUAL FLOWERS. Cut off dead flowers daily to encourage blooming. If heat causes annuals to stop producing flowers, cut the plants back by half and continue to water and fertilize; most kinds will perk up and start blooming again when the weather cools and the days shorten.

☐ CUT BACK PERENNIALS. When summer-flowering perennials such as bellflowers, geraniums, lychnis, Shasta daisies, and spiderworts finish blooming, cut back their stems to the rosettes of new foliage at the bases of the plants.

☐ HARVEST FLOWERS FOR DRYING. Cut everlasting flowers for fall arrangements. Baby's breath, globe amaranth, immortelles, statice, and strawflowers should be harvested just before they open fully. Strip off the leaves, bind the bunches with rubber bands, and hang them upside down in a basement, garage, or other cool, dark place.

☐ HARVEST POTATOES. Dig new potatoes when the plants flower. Harvest the main crop after the foliage turns brown, or leave the spuds underground until fall.

☐ START HARDENING-OFF PLANTS. New growth this late in the season is highly susceptible to early frost damage. To discourage such growth, stop fertilizing perennials, roses, shrubs, and trees by midmonth. Gradually cut back on irrigation to harden off plants for winter.

☐ TRANSPLANT PEONIES. This is the best time to divide established plants. Cut the clump into large sections and replant the divisions in amended soil at the depth at which the mother plant grew.

PEST CONTROL

☐ ASTER YELLOWS. Stunted, twisted growth and oddly distorted flowers are the symptoms of aster yellows, a disease that often shows up in midsummer, infecting not only asters but also many other ornamental plants. Sucking insects, primarily leafhoppers, transmit this disease; pull up and discard affected plants to stop its spread.

☐ GERANIUM BUDWORMS. Missing or chewed flowers on geraniums and petunias are usually the work of these small caterpillars. Handpick the pests early in the morning or spray *Bacillus thuringiensis* to kill them. Ivy geraniums are seldom bothered by budworms. — *M.T.* ◆

WHAT TO DO IN YOUR GARDEN IN AUGUST

PLANTING

☐ **PLANT COOL-SEASON VEGETABLES.** Zones 1–3: Sow seeds of lettuce, peas, short-season beans, and spinach. Set out seedlings of broccoli and cauliflower for fall harvest. Zone 10 (Albuquerque): Early in the month, sow seeds of beans, cabbage family members, corn, cucumbers, potatoes, spinach, squash, and Swiss chard; or set out seedlings of those crops at month's end. Zone 11 (Las Vegas): Sow seeds of beets, broccoli, cabbage, carrots, cauliflower, radishes, and spinach for fall harvest. Zones 12–13 (Tucson, Phoenix): Sow beans, carrots, corn, and summer squash for fall harvest.

☐ **SOW WILDFLOWERS.** Zones 1–3, 10: Sow seeds of annual and perennial wildflowers now for bloom next spring. Try bachelor's buttons, blue flax, coreopsis, Mexican hat, poppies, prairie asters, and Rocky Mountain penstemons. Cultivate soil lightly, broadcast seeds, then cover with ¼ to ½ inch of ground bark or other organic mulch.

MAINTENANCE

☐ **CARE FOR ROSES.** Zones 1–3, 10: Discontinue feeding and pruning plants to avoid stimulating tender new growth that might be damaged by early frost. Zones 11–13: To prepare plants for strong fall bloom, feed now with complete fertilizer. If leaves show signs of chlorosis (yellow leaves and green veins), apply iron chelate.

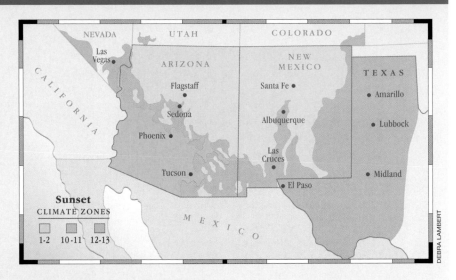

Sunset CLIMATE ZONES
1-2   10-11   12-13

☐ **FEED CITRUS.** Apply a complete fertilizer to all citrus this month, following instructions on the package. Thoroughly soak the soil before you apply the fertilizer and water immediately after. This late-summer feeding is essential for navel oranges and mandarins (or tangerines).

☐ **FERTILIZE SHRUBS.** Zones 11–13: Apply a half-strength dose of complete fertilizer to summer- and fall-blooming shrubs; water it in thoroughly. Do not feed desert shrubs such as black dalea and Texas ranger.

☐ **WATER.** Take care not to overwater desert shrubs—many are susceptible to root rot if given too much water in hot weather. For other shrubs and herbaceous plants, continue to water weekly, using a drip system, a soaker hose, or a standard hose running slowly into basins built around plants.

CONTROL PESTS

☐ **OLEANDER GALL.** Cut out affected parts and throw them away. Between cuts, disinfect pruning shears in a bleach solution (1 part bleach to 10 parts water).

☐ **SOUTHWESTERN CORN BORERS.** Translucent, skeletonized patches appearing on corn leaves are usually the work of corn borer larvae. Spray plants, especially where leaves join the stalk, with *Bacillus thuringiensis*.

— *Mary Irish* ◆

raised bed
rewards

From Alaska to Colorado, they solve gardening problems across the West

By Jim McCausland

■ We haven't yet met a raised-bed gardener who would go back to flat-earth gardening. There are just too many advantages to raised beds. Filled with organically rich soil, they warm up quickly in spring, provide perfect drainage, and often yield heavier crops of vegetables. They make it possible to garden over heavy clay soil or rock-solid caliche. They can be underlined with hardware cloth to foil gophers and moles. On sloping terrain, they can create level terraces to extend the cultivated area.

In most cases, you can turn any plot of ground into a fairly substantial raised-bed garden—in little time and for a modest cost. For less than $500, including lumber, soil, and gravel for paths between the beds, we made five raised beds on a Saturday.

Because you reach in to plant and maintain most raised beds, the center of each bed should be no more than an arm's length from the edge, making the width around 4 feet. Eight to 10 feet is a good length. The height should be at least 10 inches; for wheelchair gardening, which is facilitated by raised beds, make the height about 24 inches.

Framing and filling the beds

Wood is used to frame most raised beds. Since untreated wood rots fairly quickly where it contacts soil, most people use rot-resistant cedar or redwood, pressure-treated lumber, creosote-treated railroad ties, or composite lumber (such as TimberTech and Trex) made from recycled wood and plastic. Studies suggest that pressure-treated

NORM PLATE

Homer, AK. Because summer high temperatures average only 68° in this part of Alaska, Gabriela Husmann and Konrad Schaad needed beds that would warm up quickly in spring and get flowers off to a faster start than in flat ground. They made 2-foot-tall beds with large rocks that soak up heat during the day and radiate it into the soil at night. The upper bed is mostly for perennials, including red-and-white columbines, purple blue campanulas, and tall blue delphiniums fronted by yellow and orange Iceland poppies. The lower bed holds mostly annuals, including yellow and orange nemesias, and pink godetias.

Port Orchard, WA. Kirk and Teri Doughty wanted to make room for a productive vegetable garden without losing the lawn their children love to play on. Landscaper David Tubberville helped them develop a series of raised beds that step down the slope. All are made from pressure-treated 4-by-6s. The timbers are held together—and staked into the ground—with lengths of rebar pounded through ½-inch holes drilled into the ends of each piece. Posts support overhead trellises that will eventually carry fruit like grapes and kiwis. In summer, twine strung between posts supports vining crops like pole beans.

lumber is safe for raised vegetable beds, but if you're concerned about the chemicals used in treated lumber or creosote-treated railroad ties, you can opt for untreated or composite lumber.

Large timbers were used to frame many of the beds pictured on these pages. You can build smaller-scale beds with sides made from two 2-by-5s or 2-by-6s stacked on top of each other. (Don't try to make sides out of single 2-by-10s or 2-by-12s; such extrawide boards will warp and pull apart at the corners.)

Interlocking concrete blocks and dry-stacked rocks and flagstones are also commonly used to form beds. If you use stones, place the largest ones at the bottom.

You can fill a bed with amended native soil or imported topsoil. In most instances, you can improve native soil by digging in a 4- to 6-inch layer of compost, well-aged manure, or other organic material before planting. If your native soil is too hard or rocky to amend easily, bring in topsoil that contains at least one-third organic matter by volume. Since soil settles over time and organic matter decomposes, you'll need to replenish the soil every spring before planting.

Colorado Springs. Peggy Marshall designed these 24-inch-tall beds, flanking a surface of brick pavers, so they could be reached easily by someone in a wheelchair. The sides of the beds are made from pressure-treated 6- by-6-inch timbers capped by 2-by-8s, which are wide enough to sit on. Marshall placed rock on the bottom of the beds, topped by a layer of gravel, a layer of sand, and 18 inches of light potting soil. She grows low or trailing annuals like alyssum, lobelias, and petunias along the edges of the beds, with taller cosmos, poppies, and zinnias behind.

Kenmore, WA. Faced with a blackberry-covered slope that dropped away on two sides, Stephanie Brooks needed level ground for gardening. With help from her father, Robert Thomas, she outlined a 24- by 32-foot space with railroad ties, then put in a 4-foot wall made from pressure-treated timbers to divide it into upper and lower gardens. The railroad ties in the lower garden are capped with a top constructed of three 2-by-2s and two 2-by-4s. Brooks grows flowers, basil, beans, cucumbers, lettuce, onions, and peppers, plus everbearing raspberries and strawberries: "We sit and eat to our heart's content." She fertilizes with composted steer manure and alfalfa pellets.

West Linn, OR. Nancy and Jim DeClark's vegetable garden is the picture of order. Each 4- by 8-foot bed is outlined with landscaping timbers and amended with compost and rotted manure to make the soil easy to work. A 2-inch layer of crushed gravel covers the paths between the beds, so feet stay free of mud during western Oregon's frequent rains. Sweet peas are trained up wire attached to a wooden A-frame. ◆

Frost-hardy fuchsias

They sail through the Northwest's cold winters with a minimum of fuss

By Jim McCausland

When growers at Joy Creek Nursery in Scappoose, Oregon (*Sunset* climate zone 6), started winter hardiness trials on 140 hybrid fuchsia varieties, they weren't prepared for the results: After three winters—including one with temperatures dipping to 10°—they lost only two plants. The news was greeted with delight but not surprise at the Northwest Fuchsia Society. Their own list of hardy fuchsia varieties runs to four single-spaced pages, and they add to it regularly.

Heronswood Nursery in Kingston, Washington, has had similar experiences: In its woodland gardens, fuchsias compete successfully with ferns and huckleberries for the dappled light that filters through the tall Douglas firs above.

Increasing plant hardiness

The secret to getting them to over-winter? Protecting their roots. Plants that would die in containers, which freeze from the sides as well as the top, can last for years in the ground.

While fuchsias won't tolerate frozen roots, they have many traits that see them through surprisingly cold weather. Good genes help: Some of the fuchsias are native to the cloud forests and chilly, damp coasts of South America, where they are adapted to cool, wet weather.

You see this adaptation in the way hybrids react to cold—when temperatures start to approach freezing, the plants drop their leaves. Below freezing, they lose their tops well before their roots are damaged. And, since

FAR LEFT: *Fuchsia magellanica* can reach 6½ feet tall in the Northwest.

CENTER: 'Tom Thumb' has flared sepals that give its flowers the look of birds in flight.

BELOW RIGHT: *F. magellanica* 'Alba' covers itself with pale pink flowers.

Planting fuchsias in woodland settings helps improve hardiness, too; tree canopies provide several degrees of frost protection. When an exceptionally hard winter comes along, give your fuchsias an extra edge by covering their root zones with a 4-inch layer of leaves, straw, or other organic mulch.

If fuchsia tops freeze back, don't cut them out until new growth starts in spring.

The hardiest types

A couple of principles help determine which of the many fuchsias available are the hardiest ones.

• Single-flowered fuchsias are usually more cold-tolerant than doubles, and singles are more prolific bloomers. (But if you're crazy about doubles, try 'Voodoo', 'Garden News', and 'Garden Week'.)

• Most hybrid fuchsias usually have hardy *Fuchsia magellanica* or *F. regia reitzii* ancestry.

When you shop for fuchsias, ask for hardy varieties. Many nurseries and mail-order catalogs keep lists of robust hybrids and push them for landscape planting. Cold-tolerant bedding fuchsias and hybrids generally fall under *F. magellanica*.

These varieties have red or purple flowers and grow mostly into large, fountain-like shrubs. *F. m.* 'Riccartonii' is among the toughest (it has even naturalized in Ireland, and overwinters in Stockholm, Sweden). *F. m.* 'Alba' has white flowers that develop a pink blush in sun; *F. m.* 'Variegata' and *F. m.* 'Aurea' are grown for variegated and golden green foliage, respectively, and do best in shade.

BEDDING FUCHSIAS, or miniatures, are often small-flowered, and include some that fit well into mixed perennial borders. Try ones like 'Dainty Angel's Earrings', 'Little Darling', 'Papoose', and 'Tom Thumb'.

HARDY HYBRIDS, the newsmakers, include ones with red flowers like 'Cardinal' and 'Flash', red-and-whites like 'Jingle Bells' and 'Santa Claus', and then 'June Bride' (deep pink), 'Surprise' (pink and purple), 'Tessie' (pink and purple), and 'Voltaire' (red and purple). ◆

fuchsias flower on new growth, they can regrow and bloom the following season, even when tops die back.

You can help fuchsias to gain even more hardiness by planting them below soil level. Dig a planting hole that's deep enough so the plant's crown (where trunk meets roots) will sit about 5 inches below the surrounding soil. Fill in around the rootball with soil, but do not cover the top of the rootball. Instead, allow soil, leaves, and dust to naturally fill in the depression around the trunk over time. Fibrous roots will grow into it, and the plant will thrive. The basin will also catch extra water—a good thing for such a moisture-loving plant. Be sure, however, that the soil has good drainage, because fuchsias don't like wet feet.

Sources

Several mail-order nurseries have excellent hardy fuchsia lists. They include Joy Creek Nursery (503/543-7474 or www.joycreek.com), Delta Farm & Nursery (541/485-2992 or www.deltafarm.com), and Flower World (425/481-7565). Heronswood Nursery (360/297-4172 or www.heronswood.com) lists only about 20 plants in its catalog, but all are hardy and represent the best of more than 100 tested in its gardens over many years.

For a look at the Northwest Fuchsia Society's short list of hardy fuchsias, which covers more than 100 varieties, go to our website (www.sunset.com/garden/fuchsias.html). A more comprehensive list is available to members of the Northwest Fuchsia Society; you can join by sending $12 to NWFS, PO Box 33071, Seattle, WA 98133-0071.

THOMAS J. STORY (2)

FROM LEFT TO RIGHT: General-purpose trowel by Fiskars with stainless steel blade ($21.50, Denman & Company); crevice trowel with forged-steel blade by Red Pig ($14.50, Denman); transplanting trowel with aluminum blade by Corona Clipper ($4.99, Corona Clipper); folding stainless steel trowel comes with a leather belt pouch ($27, Smith & Hawken).

Trowel savvy

A buyer's guide to the most-used garden tool

By Jim McCausland

The trowel is practically the only tool you need for gardening in containers and raised beds, and for transplanting annuals, perennials, and vegetables. Considering how indispensable it is, it makes sense to spend a little time shopping for a trowel that best meets your particular needs.

Three main types

General-purpose trowels typically have 3- to 4-inch-wide blades. If you own only one trowel, this is the type to get.

Transplanting trowels have blades about 1½ to 3 inches wide. Most of these have inch/centimeter markings on their blades to help you plant bulbs or seeds at the recommended depths.

Crevice trowels have the narrowest blades, about 1¼ inches wide. They're designed for work among the crannies of rock gardens.

Blade materials

Trowels with stamped-steel blades ($1 to $5 and up) usually have short life spans. Rivets hold the blade to the tang (the shaft that joins the blade to a plastic or wood handle), but rivets aren't as durable as good welds. Avoid these trowels, except for use as scoops for potting soil.

High-carbon steel blades ($10 to $20) are strong and can last for decades. The steel may be forged, so it's less likely to bend under stress, or it is tempered (heat-treated) to make it tougher and better at holding a sharp edge. (If a tool is forged,

it's safe to assume that it's tempered as well.) High-carbon steel is easy to sharpen but prone to rust.

Stainless steel blades ($10 to $40) are slow to rust. They're also easy to clean, since soil doesn't stick to this steel. Nearly always forged and tempered, stainless steel blades hold an edge well.

Rustproof aluminum blades ($5 to $10) are perfect for work with potting soil, but they have trouble penetrating hard garden soil and are prone to chipping in rocky soil. Also, aluminum blades become dull quickly and don't hold an edge long.

Handles

Most trowels come with handles made of plastic or wood; both are comfortable, but wood is more durable. One-piece aluminum or steel trowels often have handles covered with soft rubber or plastic grips.

Sources

Most garden centers and some hardware stores sell trowels. For the best selection, try one of these mail-order specialists: Corona Clipper (www. coronaclipper.com); Denman & Company (714/639-8106); Gardener's Supply Company (800/863-1700); Kinsman Company (800/733-4146); Smith & Hawken (800/776-3336). ◆

Right-angle trowel with bicycle grip by Red Pig ($24, Denman) is ergonomically designed.

Perfuming the garden

Scented plants can enhance outdoor rooms, if you put them where you'll enjoy them most

By Sharon Cohoon

Cleopatra would never have set off to woo Mark Anthony armed with a single spritz of attar of roses. She would have used enough perfume to envelop herself in a cloud of scent. If we want our gardens to exude romance, we need to think like Cleo. A single sweetly scented rose—even one named 'Fragrant Cloud'—won't suffice; instead, plant enough perfume producers to permeate the garden with seductive scent.

Start by adding fragrant plants to the garden's energy hubs—decks, pool and spa areas, dining alcoves, gazebos, and anywhere else people naturally congregate. (Think of them as the equivalent of pulse points.) Then, lead your visitors by the nose to more hidden parts of the garden. Add jewel mint of Corsica or creeping thyme—plants that release their scent when trod upon—between a path's steppingstones, and, if you have room, put a lemon or orange tree or a mock orange (*Philadelphus*) beside the path. Or plant chocolate cosmos and chocolate daisies near a garden bench where you'd like visitors to stop and sit.

Ideally, when you've finished, the garden will smell as

intriguing as an expensive perfume. The top note will be floral—jasmine, honeysuckle, rose. The middle register will be spicy, such as the vanilla of heliotrope or the clove of dianthus. Finally, rumbling underneath will be the earthy bass tones that give perfumes their vigor, like artemisia, sage, and santolina.

Just as a woman switches from a light-hearted daytime perfume to a moody swooner at night, the garden can change character after dusk. Lavender is perfect for a summer afternoon, but a moonlit evening calls for the heady scent of gardenia or tuberose.

Where to locate fragrant plants

Does your backyard paradise lack the seduction of perfume? If so, following are ideas on where to add fragrant plants, plus a list of what is available in nurseries now.

FRONT ENTRY. Give guests a hint of what to expect from your garden the minute they approach the front door. Train a fragrant climbing rose over a pergola at the garden gate. Fill some of the containers in your entry with

LEFT: Several varieties of hyssop (*Agastache*) mingle beside a hammock in Santa Fe. RIGHT: Fragrant lavenders grow near prime areas for outdoor living—along the pathway, near the swimming pool and patio—in the Montecito, California, garden of Lucinda Lester, Lucinda Lester Designs. Blossoms and fruits on the lemon trees nearby scent the air with sweet overtones.

scented bedding plants like dianthus or stock, aromatic evergreens like rosemary and lavender, or fragrant shrubs like gardenia. Let a scented vine such as star jasmine frame the porch on an "eyebrow" of wire, as Constance Turner did at her home in Coronado, California (see the facing page). Train another over the garage door.

OUTDOOR SITTING AREAS. Let a fragrant rose such as 'Don Juan', 'New Dawn', or 'Zephirine Drouhin' cover the pergola that shades the entertainment patio. Train honeysuckle vine to twine around a trellis that serves as a privacy screen or around a fence enclosing the pool area. Plant sweet smelling shrubs such as sweet olive or Mexican orange (*Choisya ternata*) near a gazebo.

In an open courtyard, add fragrant annuals and perennials in pots. Put a plant with aromatic foliage, such as lemon verbena or rose-scented geranium, near a garden bench.

SECRET GARDENS. Don't forget your personal space—a lounge chair hidden by shrubbery where you relax in the late afternoon. Plant something there you especially en-

joy. At the Santa Fe garden shown on page 267, for instance, a hammock floats above several varieties of hyssop. Not only are the homeowners delighted by the plants' licorice scent, they also like observing the bees, butterflies, and hummingbirds attracted by the flowers.

Be sure to include in your fragrance palette blossoms that don't release their scent until evening, especially in the areas of the garden you most frequent after dark. Place pots of tuberose near the spa, for instance, or a colony of woodland tobacco (*Nicotiana sylvestris*) close to your dining deck. Since the majority of night-scented blossoms have white flowers, these plants also light up the landscape at night. One caveat: Some people find certain night-bloomers too intense, especially when situated close enough to the house for the scent to drift indoors. Night jessamine (*Cestrum nocturnum*) is the most notable example.

Not every inch of the garden needs to be fragrant, of course, but a waft or two of fragrance from the right plants in the right places can turn a garden from ordinary to enchanting.

LEFT: Lemon-scented 'Prince Rupert' geranium forms a shrubby mound of aromatic foliage beside a garden bench.
RIGHT: Sweetly fragrant white flowers of star jasmine (*Trachelospermum jasminoides*) bloom in spring.

Perfumed plants

Except where noted, the plants listed below grow in all *Sunset* climate zones.

Annuals

Common heliotrope (*Heliotropium arborescens*). Look for the white-flowered form. Not as showy as the popular dark violet version, but it's more fragrant.

Moonflower (*Ipomoea alba*). Zones 15–17, 23–24.

Nicotiana alata. Look for *N. a.* 'Grandiflora' or trust your nose (some of the hybrids are not fragrant).

Stock (*Matthiola incana*). Many kinds bear fragrant flowers.

Woodland tobacco (*Nicotiana sylvestris*). Long, tubular white flowers are intensely fragrant.

Perennials

Chocolate cosmos (*Cosmos atrosanguineus*). Zones 4–9, 14–24.

Chocolate flower (*Berlandiera lyrata*). Zones 10–13, 18–23.

Lavender (*Lavandula*). English lavender (*L. angustifolia*), zones 2–24; French lavender (*L. dentata*), zones 8–9, 12–24; sweet lavender (*L. x heterophylla*), zones 8–9, 12–24; 'Provence' and similar types (*L. x intermedia*), zones 4–24; and 'Goodwin Creek Grey', zones 8–9, 12–24.

Pinks (*Dianthus*). Many hybrids have lost their delightful clove scent, but others are reliably fragrant. These include cheddar pinks (*D. gratianopolitanus*); cottage pinks (*D. plumarius*), zones 1–24; and maiden pinks (*D. deltoides*), zones 1–24.

Fragrant foliage

Hyssop, hummingbird mint (*Agastache*). Zones vary by species.

Lemon verbena (*Aloysia triphylla*). Zones 9–10, 12–24.

Rosemary (*Rosmarinus officinalis*). Zones 4–24.

Scented geraniums (*Pelargonium*). Of the many varieties, those with scents of rose, lemon, and peppermint are the most fragrant.

Bulbs

Lilies. Madonna lily (*L. candidum*), zones 1–9, 14–24; 'Stargazer', 'Casablanca', and other Oriental hybrids, zones 1–9, 14–24.

Tuberose (*Polianthes tuberosa*). Zones 7–9, 14–24. Can be treated as an annual.

Vines

Angel-wing jasmine (*Jasminum laurifolium nitidum*). Evergreen or semievergreen. Zones 12, 16, 19–24.

Japanese honeysuckle (*Lonicera japonica*). Evergreen or deciduous. Zones 1–24.

Madagascar jasmine (*Stephanotis floribunda*). Zones 23–24.

Poet's jasmine (*J. officinale*). Semievergreen or deciduous. Zones 5–9, 12–24.

Shrubs

Gardenia. All kinds are fragrant. Zones vary by species.

Mexican orange (*Choisya ternata*). Zones 6–9, 14–24.

Mock orange (*Philadelphus*). Most kinds are fragrant, especially sweet mock orange (*P. coronarius*), all zones; *P. x lemoinei,* zones 2–17; and *P. x virginalis,* zones 1–17.

Roses. Many old roses are fragrant, including the damasks, Bourbons, hybrid perpetuals, Chinas, and rugosas, as are many David Austin shrub roses.

Star jasmine (*Trachelospermum jasminoides*). Evergreen (can also be grown as a ground cover or spreading shrub) with white, star-shaped flowers. Zones 8–24, H1, H2.

Sweet olive (*Osmanthus fragrans*). Zones 8–9, 12–24.

Summersweet (*Clethra alnifolia*). Zones 1–6. ◆

Drip watering for containers

This simple system is the easiest, most efficient way to water pots

By Tom Bressan
Photographs by Thomas J. Story

Container plants are like family pets: the more attention you give them, the better they behave. But it's not always easy to give plants the care they need, particularly when hot or dry weather means daily watering. A simple, automated drip-irrigation system, which applies water slowly and directly to roots, frees you from hand-watering and helps eliminate harmful fluctuations in soil moisture. Plants respond by growing full and lush. And you'll never have to drag around another hose.

How to get started

The system must have a backflow prevention device, which keeps irrigation water

A 2- to 4-gallon-per-hour mister sprays the soil and the foliage. Bonsai wire keeps mister head pointing in the right direction.

Installing a basic drip system

■ System components include a backflow prevention device—here, an automatic antisiphon valve (A)—a filter (B), a pressure regulator (C), and a compression fitting (D). The automatic controller (E) operates the system. A T fitting above the shutoff valve (F) accommodates a hose bibb.

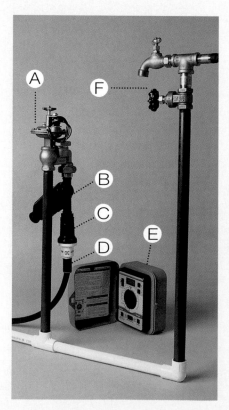

■ A single emitter provides adequate water for pots up to 10 inches wide. An elbow fitting takes the tubing over the pot edge at a 90° angle; a U stake keeps the tubing and emitter in place.

■ Here, two emitters are attached to a T fitting. This configuration will water medium-size pots up to 15 inches wide. A notched stake holds the tubing in position.

from flowing back into the household water lines; a filter, to trap particles that could clog emitters; a pressure regulator, which lowers the incoming water pressure to a level the drip system can tolerate; and a compression fitting, to connect the tubing to the pressure regulator.

The simplest way to hook up a drip system is to connect it to an existing hose bibb (with a Y attachment so you can still attach a hose). You can operate the system manually or you can add a battery-operated timer.

The other option is to connect directly to the water line using an automatic valve. This makes the most sense if you already have an automatic controller (it's usually simple to add another valve) or you plan to install other systems that will run off the same controller.

Concealing the water lines

To get water out to the containers, use either $\frac{3}{8}$- or $\frac{1}{2}$-inch black polyethylene tubing for the main line. Hide it anywhere it won't be seen. Keep $\frac{1}{2}$-inch tubing shorter than 200 feet and $\frac{3}{8}$-inch lines shorter than 100 feet, since longer lines can cause uneven water distribution.

Next, run $\frac{1}{4}$-inch microtubing into the pots (vinyl is preferable to polyethylene, since it's more flexible). You can run it over the lip of a pot or up through the drainage hole (but then the pot can't easily be moved). For hanging baskets, run microtubing up posts, under eaves, or in the joint between two walls. To prevent backflow on hanging baskets, leave 2 inches between emitters and foliage or soil, or place an atmospheric vacuum breaker on the line 6 inches above the highest emitter.

How many emitters?

All containers running off the same valve will be watered for the same amount of time, but they may not need the same amount of water. To compensate, set up the system for the smaller pots, then put extra emitters in larger ones.

Use one $\frac{1}{2}$-gallon-per-hour (gph) emitter for a pot up to 10 inches wide and two $\frac{1}{2}$-gph emitters on a T fitting for medium-size pots up to 15 inches wide. For larger containers, make a ring of emitters—four $\frac{1}{2}$-gph for a 16-inch-wide pot, more emitters and a bigger circle as pot size increases. Or use $\frac{1}{4}$-inch emitter line with factory-installed emitters at 6-inch intervals. An emitter line can also be used in a straight line to water a rectangular container or a window box. For some pots, you may want a specialty emitter such as a mister or a bubbler.

How long do you run the system?

Test your system by running it for 5 to 10 minutes. After watering, the soil should be thoroughly wet, with some water draining out of the container bottoms. If water floods out, you have run it too long; if no water comes out and the soil isn't thoroughly moist, you need to run the system longer or change to larger emitters. Most controllers allow you to run the system several times a day, which is particularly useful in hot climates. ◆

■ A circle of emitter line (with factory-installed emitters), held down by U stakes, will keep the soil moist in a large container such as this 20-inch-wide pot.

■ Multi-outlet emitter (sometimes called a bubbler) can be used to thoroughly water the soil in a large container. It can be adjusted to change the spray.

■ Quarter-inch tubing hides along the base of a wooden planter, then follows a crack to the top of the container. (For brick or concrete walls, drill holes with a masonry bit and use masonry nails.)

The dramatic bromeliads

These pineapple relatives are easy to grow, whether in patio pots or indoors or—in the mildest of climates—in borders

By Sharon Cohoon
Photographs by Steven Gunther

Guzmanias and vrieseas—two popular members of the Bromeliaceae family—are almost as low-maintenance as plastic plants. In fact, at times, you'd swear they were plastic. Water spots don't burn any of these plants, and bugs don't chomp them. Their straplike leaves, smooth, shiny, and thick, fan out symmetrically around a central cup (called a tank) to form a neat rosette. Their dramatic flower heads have the same tough perfection. Shaped like tubes, arrowheads, or stars, they come in fluorescent shades of red, pink, orange, and yellow, and they last for months without fading or wilting. Often, vrieseas also have variegated foliage, with stripes (sometimes horizontal) or blotches.

During their bloom period, these bromeliads can do well on very little care. Just fill up their tanks with water occasionally. Mist, if you remember. If you only intend to keep the plants as long as they're in bloom, which is what many people do—the mother plant dies after it finishes blooming—that's pretty much the extent of care. If, how-

ever, you want to try for another generation, you can; mother plants produce new plants called offsets, or pups, before they die. But you'll have to give the plants slightly better treatment to keep them going (see box at right).

Guzmanias and vrieseas make ideal container plants for indoors or for shady patios. In frost-free climates such as Hawaii or coastal California, you can plant them in the ground in lightly shaded spots. Dr. Leonard Kent, founder of Kent's Bromeliad Nursery, has filled his garden in Vista, California, with naturalized bromeliads. "I didn't amend the soil, I rarely feed them, and they don't need to be watered very often," he says. "If you don't have to worry about frost, they're incredibly easy."

What bromeliads need

According to Kent's Bromeliad Nursery (www. kentsbromeliad.com), these bromeliads thrive under the following conditions.

LIGHT. Ideally, both guzmanias and vrieseas should have

To start a new plant

After flowering, snip off the bloom stalk to encourage the mother plant to create pups. When an offset forms, let it grow to at least half the size of the mother plant before separating. Then remove both mother and pup from container. Gently pull away soil to see where the two are joined. Pull pup away from mother plant or prune, cutting close to the base of the mother plant.

Replant mother plant immediately so it will produce more offsets. Place pup in shady area until it forms a callus (one to two days); then repot in a loose, fast-draining potting medium such as a cymbidium mix that is about 50 percent peat moss.

LEFT: Vibrant red bracts surround the center of *Guzmania* 'Tutti Frutti'. TOP CENTER: Guzmanias come in dozens of brilliant colors, such as yellow, orange, red, and hot pink. TOP RIGHT: Bromeliads add bold textures to Mary and John McGrath's mostly foliage border in Honolulu. ABOVE CENTER: *Guzmania limones* bears clusters of yellow buds. ABOVE RIGHT: *Vriesea* 'Annie' shows off its distinctive arrowhead-shaped flower heads—these are brilliant yellow atop bright red stems.

bright light but not direct sun. The reflected light of a patio is often perfect, as is a bright room indoors. However, if you want the plants to decorate a shady outdoor alcove or a fairly dark room indoors while they're blooming, go right ahead. They'll survive gloomy conditions for months without serious harm. Just regularly rotate them back into brighter spots.

WATER. Irrigate these bromeliads by pouring water directly into their tanks. Pour enough so the excess spills out and moistens the soil below. Don't water again until the surface of the soil is dry to the touch—roughly every one to three weeks, depending on conditions.

HUMIDITY. If you're growing bromeliads in an arid climate, either indoors or outdoors, they'll appreciate having their leaves misted weekly or more often to increase humidity. As an alternative, place a couple of inches of pebbles in the saucer underneath the pot and add a little water.

FERTILIZING. Guzmanias and vrieseas are not heavy feeders. Fertilize them once in spring, twice in summer, and once more in fall by applying a 20-20-20 or 20-10-20 formula liquid fertilizer at half or one-third strength directly into the soil.

TEMPERATURE. These bromeliads flourish when air temperatures are between 40° and 90°, though they can survive temperatures outside of this range for short periods. When temperatures soar, give outdoor plants deeper shade and extra humidity. When frost is predicted, move plants indoors. ◆

SEPTEMBER IS HARVEST MONTH for the spicy 'Alkmene' apple. A good choice for home gardens, it bears a heavy crop of disease-resistant fruit on a relatively compact tree. For details, see page 279.

September

an adobe toolshed
in New Mexico

■ James Havard of Santa Fe admired the one-room adobe chapels scattered across the landscape of New Mexico. So he built one of his own. At the time the adobe walls surrounding his property were being built, it occurred to Havard that he could incorporate a toolshed resembling the style he admired. Working without architectural drawings, a Mexican artisan crafted the structure from photos in books Havard showed him.

The shed is about 10 feet wide by 14 feet long by 15 feet high at its tallest point. The ceiling is made of *vigas* (logs) overlaid with cedar *latillas* (saplings) in the traditional herringbone pattern. The floor is made of local rock. The mesquite door is an antique from Mexico found in Santa Fe. Inside, a large cupboard holds Havard's tools, which rarely get a rest during the growing season, as Havard puts them to work in his intensely planted garden—an eclectic mixture of flowering perennials, ornamental grasses, and roses.

A functional cast-iron bell crowns the shed. "I ring it when the mood strikes me and it seems right, like when the sun sets or on Sunday mornings," says Havard. His neighbors apparently like the mellow sound: "I haven't had a complaint yet."
— *Sharon Cohoon*

grand old "Fairmount Red" rose

MICHAEL MOWRY

■ Established in 1890, Fairmount Cemetery in Denver is home to at least 61 so-called mystery roses: old-fashioned varieties of unknown origin and identity. Planted around the graves, possibly by relatives of the deceased, they possess toughness and fragrance that endear them to modern gardeners.

The first mystery rose from the cemetery to be sold (discovered by this writer in 1991) is now available in limited quantities under the name of "Fairmount Red." Possibly a hybrid Bourbon with Gallica and China rose ancestry, it bears potently scented burgundy and magenta blooms on gracefully arching branches. The plant reaches 7 feet tall and wide if not pruned. Grow one as a garden centerpiece or form a dramatic hedge by spacing several plants 4 feet apart in a row. Pests and diseases ignore this tough old-timer, but birds like to roost in its dense branches and feed on the plump orange hips that form in fall.

Give "Fairmount Red" a feeding of fish emulsion or fish meal in spring. Spread a thick mulch around the plant and provide a few deep waterings each month in summer. Cutting 3-foot-long canes for elegant summer bouquets is the only pruning required.

Look for "Fairmount Red" at selected Colorado nurseries or order from High Country Roses in Jensen, Utah (800/552-2082 or www.highcountryroses.com). — *John Starnes*

sweet autumn surprise

■ Looking for a quick cover-up for an unsightly dog run or a chain-link fence? Sweet autumn clematis (*Clematis terniflora* or *C. dioscoreifolia*) can camouflage either with panache. Reaching 20 feet in two to three years, this robust vine can also shade a patio when it's trained over an arbor. It bears smaller flowers—just 1 inch across—than hybrid clematis, but the sheer volume of blossoms more than compensates for their size. Masses of sweetly fragrant, creamy white flowers smother the vines for several weeks in late summer and early fall. The silvery seed heads that follow resemble feather dusters. The glossy green foliage, sometimes mottled with silver, is deciduous in cold-winter areas but may stay evergreen in mild winters.

Sweet autumn clematis prefers a sunny

DAVID WINGER

spot in compost-enriched soil. Shade the roots with several inches of mulch or plant perennial flowers at its base. Prune only to limit size and to remove deadwood in spring. This vigorous vine needs support to climb. Provide it with a stout trellis and tie up the young shoots. It can also be planted where it will clamber up a sturdy climbing rose or 'Concord' grape. One of my neighbors trained a sweet autumn clematis onto a privacy fence, where it launched itself skyward into an Austrian pine.

Hardy in *Sunset* climate zones 2–9, 14–24, H1, sweet autumn clematis is available at most nurseries, or by mail order from Forestfarm in Williams, OR (541/846-7269 or www.forestfarm.com), or Wayside Gardens in Hodges, SC (800/845-1124 or www.waysidegardens.com).

— *Marcia Tatroe*

PAUL BOUSQUET (2)

tough enough near Boulder

This landscape resists drought, wind, deer

■ High in the foothills west of Boulder, Colorado, this property was a real challenge for the landscape designers of Marpa & Associates. Overlooking forestland along the Continental Divide, the site (7,200 feet in elevation) has a short growing season and is routinely beset by dry spells, buffeted by winds, and browsed by deer. Any landscaping had to be tough enough to withstand these conditions and still be sensitive to the natural scenery.

Most plantings are confined to small pockets protected by boulders and mulched with pea gravel—the only mulch heavy enough to stay put in the big winds that lash the site. The designers chose hardy perennials, including white snow-in-summer (*Cerastium tomentosum*), blue salvia, silvery-leafed lamb's ears (*Stachys byzantina*), and penstemons in shades of red and purple. Ornamental grasses, including

feather reed grass (*Calamagrostis* x *acutiflora* 'Stricta') and maiden grass (*Miscanthus sinensis* 'Gracillimus'), blend with native plants in an adjacent meadow.

The owners wanted a hot tub, but to preserve their view, they located it some distance from the house. And since they use the hot tub year-round, they needed a walkway that would provide safe footing in any kind of weather. To meet this challenge, designers Basho Mosko and Chester Simmons built a path (left) of red and buff flagstone surrounded by black Mexican pebbles. All the stones are set in concrete to create a solid surface, which facilitates snow removal.

For its work at the site, Marpa & Associates won a merit award in the Excellence in Landscape competition sponsored by the Associated Landscape Contractors of Colorado. — *M.T.*

'Alkmene' apple

■ While inheriting the spicy flavor of 'Cox's Orange Pippin', one of its famous parents, the 'Alkmene' apple bears even heavier crops of red-orange fruit on a more compact tree. Best of all for home gardeners, 'Alkmene' was found to be both mildew- and scab-tolerant in trials conducted by Washington State University's research and extension center in Mount Vernon. The eight-year-old tree shown at right in Anh and Frank Hnatovic's garden in Port Orchard, Washington, is 10 feet tall. They spray it with lime sulfur and horticultural oil in January or February, and it produces a great crop of disease-free fruit. The harvest comes in September; picked fruit can be stored for about a month.

'Alkmene' is partially self-fruitful, meaning that while it will bear fruit without a pollenizer, it will yield much more heavily if one is growing nearby. 'Liberty' and 'Melrose' are good pollenizers, as is any flowering crabapple.

Many nurseries and garden centers sell 'Alkmene'; you can order by mail from Raintree Nursery (360/496-6400 or www.raintreenursery.com). — *Jim McCausland*

JIM McCAUSLAND

Northwest artists and their gardens

■ There's an art to displaying art in the garden, and no one does it better than an artist—a point beautifully made by *Artists in Their Gardens* (Sasquatch Books, Seattle, 2001; $23.95; 800/775-0817 or www.sasquatchbooks.com). This 160-page softbound book, written by Valerie Easton and David Laskin and illustrated by photographer Allan Mandell, takes you into 10 gardens around the Pacific Northwest embellished by the works of the artists who own them.

In sculptor Les Bugajski's garden (left) in Vancouver, Washington, the faces of old men carved in wood (below left) and stone peer from conifers, ground covers, and ivy vines. As the authors note, "Despite their seemingly random positions, peeking out from beneath a leaf or the curve of a tree, the faces are cunningly placed to lead you deeper into the garden as surely as signposts along a hidden trail."

Glass art objects adorn Ginny Ruffner's Seattle garden in fanciful ways. Glass balls poise like bubbles around container plantings in a courtyard. A translucent glass torso serves as a pedestal for a path light. Ruffner, who admits, "I never met a color I didn't like!" dares to pair an orange begonia with green-and-white *Hosta* 'Fire and Ice'.
— *Steven R. Lorton*

ALLAN MANDELL (2)

E. SPENCER TOY

DEIDRA WALPOLE (2)

Recycled glass, as mulch

■ Who would have guessed that yesterday's water and wine bottles could find new life as decorative and long-lasting garden mulch? In the garden of Judy and Bruce Burness, a river of these lavender pebbles meanders between pools of olive green glass pebbles from recycled Chardonnay bottles. The rest of the mosaic beneath an elm tree is composed of plant material—emerald green Scotch moss, 'Black Prince' echeveria, and 'Dragon's Blood' sedum. Benderboard made from recycled plastic holds the pebbles in place, and landscape barrier cloth underneath keeps weeds from emerging.

Succulents are good choices for the dappled sunlight under these trees, says Tony Exter of BEM Design Group of South Pasadena, California, who did the design. These varieties like the shade canopy and have shallow root systems that can successfully coexist with the more extensive tree roots. Besides being a delightful surprise, the glass contributes brightness, says Exter. Judy Burness loves the result: "This area sings."

Tumbled glass pebbles are available from Glass Garden in Los Angeles. The ⅝-inch glass pebbles come in other colors as well, including cobalt blue and frosty white. A 50-pound bag—enough to make a 1-inch layer over 5 square feet—costs $70. *(213) 368-9220 or www.landscape2go.com. — S.C.*

STEVEN GUNTHER

beautiful and unthirsty

■ Only five regions of the world have a summer-dry Mediterranean climate—California, central Chile, the southwestern portion of South Africa's Western Cape, areas of southern and western Australia, and the Mediterranean basin. Together they make up less than 2 percent of the world's landmass. But that small percentage of land supports an astonishing variety of plants. Susi Torre-Bueno's front yard in Encinitas, California, is living proof. It has lavender and rosemary from Europe; lion's tail and *Melianthus major* from South Africa; bottlebrush and kangaroo paw from Australia; and Southwestern natives like Mexican grass tree (*Dasylirion quadrangulatum*) and Texas ranger (*Leucophyllum frutescens* 'Green Cloud'). Though the garden is barely two years old, 300 species were growing in it at last count. Torre-Bueno will probably double that amount before she's "planted out." Try telling her that drought-tolerant plants are boring.

The pond in the front yard and the dry riverbed that meanders through the garden are more than decorative. They're integral parts of a water collection system. The house's flat roof captures the area's sparse annual rainfall—9 to 12 inches, typically. Some of the rain is diverted to the pond, which is located under a footbridge. From the pond, the water percolates into the front garden. The rest of the rain flows directly into the dry riverbed for use in the backyard. "Not a drop is wasted," she says.

Though Torre-Bueno took a very active role in shaping her garden, she worked closely with Del Mar landscape designer Linda Chisari, who provided the basic plan, and with Tom Piergrossi, who did the installation. — S.C.

THOMAS J. STORY

stack a tower of roses

■ This trio of blue glazed bowls, filled with yellow miniature roses, has the elegance of a frosted wedding cake. Displayed on a sunny patio or deck, the roses will provide a season-long show of cheerful blooms.

Choose containers in three sizes—small, medium, and large. When they are stacked, there should be enough room around the bottom two tiers for planting. Our top pot measures 9½ inches in diameter and about 8 inches tall; the middle pot is 15 inches wide and 6 inches tall; and the bottom pot is 19 inches wide and 8 inches tall.

COST: $50 to $100, depending on pots
TIME: 20 to 30 minutes

MATERIALS

• Three **bowl-shaped pots**, sized as noted above
• One 2-cubic-foot bag of **potting soil**
• **Organic granular fertilizer**
• Nine 4-inch potted **miniature roses** (or nine 2-inch pots)
• Three sixpacks of **blue lobelia**

DIRECTIONS

1. Fill the bowls about ⅔ full with potting soil. Mix in fertilizer.
2. Plant five roses around the perimeter of the largest bowl, spacing them evenly around the edges. Set the tops of the rootballs about 1 inch below the lip of the bowl and tip the plants slightly outward.
3. Plant one lobelia between the roses.

4. Fill in the remainder of the bowl with potting soil; press to firm down well.
5. Plant three roses in the midsize bowl as described in step 2, setting lobelia plants between them. Press down soil.
6. Plant one rose in the center of the smallest bowl; set lobelia around the edges.
7. Stack the three pots, centered. Take care that they don't damage foliage (ask a friend or family member to slip on some gloves and help hold the foliage away while you place the pots). Make sure the pots sit level. If they sink too low when stacked, lift them and add more potting soil to pot centers.
8. Water all pots thoroughly.

— Lauren Bonar Swezey

designed for serenity

This small Northern California garden recalls the peaceful, all-green gardens of Japan

■ Some gardens are filled with brilliant blooms to stimulate the senses. Others—like the Japanese garden at Osmosis Enzyme Bath & Massage in Freestone, California—are green and peaceful. Designed for quiet contemplation, this garden inspires visitors to relax and connect with nature.

"The garden is an essential part of Osmosis," explains owner Michael Stusser, who designed it with landscaper Steve Stücky. "It provides a wonderful transition from the outside world into our treatment rooms." When guests arrive at Osmosis, just west of Sebastopol, they're served tea in a room with views of the garden.

After spending years apprenticing in Kyoto, Stusser is familiar with Japanese gardens. When he planned this one, he knew it had to contain the traditional elements: water, an arching bridge, beautiful stones, and striking plant textures and forms.

Fifty-year-old bonsai trees—pine, maple, and hawthorn—dot the small (24-foot-wide by 28-foot-long) garden; below them grow are low-growing shrubs and ground covers, such as azaleas, dittany of Crete, ferns, and junipers.

The garden is a truly magical place. "Guests find peacefulness there," says Stusser with delight.

— L.B.S.

LINDA HOLT AYRISS

When to use a spading fork or a spade. A spading fork (also called a digging fork) is particularly useful for cultivating clay or rocky soil, breaking up large clods, or digging up plants without slicing through the roots. Buy the kind with flat tines, front and back. Spades are good for loosening and turning the soil, for digging straight-sided holes, and for dividing perennials.

— *L.B.S.*

CLIPPINGS

• New nursery in San Francisco. Potrero Gardens specializes in rare and unusual plants from the high-altitude tropics, although you'll also find more typical garden plants here. Owner Michael Sasso's goal is to make an "urban oasis in San Francisco." *1201 17th St.; (415) 861-8220 or www. potrerogardens.com.*

• Armchair journey. *The Looking-Glass Garden: Plants and Gardens of the Southern Hemisphere,* by Peter Thompson (Timber Press, Portland, 2001; $39.95; 800/327-5680), is part travelogue, part inspiration, and part practical gardening advice. It explains which southern hemisphere plants like standard garden conditions and which ones prefer lean growing conditions.

Healthy start for newly planted trees. Young trees become established faster and form stronger trunks if their lower branches are left to develop along the trunk

LOIS LOVEJOY

for the first few years after planting. If side branches become too long or vigorous during this time, shorten them during the dormant season. Once the trunk is at least 2 inches thick, begin removing the lower branches gradually, over a period of several years.

for fern fanatics

■ Fern fanciers will find indispensable the revised and expanded edition of *Fern Grower's Manual,* by Barbara Joe Hoshizaki and Robbin C. Moran (Timber Press, Portland, 2001; $59.95; 800/327-5680 or www.timberpress.com). Although useful everywhere, this book has special relevance for Western gardeners: Hoshizaki's long experience with ferns on the West Coast makes her especially qualified to write about species that are exotic to much of the country—tree and staghorn ferns, for instance—that are familiar garden subjects here.

The 624-page book is a must-have for home gardeners, professional growers, and botanists alike. The first 140 pages explain fern structure, growth, culture, and propagation. The bulk of the book is an encyclopedia covering 700 species of ferns found in cultivation. Each species is illustrated by a black-and-white drawing or photograph that shows fern fronds and their distinguishing characteristics. Each description includes cultural notes and climate adaptability. Fifty color plates show ferns in detail or in garden situations.

— *John R. Dunmire*

E. SPENCER TOY

peony planting time
in the Northwest

■ In the 1980s, nurseries around Anchorage all seemed to carry only three kinds of peonies—a double red, a double white, and a double pink. That frustrated Judy Wilmarth, who decided that she wanted to show her friends that "you could grow more than the same three poofy peonies here."

Today, Wilmarth grows 150 varieties of herbaceous peonies on an acre of land, and a mix of early-, mid-, and late-season varieties keeps the flowers coming from early June until the middle of August. Her plants originally came from mail-order nurseries, which ship the tuberous peony roots in September for planting in early October—a good time to set out peonies anywhere in the Pacific Northwest.

Key to success is the proper planting technique. "The number one failure with peonies is planting them too deeply," Wilmarth explains. "I dig each hole 12 inches deep, throw a fistful of bonemeal in the bottom, add lime and compost to the backfill, and refill the hole. Once the earth has settled, I plant each peony root 2 inches deep."

In Wilmarth's garden, the peonies begin to emerge in early May and start flowering in June. She waters with an overhead sprinkler until flower buds show, then switches to soaker hoses to keep water off the petals. To keep their blooms out of the mud, Wilmarth cages the plants, and in August, she top-dresses them with an inch of compost mixed with kelp and bonemeal. In fall, she cuts the foliage down to the ground for winter. —*J.M.*

WHAT TO DO IN YOUR GARDEN IN SEPTEMBER

PLANTING

☐ **COOL-SEASON CROPS.** Zones 4–7: Before Labor Day weekend, sow seeds of ornamental cabbage and kale and salad crops such as arugula, leaf lettuce, mustard greens, radishes, and spinach. Or set out nursery-grown seedlings of these, plus edible cabbage and purple-sprouting broccoli to harvest next spring.

☐ **COVER CROPS.** This is a good time to replace annual crops with cover crops such as Austrian field peas, crimson clover, and vetch. These plants minimize erosion during harsh winter weather and add lots of organic matter to the soil when you till them into the ground next spring, before planting.

☐ **LAWNS.** Zones 4–7: Early September is one of the best times to sow new lawns. Or overseed thin spots in your existing lawn with the same kind of grass that grew there originally. You can also lay sod from now until mid-October.

☐ **PERMANENT PLANTS.** Plant ground covers, perennials, shrubs, trees, and vines now so their roots will become well established over winter and give you more growth and bloom next summer.

☐ **SPRING-BLOOMING BULBS.** Watch for their arrival in nurseries around Labor Day; shop early for the best selection of healthy bulbs. Plant bluebells, crocuses, daffodils, hyacinths, and tulips.

MAINTENANCE

☐ **CARE FOR ROSES.** After the fall flush of bloom, let flowers turn to hips. The process slows flower production and gets plants ready for winter.

☐ **CLEAN GREENHOUSES.** Before the first frost, empty the greenhouse and wash it down with a solution of bleach and water to get rid of moss and algae. Replace weather-stripping, check out heating and venting systems, and clean out flats, pots, and seedbeds.

☐ **DIG AND DIVIDE PERENNIALS.** Divide and replant spring- and summer-blooming perennials, including oriental poppies, peonies, Shasta daisies, and Siberian irises. Divide fall-blooming plants after flowering, or next spring.

☐ **MAKE COMPOST.** Use grass clippings, fallen leaves, weeds, and vegetable waste to build an autumn compost pile. Keep the pile as damp as a wrung-out sponge and turn it regularly so you'll have compost to dig into the soil before winter.

☐ **MULCH.** Zones 1–3: To minimize winter freeze damage and soil erosion, spread a 3-inch layer of organic mulch such as compost on top of beds that contain bulbs, perennial flowers and vegetables, or strawberries.

☐ **WEED.** Hoe weed seedlings and spread 2 to 3 inches of mulch over bare earth to keep new weeds from germinating. ◆

WHAT TO DO IN YOUR GARDEN IN SEPTEMBER

PLANTING

☐ **BULBS.** Try these less common charmers in your garden—all will give a colorful display in spring in zones 7–9, 14–17 (except where noted): African corn lily *(Ixia)*, baboon flower *(Babiana)*, dwarf narcissus, freesia (zones 8–9, 14–17), grape hyacinth *(Muscari)*, harlequin flower *(Sparaxis;* zones 9, 14–17), *Homeria,* naked lady *(Amaryllis belladonna)*, poppy-flowered anemone *(Anemone coronaria)*, *Ranunculus,* species tulips (such as *Tulipa clusiana, T. saxatilis)*, and *Tritonia* (zones 9, 14–17).

☐ **CARROTS IN CONTAINERS.** Zones 7–9, 14–17: If your soil is heavy clay, consider planting carrots in a container. 'Thumbelina' is a small, round short-season variety. Or try 'Sweetness II', which can be harvested at the baby stage (4 inches) or full size (8 inches). Both are from Nichols Garden Nursery (541/928-9280 or www.nicholsgardennursery.com).

☐ **COLORFUL CABBAGES AND KALE.** Zones 7–9, 14–17: Although not actually flowers, ornamental cabbages and kale provide striking midwinter color in the garden. Most nurseries carry several different types. Or you can grow special varieties from seed. 'Color Up' has smooth leaves, 'Nagoya' has frilly leaf edges, and 'Peacock' has feathery leaves (all are available from Park Seed Co.; 800/845-3369 or www.parkseed.com).

Sunset
CLIMATE ZONES
☐ Mountain (1-2)
☐ Valley (7-9)
☐ Inland (14)
☐ Coastal (15-17)

DEBRA LAMBERT

☐ **NEW LAWNS.** Zones 1–9, 14–17: Towards the end of the month, sow seed or lay sod over soil that's been rotary tilled and amended with plenty of organic matter. Zones 1–2: Plant new lawns early in September. At highest elevations, wait to plant seed until October; it will germinate in spring when the snow melts.

☐ **SALAD MIX.** Zones 7–9, 14–17: Instead of purchasing expensive salad mixes at the grocery store, sow seeds of a mesclun mix now, either in the ground or in a wide, low container (try Baby Mesclun Mix from Renee's Garden, available on seed racks or at www.reneesgarden.com). Moisten the soil or potting mix, sow seed thinly, and cover with ¼ inch of soil; sprinkle lightly with water. When seedlings are 1 or 2 inches tall, thin them to about ½ inch apart (save for salads). Thin once or twice more to allow room for the seedlings to develop.

MAINTENANCE

☐ **CARE FOR CITRUS.** Zones 7–9, 14–17: To prevent citrus fruit from drying out as it matures, give trees regular deep soakings during warm fall weather.

☐ **DIVIDE PERENNIALS.** Dig and divide perennials, such as agapanthus, candytuft, coreopsis, daylilies, and penstemon, that are either overgrown or not flowering well. (Zones 1–2: Do this early in the month.) You can also divide to increase the number of plants for your garden. Use a spading fork or spade to lift clumps, then cut them into sections with a spade, a sharp knife, or pruning shears. Replant sections in well-amended soil and keep moist.

☐ **PREPARE WILDFLOWER BEDS.** To help control weeds before planting, soak the soil to germinate the seeds, then hoe down or spray with a contact herbicide, such as a nontoxic kind derived from fatty acids. If time permits, repeat the process before sowing wildflowers. ◆

WHAT TO DO IN YOUR GARDEN IN SEPTEMBER

PLANTING

☐ **BULB COVERS.** Forget-me-nots, Johnny-jump-ups, lobelia, and sweet alyssum planted among bulbs provide color until the bulbs sprout and flower. After the bulbs flower, tuck their yellowing foliage beneath the cover foliage.

☐ **HERBS.** Plant mint, parsley, rosemary, tarragon, thyme, and other perennial herbs. Sow arugula, chervil, cilantro, and dill.

☐ **SEASONAL COLOR.** For long-lasting fall color, plant chrysanthemums. Or plant early-spring flowers such as calendula, Iceland poppy, nemesia, pansy, primrose, snapdragon, and stock.

☐ **SPRING BULBS.** Nurseries are well stocked now with bulbs to plant in fall. For a good selection, shop early. South African bulbs, the best naturalizers in our climates, can be planted immediately. Choices include babiana, freesia, ixia, sparaxis, and watsonia. Paper whites and other tazetta-type narcissus can be planted now too. Buy anemones, daffodils, Dutch iris, and ranunculus now, but wait until October to plant. Chill Dutch crocus, hyacinths, and tulips at least six weeks before planting; store them in paper bags in the refrigerator. In the high desert, chilling isn't necessary.

Sunset
CLIMATE ZONES

1-3 7-9 11 13 14-24

DEBRA LAMBERT

☐ **VEGETABLES.** From midmonth on, coastal (zones 22–24) and inland (zones 18–21) gardeners can plant winter crops. Sow seeds or transplant seedlings of Asian greens, beets, broccoli, brussels sprouts, cabbage, carrots, cauliflower, collards, kale, leeks, lettuce, onions, parsnips, peas, potatoes, radishes, spinach, Swiss chard, and turnips. In the high desert (zone 11), plant lettuce, radishes, and spinach.

MAINTENANCE

☐ **FEED PERMANENT PLANTS.** Fertilize established trees, shrubs, ground covers, and warm-season grasses. Feed roses one last time for a strong late-fall bloom. For cymbidium orchids, switch from a high-nitrogen fertilizer to a bloom formula, such as 15-30-15.

☐ **FORCE SUMMER CROPS.** Pinch off new blossoms and growing tips on eggplants, melons, squash, and tomatoes to force plants to ripen fruits that have already set.

☐ **REPLENISH MULCH.** To help keep soil moisture from evaporating and to protect plants from drying Santa Ana winds, renew mulch now. Apply a 3- to 4-inch-thick layer around plants, but keep mulch away from crowns, stems, and trunks.

☐ **PROTECT AGAINST BRUSHFIRES.** In fire-prone areas, before the onset of Santa Ana winds, cut and remove all dead branches and leaves from trees and shrubs, especially those that grow near the house. Clear fallen leaves from rain gutters, and remove woody vegetation that is growing against structures.

PEST & DISEASE CONTROL

☐ **PROTECT CABBAGE CROPS.** Squadrons of little white moths seem to descend on cabbage and other brassica crops the minute you plant. The easiest way to deal with them is to cover the young seedlings with floating row covers right after you plant. The next best option is to spray with *Bacillus thuringiensis* to kill the young caterpillar larvae. ◆

WHAT TO DO IN YOUR GARDEN IN SEPTEMBER

PLANTING

☐ HARDY PERENNIALS. Set out transplants of campanula, candytuft, catmint, coreopsis, delphinium, dianthus, foxglove, penstemon, phlox, salvia, and yarrow. In areas where soil freezes deeply every winter, spread a thick layer of mulch around plants to keep them from being heaved out of the ground.

☐ INSTANT FALL COLOR. As tender flowers are damaged by frost, replace them with fall-blooming asters, chrysanthemums, and pansies.

☐ TREES AND SHRUBS. Cool fall weather is perfect for planting hardy varieties of trees and shrubs. Apply several inches of organic mulch around the plants and don't let their rootballs dry out as they become established. Irrigate at least twice a month during the first winter.

☐ VEGETABLES. Sow seeds of lettuce and other salad greens, radishes, and spinach for late-fall harvest. Prepare the bed by digging 2 inches of compost or well-aged manure into the soil to a depth of 6 to 8 inches. Keep the bed evenly moist until the seeds germinate and use a floating row cover to protect the plants from early frosts. Spinach can be left in the ground for harvest in late winter or early spring; protect the plants with a thick blanket of hay or straw.

Sunset
CLIMATE ZONES
☐ 1-3 ☐ 10-11

DEBRA LAMBERT

MAINTENANCE

☐ CARE FOR HOUSEPLANTS. Bring houseplants back indoors before the first frost. Inspect them carefully for insects; if you find them, spray the foliage with insecticidal soap or a pyrethrum-based insecticide labeled safe for houseplants. Be sure to spray tops and undersides of the leaves thoroughly. This is also a good time to repot rootbound houseplants.

☐ DIVIDE PERENNIALS. Lift and divide overcrowded clumps of perennials, including campanulas, daylilies, hostas, peonies, sedums, and Shasta daisies. Cut or pull the roots apart and replant the healthiest divisions in soil amended with compost. Cover with shredded-bark mulch, evergreen boughs, hay, or straw to protect them over the winter.

☐ LIFT AND STORE SUMMER BULBS. After frost kills their foliage, dig up callas, cannas, dahlias, gladiolus, tuberous begonias, and other tender bulbs. Dry off the bulbs and pack them in vermiculite or sterile potting soil. Store in a cool, dry place and keep the medium slightly moist all winter.

☐ OVERWINTER TENDER PERENNIALS INDOORS. Take cuttings from coleus and geraniums to overwinter indoors. Root the cuttings in moist vermiculite or sterile potting soil. Bedding or wax begonias, heliotrope, impatiens, and Madagascar periwinkles can be moved indoors and grown as houseplants over the winter. Clean up the plants, cut them back by one-third, place them in containers in a sunny window or under artificial lights, and fertilize.

☐ WATER DEEPLY. Hot, dry weather can be hard on shrubs and trees, even established ones. Leaves that turn brown or drop prematurely in late summer are signs of seriously stressed plants. Water deeply by setting a sprinkler in place and letting it run for an hour, or use a root irrigator to inject water around the drip line twice a month until the ground freezes. ◆ — *M.T.*

WHAT TO DO IN YOUR GARDEN IN SEPTEMBER

PLANTING

☐ **ANNUALS.** Zones 1–3: Sow seeds of calendula, cornflower, desert marigold *(Baileya multiradiata),* larkspur, and poppies for spring bloom. Zones 11–13 (Las Vegas, Tucson, Phoenix): Set out transplants of larkspur, lobelia, pansy, snapdragon, stock, and sweet alyssum late in the month.

☐ **INDOOR PLANTS.** All zones: Begin forcing bulbs of amaryllis and paper white narcissus by month's end to ensure indoor bloom for Christmas. Kalanchoes need 12 hours of darkness for 4 to 6 weeks beginning this month to promote flowering by Christmas.

☐ **PERENNIALS.** Zone 10 (Albuquerque): Moderate temperatures and, in most places, the approach of winter rains make this a good time to set out transplants of many perennials, including campanula, catmint, coreopsis, dianthus, gaillardia, geum, penstemon, phlox, salvia, and yarrow. Zones 11–13: Plant all of the above and start seeds of aster, carnation, columbine, feverfew, hollyhock, lupine, phlox, Shasta daisy, and statice for transplanting in about eight weeks.

☐ **SPRING BULBS.** Zones 1–3, 10: Plant crocuses, daffodils, grape hyacinths, hyacinths, and tulips. Zones 11–13: Buy these bulbs now, place them in paper bags, and chill in the refrigerator until the soil cools enough to plant next month.

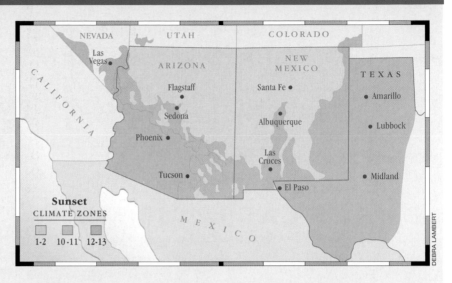

☐ **TREES, SHRUBS.** Zones 10–13: Set out hardy, container-grown trees and shrubs. Most native desert species become established better when planted in the fall.

☐ **VEGETABLES.** Zones 1–3, 10: Sow seeds of carrots, kale, radishes, and spinach; set out garlic cloves. Zones 11–13: As soon as temperatures drop below 100°, sow seeds of beets, broccoli, cabbage, carrots, cauliflower, celery, cucumbers, fava beans, kale, kohlrabi, leeks, radishes, short-season snap beans, Swiss chard, and turnips. Set out transplants of green onions, peppers, and tomatoes.

MAINTENANCE

☐ **CARE FOR ROSES.** Zones 1–3, 10: Let blossoms form hips to harden off plants as winter approaches. Zones 11–13: Prune dead canes, then fertilize and water well to stimulate fall growth.

☐ **DIVIDE PERENNIALS.** Zones 1–3, 10: Lift and divide crowded clumps of daylilies, hostas, peonies, and Shasta daisies. Zones 11–13: Lift and divide crowded iris rhizomes.

☐ **STORE SUMMER BULBS.** Zones 1–3, 10: When foliage dies down, lift cannas, dahlias, and gladiolus and let bulbs dry a few days, then store in a cool, well-ventilated place for winter. ◆ — *Mary Irish*

Many perennials deliver
dazzling blooms late
in the season,
when Western gardens
need them most

GREAT LATE-SUMMER
color

"The fullness of late summer and early fall ought to be one of the richest seasons in the garden," says Mary McBride, a horticulturist at Tom Piergrossi Landscape Nursery in Vista, California. But—and this is one of McBride's pet peeves—that's when most gardens look their worst. Summer annuals and vegetables are spent; spring-blooming perennials are growing leggy and are in need of cutting back. This time of year, when the weather is often at its most glorious and we're most inclined to linger outdoors at day's end, what do we see? Hardly a flower.

Don't blame it on Mother Nature, chides McBride. Plenty of perennials peak during this period. Their flowers come mostly in colors with character: Golden yellows that stand up to strong sun now, then later in the season burn like embers under gray skies—gloriosa daisies, coreopsis, and goldenrod, for example. Coppers, rusts, and wine reds that forecast the shades of falling leaves, such as the flowers on *Sedum* 'Autumn Joy', purple coneflower, or sneezeweed *(Helenium)* hybrids. And lots of soulful violet blues—asters, Russian sage, salvias. Colorado garden writer Lauren Springer calls this palette of burnished tones and blues "the colors of autumn in America."

Why don't we see these beauties in more gardens? Call it the catch-22 syndrome. If you saw them, you'd want them. But to see them, you have to visit nurseries now—not next spring. If you buy and plant some of the perennials listed here this month, you'll get pleasure from them immediately (on the following pages, we give plans for beds, borders, and pots, as well as a list of champion bloomers for your region). Then, next year, promises McBride, your garden will be even better: "Plants will be twice the size, so you'll get twice the display."

BY SHARON COHOON • PHOTOGRAPHS BY THOMAS J. STORY

Gloriosa daisy

Aster

Coreopsis tinctoria 'Mahogany'

Yarrow, purple
coneflower, coreopsis,
Mexican bush sage,
and other fall-blooming
beauties fill pots that
brighten this entry gate.
DESIGN: Bud Stuckey

late-summercolor

The special joy in planting late-season bloomers is the immediate reward...

...in beds

The bed pictured here, planted in Menlo Park, California, shows what you can still achieve this season. *Sunset* test garden coordinator Bud Stuckey designed and installed this border late last summer; we photographed it a few weeks later. Since the bed was already shaped and the soil already amended, all we had to do was plant. That took less than three hours. Deciding what we wanted in the border and shopping for the plants took longer. But does anyone really consider that part work?

The free-form bed measures about 22 feet long and 10 to 12 feet wide, and it contains 29 perennials—most purchased as 1-gallon plants. Perfect partners for these late-blooming plants are 11 ornamental grasses (including purple fountain grass), several nandinas, and one spectacular red Japanese maple.

The color scheme is rich yellow and dark red, from plants such as coreopsis, creeping zinnia, 'Garnet' penstemon, pineapple sage, rudbeckia, and yarrow. As an accent, we added a few traces of the cool violet blue of *Salvia* 'Purple Majesty'.

1. After amending the soil with organic matter such as compost, raking it smooth, and positioning boulders (optional), apply gypsum in lines on the soil to block out a design.

2. Position the plants, still in their nursery containers, in the bed—tallest plants in the back, lowest ones in front. Set plants of the same variety together in groups of three to avoid a confetti look. Adjust the design by moving plants as needed. Then, plant and water.

3. Three weeks later, plants are filling in and still in bloom. Winter will establish them. To ensure vigorous new growth next spring, keep spent blooms clipped, then cut back perennials just above new basal growth early in the growing season.

Don't have time or space to plant a bed or border? Then create a late-summer show...

...in pots

A single pot can add a splash of color by a path or, for a garden look on a patio, cluster three pots together. Pictured here are five sample plantings, designed by Bud Stuckey, to give you inspiration. Create your own combinations from the listings for your climate zone on page 294. Use large containers (18 to 24 inches across and as deep) and a good potting mix; buy blooming perennials in gallon cans.

Before planting, put the container where you'll display it, since finished pots can be heavy to move. Fill it about halfway with potting soil, then set the plants, still in their nursery containers, atop the soil—tallest ones in the back or center, lowest ones around the edges, adjusting the design as necessary. Remove the plants from their nursery pots, and plant. Fill in around rootballs with additional soil; firm the soil with your hands, then water.

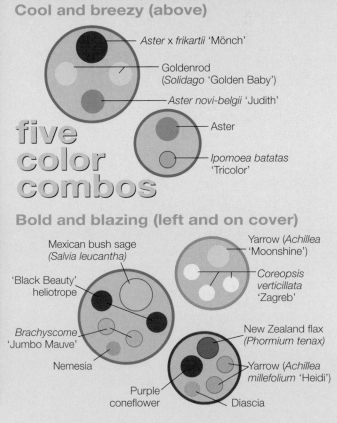

Cool and breezy (above)

- Aster x frikartii 'Mönch'
- Goldenrod (*Solidago* 'Golden Baby')
- *Aster novi-belgii* 'Judith'
- Aster
- *Ipomoea batatas* 'Tricolor'

five color combos

Bold and blazing (left and on cover)

- Mexican bush sage (*Salvia leucantha*)
- 'Black Beauty' heliotrope
- *Brachyscome* 'Jumbo Mauve'
- Nemesia
- Yarrow (*Achillea* 'Moonshine')
- *Coreopsis verticillata* 'Zagreb'
- New Zealand flax (*Phormium tenax*)
- Yarrow (*Achillea millefolium* 'Heidi')
- Purple coneflower
- Diascia

late-summer color for Sunset gardeners

- **Angelita daisy** *Tetraneuris acaulis).* Bears golden yellow daisy blooms on tufted plants about 8 inches tall. *Sunset* climate zones 1–3, 7–14, 18–24.
- **Aster.** *A.* x *frikartii* 'Mönch' is on everyone's top 10 list of lavender blue perennials; plants grow to 2 feet. *Sunset* climate zones 2B–24. New England aster (*A. novae-angliae*) has mostly blue flowers. 'Alma Potschke', an old favorite, bears salmon pink blooms. Grows to 3 feet tall. Zones 1–24. Flowers of Michaelmas daisy (*A. novi-belgii*) come mostly in shades of blue. 'Climax' has true blue flowers. Grows 4 to 6 feet tall. Zones 1–24.
- **Bat-faced cuphea** *(Cuphea llavea).* Red and purple flowers that look like bat faces appear on plants 2 to 3 feet tall. Zones 11–13, 21–24, H1–H2.
- **Boltonia asteroides.** Bears white, pink, or blue flowers on plants 5 to 6 feet tall. Zones 1–24.
- **Chrysanthemum.** Florist's chrysanthemum (*C.* x *morifolium*) bears flowers in many colors, from rust and wine red to orange and golden yellow. Grows 1 to 6 feet, depending on variety. Zones 2–24, H1. *C.* x *rubellum* flowers come in various colors; 'Clara Curtis' is bright, clear pink. Grows 2 feet tall. Zones 1–24.
- **Copper canyon daisy** *(Tagetes lemmonii).* Golden orange flowers emerge at branch ends atop mounding 3- to 6-foot-tall plants. Foliage is strongly fragrant when brushed (a blend of marigold, mint, and lemon). Zones 8–10, 12–24, H1.
- **Coreopsis.** *C. lanceolata* bears yellow flowers on plants 1 to 2 feet tall. Zones 1–24,

H1–H2 *C. verticillata* has yellow, daisylike blooms; 'Moonbeam' produces pale yellow blooms. Grows 2 to 3 feet tall. Zones 1–24.
- **Daylily** *(Hemerocallis* hybrids). Comes in various colors; look for reblooming or late varieties. Takes partial shade in hottest climates. Standard kinds grow 2½ to 4 feet tall. Zones 1–24, H1–H2.
- **Eupatorium greggii.** This aster relative is native to Arizona and Texas. Clusters of small, fluffy lavender flowers emerge on weak stems of 1½- to 2½-foot-tall plants. 'Boothill', first found near Tombstone, Arizona, is a choice form. Zones 3, 10–13.
- **False dragonhead** *(Physostegia virginiana).* Flower spikes are 10 inches tall, densely set with funnel-shaped, bluish pink blooms. Zones 1–9, 14–24, A3.
- **Gaillardia** x **grandiflora.** Daisylike flowers in golden yellows, reds, and bicolors; grows 2 to 4 feet tall. Zones 1–24, H1–H2.
- **Garden penstemon** *(P.* x *gloxinioides).* Many kinds and colors bloom most heavily in spring but will repeat bloom in fall if you cut back plants after flowering. Blooms range from fire engine red to deep purple to pale pink, depending on variety. Plants grow 2 to 4 feet tall. Zones 6–9, 14–24.
- **Globe thistle** *(Echinops).* Golf ball–size flowers look like blue pincushions above deeply cut gray blue leaves on plants 2 to 4 feet tall. Zones 1–24, A2–A3.
- **Golden dyssodia** *(Thymophylla pentachaeta).* This Southwest native bears yellow daisylike flowers on plants 4 to 6 inches high, with open, sparse,

Zones 8–14, 18–23.
- **Goldenrod** *(Solidago).* Bears feathery yellow bloom clusters atop 2- to 3-foot plants. Zones 1–11, 14–23
- **Helianthus maximilianii.** This perennial sunflower, native to the Southwest, has yellow flowers on plants to 10 feet tall. Zones 1–3, 10–13.
- **Heliotrope** *(Heliotropium arborescens).* Vanilla-scented, purple flowers on plants 1½ to 2 feet tall. Prefers partial shade in warm climates. Zones 15–17, 23–24, H1–H2.
- **Hummingbird mint** *(Agastache* hybrids). Whorls of apricot, pink, blue, and lavender flowers (favored by hummingbirds) appear in spikelike clusters on plants 1½ to 4 feet tall. Most grow in zones 4–24.
- **Japanese anemone** *(A.* x *hybrida).* Bears white or pink blooms, prefers partial shade. Grows 2 to 4 feet tall. Zones 2B–24.
- **Joe Pye weed** *(Eupatorium purpureum).* Bears big domes of pale purple flowers on 3- to 9-foot-tall plants. 'Gateway' grows to 6 feet tall with mauve flowers. Zones 1–9, 14–17.
- **Lion's tail** *(Leonotis leonurus).* Mint family relative from South Africa bears whorls of tubular, deep orange flowers along spikes on 4- to 6-foot-tall plants. Zones 8–24, H1–H2.
- **Purple coneflower** *(Echinacea purpurea).* Lavender pink, daisylike blooms with bristly, mounding centers. 'Magnus' grows to 4 feet tall. Zones 1–24, A2–A3.
- **Rudbeckia.** *R. fulgida* 'Goldsturm' bears golden yellow blooms on 3-foot-tall plants. Gloriosa daisy (*R. hirta*) grows 3 to 4 feet tall. 'Indian Summer' has single to double golden

yellow flowers. Zones 1–24.
- **Russian sage** *(Perovskia).* Velvety, lavender blue flowers grow on 3- to 4-foot-tall plants. Zones 2–24.
- **Salvia.** Many kinds bloom in late summer and early fall. Anise-scented sage (*S. guaranitica*) bears cobalt blue flowers, attractive to hummingbirds, on plants 4 to 5 feet tall. It can take partial shade in hot climates. Zones 8–9, 14–24. Autumn sage (*S. greggii*) flecks itself with flowers in many shades of red, white, and rose on shrubby, 1- to 4-foot plants. Zones 8–24. *S. azurea grandiflora* bears azure flowers, grows to 5 feet tall, and needs support. Zones 1–24. Eyelash sage (*S. blepharophylla*) puts out spikes of orange scarlet blooms on plants 1½ to 2 feet tall. Zones 14–24. Mexican bush sage (*S. leucantha*) has velvety purple flowers on plants 3 to 4 feet tall. Zones 12–24, H1–H2. Pineapple sage (*S. elegans*) has spikes of bright red flowers and fragrant foliage on plants 3 to 4 feet tall. Zones 8–24.
- **Sneezeweed** *(Helenium* hybrids). Flowers in red orange. 'Moerheim Beauty' is coppery red. Grows 3 to 5 feet tall. Zones 1–24.
- **Wine cups** *(Callirhoe involucrata).* A profusion of purplish red, mallow-type flowers on spreading plants to 6 inches tall. Zones 1–3, 7–14, 18–24.
- **Yarrow** *(Achillea).* Flowers come in various colors, including salmon and rusty red. *A. filipendulina* 'Coronation Gold' and *A.* 'Moonshine' have yellow blooms. Grows 4 inches to 5 feet tall, depending on species. Zones 1–24, A1–A3. ◆

Yellow yarrow makes beautiful companion for golden gloriosa daisies. Pictured at left (top to bottom): chrysanthemum, *Salvia* 'Purple Majesty', and *Echinacea purpurea* 'White Swan'.

Broad bronzy foliage of phormium rises over lavender-flowered catmint and heart-shaped leaves of *Houttuynia cordata.* Behind, silky flower plumes of Oriental fountain grass wave over a raised bed.

Grasses for containers

Here are 12 favorites, plus grasslike companions

By Steven R. Lorton

Asking a panel of professional gardeners to name the best ornamental grasses for containers is like asking a group of sommeliers to list their favorite wines: You'll get a different opinion from everyone you ask.

For instance, landscape designer Karen Steeb of Woodinville, Washington, raves about 'Hameln' fountain grass. Container specialist Annie Huston of Columbine Design in Denver prefers purple fountain grass grown as an annual. Gardener Les Brake of

Willow, Alaska, just can't have enough blue oat grass. Then there's nursery professional John Greenlee of Pomona, California, who has so many favorites that he wrote a book about them—*The Encyclopedia of Ornamental Grasses.*

When it comes to great grasses for containers, your main challenge will be deciding which to choose.

Indeed, grasses add a fine, often airy texture to container plantings. They dance in the gentlest breeze, bringing movement to the garden;

many of them make a rustling sound, as well. And even when cold weather turns them brown, their dry leaves and seed heads provide strong visual interest.

Grasses require less maintenance than most other container plants. Most do well in any pot of ample size. While they aren't fussy about soil, most thrive in a rich container mix that provides good drainage. Grasses tolerate drier conditions than most other plants. However, they can't stand going bone-dry (if that happens and the plants go brown, cut them back to encourage new growth).

Feed potted grasses twice monthly during the growing season with a high-nitrogen liquid fertilizer diluted to half strength. Most grasses should be cut back in late winter or early spring. About every three years, knock plants out of their pots, cut the clumps in halves or quarters, and replant the divisions, discarding the parts of the clumps (usually the centers) that have died out.

In cold-winter areas, nonhardy grasses can be grown as annuals. In the hot-summer areas of California and the Southwest, grasses that like a cool, moist climate can be grown as three-season plants, from autumn to early spring.

On the facing page, we describe favorite grasses, a palette of plants in a spectrum of colors.

Clumps of sedge (taller green *Carex secta* and *C. solandri*) and black mondo grass grow over Scotch moss.

Top 12 grasses...

Green

- Feather reed grass (*Calamagrostis* x *acutiflora* 'Karl Foerster'). Narrow, bright green leaves 2 to 3 feet tall are topped with flower plumes that can reach 6 feet. Needs partial shade in hot-summer climates.
- 'Hameln' fountain grass (*Pennisetum alopecuroides* 'Hameln'). Dark green, 12- to 20-inch leaves turn bronzy in autumn. Foxtail-like flowers are at about the same height as leaves and hang on well into winter.
- Oriental fountain grass (*Pennisetum orientale*). Fluffy pink flower plumes are borne from spring to autumn over mounds of gray green leaves reaching 2 feet tall and 2½ feet wide. The foliage turns a straw color in winter.
- Pheasant's-tail grass (*Stipa arundinacea*). Medium green leaves take on a coppery tinge in late fall and winter. Arching clumps reach 2 feet tall and wide. Good choice for hot, dry climates.

Blue

- Blue oat grass (*Helictotrichon sempervirens*). Blue gray leaves in 2- or 3-foot-tall clumps topped by straw-colored flowers in spring. Evergreen in mild-winter climates; semievergreen in colder areas. Comb out dead foliage; this grass resents cropping.
- *Paspalum quadrifolia*. This robust blue grass with a fountaining habit brings a soft, willowy look to the garden. Its ¼- to ½-inch-wide leaves reach up to 3 feet; they have a luminous quality when light passes through them. A good choice for Southern California and the Southwest.

Bronze and purple

- Leather leaf sedge (*Carex buchananii*). Clumps of narrow, reddish bronze leaves reach 2 to 3 feet tall. Makes a striking contrast to blue, silver, or green foliage.
- Purple fountain grass (*Pennisetum setaceum* 'Rubrum' or 'Cupreum'). Pinkish, foxtail-like flower plumes rise over graceful mounds of deep purple leaves. In mild climates, where it is grown as a perennial, it reaches 5 feet tall and wide. In cold climates, where it is grown as an annual, it rarely tops 2 feet. (Note: This grass is banned in Hawaii, where it is listed as a noxious weed.)

Silver

- Japanese silver grass (*Miscanthus sinensis* 'Morning Light'). A narrow band of clear white on the leaf margins turns this airy grass into a shimmering spray of silver reaching 5 to 6 feet.
- Variegated Japanese silver grass (*Miscanthus sinensis* 'Variegatus'). This grass shines like sterling when its white-striped leaves catch the low morning or evening light. Somewhat floppy clumps reach 5 to 6 feet. For hot, dry climates, *M. s. condensatus* 'Cosmopolitan' tolerates heat better; it will take some shade and keep its color.

Yellow

- Japanese forest grass (*Hakonechloa macra* 'Aureola'). Golden yellow–streaked leaves grow in gracefully arching clumps to 14 inches tall. Foliage turns rosy pink after a chill. Prefers shade and moist soil.
- Variegated moor grass (*Molinia caerulea* 'Variegata'). Green leaves with creamy yellow edges grow in 1- to 2-foot-tall clumps topped by arching 3-foot-tall yellowish flower heads.

...and companions

There are many plants with spiky, grasslike leaves that make excellent companions for grasses as long as they have the same growing requirements. Here are three good choices.

- Japanese sweet flag (*Acorus gramineus*). *A. g.* 'Ogon', the best-known variety, produces 6- to 12-inch fans of narrow, golden yellow leaves. It needs ample water and light shade in the hottest climates. Try pairing it or dwarf *A. g.* 'Pusillus Minimus Aureus' with Japanese blood grass.
- Liriope and *Ophiopogon*. These sturdy plants, commonly called lily turf, both form clumps of dark green foliage, sometimes with yellow, gold, or white edges or stripes. Black mondo grass (*O. planiscapus* 'Nigrescens') forms 8-inch tufts of stunning black foliage; try pairing it with sedges and Scotch moss, as in the planter shown on page 100.
- New Zealand flax (*Phormium tenax* and *P.* hybrids). This family of evergreen plants bears swordlike leaves in shades of green, coppery red, and yellow, plus variegations. Clumps reach 2 feet or taller, depending on the species and variety.

sources: Many nurseries stock a variety of grasses in 1-gallon cans. If you can't find what you want, ask your local nursery to place a special order for you. These mail-order sources offer a wide range of grasses.

Forestfarm, 990 Tetherow Rd., Williams, OR 97544; (541) 846-7269 or www.forestfarm.com. Catalog $5.

Heronswood Nursery, 7530 N.E. 288th St., Kingston, WA 98346; (360) 297-4172 or www.heronswood.com. Catalog $5.

Joy Creek Nursery, 20300 N.W. Watson Rd., Scappoose, OR 97056; (503) 543-7474 or www.joycreek.com. Catalog $2. ◆

Fairytale

These perennials bear
irresistible flowers. Set out
plants now for an enchanting
garden next spring

By Lauren Bonar Swezey

columbines

In springtime, when masses of colorful, long-spurred columbine flowers nod gracefully above tall stems, they resemble fluttering butterflies that dazzle the eye. "Columbine is one of those flowers you really want to get close to," says Robert Nold of Denver, who has spent three years writing a book on columbine (genus *Aquilegia*), to be published in the near future.

Columbines come in a range of forms, including single and double flowers with (or without) long or short spurs. Many flowers are classic nodding types; others are borne erectly on stems. Lately, the single-petaled, long-spurred types seem to be in favor with columbine aficionados, and the nectar-bearing spurs are a hit with hummingbirds. All types of columbines arise from mounds of bright green or variegated foliage resembling maidenhair fern.

LEFT: Long-spurred yellow hybrid columbines brighten a shady corner of designer Keeyla Meadows's garden in Albany, California.
ABOVE: Nodding lilac blue–and–white flowers of *Aquilegia flabellata* have hooked spurs.

299

Growing tips

- Grow in full sun or dappled shade. A few woodland species, such as *A. formosa,* prefer cool shade.

- Plant in well-drained soil, un-amended or lightly amended.

- Keep the soil moist but not wet.

- To extend the life of a plant, cut off old flowers before seeds form. If powdery mildew infects foliage, cutting it back may initiate a new flush of foliage.

- To control aphids in spring, spray plants with a soap solution. Robert Nold prefers to use 1 capful of Dr. Bronner's Peppermint Pure-Castile Soap to 1 quart of water.

- Columbines cross-pollinate readily. Save seed only from species grown in isolation from other columbines. The seeds from nonisolated plants often produce flowers different from the original parents.

Short-lived perennials (most last only two to four years), columbines grow in almost every Western climate except Hawaii. Some of the best are native species, including the Southwest's golden columbine *(A. chrysantha)* and Rocky Mountain columbine *(A. caerulea),* Colorado's state flower. However, many of the plants you'll find in nurseries are large-flowered hybrids; although some of these are named, others are random hybrids of unknown parentage. If you want a certain flower color or form, buy only species or named varieties.

Fall is a good time to set out columbine plants from containers, as they can get established and produce a good show of blooms next spring. (In cold-winter climates, wait until next spring to set out plants.) You can also start seeds this coming winter, but such plants may take two seasons to bloom.

TOP: *A. chrysantha* 'Yellow Queen'. ABOVE: Plum-and-white hybrid of Rocky Mountain columbine *(A. caerulea).*

THOMAS J. STORY (2)

Gallery of choice columbines

You can choose from many species and varieties. Here are some of the best.

Showy species

A. clematiflora. Nodding, nearly spurless flowers resemble clematis blossoms. Colors range from rose and white to purple and burgundy red. 'Double Purple', a striking double-flowered type, grows to 24 inches tall. Sunset climate zones 1–10, 14–24, A2–A3.

A. flabellata. Native to Japan, it bears nodding, 1½-inch-wide flowers with white petals, lilac-blue sepals, and 1-inch-long spurs. 'Alba' is a white variety. Leaves are thicker and darker than other columbines. Grows 8 to 18 inches tall. Zones 1–9, 14–24, A2–A3.

Proven varieties

A. 'Swallowtail'. Outward-facing lemon yellow flowers up to 3 inches wide with dramatic 4-inch-long spurs. Grows 3 feet tall. Native to Arizona. Zones 1–10, 14–24, A2–A3.

A. vervaeneana Woodside Variegated Mixed. Grown for its yellow-and-green variegated or all-yellow foliage. Single or double flowers come in blue, pink, purple, and white. Grows up to 30 inches tall. Zones 1–10, 14–24, A2–A3.

McKana Giants. Long-spurred hybrids with 2- to 2½-inch-wide flowers in a range of colors, including blue, pink, red, yellow, and white with contrasting petals. Grows to 3 feet tall. Zones 1–10, 14–24, A2–A3.

Songbird series. Hybrids with flowers up to 3½ inches wide. 'Redbird' has gorgeous red-and-white blooms; 'Robin' has rose-and-white flowers. Grows 1½ to 2 feet tall. Zones 1–10, 14–24, A2–A3.

Western natives

Golden columbine *(A. chrysantha).* Native to the Southwest, it bears upward-facing, fragrant yellow, 1½- to 3-inch-long flowers with 2- to 2½-inch-long spurs. Grows 3 to 4 feet tall. Vigorous plant tolerates heat and resists mildew. 'Yellow Star' and 'Yellow Queen' are two noteworthy varieties. Zones 1–24.

Rocky Mountain columbine *(A. caerulea).* Upward-facing blue-and-white flowers 2 inches wide with spurs to 2 inches long. Grows 1½ to 3 feet tall. Zones 1–11, 14–24 (at lower elevations, plant in a cool, shady location), A1–A3.

Western or red spur columbine *(A. formosa).* Native from Northern California and Utah to Alaska, it bears nodding, bright red flowers 1½ to 2 inches wide with stout spurs. Grows 1½ to 3 feet tall. Zones 1–11, 14–24 (at lower elevations, plant in a cool, shady location), A1–A3. ◆

Before & After

By Kathleen N. Brenzel

Tapestry of blooms—cosmos, dahlias, gloriosa daisies, hollyhocks, purple coneflowers, and roses (right)—covers terraced slope (shown above, before planting).

STEVEN GUNTHER

Beauty and the beast

This Carmel Valley garden cloaked a tough slope with color

■ Color is everywhere you look in Penny Wood's garden in Carmel Valley, California. Red wicker chairs and a brilliant cobalt blue birdbath add punch to the tangle of bright perennials that edges the back of her house. Lemon yellow chairs with blue cushions add cheerful notes on the deck. And throughout the garden, clusters of beautiful blooms come and go with the seasons—irises, lilacs, and peonies in spring, roses and hydrangeas in summer, and a host of perennials in fall. The effect is joyous and casual, and just what Wood wanted. "I love color, chaos, and commotion," she says.

But creating this garden on a beast of a slope took vision. Wood describes the area as "1 acre plunging straight downhill"—it is also sunny, west-facing, and buffeted by winds.

For help, Wood called on landscape designers Elaine and Mark Schlegel, who built a 10-foot-tall retaining wall about 30 feet downhill from the house and another one not far from the back of the house. Behind the walls, they installed a system of drainpipes and a layer of crushed rock to enhance drainage. Then they backfilled with layered soil (half native soil, half a quality topsoil mix). On the sides of the house, they used railroad ties to create planting beds.

"The slope is a tapestry of shades and textures," says Mark Schlegel. Plants chosen for drought tolerance as well as color thrive here, including catmint (*Nepeta* 'Blue Wonder'), ceanothus, lychnis, penstemon, purple coneflower *(Echinacea purpurea)*, rockrose *(Cistus)*, rosemary, and star jasmine. And it's always evolving, as Wood continues to plant fresh finds. She doesn't plan by color schemes. "I wing it," she says. "It all falls into place."

Lessons in color

INDULGE THE SENSES. Let tough plants carry the show, but leave room near the house for treasured plants that may need more water or care. "I wanted things I'd grown up with—hollyhocks, irises, lilacs, peonies," says Wood, who now grows some 14 lilac bushes and lots of roses for fragrance. Workhorses like Mexican bush sage and Australian tea tree (*Leptospermum laevigatum*)— "a superb privacy screen," says Mark Schlegel—grow near the garden's periphery.

BRIDGE THE COLOR GAP WITH ACCESSORIES. "When I began, the garden was so minimal that color was scarce," Wood recalls. The chairs and other accessories added bursts of color until the flowers grew and filled in around them. ◆

Mature trees, instantly

A specimen tree can
give the character of age
to a new landscape

By Jim McCausland
Photographs by Russ Widstrand

A wise gardener once said, "The best time to plant a tree was 20 years ago; the second best time is now." Trees take time to grow. But you can shave years off the process by planting large trees, often sold as "specimen" trees. A wide variety, from olives and palms to oaks and pines, is available. Most nurseries and garden centers can order specimen trees for you or suggest a local source.

We show the planting process here for an olive tree. Olives are well suited to planting as specimens; with their willowlike leaves and trunks that become beautifully gnarled with

This 'Swan Hill' olive, which looks like it has grown here for years, was actually grown in a nursery to this size, then trucked to the site in a box.

age, they give mature character to a new landscape.

Most specimen trees come in wood boxes (usually 24, 30, 36, or 48 inches square). Often they are field grown and have been dug and boxed in stages over a three-month period. This process is intended to force new feeder roots to grow so that the tree is less susceptible to transplant shock.

Many specimen trees are priced by

box size. The 'Swan Hill' shown here is in a 36-inch box and cost about $700. Other trees (especially tall ones) are priced by height. Mexican fan palms, for example, cost about $30 per foot. Still other trees are sold by diameter of the trunk (given in inches). Since diameter depends on the growth rate, which differs considerably by tree type, prices for these trees will vary widely as well.

Specimen trees are too big to plant without heavy equipment and a fair amount of experience, so don't plan on doing the job yourself. However, be sure to determine in advance how much delivery and planting will cost. These costs typically run from a hundred to several hundred dollars—depending on the distance from the supplier to your garden and how difficult it is to get into your site.

Select a site where the tree will have plenty of room. A tree in a 36-inch box will need a planting hole at least one and a half times the width of the box. In addition, most boxed trees will not have achieved their full size. An established olive, for example, grows about 2 feet per year and can top out at about 35 feet tall. ◆

The planting hole was intentionally dug larger than the box. Then the suspended tree can be rotated in the hole until its best "face" is forward; the crane sets it down.

Laying a board across the top of box indicates rootball level relative to surrounding soil. Top of rootball can be a few inches higher than existing grade, as here, but never lower.

The box's sides are removed so they won't impede root growth; the wooden bottom stays in the hole and will rot out in a few months.

Rosa 'Autumn Fire'

When roses are hip

Fall is the time to buy roses for their colorful fruits

By Jim McCausland

Like a sunset at the end of a perfect day, rose hips wrap up the season with a blend of color and natural elegance that may surprise you. The best of these fruits, which range in size from the diameter of a pea to that of a cherry tomato, can compete with blooms for beauty. And they last longer, which endears them to florists and fall gardeners alike.

This month, when summer bloom is giving way to the hips, is the best time of year to search out the ones that will work best in your garden and your flower arrangements. Just scan our list and spend a little time scouting varieties in nurseries and public rose gardens. Many come on disease-resistant rose species; old-fashioned roses, most notably, produce the showiest hips, but a few hybrids have some great hips too. Here are some of our favorites.

Rugosa rose *(Rosa rugosa)* is also called "sea tomato" for its red, patio tomato–sized fruit. This rose heads our list because it often produces both hips and flowers at the same time on disease-resistant, low-maintenance shrubs. Some (like *R. r.* 'Scabrosa') have hips of different colors, from near chartreuse to tomato red, all at once; they represent different stages of maturity. The plants flower for most of the summer, so hip production is a long-term affair. Flowers are commonly in the white or purple-red range, but there are three yellow-flowered rugosas too. Most plants grow 4 to 5 feet tall.

Moyes rose *(R. moyesii)* has hips that look like shiny, red 1½-inch-long, bottle-shaped sticks of sealing wax. Red flowers cover this rather large (8- to 12-foot) shrub in early summer. Look for 'Eddie's Jewel', 'Geranium', or 'Sealing Wax' (perhaps the best for hips).

R. glauca is one of those roses that people buy for foliage—gray-green, burgundy-tinged leaves—and keep for the bright red ½-inch hips, which come in shiny clusters. They look like (and are natural substitutes for) the shiny, red artificial clusters that show up on expensive gift wrapping around Christmas. The pink blooms cover this large (to 7 feet) disease-proof plant once a year, in spring.

Sweet briar rose *(R. rubiginosa,* often sold as *R. eglanteria)* is named for its leaves. After a rain or when they're crushed, the leaves smell like green apples. The plant can grow to 12 feet tall, but hard pruning can turn it into a dense 4-foot hedge. Single pink flowers come only once each year, in late spring, and are followed by a galaxy of ½-inch hips that turn red-orange late in the season.

Chestnut rose *(R. roxburghii)* buds and yellow-orange hips are spiny, like small chestnuts. Ferny foliage makes a soft backdrop for fragrant double spring blooms. Chestnut rose grows to 6 feet tall and wide.

Sources

You can buy roses with striking hips (especially rugosas) at most nurseries, but for some of the more unusual species, try these mail-order sources.

Heirloom Roses: (503) 538-1576 or www.heirloomroses.com.

Heronswood Nursery: (360) 297-4172 or www.heronswood.com. ◆

WINTER-TO-SPRING GARDENS can pack plenty of flower power, thanks to colorful, cool-season annuals such as the ones shown here. To learn more about these easy-to-grow season extenders, see pages 320–324.

October

SAXON HOLT

woodland wonders

Four plants that love growing under oaks

■ Gardening in an oak woodland presents challenges, since the plants you choose must be able to thrive in filtered shade, stand up to heat in summer, and get by on little or no summer water once established (oak roots are prone to rotting, especially in warm, wet soil). Marauding deer can present problems too.

Landscape architect Robyn Sherrill met these challenges with the handsome planting pictured above. For the woodland look her clients wanted in front of their Ross, California, house, Sherrill chose four shade-tolerant flowering plants that provide a long season of interest. Corsican hellebore *(Helleborus argutifolius),* with its clusters of 2-inch-wide greenish flowers, offers winter bloom that lasts for months. In late winter to spring comes flowering currant (*Ribes sanguineum* 'White Icicle'), with drooping 2- to 4-inch-long clusters of white flowers and lime green foliage. Large clusters of 8-inch-wide greenish yellow *Euphorbia amygdaloides* flowers appear midspring to early summer.

A ground cover—5-inch-tall *Rubus pentalobus*—cascades over part of the raised wall. Its salmon-colored berries follow white strawberry-like spring flowers.

As they've matured, all have stood up well to deer. Only the flowering currant needed protection the first two years; netting was used to safeguard it.

— *Lauren Bonar Swezey*

autumn encore for English delphiniums

■ It's October, but the delphiniums in Twilo Scofield's Eugene, Oregon, garden are blooming almost as heavily as if it were June again. What's the secret of this autumn show? After the summer round of blooms, instead of just nipping off the faded blossoms, Scofield cuts the whole flower stalk back to 6 inches above the ground. This stimulates the growth of new shoots that arise from the base of the plant and by September another round of blooms begins.

"It's the vigor of the new English delphiniums that allows for that second bloom," says Alice Doyle, co-owner of Log House Plants, a wholesale grower that supplies these plants to retail nurseries in the Northwest. Originally bred by the Delphinium Society of Great Britain, the hybrid plants are now widely available. Flower colors include deep purple, blue, mauve, pink, and white. Although the flower spikes average 6 feet tall, those in Twilo's garden reached 9 feet in summer and 5 feet in autumn.

Plant them in a sunny spot with well-drained soil. Cut them back three times a year—in spring, summer, and after frost in the fall. Thin to strengthen the plants once they're established by snipping off all but the five most vigorous canes when they emerge in spring. Feed with a complete organic fertilizer once in spring and again in summer after cutting back. After frost, cut the canes down. Doyle suggests capping each stem with aluminum foil; this will prevent winter rains from running down inside the stems and waterlogging the plant's crown. — *Mary-Kate Mackey*

ROBIN CUSHMAN (2)

this hypericum stars in fall

■ A few seasons ago at a yard sale in Eugene, I bought some seedlings labeled *Hypericum androsaemum* 'Albury Purple' because I admired that variety's purple leaves and black fruits. Although the young plants bore green leaves, the seller assured me that they would turn purple when they got older. They never did. Instead, they grew up to be sturdy shrubs, 4 feet tall and as wide, with gray-green foliage.

The mismarked plants turned out to be *Hypericum inodorum* 'Elstead', but I've been thrilled by their performance in my garden. Starting in late June, 'Elstead' is covered with starlike yellow flowers followed by inedible fruits resembling tiny Christmas lights, which spangle the bushes from summer until frost. The fruits start out pinkish red and eventually darken to black.

I feed my plants yearly with an application of organic fertilizer. In spring, I shear them down to 2 feet, but with regular water they bounce back to 4 feet by the end of June.

Fall is the ideal season to plant this deciduous shrub in sun or partial shade. 'Elstead' is not common in Northwest retail nurseries, but two good mail-order sources are Forestfarm (541/846-7269 or www.forestfarm.com) and Joy Creek Nursery (503/543-7474 or www.joycreek.com). — *M.-K. M.*

cool-season flower show

Set out annuals now in Phoenix and Tucson

■ One of the joys of living in the low and intermediate deserts (*Sunset* climate zones 12 and 13) is that you don't have to wait until spring to enjoy flowers. In fact, you shouldn't. If you're going to plant cool-season annuals, now through the middle of November is the time to get them into the ground. It took Diana Zorich, an East Coast transplant, a while to get used to this schedule in her Tucson garden. "Having your busiest gardening season come at the same time you're gearing up for the holidays was a shock the first few years," says Zorich. But as these photos of her backyard demonstrate, she

clearly has the hang of it now.

Because nursery annuals don't do well in the heavy alkaline soil of the Southwest, Tucson landscape designer Margaret West suggested using planter beds for seasonal color and included two in the garden's design: the 45-foot-long one in these photos and a 25-foot-long bed that wraps around a patio. But Zorich likes even more color, so she decorates the garden liberally with additional containers.

Zorich's fearless color scheme is inspired by the bright-hued Mexican tiles that are inset into her outdoor fireplace. She uses the same colors

every year but varies the plants. The palette shown here includes brick red and cherry snapdragons, lemon yellow and lavender blue pansies, salmon and white petunias, and multicolored Iceland poppies. The show goes on until late April.

— *Sharon Cohoon*

TERRENCE MOORE (2)

a backyard meadow

■ Creating a yarrow meadow is a pretty notion that led to this 10-year-old casual garden in Rancho Santa Fe, California. But is it practical? Well, as owners Shirle and Bill McConnor will tell you, there's good news and there's bad news.

Starting a meadow garden is a lot of work. Until the desired grass or ground cover fills in, weeding is a major chore. And, though the weeding gets a little easier every year if you're vigilant at the start, you still have to stay on top of it. On the other hand, the only other task required is mowing down the whole field once a year to give the meadow a fresh start.

Now for the good news. Seeding common yarrow *(Achillea millefolium)* is a very economical way to cover a large bare area because you can buy seed by the pound. Peaceful Valley Farm Supply (888/784-1722 or www.groworganic. com), for instance, sells it for $15.60 per pound. Yarrow won't affect your water bill much, either. The McConnors' meadow gets by almost entirely on natural irrigation. In addition, they have a nearly year-round supply of bouquet filler. "Though spring is yarrow's prime bloom time, there's always a batch in flower somewhere," says Shirle. And yarrow is a perfect companion for spring bulbs, she explains. "They're in bloom before the yarrow starts growing again, and when they're finished and their foliage is getting yellow, the yarrow is tall enough to hide it." — *S.C.*

flaming foliage

■ When my husband, Bob, and I drove by a grove of mature Chinese pistache trees *(Pistacia chinensis)* in front of the U.S. Forest Service Oak Grove Fire Station east of Temecula last fall (pictured at right), we thought for a moment that a prescribed fire might be burning. The trees were a blaze of flame-colored foliage. Bob couldn't resist pulling over to take pictures. According to the Forest Service, he wasn't the first; motorists pull over every fall to snap pictures of these trees or to lunch under their scarlet canopies.

Chinese pistache is one of the few deciduous trees whose foliage colors up reliably in Southern California's mild-winter climates. Its leaves turn luminous orange to scarlet red, sometimes yellow. It's most brilliant in inland valleys, where temperatures are more extreme, but it looks gorgeous even along the coast. It is also the only tree whose foliage

BOB WIGAND (2)

turns scarlet in the desert.

The tree grows fairly quickly to 25 feet tall, then slowly to 40 feet or more. It has a graceful shape and, with age, develops beautiful, deeply textured bark. It tolerates a range of soil conditions, including alkaline soil and infrequent watering.

Pistacia chinensis is widely available at nurseries. Fall is the best time to choose a tree for its color. — *Judy Wigand*

Clippings

• New book. Several years in the making, *The Trees of Golden Gate Park and San Francisco,* by Elizabeth Mc-Clintock and edited by Richard G. Turner Jr. (Heyday Books, Berkeley, 2001; $18.95; 510/549-3564 or www.heydaybooks.com), is finally a reality. This joint effort with the Pacific Horticultural Foundation, Strybing Arboretum Society, Friends of Recreation and Parks, Friends of the Urban Forest, and San Francisco Tree Advisory Board has culminated in an impressive guide detailing more than 120 trees.

Chapter 1, by landscape architect Russell A. Beatty, is a fascinating history of Golden Gate Park's transformation from windswept, marshy, almost treeless sand dunes into an urban forest, thanks to two determined men, William Hammond Hall and John McLaren. Urban forester Peter Ehrlich wrote the second chapter, which looks into reforestation issues related to the park's aging trees. The rest of the book, by McClintock—a longtime botanist at University of California at Berkeley—is a field guide to the trees.

• Looking-glass plants. Australian Native Plants Nursery in Ventura is an excellent source for Australian and South African plants. Owner Jo O'Connell, an Aussie, requests that visitors make an appointment before stopping by. *(805) 649-3362 or www.australianplants.com.*

Cheerful planter is filled with flowering kale, pansies, and dusty miller. Paint gives the 8-inch-diameter clay pots a striking finish (bottom photo); once dry, they'll sit on 5-inch diameter pots set upside down inside the wooden planter box (below).

THOMAS J. STORY (3)

two-tiered for fall plants

■ This double-decker planter is filled with festive seasonal flowers. Painted clay pots are planted with dark purple and orange pansies, dusty miller, and large heads of flowering kale, then elevated on inverted clay pots inside a long wooden planter. The materials list is ordered for ease of shopping.

DESIGN: Jill Slater (650/363-0524)
TIME: 1 hour, plus shopping
COST: $100 to $140

materials and plants

• Three 8-inch-diameter **clay pots**
• Three 5-inch-diameter **clay azalea** (short) **pots**
• Green **wooden planter box**, 36 inches long, 10 inches wide, and 10½ inches tall
• One 2-cubic-foot bag of **potting soil**
• Controlled-release **fertilizer**

• Three 4-inch **purple kale**
• Four sixpacks **Melody Purple** and **Orange pansies**
• Four sixpacks **Trick or Treat pansies** (orange with black face)
• Three sixpacks **dusty miller**
• Four 4-inch **green-and-white kale**
• One pint acrylic **burnt orange paint**
• One pint acrylic **straw yellow paint**

directions

1. Paint the 8-inch-diameter pots orange; let dry a few minutes. Paint the rims yellow. Allow to dry (10 to 15 minutes).
2. Fill painted pots with potting soil; mix in controlled-release fertilizer. Plant one purple kale in the center of a pot; around it, alternate pansies with three to four dusty miller plants; water well. Repeat for the other two pots.

3. Set the planter box in its permanent location (it's heavy when full); fill it partway with potting soil. Space three inverted 5-inch clay pots evenly in the planter box so their bottoms sit just below the rim of the box. Fill in around them with soil, leaving the tops uncovered; mix in fertilizer.
4. Set one or two green-and-white kale plants on each end of the wooden box. Along the planter sides, alternate pansies and dusty miller. Place two plants between each inverted 5-inch pot. Water well.
5. Set the 8-inch pots on top of the inverted pots. — *L.B.S.*

surefire autumn color on the vine

■ When it comes to fiery fall foliage, Virginia creeper *(Parthenocissus quinquefolia)* puts on a show that's unsurpassed by other deciduous vines. Here you see it blazing up the wall of a stately house in Denver's Seventh Avenue Historic District.

In summer, leaves composed of five 6-inch-long leaflets form a dense dark green blanket. Small purple berries resembling grapes appear in late summer (these fruits attract birds but are toxic to humans). In autumn, the leaves turn brilliant shades of scarlet before dropping.

Hardy enough to grow in nearly all *Sunset* climate zones, Virginia creeper will thrive in either full sun or filtered shade, and its low water requirement makes it a natural choice for xeriscapes. A versatile vine, it can be used to dress up a dull wall, cover a boring fence, or create a living privacy screen. Or let it sprawl on slopes as a ground cover to control erosion.

Set out nursery plants early this fall or next spring. Keep in mind, though, that a single established plant can spread 60 feet or more. The vine attaches itself with clinging tendrils, which can be difficult to remove from wood siding and mortared brick and stone surfaces. Prune as needed to keep the exuberant foliage from casting unwanted shade on neighboring plants.

— *Colleen Smith*

PAUL BOUSQUET

niche for natives

Low-maintenance native plants fill this garden in Riverside

■ Nan Simonsen's reasons for wanting a nearly self-sustaining garden at the far edge of her 2½-acre property in Riverside, California, were mostly pragmatic. "This area is too far away from the house for lugging sacks of fertilizer and bags of clippings back and forth," she says. It was a nice extra that this low-maintenance section turned out to be one of her favorite parts of the garden.

For planting suggestions, the Simonsens turned to Murrieta-based garden designer Susan Frommer, of Plants for Dry Places (909/461-9691). Because a natural stream runs through the property, Frommer suggested a California riparian theme. She developed a blueprint and a plant list, and Nan and her husband, Bob, took it from there.

They used unpeeled lodgepole pines to build the rustic ramada Frommer had suggested. They started visiting na-

tive plant nurseries and botanic gardens, and acquiring the plants on their list. And then, one exhausting three-day weekend, they put in more than 150 plants.

Now going on its third year, the native garden has proved as fuss-free as Nan hoped. Its mesa and slopes are covered with ceanothus, salvias, fremontodendrons, and mallows, none of which require feeding or grooming. Most of the plants, with the exception of the fremonto-dendrons and ceanothus, get water once or twice a summer—"just to keep them a little greener," says Nan. "They'd live without it."

Nan does visit the garden daily, but for pleasure, not chores. "When I walk the property with my dogs to see what's in bloom," she says, "this is where we always stop and rest." —S.C.

new pansy named for butterfly

■ Native to the American tropics, morpho butterflies are distinguished by their brilliant iridescent blue wings. Now, *morpho* has made its way into the name of a new pansy whose delicate blooms resemble shimmering butterflies. Bred by Sakata Seed America in Morgan Hill, California, 'Ultima Morpho' is one of the winners in the 2002 All-America Selections program.

Sunset head gardener Rick LaFrentz, who has grown 'Ultima Morpho' from seed, likes the way the plants perform in containers. The 1½- to 2-inch blossoms are pastel blue with golden yellow centers marked by dark blue rays or whiskers. The blooms are borne on 3-inch stems over plants that spread 8 to 10 inches wide.

In mild-winter areas, most major garden centers and nurseries will carry plants of 'Ultima Morpho' this fall for cool-season planting. In cold-winter areas, plants will be available next spring. You can order seeds from Park Seed (800/845-3369 or www.parkseed.com).

— *Dick Bushnell*

CHRISTINA SCHMIDHOFER

THOMAS J. STORY

Cinderella cactus

■ Every fall, my Christmas cactus *(Schlumbergera)* displays a spectacular profusion of blooms on a covered patio in San Mateo, California. A bit stark-looking for most of the year, come October, it steals my heart when its stunning cloak of pale pink flowers appears.

I first met this beauty six years ago when I moved into a house and found it hunkered down on the patio, covered with dust, splattered with house paint, and busting out of its original 6-inch plastic container. Too softhearted to give it the heave-ho, I put it out of sight behind a toolshed. Months passed, and when I noticed it again, in early fall, I was surprised to find the plant still alive. Though parched, it had sprouted a dozen tiny flower buds on its branch tips.

Touched by its tenacity, I moved it into a 10-inch terra-cotta pot, gave it a bath and a big drink of water, and moved it back into view. A few weeks later, it rewarded me with a modest, but promising, show of flowers. Since then, I've repotted this survivor once more, to the 12-inch glazed pot shown at left.

Each fall, the cactus gives me a show grander than the year before. Its first flowers pop at the end of September, and it continues to dazzle until nearly Thanksgiving. During warm months, I water regularly and fertilize occasionally with fish emulsion. It gets little water in cool weather and no fertilizer. In mild-winter areas, your plant, like mine, will live happily on a covered patio year-round.

Christmas cactus are widely sold as holiday gift plants; you can buy a small one for a few dollars. — *Alan Phinney*

BEN WOOLSEY

a masterpiece deck in Seattle

■ When you have a magnificent background, you want a foreground that underlines but doesn't overwhelm the scene. This deck on Seattle's Queen Anne Hill illustrates this principle. To complement a heavenly view overlooking the Space Needle, downtown Seattle, and Elliott Bay, landscape architect Robert Chittock underscored the horizon with an elegantly restrained blend of hardscape and softscape.

Along the side of an existing swimming pool, he designed this deck with a sunken pond. First, the concrete was poured in an irregular shape, measuring about 5 feet wide, 7 feet long, and 2 feet deep, and rocks were posi-

tioned around the pond. Then, a single weeping Atlas cedar (*Cedrus atlantica* 'Glauca Pendula') was planted in the ground near the pond. Finally, the deck of cedar 1-by-5s was built around the pond and tree.

The pond is planted with taro and water lilies and stocked with goldfish. A recirculating pump aerates the water. A few container plants are placed on the deck beneath the boughs of the Atlas cedar. This drought-tolerant native of North Africa doesn't need any extra water, even in the driest Seattle summer. However, the owners do have to prune the branches regularly to keep them from getting too long and heavy. — *Steven R. Lorton*

WHAT TO DO IN YOUR GARDEN IN OCTOBER

PLANTING

☐ **BULBS.** For the best selection of spring-blooming bulbs, shop nurseries and garden centers early in the month.

☐ **COVER CROPS.** Zones 4–7: Sow cover crops such as Austrian field peas, crimson clover, tyfon, and vetch during the first week of October. They'll grow slowly through winter; plow them under next spring to enrich the soil organically.

☐ **GROUND COVERS.** Get plants in the ground now so they'll become established over winter and will put on a burst of new growth when the weather warms up.

☐ **LAWNS.** Zones 4–7: There's still time to start a new lawn if you act early in the month. The easiest, fastest way to do it this time of year is with sod, but you can also start from seed. Begin by tilling the seedbed 6 to 8 inches deep, picking out the rocks and leveling the site. Then put down sod or sow seed, and keep the site evenly moist until fall rains take over.

☐ **PERENNIALS.** Fall-planted perennials have the entire winter to put out roots, then grow and flower next spring.

☐ **TREES, SHRUBS.** This is the best time of year to plant shrubs and trees, especially those that display fall foliage color or ornamental fruits (see page 326).

MAINTENANCE

☐ **ANNUALS.** Zones 1–3: When frost hits, pull plants, shake soil off the roots, and toss them onto the compost pile. Zones 4–7: Continue to deadhead and fertilize one last time early in the month.

☐ **CARE FOR FUCHSIAS.** Zones 1–3: Bring fuchsias into a protected, dark place for the winter (a cool basement or frost-free garage is fine). Zones 4–7: Before freezing weather arrives, bring container-grown fuchsias into a frost-free place. Spread mulch around fuchsias growing in the ground.

☐ **CARE FOR ROSES.** Continue to remove most faded flowers, but let a few blooms form hips, since that process helps plants wind down into winter dormancy.

☐ **HARVEST FRUITS, VEGETABLES.** Pick them at least every other day to keep rot from taking hold and spreading. If you haven't done so yet, pick all tomatoes that have started to show color and bring them indoors to finish ripening on a windowsill.

☐ **MAKE COMPOST.** As you clean out the summer garden, pile everything but diseased or thorny material onto the compost pile. Water enough to keep the pile as moist as a squeezed-out sponge.

☐ **WATER.** Until rains begin, water established plants deeply. Drought-stressed plants are far more likely to be damaged in hard winters than well-hydrated ones. ◆

WHAT TO DO IN YOUR GARDEN IN OCTOBER

PLANTING

☐ **ANNUALS. Zones 7–9, 14–17:** For a cheerful blend of circus colors in garden beds next spring, try planting mixed colors of annual nemesia *(N. strumosa)* (zones 15–17), ranunculus, and snapdragon this fall.

☐ **BULBS THAT NATURALIZE.** Zones 14–17: Bulbs such as daffodils, leucojum, muscari, ornamental alliums, scilla, or species tulips all naturalize in mild climates. To create an informal mass of flowers that look as if they're spreading naturally across the landscape, toss out handfuls of a single kind of bulb over a planting area, varying the density. (For a better chance of repeat bloom in following years, choose a site in full sun that doesn't get much summer water.) Repeat with a second or third kind of bulb, if desired. Plant where bulbs fall. To purchase large quantities of bulbs at a reasonable price, try Dutch Gardens (800/818-3861) or Van Bourgondien (800/622-9997 or www.dutchbulbs.com).

☐ **FRUIT SALAD TREES.** Zones 7–9, 14–17: If you're short on space for a few fruit trees, try a single tree grafted with multiple fruit types grafted onto one rootstock: You might find 'Blenheim' apricot, 'Fantasia' nectarine, 'Elberta' and 'Babcock' peaches, or 'Santa Rosa' plum. Often sold as "fruit salad" trees, they can be ordered through most local nurseries (or from Orchard Nursery & Florist; 925/284-4474).

Eureka
Redding
CALIFORNIA
NEVADA
Mendocino
Santa Rosa
Sacramento
San Francisco
San Jose
Monterey
Fresno

Sunset
CLIMATE ZONES
☐ Mountain (1-2)
☐ Valley (7-9)
☐ Inland (14)
☐ Coastal (15-17)

DEBRA LAMBERT

☐ **GARLIC. Zones 7–9, 14–17:** Break the bulbs into individual cloves and plant them, scar end down, in rich, well-drained soil. Cover regular garlic with 1 to 2 inches of soil; use 4 to 6 inches of soil for elephant garlic (not a true garlic, but a bulbing leek with mild garlic flavor). Press the soil down firmly, then water. Continue to irrigate when the weather is dry. For a wide selection of garlic varieties by mail, try Filaree Farm (catalog $2; 182 Conconully Hwy., Okanogan, WA 98840; 509/422-6940 or www.filareefarm.com).

☐ **LARGE GROUND COVERS.** Zones 7–9, 14–17: To cover banks and large expanses of ground, use wide-spreading ground covers. Try *Arctostaphylos* 'Emerald Carpet', *Ceanothus* 'Centennial', coyote brush, ivy, *Juniperus chinensis* 'Parsonii', varieties of *J. horizontalis, J. procumbens* 'Green Mound', kinnikinnick, myoporum, and 'Corsican Prostrate' or 'Huntington Blue' trailing rosemary. For fastest coverage, set plants in offset rows (use groups of four to form diamonds). To check spacing (as well as soil and sunlight requirements) for specific plants, see listings in the *Sunset Western Garden Book*.

MAINTENANCE

☐ **DIVIDE PERENNIALS.** Perennials such as asters, bellflowers, callas, daisies, daylilies, helianthus, heliopsis, rudbeckias, and yarrows that look weak and crowded—with smaller blooms than normal—probably need dividing. Use a spading fork to dig out each clump so the rootball comes up intact. Wash or gently shake off excess soil, then cut off divisions using a sharp knife, pruning shears, or shovel (for tough roots). Each division should have leaves and plenty of roots. Plant immediately. ◆

WHAT TO DO IN YOUR GARDEN IN OCTOBER

PLANTING

☐ **ANNUALS.** Cool-season bedding plants can be set out in coast, inland, and low-desert gardens (*Sunset* climate zones 22–24, 18–21, and 13, respectively). Choices include African daisies, clarkias, cyclamen, delphiniums, godetias, Iceland poppies, lobelias, nasturtiums, nemesia, ornamental kale, pansies, primroses, snapdragons, stock, and violas.

☐ **BULBS.** Continue to plant anemones, daffodils, Dutch irises, ipheion, ornithogalums, and all South African bulbs that naturalize well here, such as babiana, crocosmia, freesia, homeria, ixia, nerine, sparaxis, and watsonia. Buy hyacinth and tulip bulbs, but give them at least a six-week chill in the refrigerator before planting.

☐ **BULB COVERS.** Forget-me-nots, Johnny-jump-ups, lobelias, and sweet alyssum planted over spring-blooming bulbs provide color until the bulbs sprout, push up through them easily, then flower. After the blooms are spent, such plants cover the yellowing bulb foliage.

☐ **ORNAMENTALS.** Ceanothus, toyon, and other California natives, accustomed to our wet-winter, dry-summer climate, take hold in the garden best when planted in the fall. So do rosemary, santolina, and other Mediterranean plants. Fall is also an excellent time to plant trees, shrubs, and other permanent plants.

Sunset
CLIMATE ZONES

1-3 7-9 11 13 14-24

DEBRA LAMBERT

☐ **VEGETABLES.** Gardeners in frost-free zones can continue to sow beets, carrots, fava beans, lettuces, onions, peas, radishes, Swiss chard and other greens, and turnips, as well as set out transplants of broccoli, cabbage, and other cole crops.

MAINTENANCE

☐ **DIVIDE PERENNIALS.** Plunge a spade into the soil around crowded perennials such as Shasta daisies, then pop the plants out of ground. Wash or shake off excess soil, then divide each plants with a sharp knife or spade. Partially cut back foliage on divisions and replant them immediately. Other candidates for dividing include asters, clivia, daylilies, gazanias, rudbeckias, and yarrows.

☐ **FEED ROSES.** For a final flush of blossoms around the winter holidays, deadhead and fertilize roses after fall bloom.

☐ **OVERSEED LAWNS.** To green up warm-season lawns like Bermuda or St. Augustine, overseed with annual rye now. Cut the grass short before seeding; mulch with manure or a fine-grained soil amendment afterward. Keep the soil damp until seeds sprout.

☐ **PREPARE FOR SANTA ANA WINDS.** To prevent branch breakage, thin jacarandas and other top-heavy trees. Check stakes supporting young trees to ensure that they're strong. Also make sure ties are loose enough not to cut into bark.

☐ **PRUNE.** For bird of paradise, canna, and ginger, cut stems that have already flowered to the ground.

PEST CONTROL

☐ **MANAGE PESTS.** To control aphids and whiteflies, hose off plants or spray with insecticidal soap. Repeat every three to four days. Handpick and dispatch snails and slugs early in the morning; search through strappy-leafed plants like agapanthus and daylilies, their favored hideouts. ◆

mountain · checklist

PLANTING

☐ **AMARYLLIS INDOORS.** Plant amaryllis bulbs in containers early this month for Thanksgiving bloom or in late October for Christmas bloom.

☐ **GARLIC.** Choose hardneck types like 'Chesnok Red' or 'Korean Red'. Break bulbs into cloves; plant each clove 4 to 6 inches apart and 3 to 4 inches deep in good garden soil that receives full sun. Mulch the bed after planting.

☐ **LANDSCAPE PLANTS.** Set out hardy ground covers and container-grown trees, shrubs, and perennials no later than six weeks before the ground normally freezes in your area. From fall through winter, water the transplants often enough to keep their rootballs from drying out.

☐ **SPRING BULBS.** Before the ground freezes, set out bulbs of allium, crocus, daffodil, fritillary, hyacinth, *Iris reticulata*, scilla, and tulip. Dig holes 6 to 8 inches deep for daffodils and tulips, or 3 to 4 inches deep for small bulbs, then add bulb fertilizer at the bottom of the holes and plant the bulbs. Water the soil deeply and mulch the bed after planting.

Sunset CLIMATE ZONES
☐ 1-3 ☐ 10-11

DEBRA LAMBERT

☐ **WILDFLOWERS.** Sow seeds of bachelor's button, calendula, California desert bluebell *(Phacelia campanularia)*, California poppy, larkspur, love-in-a-mist, rose campion *(Lychnis coronaria)*, Shirley poppy *(Papaver rhoeas)*, skyrocket *(Ipomopsis aggregata)*, sweet alyssum, and sweet William catchfly *(Silene armeria)*. Broadcast seeds over soil, lightly rake them in, and cover with a thin layer of compost or soil. Fall rains and winter snows will provide moisture to germinate seeds.

MAINTENANCE

☐ **CARE FOR LAWNS.** Give lawns their last feeding of the season. Fertilizer applied before the lawn goes dormant in the fall helps the grass green up faster in the spring.

☐ **CUT BACK PERENNIALS.** After the first hard freeze, cut back perennials such as aster, campanula, daylily, phlox, and veronica, leaving 6-inch stubs above the ground.

☐ **DRAIN DRIP SYSTEMS.** Before the soil freezes, drain drip systems to prevent cracked tubing. Remove end caps from the main lines, turn the water on for a few minutes, then shut it off. Drain all the water, then replace the end caps. Roll up soaker hoses and store in a dark, protected place for the winter.

☐ **HARVEST, STORE CROPS.** Pick broccoli and brussels sprouts before a killing frost hits. Cut pumpkins and winter squash with 2-inch stems; store at 50° to 60°. Beets, carrots, potatoes, and turnips keep best at 35° to 45° in barely damp sand. Onions and shallots need cool, dry storage in mesh bags or slotted crates. Store apples and pears indoors in separate containers at 33° to 40°.

☐ **MULCH FOR WINTER.** After a hard freeze, spread 2 to 3 inches of compost, weed-free straw, or other organic matter to protect bulbs, perennial flowers, vegetables, and strawberries.

☐ **WATER.** Water deeply before a hard freeze is predicted. Continue watering flower beds, lawn, shrubs, and trees once a month if the soil is dry 2 to 3 inches below the surface. — *Marcia Tatroe* ◆

WHAT TO DO IN YOUR GARDEN IN OCTOBER

PLANTING

☐ **COOL-SEASON COLOR.** Zones 1–2 and 10 (Albuquerque): Sow seeds of larkspur, snapdragon, and sweet alyssum for early spring boom. Zones 11–13 (Las Vegas, Tucson, Phoenix): Set out calendula, dianthus, Iceland poppy, lobelia, ornamental cabbage and kale, pansy, petunia, snapdragon, and stock.

☐ **COOL-SEASON CROPS.** Zones 12–13: Sow seeds of beets, carrots, kohlrabi, lettuce, peas, radishes, Swiss chard, and turnips. Plant seedlings of broccoli, cabbage, and cauliflower. Set out transplants of bulbing-type onions and plant cloves of garlic.

☐ **GROUND COVERS.** Zone 10: Plant low-growing cotoneaster, juniper, and trailing indigo bush *(Dalea greggii)*. Zones 12–13: For fast cover, try Saltillo evening primrose *(Oenothera stubbei)* and Mexican evening primrose *(O. speciosa)*, but beware of their tendency to spread quickly. Less aggressive choices include ice plant, sundrops *(Calylophus hartwegii)*, and Goodding's and moss verbena *(V. gooddingii* and *V. pulchella gracilior)*.

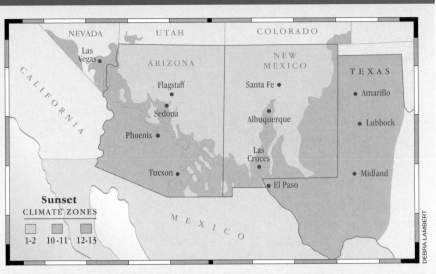

☐ **HERBS.** Zones 10–13: Set out transplants of burnet, chives, Mexican tarragon, oregano, rosemary, thyme, and winter savory. Sow seeds of cilantro, dill, and parsley.

☐ **SPRING-BLOOMING ANNUALS.** Zones 11–13: Sow seeds of African daisy, scarlet flax *(Linum grandiflorum* 'Rubrum'), Shirley poppy *(Papaver rhoeas)*, and toadflax, plus wildflowers such as California desert bluebell *(Phacelia campanularia)*, California poppy, farewell-to-spring, Mexican tulip poppy, and tidytips *(Layia platyglossa)*. Prepare soil by running a rake over the surface, spread a 1- to 2-inch layer of organic mulch, broadcast seed over the mulch, then rake it in. Water daily until the seeds germinate.

☐ **SPRING BULBS.** Zones 1–2: Plant allium, anemone, crocus, daffodil, galanthus, hyacinth, and tulip. Zones 10–11: Set out any of the above, plus freesia, iris, and ranunculus. Zones 12–13: Plant any listed above, plus amaryllis, calla, homeria, oxalis, sparaxis, and watsonia. Note: Bulbs of crocus, hyacinth, and tulip must chill in the refrigerator for at least six weeks before planting.

☐ **SPRING-FLOWERING PERENNIALS.** Zones 11–13: For spring bloom, plant blackfoot daisy *(Melampodium leucanthum)*, chuparosa *(Justicia californica)*, desert marigold, gaura, penstemon, and salvia.

MAINTENANCE

☐ **DIVIDE PERENNIALS.** Zones 10–13: Dig and divide bee balm, catmint, daylily, and Shasta daisy to reinvigorate plants and increase blooms next season. — *Mary Irish* ◆

THOMAS J. STORY LEFT: MARION BRENNER

FAR LEFT: Orange
nemesia, orange Iceland
poppies, and yellow and
red tulips turn this front
yard into a blaze of
color in early spring.
Golden feverfew and
'Red Oak Leaf' lettuce
are striking accents
between flowers.
LEFT: Yellow primroses
and ranunculus fill
the hanging basket in
the foreground; white
primroses fill the basket
behind. DESIGN: Hilda
Schwerin, Wegman's
Nursery, Redwood City,
CA (650/368-5908).

flower
power

Cool, colorful annuals
are easy to grow and
make great fillers in
winter-to-spring gardens

By Lauren Bonar Swezey

■ Not long ago, when English-style perennial gardens were all the rage, annuals fell
from favor. But now they're making a come-
back, as savvy gardeners rediscover the important role they play in beds, borders, and
containers. As season extenders, annuals are unsurpassed. • When
summer- and fall-blooming perennials
die down, cool-season annuals kick
into gear to fill gaps between established plants. There they'll grow and
bloom through winter until their
crescendo in spring. • They have other
benefits as well. "Cool-season annuals are
the easiest annuals to grow," explains horticultural consultant and garden designer
Carole Kraft, who created the planting
pictured on page 323. "They're almost
pest-free, but watch out for snails and
slugs." • If you don't have room for lots of
plants, you can still create dramatic ef-
fects. Even pocket gardens and containers
pack a lot of flower power.

MARION BRENNER (2)

A small slice of the garden shown on page 320 could be easily achieved in any size garden.
A. Orange Iceland poppy **B.** 'Yellow Emperor' tulip **C.** Red lily-flowered tulip **D.** Orange *Nemesia strumosa* **E.** Rose red and yellow-edged 'Corsage' tulip **F.** *Chrysanthemum parthenium* 'Aureum'

A garden with sizzle

The hot and spicy colors in this front yard in Piedmont, California, aren't for everyone; it takes courage to put on such a bold show. In early spring, bright orange flowers contrast beautifully with foliage in deep purple, dark green, and lime green—with tall red and yellow tulips as accents. "It's a busy garden, but the masses of orange make it work," says the designer.

DESIGN: Bob Clark, Oakland (510/633-1391)

DESIGN TIPS FROM A PRO

Oakland landscape designer Bob Clark is a master at combining annuals with other garden plants for color.

■ **Choose a color scheme.** Clark prefers hot colors (orange, red, yellow) in winter because they're more warming and vivid. But in spring, he says, "people respond to pastels."

Take existing plants into account. If gray foliage plays a major role in your garden, stick to cool-colored flowers. If lime green and variegated yellow-and-green foliage are prominent, try hot colors. On the other hand, explains Clark, "deep green foliage is more forgiving. You can go with either cool or hot colors."

■ **Buy plants with flowers in single colors, not mixes.** Mixed colors often impart a garish or spotty look to garden beds, unless they've been specifically bred for compatibility (like Antique Shades pansies). Single colors, combined with your favorite similar or contrasting colors, have more impact.

■ **Consider bloom time.** When do you want your major show of blooms? For winter bloom (in mild climates), mix in plenty of calendula, pansies, primroses, or violas. Annuals like godetia, nemesia, and schizanthus bloom in spring. For a long season of bloom, combine plants that peak in both seasons.

■ **Don't forget foliage.** To create a foil for flowers, Clark uses annual leafy vegetables (cabbage, lettuce) and herbs (fennel, feverfew, parsley) with interesting textures and colors. Since most cool-season annuals (particularly winter-blooming types) are short, some of these plants—especially fennel and mustard— also provide height until later-blooming tall flowers emerge.

■ **Consider the "visual pace."** Gardens viewed up close allow for more complexity; plantings seen by passing motorists will be more effective when simple.

THOMAS J. STORY ILLUSTRATIONS: MIMI OSBORNE

Snow white

Mild-climate gardeners needn't pine for snow in winter. It's easy to create the look of a light dusting of snow—all frosty and cool—with an all-white planting. Designed for a long season of bloom, the planting shown at left covers a two-tiered rock retaining wall. Primrose and cyclamen tucked among the stones bloom from fall through spring. Bacopa, a perennial accent, provides the lacy white flowers around them (it freezes back below 28° to 30°). Come late winter, white narcissus pop up through the garden, and by spring the garden is in its full glory. White-flowered *Chrysanthemum paludosum* and *Loropetalum chinense* fill the center pot.

DESIGN: Bob Clark

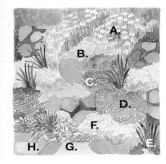

A. *Chrysanthemum paludosum*
B. *Loropetalum chinense* **C.** Bacopa *(Sutera cordata)* **D.** Baby's tears *(Soleirolia soleirolii)* **E.** 'Thalia' narcissus (foliage) **F.** *Primula obconica* **G.** Cyclamen **H.** *Ophiopogon* 'Silver Dragon'

A touch of sunshine

Although Carole Kraft specializes in perennials, she finds that annuals are her mainstay in winter; they provide abundant color when perennials are dormant. The mixed pocket garden she designed to liven up the front entry pictured at left—filled with cool, soft purples and lemon yellows—is nearly everblooming. "The owners wanted something bright and cheerful but not overwhelming, says Kraft. "Lavender and purple cool down the bright yellow, so the garden is more peaceful."

DESIGN: Natural Garden by Carole Kraft, Los Altos, CA (650/599-3379)

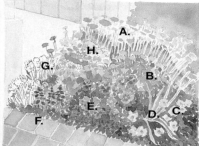

A. Pincushion flower (*Scabiosa caucasica* 'Fama') **B.** Fiesta *Calendula officinalis* **C.** Pale yellow Cream Crown pansy **D.** 'Mount Hood' daffodil (foliage) **E.** Rose Maxim pansy **F.** Catmint (*Nepeta* x *faassenii* 'Blue Wonder') **G.** Evergreen candytuft (*Iberis sempervirens*) **H.** *Sedum* 'Autumn Joy'

flowerpower

31 cool-season bloomers for fall planting

Climate zones are taken from the 2001 edition of the *Sunset Western Garden Book.*

◼ Cool colors

Bachelor's button (*Centaurea cyanus*); 1–24, H1–H2.

Canterbury bell (*Campanula medium*); 1–9, 14–24.

Chinese forget-me-not (*Cynoglossum amabile*); 1–24, A2–A3, H1–H2.

Corn cockle (*Agrostemma githago*); 1–24.

Florists' cineraria (*Senecio x hybridus*); 16–17, 22–24.

Flowering cabbage and kale; all zones.

Forget-me-not (*Myosotis sylvatica*); 1–24, A1–A3.

Honeywort (*Cerinthe major*); 1–24.

Stock (*Matthiola*); 1–24.

Sweet alyssum (*Lobularia maritima*); all zones.

◼ Warm colors

African daisy (*Dimorphotheca*); 1–24 (best in warm-summer climates).

Calendula (*C. officinalis*); 1–24, H1.

Chrysanthemum (*C. multicaule*); 1–24, A1–A3.

◼ Multicolors

Dianthus (many); 1–24, A2–A3.

English daisy (*Bellis perennis*); 1–9, 14–24.

Foxglove (*Digitalis*); zones vary by species.

Godetia (*Clarkia amoena*); 1–24.

Iceland poppy (*Papaver nudicaule*); annual in 7–9, 12–24; perennial in 1–6, 10, A2–A3.

Larkspur (*Consolida ajacis*); 1–24.

Nemesia (*N. strumosa*); 1–24.

Pansy (*Viola x wittrockiana*); all zones.

Petunia (*P. x hybrida*); winter annual only in zones 12–13.

Poor man's orchid (*Schizanthus pinnatus*); 1–9, 14–24 (best in 1–6, 15–17, 21–24).

Primrose (*Primula*); zones vary by type.

Shirley poppy (*Papaver rhoeas*); 1–24, A1–A3 (best in cool-summer areas).

Snapdragon (*Antirrhinum majus*); 1–24, A3.

Sweet peas (*Lathyrus odoratus*); all zones.

Toadflax (*Linaria*); 1–24.

◼ White

Globe candytuft (*Iberis umbellata*); 1–24.

Chrysanthemum (*C. paludosum*); 1–24, A1–A3.

Viola (*V. cornuta*); all zones.

◼ ...and their partners

bacopa • chartreuse feverfew • chives • cyclamen • daffodil • diascia • freesia • lettuce • mustard • parsley • red cabbage • tulip

THOMAS J. STORY (2)

TOP: Made for the shade, florists' cineraria adds intense color to dark corners of the garden. Here it's combined with asparagus fern in a 15-inch-wide glazed terra-cotta pot. DESIGN: Bud Stuckey. ABOVE: Light pink La Bella snapdragons and salmon ranunculus mix with lavender and purple pansies in this well-composed color symphony. DESIGN: Jackie Gray. ◆

Bag those leaves

By Jim McCausland
and Lauren Bonar Swezey

When autumn leaves carpet your lawn in shades of red, orange, yellow, or brown, you know you have a busy Saturday ahead. If you don't quickly remove the fallen leaves, rain can turn them into a sodden mat that will smother the grass beneath. A number of leaf bags are designed to help you gather and haul leaves. Made of sturdy, woven plastics, these bags are collapsible for compact storage. The ones shown here are widely sold at home and garden centers and nurseries.

Kangaroo Bags are essentially soft-sided trash cans that collapse to 3-inch-thick disks you can hang in the garage. They pop up again when you release two toggle-and-loop closures. Made from mildew- and tear-resistant vinyl-coated polyester, they come in two sizes: 10 gallon ($20) and 30 gallon ($30; shown at top left in the photo). The smaller size is fine for spot weeding, but the larger one, which can be lined with a 33-gallon plastic garbage bag, is the bag of choice for serious fall cleanup. Fiskars: (800) 500-4849 or www.fiskars.com.

Bosbag. Once this self-supporting, polyethylene container is fully open, it can hold up to 3.5 cubic feet of leaves or weeds ($15; shown at right). The manufacturer also sells a 5.3-cubic-foot version ($17). Bosmere: (888) 784-1608, (704) 784-1608, or www. bosmere.com.

Tip Bag has woven polypropylene sides with a stiff plastic hoop that you insert to hold the top open. It's available in capacities from 1.2 to 9.5 cubic feet. We found the 4.6-cubic-foot bag ($21.50; shown in photo) big enough for most tasks. Also from Bosmere (see above).

Kangaroo

Tip Bag

Bosbag

JIM McCAUSLAND

What to do with fallen leaves

If you want to recycle leaves for compost or mulch, rake them up and run them through a shredder. If you have a strong, large-capacity bagging mower, you can use it to pick up and shred leaves. On the compost pile, alternate layers of leaves and green matter like grass clippings to hasten decomposition. Not all leaves make good mulches: Black walnut leaves, for example, contain a chemical that retards the growth of other plants. And don't use diseased leaves as mulch; shred and compost them. ◆

BERRIES
to decorate your garden

These shrubs and trees bring color
and often birds to Western landscapes

By Steven R. Lorton

■ We often add plants to our gardens in fall because they bear showy flowers or have gorgeous color. But we tend to overlook plants that display ornamental berries. Yet many shrubs and garden-scale trees that bear small fruits can bejewel a landscape from early autumn well into winter.

Berried plants make handsome focal points in the garden, adding bursts of color to otherwise dull spots. Some, like pyracantha, work well as espaliers, bringing lush greenery and seasonal color to a blank wall or fence. Also, it's fun to prune berry-laden branches for indoor arrangements.

There's another good reason to grow these plants: The berries will attract wild birds to your garden. Avian visitors gobble beautyberry, cotoneaster, pyracantha, toyon, and viburnum, among others.

Now is the time to shop for such plants in garden centers and nurseries. You can plant them in the ground immediately or pop their nursery cans into larger containers and display them on a front porch, patio, or deck during the holiday season.

CLOCKWISE FROM TOP LEFT: Harlequin glorybower, strawberry tree, Oregon grape, green hawthorn 'Winter King', and beautyberry.

16 berry worthy plants

Besides carrying showy berries, they make handsome additions all year. Here are choices for sun or shade.

ABOVE LEFT: Pyracantha dangles dense clusters of pea-size berries. ABOVE RIGHT: Arching branches of *Cotoneaster lacteus* bow with a heavy crop of red fruit. BELOW LEFT: Berries of Himalayan honeysuckle turn from red to purplish black.

BEAUTYBERRY (*Callicarpa bodinieri* 'Profusion'). Round clusters of amethyst to purple berries remain on bare stems after willowlike leaves turn color and drop. This deciduous shrub grows 6 feet tall (sometimes more) and almost as wide. Full sun or light shade. *Sunset* climate zones 3–9, 14–24.

COTONEASTER. Of the more than 70 species in this genus, these four have exceptionally showy berries.
C. dammeri. Commonly called bearberry cotoneaster, it displays bright red fruits among dark evergreen leaves. Often used as a ground cover; it reaches only 6 to 12 inches tall but will spread 10 feet wide and cascade down a slope. Full sun or partial shade. Zones 2–24.
C. divaricatus. Bright red, egg-shaped fruits deck the branches of this deciduous shrub, whose dark green leaves turn orange red in fall. After the leaves drop, the berries last until the birds devour them. Grows 6 feet tall and wide. Full sun. Zones 1–24.
C. horizontalis. Red fruits hang on after round green leaves turn orange, then red before dropping. The stiff horizontal branches are set in a herringbone

pattern. This deciduous shrub grows 2 to 3 feet tall and up to 15 feet wide. Full sun. Zones 2B–11, 14–24, A3.

C. lacteus. Clusters of red fruits last a long time among the dark green leaves of this evergreen shrub. Full sun. Zones 4–24.

HARLEQUIN GLORYBOWER (*Clerodendrum trichotomum*). Shiny blue or turquoise berries framed by scarlet calyxes form in late summer and hang on after leaves drop. This deciduous shrub reaches 10 to 15 feet tall and wide. Partial shade. Zones 15–17, 20–24; can be grown in zones 5 and 6 but may freeze to the ground.

HAWTHORN (*Crataegus*). These two deciduous trees are standouts in the berry department. Give them full sun.

Carriere hawthorn (*C.* x *lavallei*). Clusters of orange red fruits the size of small crabapples hang on the plant from autumn through winter. The dark green leaves turn bronzy red after the first deep frost and may stay on the tree all winter long. Grows to 25 feet tall and 15 to 20 feet wide. Zones 3–12, 14–21.

Green hawthorn (*C. viridis* 'Winter King'). Masses of red berries are displayed on naked branches after leaves turn yellowish and drop. Grows 25 to 30 feet tall and wide. Zones 2–12, 14–17.

HIMALAYAN HONEYSUCKLE (*Leycesteria formosa*). This deciduous shrub's other common name—Himalayan pheasantberry—hints at the appeal its fruits have for birds. The berries start out green but quickly turn red, then deep purplish black. Grows 6 feet tall and wide. Full sun or light shade. Zones 4–6, 14–17, 20–24.

OREGON GRAPE (*Mahonia aquifolium*). Native along much of the Pacific Coast, this evergreen shrub bears clusters of deep blue fruits among shiny, hollylike leaves. The species grows 6 feet tall and 5 feet wide; the variety 'Compacta' grows only 2 to 3 feet tall, but spreads 5 feet or more. Tolerates any exposure, although it prefers shade in hottest climates. Zones 2–12, 14–24.

Berried plants make handsome focal points, adding bursts of color to otherwise dull spots in the garden.

PYRACANTHA. Commonly called firethorn, this shrub bears clusters of red, orange, or yellow berries that are the size of peas. Glossy foliage is evergreen (semi-evergreen in cold-winter climates). Species and varieties grow 3 to 15 feet tall and 4 to 10 feet wide. Full sun. Zones 3–24.

STRAWBERRY TREE (*Arbutus unedo*). Puffy fruits the size of olives turn from yellow when young to red when mature. The fruits are borne at the same time as urn-shaped flowers among dark evergreen leaves. The species ranges from 8 to 35 feet tall and wide; compact varieties reach only 5 to 8 feet tall. Full sun or partial shade (essential in desert areas). Zones 4–24.

TOYON OR CALIFORNIA HOLLY (*Heteromeles arbutifolia*). Clusters of bright red, pea-size fruits are borne among glossy dark green leaves. Grow this evergreen as a dense shrub (6 to 10 feet tall and wide) or pruned as a single-trunk tree (15 to 25 feet tall and nearly as wide). Full sun or partial shade. Zones 5–19, 14–24.

VIBURNUM. Among the many species, these three are top performers.

V. davidii. Clusters of metallic blue fruits appear among glossy dark green leaves. This evergreen shrub reaches 3 to 4 feet tall and wide. Partial shade. Zones 4–9, 14–24.

V. opulus. Upright clusters of fleshy red fruits hang on from autumn into winter. Its dark green leaves turn yellow, red, or reddish purple in fall before dropping. This deciduous shrub reaches 8 to 15 feet tall and wide. Full sun or partial shade. Zones 1–9, 14–24, A2–A3.

V. rhytidophyllum. Clusters of fruit turn from scarlet to black as they age. Commonly called leatherleaf viburnum, it bears deep green leaves, 4–10 inches long, that have wrinkled tops and fuzzy undersides. This evergreen shrub grows 8 to 15 feet tall and 6 to 12 feet wide. Tolerates deep shade. Zones 3–9, 14–24. ◆

do this now...

...to get this in spring...

LATE FALL: Perennial bed shown after fall cleanup and pruning.

MID-MAY: Roses are in peak bloom. Blue catmint and other billowy perennials surround them.

Renewal time for perennials

Follow tips from *Sunset's* test garden for easy-care flower beds that keep on blooming

By Kathleen N. Brenzel • Photographs by Thomas J. Story

Imagine a garden that pumps out gorgeous blooms over a long season. All the flower colors you've ever dreamed of are here—red, yellow, and apricot roses, orange and purple dahlias, candy pink phlox, blue catmint, lavender buddleja—weaving a rich tapestry that's frequented by birds, butterflies, and bouquet makers. Imagine it's easy to care for, too, with soaker hoses taking care of watering a couple of times a week during the growing season, and only an occasional need for feeding. Sound too good to be true?

Bud Stuckey, coordinator of *Sunset's* test garden in Menlo Park, California, doesn't think so. More than seven years ago, he set aside an 18- by 25-foot section of the garden just for cut-and-come-again blooms. There, after tilling and amending the soil, he planted roses, perennials, and a smattering of seasonal tubers, such as dahlias and tuberoses.

The payback for his initial efforts has been enormous: buckets of blooms daily, April through October, for six years.

On woody perennials, make cuts just above a growth node. Using sturdy loppers, cut back buddlejas, like the one shown here, by two-thirds.

After dahlia foliage has turned brown, shorten the stalks almost to the base. Dahlia stems are hollow; sharp hand pruners work well on them.

Cut back herbaceous perennials, such as this catmint, to just above new growth at the base (the small gray leaves poking through woody stems).

Remove old or crossing rose canes. Cut back remaining canes by one-third to one-half, making cuts at a 45° angle above outward-facing buds.

Postseason wrap-up

October

CUT BACK PERENNIALS. Make cuts as shown above. If perennials such as daylilies have become crowded, dig each clump with a spading fork so the rootball comes up intact, then use a spade or sharp knife to divide them (each division should have plenty of leaves and roots). Replant divisions immediately. In cold-winter climates, divide plants by mid-October.

CUT BACK BULB FOLIAGE. After the foliage on dahlias and other summer bulbs dies, cut plants back as shown above. In mild climates, dahlia tubers can overwinter in the ground; in cold climates, dig and store them in a frost-free place until planting time in spring.

PULL WEEDS. Pull kinds such as crabgrass. Discard those with seed heads and compost the rest.

REMOVE SOAKER HOSES. Lay them flat on the pavement, cap the ends, then flush them clean with water. Coil and store them for winter.

ADD MULCH. Apply a 6-inch-deep layer of compost to the soil surface around plants.

December

PRUNE ROSES. In mild-winter climates, remove dead or old canes and make cuts as shown above right. In cold-winter areas, it's safer to wait until April.

March

BEGIN FERTILIZING. After new growth appears, broadcast granular flower food such as a 6-2-5 formulation; water it in with a dilute fish emulsion from a hose-end sprayer. In mild climates, put down soaker hoses.

The secret to this garden's continuing productivity is autumn renewal. Beginning each October, Stuckey follows the simple strategy detailed above—cutting, pruning, weeding, mulching—to freshen the plantings. Follow his program (adapt it to your garden's special needs and to your climate) for a robust flower bed next spring. Then, says Stuckey, "get out of the way and watch the plants grow." ◆

...with a big surprise in July

JULY: Candy pink 'Bright Eyes' summer phlox steals the show.

STRIKING ORANGE FRUIT dangles from the branches of this harvest-ready persimmon. For tips on selecting a tree and air-drying the tasty fruit, see page 337.

November

NORM PLATE

gracious entry
in Paradise Valley

■ The layout of Bette Stofft's house in Paradise Valley, Arizona, is the opposite of most homes. Stofft's front entrance is actually at the rear of the property, and what would normally be considered the backyard faces the street. Visitors found this arrangement disorienting: When they drove up to the house, they couldn't immediately find the entrance; once they found it, it wasn't a welcoming space.

Landscape architect Chad Robert of Phoenix (602/307-0010) transformed this uninviting area into a gracious courtyard. First, he expanded the space to 70 feet wide by 30 feet deep by pushing its boundaries out into a parkway. Then he enclosed the courtyard with a stucco wall

with a dramatic portal that houses a gate with two rustic wood doors. Robert paved the courtyard with Saltillo tiles. A few deftly placed boulders look as if they might have tumbled off nearby Camelback Mountain. To provide a bit of shade, Robert added a pair of Chilean mesquite trees. Bougainvillea spilling over the wall accentuates its sinuous curves.

Sheltered by the house on one side and the mountain on the other, the courtyard is well protected from wind. Heat reflected from the mountainside makes it especially cozy in late fall, says Robert. In the evening, a fireplace built into the wall provides additional warmth for outdoor dining and entertaining. — *Sharon Cohoon*

BOOKSHELF

classic look at Japanese maples

■ At his nursery and garden in Roseburg, Oregon, the late J.D. Vertrees (1915–1993) cultivated hundreds of kinds of Japanese maples, at one point amassing the largest collection in the United States. In 1978, Vertrees shared his knowledge of these trees by authoring a title that has become one of the classic American garden books. Now in its third edition, *Japanese Maples* (Timber Press, Portland, 2001; $49.95; 503/227-2878 or www.timberpress.com) has been revised and expanded by British maple expert Peter Gregory. The latest edition adds nearly 100 cultivated varieties, resulting in descriptions of more than 400 plants, many of which are illustrated with color photographs. If you're looking for trees with brilliant autumn color, among the standouts you'll see *Acer palmatum* 'Osakazuki' and *A. japonicum*, whose leaves are pictured on the front cover of the book. — *Steven R. Lorton*

'Red Pygmy' leaves turn from maroon in spring to bronze in fall.

markers with staying power

■ Plant markers have to put up with a lot of abuse: The sun beats on them, water pelts them, errant feet trample on them, and sometimes they just disappear. Now a California firm has designed a series of stamped steel markers designed to withstand such stresses. The 1-foot-tall markers shown at left come in 11 different silhouette forms mounted on stakes. The forms are designed to hold either a seed packet or a vinyl card inscribed with the plant's name. You can also write directly on the coated steel. The company sells a marking pen that resists fading from sun and water. The steel markers cost about $6.50 each. They're sold at some nurseries and garden centers, or you can contact the manufacturer directly. *What's Growing: (707) 795-8851 or www.whatsgrowing.net. — Jim McCausland*

cool color schemes for pots

■ To grace the entry of her home, Robin Cushman of Eugene, Oregon, creates elegant containers that pair cool-season plants with similar or complementary colors of flowers and foliage. Planted in November, Cushman's containers look good all winter.

For the container shown at right, Cushman chose a monochromatic scheme, matching white flowering kale with white violas, variegated ivy, and the light green foliage of curry plant (*Helichrysum italicum*).

In the other container, she used complementary colors, planting purple flowering kale with viola Sorbet Lilac Ice and Antique Shades pansies among the deep pink foliage of *Ajuga reptans* 'Burgundy Glow', the purplish pink and gray green leaves of 'Tricolor' sage, and the

frosty-looking foliage of *Senecio cineraria* 'Silver Lace'.

For combinations like these, choose a generous container (Cushman uses 18-inch-diameter pots). Fill it with a good potting soil and mix a complete organic fertilizer into the top 8 inches of soil. Arrange plants from nursery sixpacks and 4-inch pots with their rootballs still intact atop the soil. Plant the ornamental kale or cabbage first in the center and the others around the edges. Water thoroughly after planting, then whenever the top inch of soil is dry.

— *Mary-Kate Mackey*

ROBIN CUSHMAN (2)

it's persimmon time

■ Beautiful fall foliage and striking orange fruit make persimmons *(Diospyros kaki)* highly ornamental garden trees. Besides being decorative, their fruit is tasty in breads, cookies, and puddings. When air-dried, it is chewy and datelike.

If you want to plant a persimmon tree this fall, here are some choices.

'**Coffee Cake**' has brown, nonastringent fruit with intense flavor. It does well in cool climates, and fruit ripens early.

'**Fuyu**' has flattened, baseball-size nonastringent fruit that can be eaten when hard, but its flavor improves when it's softened slightly off the tree.

'**Hachiya**' has large astringent fruit that tastes bitter until it's fully ripe and soft. The tree has an attractive form.

'**Izu**' produces nonastringent fruit on a tree to 15 feet tall. Fruit ripens early.

To air-dry fruit: Clip the ripe but still firm fruit from the tree, leaving a 1½-inch-long stem. Peel the fruit, tie a string onto each stem, then hang the persimmons on a rack in a warm, dry place. As the persimmons hang, moisture evaporates (unpeeled fruit softens and ripens instead of drying). Dry the fruit just until it's leathery but still pliable. Then snap off stems

and store fruit airtight in the freezer.

'Hachiya' persimmons lose their astringency, becoming very sweet and dense—almost like candy. Crisp, flat-bottomed 'Fuyu' and other nonastringent types dry equally well.

Persimmon trees are sold at nurseries. Hard-to-find kinds are available from Raintree Nursery (360/496-6400 or www. raintreenursery.com).

— *Lauren Bonar Swezey*

CLIPPINGS

• Common Ground news. Common Ground, an education center and an organic garden supplier of seeds, seedlings, soil amendments, and tools, has moved within Palo Alto from El Camino Real to 559 College Avenue. *10–5:30 Tue–Fri, 10–5 Sat–Sun. (650) 493-6072.*

• Natural insect control. Indoor/Outdoor IGR, an insect growth regulator with very low toxicity to mammals (about the same as table salt), is now available from Monterey Lawn and Garden Products. When diluted in water and sprayed on an infested area, it prevents immature insects from becoming adults, so they cannot reproduce. It controls young fleas for more than 210 days and young cockroaches for 180 days. It's also effective against ants, flies, mosquitoes, and other insects. (It doesn't kill adult insects.) The product is available at retail nurseries for $29.95 per pint (distribution is still limited) and from www. montereylawngarden.com.

everything's coming up daisies

■ For the past five years, Harry and Carol Saal have been trying to reestablish the daisy meadow that landscape designer Jonathan Plant created for them in the front yard of their Palo Alto home. He had seeded their meadow grass lawn with English daisies *(Bellis perennis),* which thrived until the gardener thatched the lawn.

Finally, contractor Frank Manocchio found a West Coast source in Sunmark Seeds (catalog free; 888/214-7333 or www.sunmarkseeds.com), and planted 2 ounces of seed last fall. He scratched the soil surface with a rake, then scattered the seed and covered it with a light layer of compost. The area was watered regularly. And the riot of daisy flowers returned. The only maintenance the daisies and grass get is a mowing after the flowers fade. — *L.B.S.*

worth the wait

A beautiful border blends foliage colors and textures

■ If Larry Free had been able to landscape the front yard at his family's new home in El Segundo right after moving in, as he wished at the time, the results probably wouldn't be as spectacular. A year's delay—because of reroofing and other disruptive projects—turned into a blessing. Free learned a lot about gardening before planting a thing. The biggest lesson? Foliage makes the garden.

He wanted a woodland theme to complement the liquidambar and birch trees already on the property, so—while still working on unrelated projects around the house—he started acquiring plants with similar looks, such as oakleaf hydrangeas, astilbes, and *Carpenteria californica* (bush anemone).

He'd always loved burgundy foliage, so he bought red flax, loropetalum, and Japanese barberry. He emphasized his favorite color combinations with red and purple salvias and penstemons.

As the collection accumulated, he tried out different compositions, with the plants still in their nursery pots, and he decided he wasn't satisfied. The somber burgundy foliage seemed to call out for a brighter contrast.

He kept shopping and found showy 'Pink Splendor' mirror plant *(Coprosma repens)*, plus a few other variegated plants. But something was still missing. Movement, he decided. So he added ornamental grasses and breath of heaven. Finally he planted.

Now the play of foliage colors, sizes, and shapes is what he likes best about his garden. "Look at that texture," he says, with justifiable pride. "Isn't it awesome?"

— *S.C.*

bring your autumn cuttings indoors

■ Late autumn brings about magical transformations in gardens throughout the West. As the days grow shorter and cooler, plants take on new personas, ripening into warm gold, russet, and sepia tones. Textures become more pronounced, with many perennials, ornamental grasses, and shrubs displaying a rich variety of seed heads, seedpods, and dried foliage. You can capture the beauty of this second season indoors by gathering up armloads of plants to display in lasting arrangements.

The only tool you need is a pair of pruning shears. A block of florist's foam can be wedged into a container to prop up more complex arrangements. You may not even need florist's foam, since most dried material is stiff enough to stay put on its own.

Group cuttings of one kind together in bunches tied with rustic bows of raffia or garden twine, as shown in the photos. Or arrange an assortment in elaborate bouquets. Baskets or containers made of stoneware or wood complement the natural mood.

For a ready supply of natural materials for arrangements, consider adding some of these plants to your landscape. Even if you don't harvest them every year, they'll lend greater fall and winter interest to your garden.

— *Marcia Tatroe*

Rabbitbrush
(*Chrysothamnus nauseosus*)

Sedum 'Autumn Joy'

Bear's breech (*Acanthus balcanicus*)

Giant allium (*A. giganteum*)

Rattlesnake master (*Eryngium yuccifolium*)

Blue false indigo (*Baptisia australis*)

Siberian iris

Four-wing saltbush (*Atriplex canescens*)

Sand love grass (*Eragrostis trichodes*)

the late show

STEVEN GUNTHER

■ A good garden has something of interest in all four seasons, says landscape architect Shirley Kerins. Take the scene at right, for example, which Kerins designed for the Grace Kallam Perennial Garden, at the Arboretum of Los Angeles County.

The star of this winter show is rock cotoneaster *(C. horizontalis),* a low, wide shrub (in foreground) that carries an abundance of decorative red berries. It grows just 2 to 3 feet tall by 6 feet wide. The compact heavenly bamboo in the background *(Nandina domestica* 'Woods Dwarf') is also at its brilliant best in winter. A band of low-growing rockcress *(Arabis caucasica* 'Variegata') separates the two, while *Helianthemum* 'Wisley Primrose' adds a dash of bright yellow at the back.

Arboretum of Los Angeles County: 9–4:30 daily. 301 N. Baldwin Ave., Arcadia.— S.C.

BACK TO BASICS

Cool-season watering tips. Fall rains are sometimes unpredictable, even in the wettest climates. To irrigate new plantings, make sure the rootball and surrounding soil stay moist. For established plants, water when the soil feels dry—1 to 2 inches deep for shallow-rooted plants, such as annuals and ground covers, and 2 to 6 inches deep for small to medium shrubs. Give supplemental water to plants growing under wide eaves. — *L.B.S.*

geodesic greenhouses

■ Practically impervious to heavy snow and high wind, the greenhouse dome pictured here keeps winter temperatures inside about 25° higher than they are outside—with no supplemental heat. The 22-foot-diameter dome, in Pagosa Springs, Colorado, lets its vegetarian owners grow much of their own food all through winter, although they once had to dig a path through 4 feet of snow to bring in the day's harvest.

Adapted from Buckminster Fuller's geodesic dome design, the wood-framed structure is glazed with double- or triple-walled polycarbonate triangles. Sunlight streams through the glazing and heats up water in a 1,200-gallon tank during the day, while a solar-powered fan pumps air through ducts in planting beds, warming the soil. At night, the water tank releases its warmth back into the air, keeping plants toasty until the morning sun takes over. When the temperature in the dome gets too high, automatic vents open and let the warm air out.

You can buy geodesic dome greenhouses in a variety of sizes from Growing Spaces (800/753-9333 or www. growingspaces.com). The cost of a complete kit for a 350-square-foot dome is $5,950 for a model with double-wall glazing (shown in the photos) and $7,495 for a model with triple-wall glazing. You can also buy a kit that doesn't include pressure-treated lumber, if you want to purchase the lumber to frame it yourself. Lumber for planting beds isn't included. —*J.M.*

ARNOLD OKERMAN (2)

oasis gardening

Smoke Tree Ranch was way ahead of its time. This Palm Springs development followed xeriscape principles as early as 1936, almost a half century before the term was coined. That's still true: Homeowners must use native plants wherever their property is visible to the public; they can plant what they want in their backyards. This policy gives the development its strong character—homes and gardens seem to blend right into the desert landscape. But it's also a sensible water-conservation measure. Save your oasis for the area where you'll spend the most time, and make your public spaces nearly self-sustaining.

Here's how Palm Desert landscape architect Michael Buccino (760/772-7166) interpreted that policy at the home of Bob and Roxy Engle. In the front, Buccino installed a gravel parking area that blends into a flagstone path; the path meanders through vegetation to an entrance gate. Walking it feels like a stroll through a desert wash at the end of a paved road. In the back, he created an unapologetic oasis—palm trees, roses, and perennials. "Roxy wanted an English garden," says Buccino. "I gave her a Scotch one instead." It's less formal and a bit wilder, he explains.

The Engles love the contrast between the native garden and the oasis. So does Buccino. "You find similar situations in the canyons," he says. "All of a sudden there's a water source and trees and grass and flowers, and then a few feet later it's dry again. So I find that sharp differentiation perfectly natural." — *S.C.*

STEVEN GUNTHER (2)

SAXON HOLT

rustic retreat

This outdoor room in Sonoma started with an arbor

■ When Sandy Donohue purchased property in Sonoma, California, a rickety old arbor in an unimproved area of the garden seemed an unlikely place for an intimate garden room. It was shorter than normal—about 7 feet tall instead of the typical 8 feet or taller. Nevertheless, landscape designer Nancy Driscoll was able to use it to create an informal retreat.

A Lady Banks' rose and grapes (a red table grape and a merlot) sprawl across the arbor's top. The patio beneath it is paved with randomly cut flagstone that's mortared in place for easy maintenance. An unmortared flagstone path, designed to match the arbor's rustic style, leads to the patio. Colorful perennials—including purple sea lavender *(Limonium perezii)* in foreground—and soft grasses such as miscanthus (rear) enhance the country feel around it.

"Nancy brought it all together," says Donohue. "Now it's my favorite place to sit in the evening."

— *L.B.S.*

pacific northwest • checklist

PLANTING

☐ **AMARYLLIS.** Buy amaryllis bulbs or growing plants. If you buy plants in bud, you'll get exactly the color and size you want. Some will flower within a few weeks, while others may take three months or more to bloom. Just give them plenty of light and regular water.

☐ **AUTUMN COLOR.** Go nursery shopping now for trees and shrubs aglow with colorful autumn foliage, including fothergilla, many maples, sourwood *(Oxydendrum arboreum)*, Persian parrotia *(Parrotia persica)*, and winged euonymus *(E. alatus)*.

☐ **CAMELLIAS.** Winter camellias (mostly sasanqua and hiemalis types) start to flower later this month, and continue blooming through the dark months. Plant and mulch right away to protect roots from freezing. Grow them as espaliers against a wall or plant under the eaves so rain can't batter their blossoms.

☐ **GARLIC.** Plant garlic for harvest next summer. Break the mother bulb into individual cloves, then plant each clove with pointed end up 1 to 2 inches deep in mild-winter climates or 3 to 4 inches deep in areas where the ground freezes. In colder climates, grow hardneck varieties like 'Spanish Roja'.

☐ **PEONIES.** As early in the month as possible, set out peony roots in rich, deeply tilled soil amended with compost and high-phosphorus fertilizer. Plant the roots no deeper than 2 inches with reddish growth buds pointing up.

☐ **SPRING-BLOOMING BULBS.** Plant anemones, bluebells, crocuses, daffodils, grape hyacinths, hyacinths, *Iris reticulata*, ranunculus, and tulips in drifts outdoors. Pot up crocuses, freesias, hyacinths, and paper white narcissus for forcing.

☐ **WILDFLOWERS.** Fall-sown wildflower seeds always come up earlier than those sown in spring. Just scatter them in amended, weeded beds.

MAINTENANCE

☐ **CLEAN UP GARDEN BEDS.** Weed, till, and amend garden beds now so they'll be ready for planting early next spring.

☐ **MAINTAIN TOOLS.** Before you put them away for the winter, sharpen shovels, hoes, pruners, and knives. Wipe metal blades with machine oil to protect against rust; rub wood handles with linseed oil.

☐ **MAKE COMPOST.** Shred fallen leaves and chop other garden waste before you put it on the compost pile so it will decompose completely by spring.

☐ **MOW ONE LAST TIME.** On a dry weekend, mow the lawn; you shouldn't have to mow again until grass starts growing next spring.

☐ **OVERWINTER TENDER PLANTS.** *Dahlias:* Dig up dahlia tubers, shake off the dirt, and let them dry before you store them for winter. *Fuchsias:* In zones 4–7, most kinds can be left in the ground for the winter with a 3-inch organic mulch over the crown. In zones 1–3, bring plants inside, preparing them as you would pelargoniums; see following. *Pelargoniums:* Before a hard freeze hits, dig plants and bring them into a cool, dark, frost-free place for the winter.

☐ **WEED.** Hoe weeds as they appear. In cold-winter zones, the mulch you apply to protect roots from ground-freezing frosts will also control weeds. ◆

northern california · checklist

PLANTING

☐ **BULBS. Zones 7–9, 14–17:** Even though nurseries begin selling bulbs much earlier, November—when the soil has finally cooled—is one of the best times to plant them in Northern California. If you still need to shop for bulbs, check them carefully; choose only firm ones that aren't sprouting. To get the longest stem lengths on tulips and hyacinths, chill them for four to six weeks and plant them in December.

☐ **BUTTERFLY PLANTS. Zones 7–9, 14–17:** To attract butterflies to your garden, try some of the following plant groups that provide nectar and larval food: buckwheat, butterfly bush, California Dutchman's pipe *(Aristolochia californica)*, coffeeberry, mallow *(Lavatera or Sidalcea malviflora)*, milkweed *(Asclepias incarnata* for wet gardens, *A. speciosa* for dry gardens), native grasses *(Carex barberae, Festuca californica,* or *F. idahoensis)*, native oak (such as coast live oak), penstemon, and willow. Recommendations come from Hallberg Butterfly Gardens, a nonprofit organization that cares for and maintains the Hallberg Gardens in Sebastopol. To join the friends of HBG, call (707) 823-3420.

☐ **CRAPE MYRTLE. Zones 7–9, 14–17:** Three of the best varieties for fall color are 'Near East', 'Pecos', and 'Zuni'. Look for these trees at your local nursery. (If you can't find one, ask the nursery to order one for you from Monrovia Nursery, which is wholesale only.)

Sunset
CLIMATE ZONES
☐ Mountain (1-2)
☐ Valley (7-9)
☐ Inland (14)
☐ Coastal (15-17)

DEBRA LAMBERT

☐ **PERENNIALS. Zones 7–9, 14–17:** Some choices include alstroemeria, artemisia, campanula, catmint, columbine, coral bells, delphinium, dead nettle, dianthus, diascia, Oriental poppy, penstemon, perennial foxglove *(Digitalis mertonensis)*, phlox, salvia, scaevola, and true geraniums. Nurseries have a wide assortment in sixpacks, 4-inch pots, and 1-gallon containers.

MAINTENANCE

☐ **COMPOST.** Start a simple compost pile by layering greens (grass, plant debris, and weeds without seed heads) with browns (straw and dried leaves). Build a simple composter by bending a 4-foot-wide piece of 12- to 14-gauge wire fencing into a cylinder about 4 feet in diameter; hook the cut edges together. Chop up plant debris, then alternate a 2- to 8-inch-thick layer of brown material with a 2- to 8-inch-thick layer of green material, sprinkling each brown layer with water as you go. To heat up the pile and speed composting, top each brown layer with a shovelful of ma-

nure or soil. Keep the pile evenly moist. Aerate it by turning the material every few weeks or so.

☐ **DIG TUBEROUS BEGONIAS. Zones 7–9, 14–17:** Continue watering plants through fall. Cut back on watering when blooms stop developing and leaves begin to yellow. After the stems start falling off the tubers, allow the soil to dry out, then lift the tubers, shake off the soil, and let dry for a few days in a protected area. Store them in a cool, dry place.

☐ **FEED COOL-SEASON CROPS. Zones 7–9, 14–17:** If you didn't use a timed-release fertilizer at planting time, your annuals and vegetables probably need feeding. Use fish emulsion bimonthly.

☐ **PROTECT COLE CROPS. Zones 7–9, 14–17:** Cabbage loopers (small green caterpillars) can damage young seedlings. Cover crops with floating row covers to keep the adults—white butterflies—from laying eggs on leaves. Or dust leaves with Bt *(Bacillus thuringiensis)*.

☐ **SPRAY FRUIT TREES.** After leaves have fallen, spray peach trees with lime sulfur to control peach leaf curl, a fungal disease. Spray the entire tree, including the trunk, branches, and twigs. ◆

WHAT TO DO IN YOUR GARDEN IN NOVEMBER

PLANTING

☐ **ANNUALS.** Except in the mountains, there's still time to set out early-blooming annuals such as African daisy, calendula, Iceland poppy, ornamental cabbage, pansy, schizanthus, snapdragon, and stock. For shady areas, try cineraria, cyclamen, and English and fairy primrose.

☐ **BULBS.** Continue to plant anemones, daffodils, Dutch irises, ipheions, ornithogalums, and all the South African bulbs that naturalize so well here, such as babiana, crocosmia, freesia, ixia, homeria, nerine, sparaxis, and watsonia. Buy hyacinth and tulip bulbs now, but give them at least six weeks' chill in the refrigerator before planting.

☐ **VEGETABLES.** Early November is a great time to start cool-season crops in most areas. In zones 13 (low desert) and 14–24, sow seeds of beets, carrots, onions, parsley, peas, radish, Swiss chard, and turnips, and set out transplants of broccoli, cabbage, and other cole crops. Coastal gardeners can continue to plant lettuces and other leafy crops. In the foothills and central valley (zones 7–9, 14), sow peas and spinach and plant garlic and onions.

☐ **WILDFLOWERS.** Broadcast seeds of baby blue eyes, clarkias, desert five spots, flax, godetias, California poppies, and other wildflowers in weed-free soil. (Before sowing them, irrigate the soil in planting areas thoroughly to encourage

weeds to sprout; then hoe out emerging weeds.) After sowing seeds, rake the area lightly to cover them with soil. Keep surface consistently moist (if rains don't come) until seeds germinate.

MAINTENANCE

☐ **OVERSEED LAWN.** If you have warm-season grasses such as Bermuda or St. Augustine in your lawn and you want them to look green over winter, overseed with annual rye now. Cut the grass short before seeding and mulch with manure or a fine-grained soil amendment afterward. Keep the ground damp until seeds sprout.

☐ **PRUNE CANE BERRY PLANTS.** Old canes of blackberry, boysenberry, and loganberry should be cut back to the ground. Leave the new, smooth-barked canes that grew this year to bear fruit. Don't cut back low-chill raspberry canes until December or January.

☐ **START COMPOST.** Fallen leaves, spent crops, and prunings are good fodder for a compost pile. Or build a simple wire bin: Bend a 4-foot-wide piece of 12- to 14-gauge wire fencing into a cylinder about 4 feet in diameter. Try to alternate green things (grass, vegetable peels) with brown (dried leaves, straw). To speed decomposition, keep the pile slightly moist.

☐ **WEED.** Pull out annual bluegrass, chickweed, spurge, and other young weeds as they emerge.

PEST CONTROL

☐ **CONTROL SNAILS, SLUGS.** Put collars or sleeves around vulnerable plants and copper bands around beds. Handpick slugs or snails early in the morning.

☐ **PROTECT COLE CROPS.** Cabbage loopers are small green caterpillars that can damage young seedlings. Cover cole crops with floating row covers to keep the adults—white butterflies—from laying eggs on leaves. Or dust leaves with Bt *(Bacillus thuringiensis)*.

☐ **SPRAY FRUIT TREES.** Around Thanksgiving, after leaves have fallen, spray peach and nectarine trees with lime sulfur or 50 percent copper to control peach leaf curl, a fungal disease. (Before spraying, rake up debris under trees.) Spray the entire tree, including the trunk, and lightly spray the ground beneath the tree. ◆

mountain · checklist

PLANTING

☐ **COVER CROPS.** After vegetables are harvested, spade several inches of manure into beds and sow seeds of white Dutch clover or winter rye to grow as a cover crop. The plants will prevent soil erosion during the winter and add nutrients to the soil when tilled into the bed next spring.

☐ **PAPER WHITE NARCISSUS.** Plant bulbs in a pot filled with horticultural sand, pebbles, or potting soil and store in a cool place (50° to 60°) until shoots emerge, then move the pot into a bright, cool window. Bulbs planted by midmonth should bloom during the holidays.

☐ **SPRING-BLOOMING BULBS.** If you haven't set out hardy bulbs yet, get them into the ground immediately. Pot up extra bulbs for forcing indoors. Put the pots in a dark, cold place (33° to 40°) for 12 weeks, then bring them into a brightly lit room to bloom.

MAINTENANCE

☐ **CONTROL INSECTS ON HOUSE-PLANTS.** If aphids, mites, scales, or other insects infest any of your houseplants, slip a plastic garment cover (the kind you get from a dry cleaner) over the plant and spray with insecticidal soap. The plastic tent will contain the spray.

☐ **MAINTAIN TOOLS.** Sharpen blades of hoes, spades, and pruning shears, then wipe them with oil (machine oil for metal parts, linseed oil for handles) and store in a dry place for the winter.

Sunset
CLIMATE ZONES
☐ 1-3 ☐ 10-11

DEBRA LAMBERT

☐ **PREPARE BEDS.** Before the ground freezes, till a 2- to 3-inch layer of composted manure or mushroom compost into planting beds. Leave the soil in large clumps; freezing and thawing will break them down, and the bed will be ready to plant as soon as the soil warms in spring.

☐ **PREVENT DEER DAMAGE TO TREES.** To prevent damage by deer, surround young trees and shrubs with wire cages made from poultry wire or hardware mesh. Use stakes to hold cages in place.

☐ **PROTECT WATER FEATURES FROM FREEZING.** To prevent damage to fish and hardy aquatic plants in ponds, use a stock tank heater (available from farm supply stores) to keep the water from freezing solid. Leaving a fountain running also prevents the water from freezing in all but the coldest weather.

☐ **PROTECT YOUNG TREES FROM SUNSCALD.** Trees with trunks less than 4 inches in diameter are vulnerable to sunscald, a damaging form of sunburn caused when the low winter sun shines on the tender bark. Paint the trunks with white latex or protect them with a commercial tree wrap.

☐ **PROVIDE AID FOR WILD BIRDS.** As colder weather sets in, birds have greater difficulty finding natural food. They seek out bird feeders. Seedeaters such as evening grosbeaks, goldfinches, and pine siskins prefer black oil sunflower and niger thistle. Insect-eaters like flickers and nuthatches favor suet. To provide fresh water in freezing weather, install an electric heater in your birdbath. Avian Aquatics (800/788-6478 or www.avianaquatics.com) sells a variety of birdbath heaters.

☐ **SPREAD MULCH.** If you haven't done so already, spread a 3- to 4-inch layer of organic mulch around half-hardy plants, over bulb beds, and under trees and shrubs. Shredded leaves, conifer boughs, or straw all work well as winter mulch. Keep mulch 12 inches away from the base of trees and shrubs to discourage rodents from gnawing the bark.

☐ **START A COMPOST PILE.** Speed up the composting process by grinding plant waste before you toss it on the compost pile. ◆ — *M.T.*

southwest · checklist

PLANTING

☐ **COOL-SEASON FLOWERS.** Zones 11–13 (Las Vegas, Tucson, Phoenix): Set out plants of ageratum, aster, bells-of-Ireland, calendula, candytuft, coreopsis, dianthus, English daisy, foxglove, hollyhock, larkspur, lobelia, painted daisy, pansy, petunia, phlox, scabiosa, snapdragon, stock, and sweet alyssum. Sow seeds of clarkia, nasturtium, and sweet pea.

☐ **COOL-SEASON VEGETABLES.** Zones 11–13: Set out transplants of asparagus, broccoli, brussels sprouts, cabbage, and cauliflower. Continue to sow seed of beets, carrots, lettuce, peas, radishes, spinach, Swiss chard, and turnips.

☐ **PERENNIALS.** Zones 10 (Albuquerque) and 11–13: Through midmonth continue to plant perennials such as autumn sage *(Salvia greggii),* bush morning glory, globe mallow *(Sphaeralcea* species), Mexican evening primrose *(Oenothera speciosa),* Mexican honeysuckle, penstemon, red justicia *(J. candicans),* and verbena.

☐ **SHRUBS, TREES.** Zones 11–13: Continue to plant frost-hardy and native woody shrubs and trees, including acacia, Apache plume, jojoba, mesquite, ocotillo, palo verde, Texas mountain laurel, and Texas ranger.

☐ **SPRING BULBS.** Continue to plant spring-flowering bulbs, including crocus, hyacinth, and tulip bulbs that you have already chilled in the refrigerator for at least six weeks.

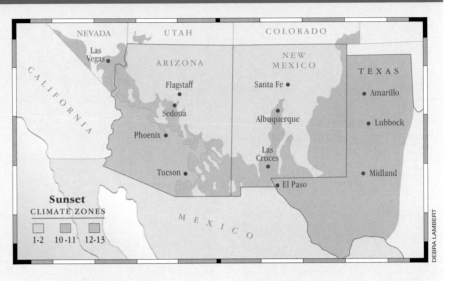

Sunset
CLIMATE ZONES
1-2   10-11   12-13

DEBRA LAMBERT

☐ **SUCCULENTS.** Zones 11–13: It's still not too late to set out cold-hardy or native succulents, such as agave, desert spoon, and yucca.

MAINTENANCE

☐ **ADJUST WATERING.** As temperatures cool, adjust irrigation controls to reduce watering frequency. Shift watering time to daylight hours for lawns, roses, and most ornamentals. This allows foliage to dry off quickly rather than remaining wet at night, which only encourages the growth of powdery mildew and other fungus.

☐ **CARE FOR CITRUS.** Zones 12–13: Remove split or fallen fruit from the ground around trees to discourage fungus and injurious insects.

☐ **CARE FOR ROSES.** Zones 11–13: Continue to remove faded flowers, pruning lightly as you go. Give plants their last feeding of the year, watering the fertilizer in well.

☐ **CONTROL APHIDS.** Zones 12–13: Blast them off new growth with a jet of water from a hose, then spray insecticidal soap.

☐ **CONTROL HOLLYHOCK WEEVILS.** Zones 10–13: This weevil spends the winter inside the seed heads of the hollyhock, then lays eggs in the emerging flower buds in spring. To prevent adult weevils from overwintering, remove and discard all spent seed heads.

☐ **PRUNE HERBS.** Zones 11–13: This is a good time to cut back established Mediterranean herbs such as rosemary, sage, and thyme that have become overgrown or too woody. Prune back to the lowest new growth and remove all dead stems. Keep plants well watered as they recover from pruning. ◆

— Mary Irish

Fall planting, spring glory

Put in now, tulips and other bulbs can create a grand color show next spring—in the ground or in pots

By Sharon Cohoon and Jim McCausland

Late November brings tulip-planting day, an annual ritual at the Crawford residence in Covina, California. Paula Meyer prepares to plant the first of thousands of tulip bulbs. FAR RIGHT: The glorious results of fall planting, shown the following spring.

Around March 1, 'Fortissimo' daffodils burst into flower among New Zealand flax and pansies in this pot; they bloom for about three weeks. See page 352 for planting directions.

■ To plant spring-flowering bulbs is to witness a miraculous transformation. Think about it: You go to the nursery in fall, pluck homely lumps from the bins, drop them into brown paper bags. The glossy color photos above the bins promise beautiful spring blooms in a rainbow of hues—elegant, cup-shaped tulips in hot pink and orange, soft pink and lavender; cheerful yellow daffodils; voluptuous blue hyacinths. Still, it's difficult to imagine these hard, brown things with bristly bottoms pushing out such incredible blooms.

But plant them well, either by type en masse or with other bulbs, and they'll surprise you. Plant them in large beds, as shown at right, or in smaller containers, as pictured above. Either way, the results are sure to be spectacular come spring.

FAR LEFT: Helen Crawford and her granddaughter Robin Hamilton join neighbors and friends before planting. NEAR LEFT: Volunteers place bulbs in dug-out bed. BELOW: Tulips, along with a sprinkling of hyacinths and daffodils, bloom the following spring.

"The party has made us an extended family," says Crawford. "Maybe the bulbs are just an excuse to get together."

Tulip day

Helen Crawford must have taken lessons from Tom Sawyer. No, she didn't talk her friends into painting her fence, as Tom did, by convincing them she was doing them a favor. Instead, for years she has invited relatives, neighbors, and friends to plant her tulips for her, and every year they come, willingly. Unlike Tom—who only managed this trick once—Crawford has pulled this off for three decades.

Each November, Crawford and her crew plant at least 2,400 tulip bulbs in a 55- by 10-foot bed in front of her house in Covina, California. The planting date is always the same—the Friday after Thanksgiving (in this warm

Southern climate, bulbs do not winter over). Her guests clear their calendars months in advance and often travel great distances to join the fun. (The Crawfords' son, Mark, and his wife only have to drive from Pasadena, but their daughter, Tracy, and her family fly in from Washington State.)

Doris and Paul Meyer just walk across the street. They sauntered over out of curiosity in 1973, during Crawford's third planting party, and ended up pitching in. They have been back

every year since, accompanied by their sons, Greg and Matthew, and daughter, Paula. "Through babies, college, marriage, travel—no matter how widely [our family is] scattered—we have a bond with that November Friday," Doris says. "We don't miss it."

What's the draw? "I think people today miss traditions," says Doris. "Many of the old rituals of our ancestors have lost their meaning, and we haven't replaced them. It's up to us to invent new ones, as Helen has."

Potted tulips, hyacinths, and daffodils extend the color show right up to the front door (note the stained-glass tulips). Containers are planted four to five weeks later than the rest of the tulips for simultaneous bloom.

Happy memories of previous planting parties also keep people coming. "I remember how Matthew's chest swelled with pride when he shoveled dirt with the men for the first time," says Crawford. It was a rite of passage.

"The party has made us an extended family," says Crawford. "Maybe the bulbs are just an excuse to get together."

In most parts of the West, November is not too late to buy bulbs. Whether you copy Crawford's party idea and gather a group together or plant on your own, you can adapt her techniques.

Planting a tradition

Here's how Crawford plans this annual planting party.

■ JULY. Crawford orders tulip bulbs from a mail-order bulb company (she prefers Dutch Gardens, in New Jersey; 800/818-3861). By ordering early, she ensures she'll get the bulbs she wants in the quantities she needs. She orders the full range of colors and some of every type (singles, doubles, fringed, parrot, and so on). To extend the color show, she also requests some early- and late-blooming varieties. Until the day of the party, she chills the bulbs in the refrigera-

tor. (In mild climates, tulips need a minimum of six weeks' chill before planting. Place them in a paper bag in the crisper section of your refrigerator; keep bulbs away from apples.)

■ NOVEMBER. A few days before the party, Crawford contracts with a manual laborer to help her double-dig half of her tulip bed. She divides the plot into six sections, then has the worker shovel out 8 inches of soil from every other section, piling the excavated dirt atop the remaining three. A generous amount of compost, usually homemade, is shoveled into each of the dug-out sections and worked into the next 8 inches of soil, along with a handful of bulb food. This preparatory step means guests can begin planting immediately the day of the party.

■ PARTY DAY. Once everyone arrives, Crawford distributes bulbs and a few suggestions. "Plant at least 25 of each variety in a group or else the color won't read," she says. She also tells them to plant closely but not too orderly—"This isn't school; you don't have to stay in rows." And leave an exit route: "Start in the center and work to a corner so you can get out without tromping on bulbs."

After the first three sections of the bed are planted, the soil excavated from them is replaced. The men and older boys usually volunteer for this job.

Helpers dig out 8 inches of soil from the remaining three sections, piling it atop the soil covering the three planted sections. They add compost and bulb food to each newly dug-out section, plant the bulbs, and cover them with the excavated soil. Then the soil over the whole bed is gently evened out with rakes.

Dispensing rewards is the final step. Appreciation of the ritual may be the main reason guests return to West Palm Drive every year, but the promise of homemade cookies and good English tea afterward doesn't hurt.

(Continued on page 352)

In fall (left), after everything is planted, grape hyacinth bulbs are poked into the spaces between heather and pansies. **In April** (above), 'Princess Irene' tulips bloom for three to four weeks. The chartreuse flowers behind are *Euphorbia amygdaloides* 'Purpurea'.

Nonstop flowers … winter through spring

Tina Dixon, of Plants à la Cart in Bothell, Washington, and Marsha Davis-Thomsen of Seattle are not easily discouraged by short days, rain, and persistently chilly weather. Each fall, just when everyone else in the Northwest is giving up on gardening for the season, the two designers whip up winter-into-spring plantings in containers.

Take the sumptuous mix of perennials, grasses, heathers, and spring-blooming bulbs they planted last fall in the sandstone urn pictured above. It looked good almost instantly after planting—and heather foliage and pansy blooms provided color on a front porch through winter. Then, in spring, successive bursts of daffodil, grape hyacinth, and tulip flowers heightened the show.

Winter weather near Lake Washington did not faze this collection of plants; New Zealand flax, the most tender of the plants in the arrangement, is hardy to about 20°. Throughout the cool season, the plants needed no supplemental feeding, and weekly watering was only necessary during dry spells between rains.

Costs for this project (including soil, bulbs, perennials, and fertilizer) came to about $110. The sandstone urn costs more, but you can use any large container that catches your fancy, including terra-cotta.

Plant list

5-gallon size (1 plant)
• New Zealand flax (*Phormium* 'Amazing Red')

4-inch nursery pots (1 each, unless noted)
• Creeping Jenny (*Lysimachia nummularia*)
• English ivy (*Hedera helix* 'Gold Dust')
• *Euphorbia amygdaloides* 'Purpurea', 2 plants
• Pansy (*Viola* x *wittrockiana* Delta Tapestry mix), 4 plants
• Pansy (*V.* x *w.* Clear Sky Orange pansy), 3 plants
• Scotch heather (*Calluna vulgaris* 'Firefly')
• Scotch heather (*C.v.* 'Wickwar Flame')
• Tassel fern (*Polystichum polyblepharum*)
• Variegated Japanese sweet flag (*Acorus gramineus* 'Variegatus')

2-inch nursery pot (1 plant)
• Variegated Japanese sedge (*Carex morrowii expallida*)

Bulbs (12 each)
In mild climates, chill tulips in the refrigerator for six weeks before planting.
• Daffodil (*Narcissus* 'Fortissimo')
• Grape hyacinth (*Muscari latifolium*)
• Tulip (*Tulipa* 'Princess Irene')

Planting strategy

1. Fill the bottom of the 21-inch urn or pot with commercial potting soil.
2. Knock the largest plant out of its nursery pot, rough up its rootball, then plant it in the center or back of the large container.
3. Set the smaller plants—still in their nursery pots—atop the soil around the first plant. Move them around to fine-tune the design, then remove them.
4. Mix 9-9-6 bulb fertilizer into the soil (follow label directions), then plant the tulip and daffodil bulbs around the periphery of the container.
5. Remove the rest of the plants from their nursery pots, rough up the rootballs, and plant them over the bulbs according to your plan. Fill the spaces between plants with potting soil; tuck in tiny grape hyacinth bulbs.
6. Water thoroughly. ◆

Turn a lawn into a bed

Nature does most of the work over winter

By Jim McCausland

When Portland landscape designer Margaret de Haas van Dorsser wants to transform a lawn into a new garden bed, she avoids the hassles of stripping sod. Instead, she simply smothers the turf under four to six layers of newspaper and a load of manure, and lets the grass decompose naturally. When the manure is applied in fall and allowed to sit all winter, the underlying grass disappears, roots and all. Then, at planting time in spring, she plants directly through the rotted manure without having to till it or other amendments into the soil. In fact, she strongly advises that the manure not be tilled in, so as not to encourage weed seeds to germinate.

This technique works well on cool-season grasses such as bent, blue grass, and fescue, but is *not* recommended for lawns of Bermuda grass, St. Augustine grass, or zoysia.

TIME: About 2 hours for a 10- by 20-foot bed

COST: About $50 for 4 yards of cow or steer manure (horse manure contains too many weed seeds)

MATERIALS
• 50- to 100-foot hose
• Garden spade
• Newspaper
• Manure

DIRECTIONS

1. With a hose, outline the perimeter of the new garden bed on the lawn (**A**).
2. With a sharp spade, dig a 2-inch-deep, V-shaped groove around the outlined area (**B**, **C**). Remove the sod from the groove and toss it on the part of the lawn you plan to smother.
3. Cover the outlined area with four to six layers of newspaper, tucking the edges into the groove in the sod (**D**).
4. Spread a 6-inch layer of manure over the newspaper (**E**).
5. After the grass beneath has decomposed (in two to four months), plant through the manure (**F**). ◆

Small yards renewed for outdoor living

These Phoenix gardens make the most of limited space

By Lauren Bonar Swezey

■ A large garden filled with gorgeous plants and areas for outdoor entertaining would be a dream come true for many homeowners. For most of us, however, small yards are the reality. But having limited space doesn't mean you can't enjoy amenities. It just requires a little more imagination during the design process and knowing a few tricks of the trade.

Landscape architect Greg Trutza of Phoenix is particularly successful at addressing the challenges of small gardens. Not only does he own one himself, but he recently remodeled three others: backyards measuring 50 feet wide by 40 to 50 feet deep. The properties are situated in a historic neighborhood, and although the houses are quaint, the yards are boxy with detached garages.

Trutza undertook the challenge of making each garden unique. "The key was understanding the owners' lifestyles and tastes," he says. Still, some requirements were common to all three couples: They wanted privacy and areas for outdoor dining and entertaining. In response, Trutza designed three very functional gardens, each in a different style. In all cases, he took cues from the interiors and continued the themes outdoors.

A firepit underscores a moon window framing a view of giant timber bamboo. ABOVE RIGHT: A ramada shades a sitting area edged by a pond. RIGHT: Water trickles from a bamboo pipe into the koi-stocked pond.

NORM PLATE (3)

Asian elegance

Tom and Genni Houlihan like clean, simple lines. In their home, the furnishings are contemporary and the colors are soft. "We wanted a calm, contemplative space with multiple areas for outdoor living," says Genni. An Asian-inspired garden met their needs perfectly.

Within the small yard, Trutza incorporated areas for lounging, dining, grilling, and gardening. Each of these areas has a different focal point. A view to the sitting area at the back of the garden offers a glance at giant timber bamboo through a moon window. Below the window, a firepit burns on cool nights. Off to the side, a serene koi pond offers ___ ers a visual treat. Bordering it, a

grid-patterned block wall accents the edge of a gravel and sculpture garden. "With each new view, the garden has an element of discovery," says Genni.

The Houlihans played an integral role in selecting the plants and materials. They chose trees with colored foliage and interesting form—purple plum and weeping willow, for instance—as focal points, and pale pink flagstone for its clean, spare feel. Lime washes in pastel hues on walls match the soft colors inside the home. "The sculptural quality of the materials and their simplicity of form were key to the design's success," says Genni.

A touch of old Mexico

TOP: Mature agaves, ocotillo, prickly pear cactus, and yuccas transplanted from the old yard give the new garden an established look. ABOVE: The brick-paved patio embraces a spa backed by a sturdy ramada. LEFT: A rock-lined waterfall cascades into the spa.

Don Steinman and Ruth Greenspan enjoy spending time outdoors. "We live in a place where the climate is so wonderful much of the year, we wanted to make the backyard an extension of our home," explains Greenspan. They're also a busy working couple, so they wanted a low-maintenance garden.

Picking up on the theme of the couple's 1920s stucco house, which is decorated with Mexican tile wall murals, Trutza created a landscape with the feel of old Mexico. An old patio that was crammed against the house was removed and replaced with a much larger ramada-covered patio at the back of the garden. "It changed the visual focus from the back wall to the back of the house, which is a much more pleasant view," says Greenspan.

Trutza then covered the patio and walkways with used brick to give them the look of adobe. By mixing brick patterns (herringbone and running bond), he was able to direct the eye to different areas of the garden.

Mature cactus saved from the original garden were transplanted into a charming miniature botanical garden that wraps around the east side of the house. The rest of the garden is filled with a mix of desert-adapted plants.

In front of the patio, a spa accented with a waterfall is a pleasant spot to relax and enjoy the garden.

The spa is framed by Saltillo tiles laid upside down. BELOW RIGHT: A sunken firepit glows at the far edge of the patio.

Design tips for small spaces

Trutza uses these techniques to make a small garden seem larger.

• **Change the level.** Add arbors, raised beds and planters, and other structures for vertical interest.

• **Create a sense of mystery.** Develop rooms or hidden views so the entire garden can't be seen at one glance.

• **Direct the eye.** Use meandering paths, ramadas, sculptures, water features, or other focal points to steer the eye to different areas of the garden.

• **Use color to add depth.** Paint a dark color on the rear wall of a garden to add visual depth.

• **Pick the right plants.** Know the size of plants at maturity so you won't choose any that will outgrow your garden. Avoid massive shrubs and trees that look out of scale in a small yard.

Contemporary Mediterranean

Garden remodels can be especially challenging when you have to work around existing fixtures. In this garden, now owned by Nancy and Michael Alexander, Trutza retained a huge, beautiful old cork oak that dominates one side of the yard. But a glaring white-bottomed spa surrounded by white decking created a bigger challenge, and behind the spa was a plain block wall bordering another yard.

Since the spa was so prominent, Trutza decided to turn the eyesore into a handsome focal point by adding a fountain, covering the spillway with tasteful gray green tiles, and refinishing the bottom of the spa in black pearl Pebble Tec.

Behind the spa, Trutza installed a new raised planter and filled it with a mix of gray-leafed and flowering plants. He covered the block wall with stucco and applied an ocher-colored lime wash to play off the gray foliage.

As a finishing touch, the Alexanders paved the patio with manganese-colored Saltillo tiles, laid upside down to create a nonslip stonelike surface. "The new paving provides the perfect connection to the house's interior, where the same pavers are placed right side up," says Trutza. ◆

The right rosemary for you

Choose the varieties that suit your landscape—and taste

By Sharon Cohoon

'Collingwood Ingram' is a good choice for slopes. DESIGN: Christine Mulligan

Rosmarinus officinalis should be a simple plant to explain. It's easy enough to describe: an evergreen shrub native to the Mediterranean with dark green, needlelike leaves that have a resinous aroma. From late winter through spring, the plant displays blue flowers. There are two basic types: upright forms useful as shrubs, and prostrate types that will spill down slopes and cascade over walls. So far, so good.

Care is also straightforward. Once rosemary is established, occasional deep watering is almost all it needs. Prune lightly to shape, if desired. Feed little, if at all. The plants will endure drought, heat, wind, and salt spray. Insects leave them alone (the aromatic oils in the foliage act as a natural repellent). And deer and rabbits don't like the taste.

Rosemary has only two weaknesses. It is somewhat tender—most varieties suffer damage when temperatures dip below the teens. And it is susceptible to root rot—usually a consequence of poor drainage, often exacerbated by overwatering.

Now comes the tricky part: distinguishing between the many varieties on the market. They don't look much different in nursery containers, and catalog descriptions sound similar too. The fact that one variety may be sold under several names (for example, 'Collingwood Ingram', 'Ingramii', and 'Benenden Blue' are all the same plant) adds to the confusion.

To sort out the differences, we spoke with expert growers. They recommended the varieties listed below and on the facing page.

Proven winners for the West

UPRIGHT SHRUBS (FROM TALLEST TO SHORTEST)
'Tuscan Blue', 6 to 7 feet tall. Leaves are wider than average and very aromatic; dark blue flowers. Good shrub for many situations. "The workhorse of the industry," says David Fross of Native Sons Nursery (wholesale only), in Arroyo Grande, California.
'Blue Spires', 5 to 6 feet tall and 4 to 6 feet wide. Strong vertical habit; clear blue flowers. "It looks like a miniature Italian cypress," says landscape designer Christine Mulligan of Long Beach, California. "If you want a formal look, it's the best choice."
'Miss Jessup's Upright', 4 to 6 feet tall and about half as wide. Slender branches; pale blue flowers. Good choice for formal herb garden or confined spaces.
'Gorizia', 4 to 5 feet tall and nearly as wide. Stiffly upright and rather open form. Leaves are larger, longer, and brighter green than typical; pale blue flowers. Good specimen or accent plant. "Very architectural-looking," says Jeff Rosendale of Sierra Azul Nursery & Garden, in Watsonville, California.
'Golden Rain' ('Joyce DeBaggio'), 2 to 3 feet tall and as wide. Yellow gold leaves; dark blue flowers. Use for contrast against darker green foliage.

STEVEN GUNTHER

'Prostratus' spills down retaining walls in this Southern California garden. DESIGN: Carole McElwee

GROUND COVERS

'Prostratus', 2 feet tall and 4 to 8 feet wide. Pale blue flowers. Most commonly used rosemary for cascading down walls, as in the photo at left of the garden designed by Carole McElwee of Capistrano Beach, California. Fairly frost tender.

'Irene', 1½ feet tall; spreads 2 to 3 feet per year. More hummocky form than 'Prostratus' or 'Huntington Carpet' (see below). Showy violet blue flowers. Good choice for draping slopes or walls. Hardier (to 15°) than most trailing types.

'Huntington Carpet' ('Huntington Blue'). About half as tall and wide as 'Prostratus' (above). Leaf nodes are closer, so the ground cover has a denser appearance. Pale blue flowers. Excellent choice for covering slopes or trailing down walls.

BEST KINDS FOR COLD OR WET CLIMATES

'Arp', 4 feet tall and wide. Rather open habit but can be kept denser with frequent pruning. Gray green leaves; bright blue flowers. Hardy to −10°.

'Hill Hardy' ('Madalene Hill'), 3 to 5 feet tall and as wide. Foliage denser and brighter green than 'Arp'. Hardy to at least 0°.

'Salem', 2 feet tall and wide. Fairly tolerant of wet soil, it's a popular choice in moist areas of the Pacific Northwest.

SEMIUPRIGHT SHRUBS

'Boule', 3 feet tall and wide. A new introduction from Native Sons, it forms a neat dome (*boule* means "ball" in French).

'Collingwood Ingram' ('Ingramii' or 'Benenden Blue'), 2 to 2½ feet tall and 4 feet wide or wider. "Because it's always putting out new side growth, you never see woody trunk," says Mulligan. This habit makes it suited for slopes (the garden shown on the facing page is a good example). This rosemary also mixes nicely with ceanothus, rockrose, and other drought-tolerant shrubs.

'Ken Taylor'. Similar to 'Collingwood Ingram' but slightly shorter and somewhat trailing. Showy dark blue flowers. Best on slopes. Sensitive to root rot.

BEST CULINARY KINDS

You can use any *R. officinalis* for cooking, but upright kinds with broader leaves contain more aromatic oil. 'Tuscan Blue' is the favorite of many chefs, but 'Blue Spires' and 'Miss Jessup's Upright' are also good. So is 'Spice Island', which is normally sold in the herb section; it grows into an upright, 4- to 5-foot-tall shrub.

Sources

Garden centers and nurseries may carry only a few kinds of rosemary, but most can usually order other varieties from wholesale growers on request. Or order plants from the following mail-order suppliers.

Forestfarm: *www.forestfarm.com* or *(541) 846-7269.* Sells 'Arp', 'Blue Spires', 'Golden Rain', 'Spice Island', and 'Tuscan Blue'.

Goodwin Creek Gardens: *www.goodwincreekgardens.com or (800) 846-7359.* Sells 'Arp', 'Blue Spires', 'Collingwood Ingram', 'Golden Rain', 'Gorizia', 'Hill Hardy', 'Miss Jessup's Upright', 'Prostratus', and 'Tuscan Blue'.

Mountain Valley Growers: *www.mountainvalleygrowers.com or (559) 338-2775.* Sells 'Arp,' 'Golden Rain', 'Hill Hardy', and 'Spice Island'.

Territorial Seed Company: *www.territorialseed.com or (541) 942-9547.* Sells 'Arp' and 'Salem'. ◆

STEMS OF SILVERY 'LADY FRANCES' ivy entwine this tree-shaped trellis. For a closer look at the many faces of ivy, see pages 372–375.

December

PAUL BOUSQUET (2)

Holiday delights in Denver

■ Even in the dead of winter, Denver Botanic Gardens springs to life with Blossoms of Light. Each December since 1989, the gardens' 23 acres are decorated with more than 250,000 lights. Along with traditional evergreen Christmas trees, the gardens gleam with illuminated weeping willows and other deciduous species strewn with strands of lights. Several animated lightscapes delight: A green frog leaps between lily pads that seem to float on an actual pond; morning glories twine up a snowy hillside; orange koi swim in a stream of blue lightbulbs in the Japanese Garden.

The grounds also are dotted with dozens of natural topiaries ensconced in containers. These stunning arrangements are designed by horticulturist Ebi Kondo to show people a simple, more organic way to celebrate the sea-son. Kondo begins with sturdy, ready-made metal frames. He stuffs and covers the frames with Spanish moss, secured by wrapping it with fishing line. Using a glue gun, Kondo affixes organic materials to the topiary frame, including pinecones and dried flowers, fruits, seed heads, and leaves. He fills in with a few artificial decorations (plastic apples and grapes), then adds ribbons, ropes, and tassels as a finishing touch. The photo at left shows one of Kondo's favorite topiary materials: magnolia leaves, which have glossy tops and velvety undersides. The leaves are studded with dried elder catkins and globe amaranth.

Blossoms of Light runs from 6 to 9 nightly during December. Musical entertainment is provided; hot chocolate and cider are available. *$7. (720) 865-3544. — Colleen Smith*

rosemary for Yuletide

■ During the holiday season, many nurseries and garden centers sell rosemary plants that are pruned into topiary cone shapes. These upright varieties of *Rosmarinus officinalis* are sheared to look like traditional trees. You can find everything from tabletop dwarf-size plants to 2-foot-tall specimens. Here, you see one such plant greeting visitors outside a front door in Eugene, Oregon. The owner transplanted it into an 18-inch-diameter terra-cotta pot. Using French shaping ribbon (the kind with fine wire woven into the edges), she tied blue-and-magenta bows to the branches and placed a silver star on top.

You can display rosemary outdoors in a mild-winter climate. The plant is hardy to around 15°. In colder areas, bring it indoors to a sunny location. For easy watering, dump a dozen ice cubes on the soil surface every other day.

This plant needs well-drained soil, moderate water, and a light feeding with an organic fertilizer in spring. To keep the compact shape, pinch back new growth several times a year

ROBIN CUSHMAN

(use trimmings to season foods). Stop tip-pinching in August to encourage a bloom of small blue flowers by Christmas.

— *Mary-Kate Mackey*

good **gear** for rose pruners

■ Gloves made of tough, thorn-resistant materials do more than protect your hands and arms from cuts when you're pruning roses; they help prevent infections that can occur when dirt, broken bits of thorn, or even bacteria naturally occurring on your skin gets into a wound.

In our tests of a variety of available garden gloves, the ones pictured at left offered the best protection. They are available at some nurseries or by mail.

A. Rose Pro's ($7.99): Waterproof nitrile coating; handle the toughest thorns. Unisex sizing. From Garden Works (425/455-0568 or www.createagarden.com).

B. Deluxe Rose Gauntlet Gloves ($39.50): Of heavy-gauge washable leather. Men's and women's sizes. From Stillbrook Horticultural Supplies (800/414-4468 or www.stillbrook.com).

C. Deluxe Rose Pro's ($21): Snug-fitting goatskin. Sized for women. From Garden Works.

D. Arm Savers ($16): Sturdy nylon cuffs. Particularly useful when trimming thorny vines or climbing roses. Use them with heavy-duty leather gloves or short-cuffed rose gloves. From Wildflower Seed Company (800/456-3359 or www.wildflower-seed.com). — *Lauren Bonar Swezey*

NORMAN A. PLATE; ABOVE: E. SPENCER TOY

greens
that celebrate the season

■ Evergreen cuttings bring garden-fresh color, texture, and often fragrance indoors for the holidays. You can prune greens from your own landscape or buy them from garden centers. Bulk greens are often priced by the pound; swags already strung on wire are sold by the foot. Below are the most reliable greens for indoor display. Mix several kinds of greens for best effect.

Most evergreen cuttings will last up to three weeks indoors if you embed the stem ends in moist florist's foam. To prolong the life of swags and wreaths, you can spray them with an anti-transpirant product like Cloud Cover or Wilt-Pruf (keep the spray off berries).

A. Cedar. Western red cedar (shown at bottom right), with its flexible and fragrant foliage, is the perfect material for classic swags. Rich green sprays of incense cedar and deeper green Port Orford cedar (bottom left) are also fragrant; both kinds work well in wreaths.

B. English holly. Glossy green or variegated leaves with silver or gold markings make a perfect foil for bright red berries.

C. Fir. Needles and branches tend to be stiff, so firs are better

used in wreaths and tabletop centerpieces than in swags. We show silver fir (top) and blue green noble fir (far right).

D. Juniper. Their fragrant foliage comes in a variety of colors, including green, silvery blue, and golden yellow. Rocky Mountain juniper (pictured) and some other kinds carry berrylike cones in blue gray shades.

E. Pine. Short-needled varieties usually work best in smaller wreaths and centerpieces; most kinds deliver a pungent pine scent. Western white pine is shown at top right.

— *Jim McCausland*

BOOKSHELF

**Anemone-flowered
C. japonica 'Tinsie Two'**

a gift for
camellia lovers

■ The opportunity to grow camellias is one of the rewards of gardening in mild climates of the West. Now, one of the finest camellia collections is spotlighted in a new book: *Camellias: A Curator's Introduction to the Camellia Collection in the Huntington Botanical Gardens,* by Ann Richardson (Huntington Library Press, San Marino, CA, 2001; $27.95; 626/405-2172 or www.huntington.org). This volume offers a succinct overview of the genus *Camellia,* including its history, flower forms, plant descriptions, and culture. You'll learn about species ranging from *C. sinensis,* the source of tea, to the three most commonly planted kinds in this country—*C. japonica, C. reticulata,* and *C. sasanqua.* A chapter on camellia culture covers planting, pruning, disbudding, and common problems. The book is illustrated with exquisite photographs by Don Normark and antique paintings from the Huntington archives. — *J.M.*

ice lanterns
from Alaska

JEFF SHULTZ (4)

■ Not every gardener gets a kick out of working outdoors when the thermometer falls to 18° or lower. But in Willow, Alaska, Les Brake takes advantage of freezing temperatures to make ice lanterns. Brake displays as many as 50 of these illuminated ice arrangements in his front yard.

The clear ice cylinder at right was made by filling a bucket with water and letting it stand outdoors until the top and sides froze. Then Brake brought the bucket indoors for about a half hour to thaw it out a bit. Outside again, he turned the bucket upside down to drain the unfrozen water from the center. He removed the frozen cylinder from the bucket and placed a candle inside.

The ice castle and the crescent moon at far right are formed from molds that Brake finds around the house (plastic storage containers for the castle, a snack tray for the moon). To keep the ice from sticking, he sprays the molds lightly with vegetable oil before filling them with water tinted with food color (red for the castle, green for the moon). The frozen shapes are then cemented to solid ice bases using a slurry of snow and icy water. When candles are placed behind the shapes, the translucent ice glows like stained glass. — *Steven R. Lorton*

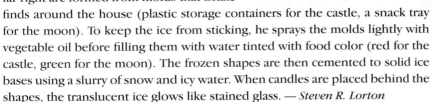

As night falls, candlelit forms brighten the covered deck of Les Brake's home in Willow, north of Anchorage.

geranium bouquet

■ Each winter, I cut back my geraniums so that their spring growth will be lush and shapely. I don't toss the trimmings; instead, I tuck them directly into garden beds or use them to make holiday arrangements to give to gardening friends.

Bouquets like the one pictured here need no flowers to look good, because many *Pelargonium*-type geraniums, including zonals (named for the zone of pigment that forms a ring on each leaf), have very decorative foliage. Leaf colors range from bronze or apple green to gold or chartreuse, often with white or yellow margins. Some leaves are velvety to the touch; others are glossy and crinkled.

The bouquets stay fresh for a week or two in moist florist's foam. Then they can be taken apart and the cuttings rooted in water or moist perlite for planting in pots or garden beds several weeks later.

Showy geranium foliage in this mix includes (from left to right) bronze and green 'Vancouver Centennial', a stellar type; green 'Mandarin', an ivy type; red, green, and cream 'Henry Cox', a zonal; and lime green 'Crystal Palace Gem'.

Well-stocked nurseries carry a selection of geraniums. One local specialist is the wholesaler New Leaf Nurseries (2456 Foothill Dr., Vista, CA; 760/726-9269). The nursery is open to the public for retail sales in December on Fridays and Saturdays from 10:30 to 4.

— *Debra Lee Baldwin*

DIRECTIONS

1. Soak a block of florist's foam in a bucket of water.
2. Place the foam in a shallow container; secure it with florist's tape.
3. Clip the cuttings to about 8 inches long; pick off lower leaves, then insert the cuttings into the foam.
4. Attach a gift card; on it, remind the recipient to keep the foam moist and the bouquet in bright light but not direct sunlight.

What to do in your garden in December

Shop for trees, prune greens, celebrate seasonal plants

PLANTING

☐ CAMELLIAS. Zones 4–7: Sasanqua camellias and other winter-flowering types (mostly *C. hiemalis*) are in bloom now. Plant them immediately and spread mulch around the plants to keep roots from freezing or provide frost-free shelter for container plants.

☐ TREES, SHRUBS. Zones 4–7: Plant hardy varieties anytime, watering them in well. It's prime shopping time for conifers, either as living Christmas trees or as specimens for your landscape. Good candidates for living Christmas trees include alpine fir, Douglas fir, noble fir, and white fir.

MAINTENANCE

☐ CARE FOR HOUSEPLANTS. Fertilize winter-flowering plants lightly at bloom time, but wait until spring growth begins to feed other kinds. Check for aphids, mites, and scales; if you find infestations, rinse the plant in lukewarm shower water, then spray with insecticidal soap. To contain the spray, first place the infested plant inside a plastic garment bag (the kind you get from dry cleaners).

☐ CARE FOR LIVING CHRISTMAS TREES. If you buy a living Christmas tree, leave it in its nursery container and try to limit its indoor stay to 10 days. Water regularly; one easy way is to dump two trays of ice cubes on top of the soil daily. After Christmas, move the tree to a cool, bright porch or other protected place where the rootball won't freeze. Transplant the tree into the garden or grow it in the container until next Christmas.

☐ PROPAGATE EVERGREENS. Use the ground-layering method to propagate new plants from broadleaf evergreens (azalea, camellia, daphne, holly, mahonia, or rhododendron). Slice a fingernail-size patch of bark off the underside of a low-hanging branch of an existing plant, then dust the wound with rooting hormone and press it into the soil below. Firm a little more soil over the branch, leaving the tip and leaves exposed; lay a stone or brick on top of the branch to hold it firmly on the ground. Keep the soil moist. The branch will form roots where it contacts the ground. Next autumn, sever the branch from its parent and transplant the rooted shoot.

☐ PRUNE CONIFERS, HOLLY. By happy coincidence, pruning season coincides with holiday needs for evergreen cuttings that make up wreaths and swags (see the item on page 364). Make each cut just above a side branch (don't leave stubs). Work from the bottom of the plant to the top and from the inside out, keeping the plant's finished form in mind.

☐ TEND GIFT PLANTS. To prolong the bloom of Christmas cactus, cyclamen, kalanchoe, and poinsettias, remove decorative foil or wrap from pots so water won't pool up inside. Keep plants away from heat vents and fireplaces. Water when the top ½ inch of soil dries out. ◆

What to do in your garden in December

Plant color, harvest greens, water wisely, and celebrate the season

Sunset
CLIMATE ZONES
- ☐ Mountain (1-2)
- ☐ Valley (7-9)
- ☐ Inland (14)
- ☐ Coastal (15-17)

DEBRA LAMBERT

PLANTING

☐ **BARE-ROOT ROSES. Zones 7–9, 14–17:** Shop nurseries now while selections are good. Choices may include climbing roses, floribundas, hybrid teas, and easy-care shrub roses. Try one of these favorite varieties: 'Bonica' (pink shrub rose), 'Brandy' (apricot blend hybrid tea), 'Double Delight' (red and white bicolor hybrid tea), 'Iceberg' (white floribunda or climber), 'Just Joey' (apricot hybrid tea), 'Kaleidoscope', (orange tan to lavender shrub rose), 'Knock Out' (cerise shrub rose), 'Mister Lincoln' (red hybrid tea), or 'Peace' (yellow hybrid tea).

☐ **NEW PRIMROSE.** A chemical found on the hairs of *Primula obconica* stems and leaves can cause a skin rash for some susceptible people after the plants have been handled. The irritant is called primin, and if you've discovered you're sensitive to it, look in nurseries for a relatively new series of *P. obconica* called Libre, which is primin-free. Flower colors include blue, light salmon, magenta, pink, and white.

DECORATING

☐ **CARE FOR LIVING CHRISTMAS TREES.** Most nurseries carry the following kinds: aleppo pine, Colorado blue spruce, dwarf Alberta spruce, giant sequoia, and Monterey pine. Before bringing the tree indoors, water the pot thoroughly and hose down the foliage. Indoors, set the pot in a cool location in a plastic waterproof saucer or in a clay saucer set on plastic or a waterproof cork mat. Camouflage the nursery can by surrounding it with corrugated metal sheeting or drape it with festive fabric. Check soil moisture daily.

☐ **MAKE A WREATH OR SWAG.** Nurseries are stocked with plenty of greenery for adorning a door and draping on a mantel. Spray untreated greens with an antitranspirant to delay drying. Add natural cones and pods or dried berries, and finish it with a raffia bow. Or attach an elegant wired ribbon bow.

☐ **PREPARE CUT TREES.** Christmas trees purchased on lots are sometimes dusty and dirty. Before bringing your tree indoors, shake out the old needles, then spray the tree down with water and allow it to dry. Slice 1 inch off the bottom of the trunk before setting the tree in the stand.

MAINTENANCE

☐ **PROTECT CITRUS FROM FREEZES. Zones 7–9, 14–17:** Young trees are more susceptible to injury than older ones. Regardless of the tree's age, small fruits (such as immature lemons up to $1/2$ inch in diameter) are damaged at 30° to 31°, while larger, ripe citrus fruits (especially grapefruits, oranges, and mandarins) can usually handle temperatures down to 26° for short periods of time. If a heavy freeze is predicted, cover trees with burlap draped over stakes, if practical. Harvest mature fruit.

☐ **ADJUST IRRIGATION SYSTEM. Zones 7–9, 14–17:** Now that the weather has cooled down, soil dries out more slowly. Adjust your automatic irrigation system to operate less frequently (test soil moisture between irrigations to determine frequency). If rainfall is ample, set your controller on rain delay (if it has a rain sensor) or simply turn it off. Otherwise, continue to water as needed until rains come. ◆

What to do in your garden in December

Plant, prune, water, weed, and celebrate the season

Sunset
CLIMATE ZONES
1-3 7-9 11 13 14-24

PLANTING

☐ BARE-ROOT. For the best selection in bare-root roses, visit nurseries this month. Deciduous fruit trees, cane berries, grapes, and perennial vegetables will arrive later this month and next. Plant anything bare-root as soon after purchase as possible.

☐ BULBS. Coastal, inland, and low-desert gardeners (zones 22–24, 18–21, and 13, respectively) can continue to plant spring-blooming bulbs. Tulips and hyacinths that have been chilled at least six weeks can go into the ground too.

☐ FLOWERING SHRUBS. Sasanquas and other types of early-flowering camellias are good choices for winter color and readily available in nurseries now. Also look for breath of heaven (*Coleonema*), *Erica canaliculata*, Geraldton waxflower, New Zealand tea tree (*Leptospermum scoparium*), pink powder puff (*Calliandra haematocephala*), and spotted emu bush (*Eremophila maculata*).

☐ VEGETABLES. Beets, carrots, kale (and other cooking greens), lettuces, peas, radishes, and Swiss chard can go in from seed. Cauliflower, cabbage, broccoli, and brussels sprouts do best started as seedlings.

MAINTENANCE

☐ ADJUST IRRIGATION. If rainfall is light, water just enough to compensate; don't forget plants under eaves. Also irrigate container plantings when necessary. If rains are adequate, shut off your automatic controller.

☐ CARE FOR CHRISTMAS TREES. To prolong freshness of a cut tree, saw an inch off the bottom of the trunk, then store the tree in a bucket of water in a shady spot outdoors. Before bringing it indoors, saw off another inch. Use a stand that holds lots of water and keep the reservoir full. (Check daily the first week.) Keep living trees outdoors until shortly before the holidays. Restrict indoor time to two weeks or less.

☐ FERTILIZE CYMBIDIUMS. Feed with a bloom-promoting fertilizer, such as a 15-30-15, until buds open.

☐ PRUNE FOR HOLIDAY GREENS. Prunings from cedars, pines, and other conifers can be used for holiday swags and wreaths. Cotoneaster, holly, magnolia, pyracantha, and toyon are useful too. Cut to side branches or to about ¼ inch above buds.

☐ WEED. Pull out annual bluegrass, chickweed, spurge, and other weeds as they emerge. If annual weeds are prevented from setting seed and multiplying, next year's weeding will be easier.

PEST AND DISEASE CONTROL

☐ PREVENT BEETLE DAMAGE. Prune eucalyptus, pine, and other trees susceptible to bark beetles now, before the beetles become active again in the spring. Chip the prunings or cover the firewood tightly with a tarp to prevent beetles from laying eggs. (Beetles lay eggs on dead as well as live wood.)

☐ SPRAY FRUIT TREES. As soon as their leaves fall, spray deciduous flowering and fruit trees with dormant oil to smother overwintering aphids, mites, and scale. If you haven't done so already, treat susceptible trees for peach leaf curl. Add lime sulfur or fixed copper to the dormant oil. (Don't use lime sulfur on apricot trees, however). Spray branches, crotches, the trunk, and the ground beneath the tree's drip line. If it rains within 48 hours of spraying, repeat the treatment. Spray again at the height of dormancy and at first bud swell. ◆

What to do in your garden in December

Shop for trees, prune conifers, protect roses

SHOPPING

☐ **BUY LIVING CHRISTMAS TREES.** Good choices include alpine fir (*Abies lasiocarpa*), Colorado blue spruce (*Picea pungens glauca*), Engelmann spruce (*Picea engelmanii*), and white fir (*A. concolor*). Keep the tree in its nursery container and try to limit its indoor stay to 10 days. Water regularly. If you don't have space to plant one of these trees in the garden (all of those listed above grow into large specimens) but still want a live tree, choose a subtropical Norfolk Island pine; it can be grown as a houseplant after the holidays.

MAINTENANCE

☐ **CARE FOR GIFT PLANTS.** *Christmas cactus.* After plants stop flowering, move them to a sunny east- or north-facing window. Let the soil dry out between waterings and fertilize every two weeks. After all danger of frost is past, move the plants outside to a shaded porch and water sparingly. In late summer, bring the plants indoors and within a few weeks they will form new flower buds. *Poinsettias.* Display them in a cool room, away from doorways or heating vents, where they'll receive bright, indirect light. Check the soil often, and when it feels dry, water, soaking the root mass. Drain any water that collects in the saucer.

☐ **HARVEST GREENS.** Prune evergreen conifers and use the boughs for holiday wreaths or swags (see "Holiday Greens" on page 364). Don't leave stubs; cut just above side branches that you want to grow. While you're at it, remove dead, diseased, and injured branches. Then prune for shape, working from the bottom of the tree to the top and from the inside out.

☐ **INSULATE ROSES.** Don't prune roses this time of year except to remove broken or dead canes. After temperatures drop below freezing for a few nights, mound soil over the plant base; if it's a grafted rose, be sure the soil covers the bud union (the enlarged knob from which the canes emerge). Once soil surface freezes, set a cylinder of chicken wire or a tomato cage around each plant and fill with a mulch of leaves, pine boughs, or straw. In spring, remove mulch and add it to compost.

☐ **MULCH.** Spread a 3- to 4-inch layer of organic mulch around perennials and shrubs and over bulb beds.

☐ **PROPAGATE HOUSEPLANTS.** Chinese evergreen, philodendron, pothos, and other indoor plants can become leggy in winter. To start new plants, snip off elongated stems and immerse the cut ends in water until roots form, then transplant rooted cuttings into fresh potting soil.

☐ **SPRAY BROADLEAF EVERGREENS.** Dwarf conifers and broadleaf evergreens such as holly and rhododendron are susceptible to dehydration and windburn in winter. To protect them, spray the foliage with an antitranspirant product like No Wilt or Wilt-Pruf, following instructions on the label. One application lasts for several months. You can also use these products to prolong the life of cut greens in holiday arrangements.

☐ **WATER.** When temperatures stay above freezing, water dry spots in the garden, especially plants in containers and under house eaves. ◆

— *Marcia Tatroe*

What to do in your garden in December

Shop for roses,
set out bulbs, celebrate
seasonal plants

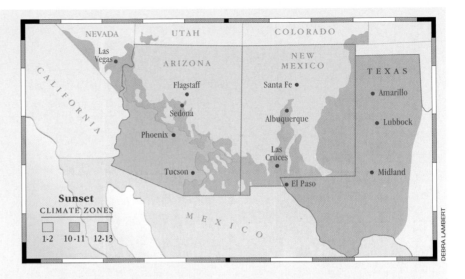

DEBRA LAMBERT

PLANTING AND SHOPPING

☐ **BUY LIVING CHRISTMAS TREES.**
Choose a tree you can transplant into the garden. Zones 1A–3B: Consider Colorado spruce *(Picea pungens)* and Douglas fir *(Pseudotsuga menziesii)*. Zone 10 (Albuquerque): Try Arizona cypress *(Cupressus arizonica)*, Colorado spruce, deodar cedar *(Cedrus deodara)*, Douglas fir, and piñon *(Pinus edulis)*. Zones 11–13 (Las Vegas, Tucson, Phoenix): Good choices include Aleppo pine *(P. halepensis)*, Goldwater (or Mondell) pine *(P. eldarica)*, and Italian stone pine *(P. pinea)*. Keep trees in their containers, water them regularly, and try to limit their indoor stay to 10 days.

☐ **PLANT BARE-ROOT ROSES.**
Zones 12–13: Buy bare-root plants at nurseries; ask the staff to pack the roots in damp burlap or sawdust and wrap them in a plastic bag to prevent them from drying out before you get home. Soak the plants in water for a day before planting.

☐ **PLANT SPRING BULBS.** Zones 11–13: Early in the month, you can still plant anemones, callas, daffodils, freesias, and ranunculus, plus crocuses, hyacinths, and tulips that have chilled for at least six weeks.

☐ **START PEPPERS AND TOMATOES.** Zones 11–13: Sow seeds of peppers and tomatoes in containers filled with sterile potting soil in a warm, bright spot indoors. Seedlings will be ready to transplant outdoors eight weeks after sowing.

MAINTENANCE

☐ **APPLY WINTER MULCH.** Zones 1–2: Spread a 3- to 4-inch layer of organic mulch over beds of bulbs and perennials to protect roots from being heaved out of the ground during freezing and thawing cycles.

☐ **CARE FOR GIFT PLANTS.** To keep drainage free-flowing, remove decorative wrapping from potted plants such as Christmas cactus, kalanchoe, and poinsettia. Place them away from heater vents and fireplaces. Check plants daily and keep soil moist.

☐ **PREVENT GIRDLER DAMAGE.**
Mesquite twig girdlers are beetles that eat the bark off limbs in a circular pattern, which will kill the tree. To reduce girdler infestations, clean up fallen twigs and remove hanging deadwood.

☐ **PROTECT CITRUS.** Zones 12–13: When temperatures are forecast to drop below 28°, cover tree canopies with burlap, blankets, or old sheets. Wrap the trunks of young trees with a blanket or cloth to protect their thin bark from splitting.

☐ **WATER.** Zones 1–2, 10: Water plants when the temperature is above freezing. Zones 11–13: Irrigate established trees and shrubs deeply one time this month if there has been no rain. ◆

— *Mary Irish*

'Golden Ingot'
Suffused with gold

'Fluffy Ruffles'
Self-branching

'Kolibri'
Mutates freely

'Teardrop'
2002
Ivy of the
Year

'Perkeo'
Rounded leaves

'Spetchley'
Smallest leaves

'Cascade'
Classic trailer for pots

'Calico'
Multicolored

'Henriette'
Snowlike splotches

THE MANY FACES OF
IVY

It's the "do anything" holiday plant. Green or golden,
leaves are oval, heart shaped, or three pointed

By Jim McCausland • Photographs by Christina Schmidhofer

'Ivalace'
A favorite curly

■ Whether trailing along a bookshelf, spilling out of a hanging basket, or covering the soil around a potted palm, ivy is one of the easiest, most successful plants. It reacts to too much shade by sending out a tendril toward whatever light it can find. It grows willingly on any type of support—a fence, wreath, or wire topiary frame. Its leaves come in hundreds of shapes, from birdfoot to heart, fan to curly—each overlaid with colors that range from solid green to green with snowy white spots or pale yellow edges. Stems can be green or red; on a few varieties, leaves blush pink in cold weather.

Ivies have a mythical history: Both Bacchus and Nero were said to have worn ivy wreaths, and Nero wore his around his head while Rome burned. Today, these graceful vining plants

LEFT: Young ivy trails gracefully. RIGHT: Stems of silvery 'Lady Frances' entwine a tree-shaped trellis.

are so ubiquitous that many people overlook them.

So take a second look at the sprig of ivy that trails out of your holiday flower basket. Its intricate leaf pattern may startle you—at least until you realize that horticulturists have been improving this plant for centuries. The breeder's art has com-bined with ivy's natural tendency to mutate, resulting in a breathtaking array of gold, green, cream, gray, and white leaf patterns. All make hand-some topiaries during the holidays or versatile container plants anytime.

Ivy's ages and stages
In its juvenile stage, English ivy runs and roots with all the reckless aban-don of youth. It can quickly become a lovely trailing pot plant, a dense ground cover, or the leafy hide for a fat topiary elephant.

Unpruned, most varieties eventually reach the adult stage (except in cold-winter climates). They then change leaf form, stop making aerial roots, stop climbing, and start flowering and producing black berries that are edible for birds but toxic to people.

At any stage, ivy is usually happiest in places that get partial to full shade.

Given monthly doses of liquid fertil-izer and enough water to keep the soil from drying out, ivies grow well. Mites and worms can occasionally damage them, but ivies are trouble-free in most areas.

There's a fair chance that the ivy you buy for your mantel will send out a shoot that doesn't look like the mother plant. It could be a simple re-version—a change from variegated to solid green—or it might be a new pat-tern that's more beautiful than the parent. If you like what you see, prop-agate it (see "Garden Tip" at left).

Plants and information
A variety of ivies (including most of the ones shown here) is available at nurseries, florists, and supermarkets throughout the West. Or you can order plants by mail from Heritage International (805/484-5262) or

garden tip
To root ivy, take a 6- to 8-inch sprig, strip off the lower leaves, and plant the cutting in a pot full of loose, moist planting mix. Put it on a windowsill and roots will form within a month or two. Ivy also roots easily in a glass of water, but water roots break easily. Transplant them with care.

Keeping ivy in its place

In mild parts of the Pacific Northwest and along the California coast, English ivy grows too well. It crawls into the woods from adjacent gardens, spreads by bird-transported seed, and starts from trimmings gardeners dump at the forest's edge. In Oregon, the problem is so serious that the Department of Agriculture there may forbid the sale of plain English ivy next year (they've already declared it a noxious weed). Sale of numerous small-leafed and variegated cultivars would still be allowed, and gardeners who have ivy could keep it.

To protect woodlands, keep ivy indoors, or outdoors only as a potted plant or in a contained area. If your ivy blooms, cut off flowers and seed heads, and consider replacing the ivy with a noninvasive ground cover like *Epimedium*.

Also keep ivy out of trees. It can weaken them by causing crown rot and by overtaking and killing leaves. To remove ivy from a tree, cut vines off at the base. After the vine above the cut dies, strip it off by hand.

ABOVE: 'Duckfoot', aptly named for its distinctive leaf shape, fills this hanging basket. RIGHT: Variegated ivy softens the edges of this long container, planted with three dwarf Alberta spruce trees.

Samia Rose Topiary (760/436-0460 or www.srtopiary.com).

To learn more about ivies, join the American Ivy Society ($20 per year; Box 2123, Naples, FL 34106-2123; www.ivy.org). You can also find out more from *The Ivy Book,* by Suzanne Warner Pierot (Garden by the Stream, Willow, NY, 1995; $15.95; 845/688-5318). ◆

A

B

Coast
redwood

Blue atlas
cedar

THOMAS J. STORY (3)

Make mini-trees from prunings

By Jill Slater and Lauren Bonar Swezey

Conifer branches, trimmed from the bottom of your Christmas tree or gathered from your garden's evergreens, make charming holiday displays. Simply arrange them in moistened florist's foam set in a decorative pot, and they'll delight you for weeks. You can make one in an hour, for $20 or less.

You'll need branches of various lengths; try blue atlas cedar, Douglas fir, juniper, pine, or redwood. If you don't have access to holiday greens, you can buy them at nurseries and florists' shops. To add a little color, use small dried pepper berries, ornaments, ribbons, or lights.

For each tree, you'll also need two bricks of **florist's foam**, an 8-inch-diameter **decorative pot with saucer**, a clear plastic **pot liner** (or heavy-duty garbage bag and double-stick tape), a handful of **sphagnum moss**, a ½-inch-thick **wood dowel** or a piece of bamboo about 24 inches long, and **18-gauge wire**.

DIRECTIONS

1. Soak florist's foam in water for at least 30 minutes.
2. While the foam is soaking, insert the pot liner into the pot. (Or cut a garbage bag to fit and secure it to the inside of the container with double-stick tape.)
3. Using a knife, trim the florist's foam to fit inside the pot. (The top of the foam should be even with the pot's top.) Place the foam inside the pot, then cover it with moss.
4. Insert the dowel about 6 inches down through the center of the foam.
5. Trim the branches to about 20 inches long. Place one next to the dowel and insert it about an inch into the foam. Wire it to the dowel's top, middle, and bottom (see photo **A**). Set two or three more branches (depending on how bushy they are) around the dowel, wiring them in place (**B**).
6. Fill in with shorter pieces to form a Christmas tree. Wire branches onto the dowel in one or more places. ◆

Flower trees

Tabletop trees made from your favorite flowers

By Kathleen N. Brenzel

Floral Trees

COST: About $20 or more, depending on the flowers

TIME: About 1 hour each

TOOLS AND MATERIALS
- 1 block **florist's foam** (4 by 9 by 3 inches thick)
- **Bucket**
- Flowers: **Chrysanthemum trees** (white, green): 75 stems
  Red gerbera tree: about 20 stems
- **Knife** for shaping florist's foam
- **Small pot** or urn, about 4 inches diameter
- **Plastic spray bottle** of water
- **Flower clippers** or scissors

DIRECTIONS

1. Soak the florist's foam in water until moistened, about 20 minutes. Place flowers in water-filled bucket.

2. Using knife, slice off enough foam to round each corner on one end of the foam block. Slip this end into the container, pushing and twisting until it is snug.

3. With the knife, starting at the top corners, shave downward on all sides of the foam block to form a flat-topped cone. If edges begin to dry, spray with water.

4. With scissors or clippers, cut several flower stems about 3 inches long, cutting on an angle. Poke stems about an inch deep into the foam cone. Continue until the foam is totally covered with flowers. ◆

It's a simple fact: Flowers are gorgeous any time of year. And when winter quiets the color in many Western gardens, florists and grocery stores stock plenty of blooms for holiday decorating—frosty white chrysanthemums that look like snowflakes, mums the color of fresh limes. Ruby red gerberas and even fragrant lilies and roses are abundant.

To celebrate the beauty and diversity of cut flowers at this time of year, floral designer Jill Slater created the trees pictured above, each about 10½ inches tall. Made of moistened florist's foam carved into cones and studded with flowers, they're great for decorating a dining or buffet table. The best-looking trees use one or two kinds and colors of flowers. You can opt for the lacy, elegant look with white mums or go with vibrant, south-of-the-border hues like orange and purple. Either way, choose long-lasting varieties with strong stems. And keep in mind that large flowers such as gerberas are less time-consuming to work with than small ones like button mums, as you'll need fewer stems to cover the foam base. Any container will do to hold the tree; ceramic urns give them some height.

The trees last about a week. Check the foam every other day; if it feels dry, move the tree to the kitchen sink and pour a gentle stream of water on top (you may have to remove a bloom or two to do this), allowing it to soak in. Display the trees away from furnace vents and drafts.

JAY GRAHAM

This tropical bouquet contains orange pincushions *(Leucospermum),* 'Madame Butterfly' obake anthuriums, yellow oncidium orchids, deep red vanda orchids, croton leaves, and a spray of bear grass stems. All are secured in a brick of moist florist's foam inside a plastic-lined gourd. DESIGN: Jill Slater

Blooms from Hawaii

By Kirsten Whatley

At dawn, the brilliant tropical blooms that fill the farms along Maui's Hana coast burn deep orange, red, and frosted pink, like the rising sun. Lush green foliage surrounds them and sets off their dazzling hues.

But the beauty of these waxy-plumed heliconias, vivid torch gingers, heart-shaped anthuriums, elegant orchids, and spiky proteas lasts far longer than the morning. On a recent tour of the farms listed at right, I watched as these captivating blooms were harvested and gathered into bouquets for sending to the mainland. Floral gift boxes, which range from $45 for a dozen stems to more than $125 for 35 to 40 stems (plus greenery as stunning as the flowers), arrive at far-flung destinations within one to two days. Once arranged, the flowers can last for a week or more in water-filled vases.

If your holiday decorating or gift list calls for flowers from paradise, order as soon as possible to ensure delivery by Christmas (call ahead for a brochure and price list). Many farms are also open to visitors; call first for directions. All flowers and plants are approved for agricultural export.

Where to shop

Hana Tropicals. Tropicals flourish in Susie and Tony Pu's shade houses and fields. Cut flowers are shipped in boxes or in carefully packed glass vases tied with raffia. For Christmas decorations, ask about hanging bromeliad balls. *Open by appointment. Box 247, Hana, HI 96713; (800) 456-4262 or www.hanatropicals.com.*

Maui Floral. Carver and Maureen Wilson have grown proteas on the slopes of Haleakala Volcano for 26 years. Besides incorporating other growers' tropicals into their gift boxes and leis, they sell protea wreaths. *8–3:30 Mon–Fri. 310 Copp Rd., Kula, HI 96790; (800) 543-2727 or www.mauifloral.com.*

Nahiku Tropicals. Brad and Nedia Reid grow orchids and bromeliads. Cut-flower boxes can be bought at their gift shop or ordered over the Internet. *8–5 daily; call before visiting. Box 324, Hana, HI 96713; (800) 250-3743 or www.maui.net/~reid.*

Na Pua 'Ohana. John and Dawn Lono grow 20 varieties of heliconia and offer cut-flower boxes and leis. Their store, 'Ohana Lei & Flowers, is located in the Hana Town Center. *10–5 Mon–Sat. Box 495, Hana, HI 96713; (800) 438-9479, (808) 248-7064 (store), or www.maui.net/~napua.*

Na Pua O Helani and Helani Farm. On more than 70 acres, Matt and B.J. Keiley grow vibrant-hued tropicals for their cut-flower boxes. *By appointment. Box 571, Hana, HI 96713; (800) 385-5241 or BJ4flowers@aol.com.*

Sunset Tropicals. For Terrie Roberts, proteas are a specialty, but her most popular gift box contains proteas, orchids, anthuriums, and other tropicals. *8–3 Mon–Fri. Box 451, Kula, HI 96790; (800) 343-2243 or www.sunsettropicals.com.*

Tradewind Tropicals. Rebecca Buckley grows gingers, heliconias, and calatheas. She ships cut flowers and arrangements in vases. *Not open to visitors. Box 385, Hana, HI 96713; (800) 327-8097.*

Tropical Flowers and Bouquets of Hawaii. Virginia and Moses Timbal sell a variety of homegrown tropicals. *10–4 Sat–Thu. SR Box 36A, Hana, HI 96713; (800) 654-7956.* ◆

Miniature amaryllis for winter color

They bear more blooms than giant kinds

By Sharon Cohoon

If giant amaryllis are the tubas in the flowering bulb band, miniature amaryllis are the French horns. The large-flowered amaryllis we're used to seeing at this time of year carry huge blossoms—8 and even 10 inches across. By comparison, miniature amaryllis flowers are only one-third as wide. Yet what these smaller blooms lack in breadth they make up for in volume. Miniature kinds not only put out more flowers per stem than their bigger cousins but produce more stems, which tend to come one at a time, so you get a long performance from each bulb.

While large-flowered kinds can look rather stiff and formal, miniature amaryllis, with their wavy blooms, have a graceful informality that fits anywhere in the house—on the kitchen table, sideboards, even bathroom counters.

Many nurseries now carry miniature amaryllis. Christmas-flowering amaryllis, usually bulbs grown in South Africa (or elsewhere in the southern hemisphere), bloom sooner after planting—in 4 to 6 weeks—and are available as early as September. Dutch-grown bulbs take longer to bloom—from 8 to 12 weeks.

If you can't find miniatures locally, order bulbs from McClure & Zimmerman (800/883-6998 or www.mzbulb.com) and John Scheepers (860/567-0838 or www.johnscheepers.com).

For more tips on indoor bulbs, go to www.sunset.com/winterbulbs.html.

THOMAS J. STORY (3)

Three popular varieties are 'Fairy Tale' (left), 'Green Goddess' (top right), and 'Carina' (bottom right).

Planting tips

Choose containers just large enough to hold the bulbs with an inch or so to spare all around. Typically, you can fit one bulb in a 6-inch pot and three bulbs in an 8-inch pot. Make sure containers are deep enough to accommodate all the roots and are heavy enough to counterbalance the substantial top growth. Miniature amaryllis stems are almost as tall as those of large-flowered kinds.

Fill containers halfway with potting soil. Set bulbs stem ends up and partially cover with additional potting soil. The widest part of the bulb should be at soil level, leaving up to half the bulb above the soil. Firm soil around the bulb and water well. Then keep soil barely moist until shoots emerge.

Once growth begins, give the plant bright, indirect light and more water.

Turn frequently so the stalk won't lean toward the light. When buds open, move the container to a cooler location to prolong flower life. Cut off individual flowers as they fade. After all flowers have withered, cut off the entire stem.

After-bloom care

If you want to maintain the plant after bloom, encourage growth by watering regularly and feeding bimonthly with liquid fertilizer diluted to half strength. (If foliage did not appear with the bloom, it will now.)

Once the danger of frost is past, move the plant outdoors, preferably in a spot where it will get morning sun and afternoon shade.

Allow it to dry out and go dormant in late summer. Repot in late fall or early winter, and as new flower buds emerge, resume watering. ◆

Before & After

By Sharon Cohoon

From ho-hum to heavenly

New outdoor living spaces transform a tired garden

before

BEFORE: Tired lawn and glaring broken concrete pavers filled the backyard. AFTER: Small patios such as this one provide outdoor dining space. Limestone pavers echo the earthy hues of purple fountain grass and lavenders around it.

after

■ When Paul and Susan Robbins bought their 1926 Craftsman house in Los Angeles last year, it's a safe bet that their realtor didn't think the backyard was one of the property's selling points. To most prospective buyers, it must have looked discouraging, with a worn-down lawn, rough-hewn pond, and vast sweeps of broken concrete paths.

But Paul is a garden designer, and when he looked at the space, he saw potential. He liked the garden's simple shape—a perfect 50-foot square. "A garden like that is easy to divide up into areas, which is what I wanted to do," he says. He imagined the garden as it looks today, sectioned into inviting spaces for entertaining or to retreat to alone—the whole softened and sensualized with flowing ornamental grasses, aromatic Mediter-

ranean lavender and rosemary, and fragrant citrus trees.

Paul recognized the mature plants that were worth hanging on to, including a handsome pepper tree that screened out the telephone pole in the alley, and pittosporum shrubs tall enough to hide most of the concrete block wall that borders the garden. "They made the space feel sheltered and quiet," he says. There were no expensive mistakes to correct; all he needed to do for a fresh start was to drain the pool and haul away the concrete.

The backyard includes four new spaces: a 12-foot redwood deck off the master bedroom; a dining terrace of limestone tile set in sand immediately below the deck (shown here); a gravel terrace seating area under the shade of the pepper tree (with a new

retaining wall around the tree for additional seating); and a citrus grove–herb garden with an inviting bench. "We wanted lots of options—sunny spots and shady retreats; areas large enough to entertain in and hideouts only big enough for one or two people," says Paul.

Of the $26,000 in total renovation costs, about $8,000 was for plants. "I brought in quite a few fairly mature trees, which added to the cost," he says. "But they gave the garden instant age." Among his choices were olive, lemon, lime, apricot, peach, and chinaberry.

It was well worth every penny, says Paul. "We're out in the garden some part of the day a good part of the year," he says. "Having so many rooms outdoors makes the house seem twice as large." ◆

Article Titles Index

General Subject Index